THE
QUOTABLE
OSWALD CHAMBERS

THE
QUOTABLE
OSWALD CHAMBERS

COMPILED AND EDITED BY
DAVID MCCASLAND

DISCOVERY HOUSE
PUBLISHERS®

Feeding the Soul with the Word of God

The Oswald Chambers material is published and licensed exclusively by Discovery House Publishers through arrangement with the Oswald Chambers Publications Association, Ltd.

Discovery House Publishers is affiliated with RBC Ministries, Grand Rapids, Michigan.

Discovery House books are distributed to the trade exclusively by Barbour Publishing, Inc., Uhrichsville, Ohio.

Interior design by Veldheer Creative Services.

Library of Congress Cataloging-in-Publication Data

Chambers, Oswald, 1874–1917.
    The quotable Oswald Chambers / compiled and edited by David McCasland.
        p. cm.
    Includes bibliographical references and index.
    ISBN 978-1-57293-194-7
    1. Chambers, Oswald, 1874–1917— Quotations. I. McCasland, David. II. Title.
    BR1725.C43A25 2008
    230—dc22

                                          2008004936

08 09 10 11 12 / DP / 10 9 8 7 6 5 4 3 2 1

Printed in the United States of America

~ CONTENTS ~

CONTENTS

CONTENTS

A WORD ABOUT
～ OSWALD CHAMBERS ～

Oswald Chambers sometimes startled audiences with his vigorous thinking and his vivid expression. Even those who disagreed with what he said found his teachings difficult to dismiss and all but impossible to ignore. Often his humor drove home a sensitive point: "Have we ever got into the way of letting God work, or are we so amazingly important that we really wonder in our nerves and ways what the Almighty does before we are up in the morning!"

Oswald Chambers was not famous during his lifetime. At the time of his death in 1917 at the age of forty-three, only three books bearing his name had been published. Among a relatively small circle of Christians in Britain and the U.S., Chambers was much appreciated as a teacher of rare

insight and expression, but he was not widely known.

Chambers was born in Aberdeen, Scotland, in 1874, the youngest son of a Baptist minister. He spent his boyhood years in Perth; then his family moved to London when Oswald was fifteen. Shortly after the move to London, Oswald made his public profession of faith in Christ and became a member of Rye Lane Baptist Church. This marked a period of rapid spiritual growth, along with an intense struggle to find God's will and way for his life.

A gifted artist and musician, Chambers trained at London's Royal Academy of Art, sensing God's direction to be an ambassador for Christ in the world of art and aesthetics. While studying at the University of Edinburgh (1895–96), he decided, after an agonizing internal battle, to study for the ministry. He left the university and entered Dunoon College, near Glasgow, where he remained as a student, then a tutor for nine years.

In 1906 he traveled to the United States, spending six months teaching at God's Bible School in Cincinnati, Ohio. From there, he went to Japan, visiting the Tokyo Bible School, founded by Mr. and Mrs. Charles Cowman. This journey around the world in 1906–07 marked his transition from Dunoon College to fulltime work with the Pentecostal League of Prayer.

During the last decade of his life, Chambers served as:

• traveling speaker and representative of the League of Prayer, 1907–10

• principal and main teacher of the Bible Training College, London, 1911–15

• YMCA chaplain to British Commonwealth soldiers in Egypt, 1915–17

He died in Cairo on November 15, 1917, of complications following an emergency appendectomy. The complete story of his life is told in *Oswald Chambers: Abandoned to God* (1993), available from Discovery House Publishers, Box 3566, Grand Rapids, MI 49501 or at www.dhp.org.

During the seven years of their marriage, his wife, Gertrude (Biddy) Hobbs, took verbatim shorthand notes of nearly all his lectures and sermons. After his death, she spent the rest of her life publishing her husband's spoken words. His best-known book, *My Utmost for His Highest*, has been continuously in print since it was first published in 1927. From the earliest days of publication, following World War I, Mrs. Chambers was advised and assisted by a small group of personal friends. In later years this group became known as the Oswald Chambers Publications Association, which was incorporated in 1942, and exists today as a Registered British Charity. It oversees the publication and distribution of Oswald Chambers' material around the world. Mrs. Chambers worked constantly and creatively to make Oswald's words available in new forms to new readers. In *My Utmost for His Highest* she combined excerpts from hundreds of lectures into succinct daily readings. This book's enduring popularity testifies to her intimate knowledge of the material and her editing skill. In later years she compiled *Called of God* from thoughts on the missionary calling taken from *My Utmost for His Highest*. While many of these books contained a topical index, she never compiled a comprehensive topically arranged volume of quotations.

We offer this book in the innovative spirit of Biddy Chambers, with the prayer that this arrangement of Oswald's teaching will open the door to new readers, and point us all to the person of Jesus Christ, "Who alone can satisfy the last, aching abyss of the human heart."

⟶ The Last Picture ⟵

This is likely the last photo of Oswald and Biddy Chambers together, taken by a colleague at Zeitoun, who captured them near the rose trellis in late summer. Few people in the early twentieth century smiled for the camera, so their rather stern expressions reflect a common pose of the day, and they are wearing the thick clothing that offered protection from the searing sun and biting insects of the Egyptian desert. Oswald and Biddy were busy people, fully engaged in reaching out to British Commonwealth troops stationed in Egypt during World War I. A few weeks after this photo was taken, however, Oswald was gone and Biddy was a widow and single mother at age thirty-four.

Sometime after Oswald's death on November 15, 1917, Biddy wrote on the back of this photograph the following lines from Robert Browning's poem, "Abt Vogler":

Well, it is gone at last, the palace of music
    I reared;
  Gone! and the good tears start, the praises
    that come too slow;
For one is assured at first, one scarce can say
    that he feared,
  That he even gave it a thought, the gone thing
    was to go.
Never to be again! But many more of the kind
  As good, nay, better perchance: is this your
    comfort to me?
To me who must be saved because I cling with
    my mind
  To the same, same self, same love, same
    God: aye, what was, shall be.

There shall never be one lost good! What was,
    shall live as before;
  The evil is null, is naught, is silence implying
    sound;
What was good shall be good, with, for evil, so
    much good more;
  On the earth the broken arcs; in heaven, a
    perfect round.

All we have hoped or thought or dreamed of
    good shall exist;
  Not its semblance, but itself; no beauty, nor
    good, nor power
Whose voice has gone forth, but each survives
    for the melodist
  When eternity affirms the conception of
    an hour.

    —"Abt Vogler," by Robert Browning
    (from stanzas 8, 9, 10)

Georg Joseph Vogler, a German priest and musician, was famous for his extemporaneous compositions at the organ. In this poem, Browning pictures Vogler joyfully improvising a piece of music, then lamenting its short-lived existence and pondering how it might relate to the purposes of God on earth and in heaven.

Browning was a favorite poet of Oswald's, and one he quoted often. If Biddy had not known Browning's writing before they married, she had come to know and love it during their seven years together.

Below the poem excerpt, she jotted six Bible references:

Psalm 21:6 - For thou hast made him most blessed forever: thou hast made him exceeding glad with thy countenance.

Revelation 22:4 - And they shall see his face; and his name shall be in their foreheads.

Psalm 41:12 - And as for me, thou upholdest me in mine integrity, and settest me before thy face for ever.

Psalm 34:5 - They looked unto him, and were lightened (radiant); and their faces were not ashamed.

Psalm 44:3-4 - For they got not the land in possession by their own sword, neither did their own arm save them: but thy right hand, and thine arm, and the light of thy countenance, because thou hadst a favour unto them.

2 Corinthians 4:6 - For God who commanded the light to shine out of darkness, hath shined in our hearts, to give the light of the knowledge of the glory of God in the face of Jesus Christ.

This small photo in a simple frame sat on Biddy's desk for the rest of her life.

It was more than sheer will and determination that carried her through the rigors of the next half-century as she put her husband's words into print. Like Oswald, she believed that in the great purposes of a loving God, "the best is yet to be."

Photo of Oswald and Biddy Chambers in Egypt, circa 1917.

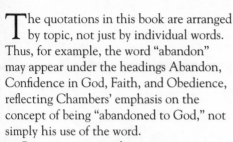

HOW TO USE THIS BOOK

The quotations in this book are arranged by topic, not just by individual words. Thus, for example, the word "abandon" may appear under the headings Abandon, Confidence in God, Faith, and Obedience, reflecting Chambers' emphasis on the concept of being "abandoned to God," not simply his use of the word.

Because many similar statements appear in more than one published book, each quotation is identified by the book from which it is taken. The Annotated Bibliography on pages 326–329 gives the publication date, theme, and spoken source for each of these books.

For readers wanting to explore the context of a statement, each quotation is keyed to the page number and column (L for left and R for right) on which it appears in the printed text of *The Complete Works of Oswald Chambers*. For example:

There is no condition of life in which we cannot abide in Jesus. We have to learn to abide in Him wherever we are placed.

Our Brilliant Heritage, 946 R

This indicates where the quotation begins, although it may carry over into the next column or page.

On the searchable CD-ROM, all Scripture quotations in the text appear as blue links. Clicking on a link will take you to the passage and its reference in the King James Version of the Bible.

We have retained the British spellings used in the original books as well as in *The Complete Works of Oswald Chambers* (for example, "judgement" and "civilisation").

Also, in the accepted grammatical style of his day, Oswald Chambers used man/men as the generic term for person/people. The notation RV following a text refers to

The Revised Version (or English Revised Version) of the Bible, a late-19th-century British revision of the King James Version of 1611.

Any reference to war in these quotations is generally to World War I (1914–1918).

Source of the Quotations

The quotations in this volume are drawn from the talks, sermons, and lectures given by Oswald Chambers from 1907–1917 and later published by his wife, Gertrude "Biddy" Chambers. Like most teachers, Chambers' thought revolved around a number of recurring themes, which he wove throughout his teaching. Three of these are prayer, redemption, and obedience. For example:

We take for granted that prayer is preparation for work, whereas prayer is the work.

Christian Disciplines, Volume 2,
The Discipline of Prayer, 317 L

The basis of life is tragic, and the only way out is by a personal relationship to God on the ground of Redemption.

Shade of His Hand, 1198 R

The spirit of obedience gives more joy to God than anything else on earth. . . . The best measure of a spiritual life is not its ecstasies, but its obedience. "To obey is better than sacrifice."

Not Knowing Whither, 904 L

The selections in this book reflect these and other major themes in the thought and teaching of Oswald Chambers.

The Teacher and His Audience

A colleague once dubbed Chambers "the apostle of the haphazard" because of his repeated emphasis on the importance of what seem to be the random events of life:

One great thing to notice is that God's order comes to us in the haphazard. We try to plan our ways and work things out for ourselves, but they go wrong because there are more facts than we know; whereas if we just go on with the days as they come, we find that God's order comes to us in that apparently haphazard way.

He Shall Glorify Me, 480 L

Chambers discovered the truth of this in his own varied experiences of life. During the decade of his public speaking and teaching, the audiences for Chambers' spoken words differed widely:

From 1907–1910 he spoke primarily to meetings of the Pentecostal League of Prayer in Britain, and to students at God's Bible School in Cincinnati, Ohio. His emphasis on sanctification and the baptism of the Holy Ghost reflects the vocabulary of his audience as well as the importance of this teaching to Chambers himself and the holiness groups to which he was speaking.

During 1911–1915 Chambers served as principal of The Bible Training College in London. While he sought to prepare the students for practical Christian service, his previous themes of holiness and personal commitment to Christ remained prominent. He emphasized study, preparation, and the need to think, but reminded his students:

One student a year who hears God's call would be sufficient for God to have called this College into existence. This College as an organisation is not worth anything, it is not academic; it is for nothing else but for God to help Himself to lives. Is He going to help Himself to us, or are we taken up with our conception of what we are going to be?

My Utmost for His Highest, November 3, 840 R

The years 1915–1917 required Chambers to address the issues of doubt and disillusionment in a world turned upside-down by the slaughter of World War I. His talks to the soldiers in Egypt centered on the redemption of Jesus Christ and its meaning in a world where the basis of life is not rational, but tragic. Two of his books, *Baffled to Fight Better* (Job) and *Shade of His Hand* (Ecclesiastes) were compiled from his talks at the YMCA camps during these years.

As you read these words of Oswald Chambers, may they bring you personal encouragement as well as useful resource material.

My thanks to Discovery House Publishers for the unique opportunity to compile this volume.

David McCasland, Editor

ABANDON

I am convinced that what is needed in spiritual matters is reckless abandonment to the Lord Jesus Christ, reckless and uncalculating abandonment, with no reserve anywhere about it; not sad, you cannot be sad if you are abandoned absolutely.

The Philosophy of Sin, 1112 R

When God's voice will come you do not know, but whenever the realisation of God comes again in the faintest way imaginable, recklessly abandon. It is only by abandon that you find Him. Never make the mistake of thinking that God speaks unmistakably clearly; He speaks in the gentlest of whispers, so unutterably quiet that it is not easy to hear Him. We only realise His voice more clearly by recklessness.

God's Workmanship, 434 R

Jesus Christ is always unyielding to my claim to my right to myself. The one essential element in all our Lord's teaching about discipleship is abandon, no calculation, no trace of self-interest.

Disciples Indeed, 395 L

"Do your utmost to let God see that you at least are a sound workman, with no need to be ashamed of the way you handle the word of the Truth" (2 Timotheus 2:15 Moffatt).

There is no royal road to becoming a worker for God. The only way is to let God in His mighty providence lift the life by a great tide, or break it from its moorings in some storm, and in one way or another get the life out to sea in reckless abandon to God. . . . We say, "Let me get back to the 'duck pond,' to its limitations, where all is so simple and placid and easy to understand." We may go back to our "duck pond" and be a success there, but God wants to launch us out into the ocean.

God's Workmanship, 459 L

Abraham's obedience was far from perfect, but its great characteristic was its unreservedness. Abandon in the profound sense is of infinitely more value than personal holiness.

Our Portrait in Genesis, 967 R

The note of the Christian life is abandonment to Jesus Christ. That life is not a hole-and-corner business whereby I look after my own speckless whiteness, afraid to do this and that, afraid to go anywhere in case I get soiled. The whole life is summed up in a passionate absorbing devotion to Jesus and the realisation of His presence.

The Place of Help, 1036 L

If we have not abandoned to Jesus Christ we are likely to be trapped on every hand by our complete ignorance of ourselves, and panic will result. Panic leads us away from the control of God and leaves us not only beyond our own control but possibly under the control of other forces. The one safeguard is abandonment to the Lord Jesus, receiving His Spirit, and obeying Him.

The Servant as His Lord, 1272 L

The great word of Jesus to His disciples is *Abandon*. When God has brought us into the relationship of disciples, we have to venture on His word; trust entirely to Him and watch that when He brings us to the venture, we take it.

Studies in the Sermon on the Mount, 1459 R

ABIDING IN CHRIST

Never be hurried out of the relationship of abiding in Him. It is the one thing that is apt to fluctuate but it ought not to. The severest discipline of a Christian's life is to learn how to keep "beholding as in a glass the glory of the Lord."

My Utmost for His Highest, January 23, 742 L

There is no condition of life in which we cannot abide in Jesus. We have to learn to abide in Him wherever we are placed.

Our Brilliant Heritage, 946 R

"*Abide in Me*" (*John 15:4*).

Think of the things that take you out of abiding in Christ—"Yes, Lord, just a minute, I have got this to do; Yes, I will abide when once this is finished; when this week is over, it will be all right, I will abide then." *Get a move on;* begin to abide *now*. In the initial stages it is a continual effort until it becomes so much the law of life that you abide in Him unconsciously. Determine to abide in Jesus wherever you are placed.

My Utmost for His Highest, June 14, 791 L

ABRAHAM

The life of Abraham does not stand for the life of a saint but for the life of the Father of the Faithful, consequently every error he committed, as well as every glorious thing he did, is recorded and traced out in its consequences through the history of his people. We are not to follow all the steps of Abraham, but to follow the steps of his faith (cf. 1 Corinthians 4:17).

Not Knowing Whither, 881 R

Abraham's defects are clear and his sins obvious, but his nobility is extraordinary. Abraham is never presented as a saint or as a type of sanctification. Phases of his life may be used to present these, but Abraham himself is the type of the life of faith in its failures and in its successes.

Not Knowing Whither, 893 R

The life of Abraham is an illustration of two things: of unreserved surrender to God, and of God's complete possession of a child of His for His own highest end.

Not Knowing Whither, 901 R

The great point of Abraham's faith in God was that he was prepared to do anything for God.

Not Knowing Whither, 903 R

The greatest thing in Abraham's life is God, not "Abraham-ism." The whole trend of his life is to make us admire God, not Abraham.

Not Knowing Whither, 912 R

AGING

Am I getting nobler, better, more helpful, more humble, as I get older? Am I exhibiting the life that men take knowledge of as having been with Jesus, or am I getting more self-assertive, more deliberately determined to have my own way? It is a great thing to tell yourself the truth.

The Place of Help, 1005 R

There is nothing, naturally speaking, that makes us lose heart quicker than decay— the decay of bodily beauty, of natural life, of friendship, of associations, all these things make a man lose heart; but Paul says when we are trusting in Jesus Christ these things do not find us discouraged, light comes through them.

The Place of Help, 1032 L

The mature saint is just like a little child, absolutely simple and joyful and gay. Go on living the life that God would have you live and you will grow younger instead of older. There is a marvellous rejuvenescence when once you let God have His way. If you are feeling very old, then get born again and do more at it.

The Psychology of Redemption, 1074 R

(Continued)

AGING (Continued)

Paul faces the possibility of old age, of decay, and of death, with no rebellion and no sadness. Paul never hid from himself the effect which his work had upon him; he knew it was killing him, and, like his Master, he was old before his time; but there was no whining and no retiring from the work. Paul was not a fool; he did not waste his energy ridiculously, neither did he ignore the fact that it was his genuine apostolic work and nothing else that was wearing him out. Michelangelo said a wonderful thing—"the more the marble wears, the better the image grows," and it is an illustration of this very truth. Every wasting of nerve and brain in work for God brings a corresponding uplift and strengthening to spiritual muscle and fibre.

The Love of God—The Message of Invincible Consolation, 670 L

The Hebrews regarded life as complete when it was full of days and riches and honour. Age was looked upon as a sign of favour. Whenever a nation becomes unspiritual, it reverses this order; the demand is not for old age but for youth. This reversal in the modern life of to-day is indicative of apostasy, not of advance.

Not Knowing Whither, 913 R

In the case of people with an impaired memory, as it is termed, some say it would be better to remove them; to put them to sleep if that were legal. Why do they say this? Because they estimate wrongly; they estimate according to the perfection of the machine. God looks at what we cannot see, viz., at the heart. God does not look at the brain, at what man looks at, neither does He sum men up in the way we do.

Biblical Psychology, 174 R

AGNOSTIC (See REVELATION OF GOD)

AGONY

Agony means severe suffering in which something dies—either the base thing, or the good. No man is the same after an agony; he is either better or worse, and the agony of a man's experience is nearly always the first thing that opens his mind to understand the need of Redemption worked out by Jesus Christ.

The Shadow of an Agony, 1161 R

When you hear a man talk in agony, remember he is hurt. Be patient and reverent with what you don't understand.

The Shadow of an Agony, 1159 L

To those who have had no agony Jesus says, "I have nothing for you; stand on your own feet, square your own shoulders. I have come for the man who knows he has a bigger handful than he can cope with, who knows there are forces he cannot touch; I will do everything for him if he will let Me. Only let a man grant he needs it, and I will do it for him."

The Shadow of an Agony, 1166 R

If Our Lord had never known the "vanishing vision of God" He could not have been a complete Saviour. Agony which has God behind it can be turned into triumph; but think of agony in which there is no God, neither in Heaven above nor earth beneath, only the terror of an accusing conscience. No human sympathy can touch that desolation. In all probability the man is to blame for it, and just because he is, no human sympathy can reach him. Anyone can have a fellow-feeling for a poor unfortunate being and can sympathise with him, but who among us can understand agony which goes deeper down than can be put into words? Who but Jesus Christ?

Bringing Sons Unto Glory, 234 L

"Through the shadow of an agony cometh Redemption." The majority of us live our lives untouched by an agony; but in war, the chances are that all are hit somewhere, and it is through a personal agony that a man is likely to begin to understand what the New Testament reveals.

The Shadow of an Agony, 1174 L

AMATEUR PROVIDENCE
(*See MEDDLING*)

AMBITION

Ambition means a set purpose for the attainment of our own ideal, and as such it is excluded from the Kingdom of Our Lord.

So Send I You, 1319 R

Am I set on my own way for God? We are never free from this snare until we are brought into the experience of the baptism of the Holy Ghost and fire. Obstinacy and self-will will always stab Jesus Christ. It may hurt no one else, but it wounds His Spirit. Whenever we are obstinate and self-willed and set upon our own ambitions, we are hurting Jesus. Every time we stand on our rights and insist that this is what we intend to do, we are persecuting Jesus. Whenever we stand on our dignity we systematically vex and grieve His Spirit.

My Utmost for His Highest, January 28, 743 R

APOSTASY
(*See BACKSLIDERS / BACKSLIDING*)

APPROVAL (*See RECOGNITION*)

ARGUE / ARGUMENT

God is the only Being who can afford to be misunderstood; we cannot, Job could not, but God can. If we are misunderstood we "get about" the man as soon as we can. St. Augustine prayed, "O Lord, deliver me from this lust of always vindicating myself." God never vindicates Himself; He deliberately stands aside and lets all sorts of slanders heap on Him, yet He is not in any hurry.

Baffled to Fight Better, 54 R

It is perilously possible to make our conceptions of God like molten lead poured into a specially designed mould, and when it is cold and hard we fling it at the heads of the religious people who don't agree with us.

Disciples Indeed, 388 R

If you are a logician you may often gain your point in a debate and yet feel yourself in the wrong. You get the best of it in disputing with some people because their minds are not clever, but when you get away from your flush of triumph you feel you have missed the point altogether; you have won on debate, but not on fact.

Baffled to Fight Better, 57 L

You cannot get at the basis of things by disputing. Our Lord Himself comes off second best every time in a logical argument, and yet you know that He has in reality come off "more than conqueror." Jesus Christ lived in the moral domain and, in a sense, the intellect is of no use there. Intellect is not a guide, but an instrument.

Baffled to Fight Better, 57 L

(Continued)

ARGUE / ARGUMENT
(Continued)

"Being ready always to give answer to every man that asketh you a reason concerning the hope that is in you" (1 Peter 3:15 RV).

To give "a reason concerning the hope that is in you" is not at all the same thing as convincing by reasonable argument why that hope is in us . . . The line we are continually apt to be caught by is that of argumentative reasoning out why we are what we are; we can never do that, but we can always say why the hope is in us.

God's Workmanship, 451 L

Jesus Christ can afford to be misunderstood; we cannot. Our weakness lies in always wanting to vindicate ourselves.

The Place of Help, 1051 L

Only one man in a thousand can maintain his spiritual life and controvert; he may increase his intellectual vim, but he does not increase his spiritual grasp of things. Dr. Alexander Whyte put this better than any other when he said:

Oh, the unmitigated curse of controversy! Oh, the detestable passions that corrections and contradictions kindle up to fury in the proud heart of man! Eschew controversy, my brethren, as you would eschew the entrance to hell itself. Let them have it their way; let them talk; let them write; let them correct you; let them traduce you; let them judge and condemn you; let them slay you. Rather let the truth of God suffer itself, than that love suffer. You have not enough of the divine nature in you to be a controversialist. "He was oppressed

and He was afflicted, yet He opened not His mouth; He is brought as a lamb to the slaughter, and as a sheep before its shearers is dumb, so He openeth not His mouth." "Who when He was reviled, reviled not again; when He suffered, He threatened not; . . . by whose stripes ye were healed." "Heal me," prays Augustine, again and again, "of this lust of mine of always vindicating myself."

Baffled to Fight Better, 62 L

You can never argue anyone into the Kingdom of heaven; you cannot argue anyone any where. The only result of arguing is to prove to your own mind that you are right and the other fellow wrong. You cannot argue for truth; but immediately Incarnate Truth is presented, a want awakens in the soul which only God can meet.

The Moral Foundations of Life, 693 R

(Alexander) Pope is often misquoted; he did not say, "Convince a man against his will, he is of the same opinion still," but "compel a man against his will, he is of the same opinion still." God has so constituted man that it is not possible to convince him against his will; you can compel him and crush him, but you cannot convince him against his will.

The Moral Foundations of Life, 699 L

The reason Paul tells Timothy not to argue, and the reason he tells me not to argue, and the reason he tells you not to argue, is that we argue from our own point of view. We argue not for the truth's sake; we argue to prove we are right.

Workmen of God, 1363 R

A man may increase his intellectual vim by controversy, but only one in a thousand can maintain his spiritual life and controvert. Never denounce a thing about which you know nothing.

Approved unto God, 13 L

Defenders of the faith are inclined to be bitter until they learn to walk in the light of the Lord. When you have learned to walk in the light of the Lord, bitterness and contention are impossible.

Biblical Psychology, 199 R

ATONEMENT

Be careful not to be caught up in the clap-trap of to-day which says, "I believe in the teachings of Jesus, but I don't see any need for the Atonement." Men talk pleasant, patronising things about Jesus Christ's teaching while they ignore His Cross . . . but the teaching of Jesus apart from His Atonement simply adds an ideal that leads to despair. The purity God demands is impossible unless we can be re-made from within, and that is what Jesus Christ under-takes to do through the Atonement.

Biblical Ethics, 90 R

And here comes the wonder—let the blunders of lives be what they may, let hereditary tendencies be what they like, let wrongs and evils crowd as they will, through the Atonement there is perfect readjust-ment to God, perfect forgiveness, and the gift of a totally new disposition which will manifest itself in the physical life just as the old disposition did (see Romans 6:19). Jesus Christ comes as the last Adam to take away the abnormal thing (which we call natural), the disposition of my right to myself, and He gives us a new disposition, viz., His own heredity of unsullied holiness, *Holy Spirit*.

Biblical Ethics, 130 R

The Bible reveals that there is anarchy somewhere, real thorough-going anarchy in the heart of men against God; therefore the need is strong that something should come into us from the outside to readjust us, to reconcile us, to turn us round, to put us right with God. The doctrine of the

Atonement is the explanation of how God does that. The doctrine of the Atonement is that "while we were yet sinners, Christ died for us."

Biblical Ethics, 130 L

AUTHORITY

Other men exercised authority by coercive means; Jesus Christ never did; His authority was *worthy*. He proved Himself worthy not only in the domain of God, which we do not know, but in the domain of man, which we do know; He is worthy there, conse-quently He prevails to open the Book (see Revelation 5). Authority to be lasting must be of the same order as that of Jesus Christ, not the authority of autocracy or coercion, but the authority of worth, to which all that is worthy in a man bows down. It is only the unworthy in a man that does not bow down to worthy authority.

Baffled to Fight Better, 76 L

Any theology which ignores Jesus Christ as the supreme Authority ceases to be Chris-tian theology. "I am the Way," said Jesus, not the road we leave behind us, but the Way we stay in: "no man cometh unto the Father, but by Me." On the ground of His absolute, not coercive, authority, every man recognises sooner or later that Jesus Christ stands easily first.

Baffled to Fight Better, 78 L

BACKSLIDERS / BACKSLIDING

He [a backslider] is worse than a person who is degenerating, and worse than a person who has committed sin; he has forsaken God and taken up with something else.

Workmen of God, 1348 L

(Continued)

BACKSLIDERS /
BACKSLIDING (Continued)

Spiritual revolt means the deliberately forsaking of God and signing on under another ruler. . . . "For My people have committed two evils; they have forsaken me the fountain of living waters"—that is not backsliding; that is degeneration; "and have hewed them out cisterns, broken cisterns, that can hold no water"—these two things together constitute backsliding. The words God uses in connection with backsliding are terrible. He uses words that shock us as moral individuals in order to portray what backsliding is in His sight (e.g. Jeremiah 3:8).

The Philosophy of Sin, 1123 R

When a soul realises the truth of God and fails to attain it, there lies within him a power of reaction which not only means he will try no more but he will dissuade others. If once we deliberately stop short and refuse to let God's life have its way with us, we shall revile the truth because it has not been reached.

The Philosophy of Sin, 1124 L

The best example of a backslider in the New Testament (the word "backslider" is never used in the New Testament, it is an Old Testament word) is in 2 Timothy 4:10. "For Demas forsook me, having loved this present world" (RV)—he has gone back to where he prefers. Couple with that Jeremiah 2:13, and you will have a good indication of what a backslider is: "For My people have committed two evils; they have forsaken Me the fountain of living waters, and hewed them out cisterns, broken cisterns, that can hold no water." Backsliding is twofold, and the term can only be applied to people in this condition.

Workmen of God, 1348 L

More awful things are said about backsliding than about any other sin. If we do not maintain a walk in accordance with the perception given, we shall fall as degradingly low as we were high before. The depth of degradation is measured by the height of attainment. Don't deal with it on the surface and say, "I'm not built that way, I have none of those sordid tastes." The nature of any dominating lust is that it keeps us from arriving at a knowledge of ourselves. For instance, a covetous man will believe he is very generous. Thank God for the surgery of providence by means of which He deals with these absurdities. The way God brings us to know ourselves is by the kind of people He brings round us. What we see to condemn in others is either the discernment of the Holy Ghost or the reflection of what we are capable of ourselves.

The Servant as His Lord, 1271 R

The parable in the fifteenth chapter of St. Luke . . . is used in many ways, but I want to use it as a picture of the backslider. It is obvious why it is called "The Parable of the Prodigal Son," but it is not called so in the Bible, it is called "The Parable of the Two Sons." One son went away and spent his substance in riotous living, the other son stayed at home. Both are as bad as each other. The spirit of the stay-at-home was every bit as bad as the wild riot of the younger boy who went away.

Workmen of God, 1349 R

Backsliding is turning away from what we know to be best to what we know is second-best. If you have known God better than you know Him to-day and are deliberately settling down to something less than the best—watch, for you will not escape; God will bring embarrassments out against you, in your private life, in your domestic life; He will enmesh you on the right hand and on the left.

The Place of Help, 1054 L

BAPTISM OF JESUS

The experience of Jesus at His Baptism is as foreign to us as His Incarnation. Read the so-called "Lives" of Jesus, and see how little is made of His baptism, the reason being that most of the writers take the Baptism to be something to teach us, or as an illustration of the rite of baptism. In the New Testament the Baptism of Jesus is not taken as an illustration of anything which we experience; it is recorded as a manifestation of Who Jesus was. He stands forth consciously—Son of God, Son of Man, God-Man—having come for one purpose, to bear away the sin of the world.

Bringing Sons Unto Glory, 224 R

Our Lord's baptism is not an illustration of the Christian rite of baptism, nor of the baptism of the Holy Ghost. At His baptism our Lord accepted His vocation, which was to bear away the sin of the world. We have no corresponding experience to that.

The Psychology of Redemption, 1074 L

All through the Bible it is revealed that our Lord bore the sin of the world by *identification*, and not by *sympathy*. He deliberately took upon His own shoulders, and bore in His own person, the whole massed sin of the human race. Our Lord knew what He had come to do, and His baptism is the first public manifestation of His identification with sin with a conscious understanding of what He was doing. At His baptism He visibly and distinctly and historically took upon Him His vocation.

The Psychology of Redemption, 1074 R

BAPTISM OF THE HOLY SPIRIT (See HOLY SPIRIT, BAPTISM OF)

BEATITUDES, THE
(See SERMON ON THE MOUNT)

BEHAVIOR

Paul's advice to Timothy was—"Let no man despise thy youth." "Don't try to make up for your youth by dogmatism and talk, but see that you walk in such a manner that you are an example to the believers." No really wise, liberal-minded person ever needs to say, "Remember how old I am."

Baffled to Fight Better, 65 L

> We are not to preach the doing of good things; good deeds are not to be preached, they are to be performed.

So Send I You, 1330 L

There is no allowance whatever in the New Testament for the man who says he is saved by grace but who does not produce the graceful goods. Jesus Christ by His Redemption can make our actual life in keeping with our religious profession.

Studies in the Sermon on the Mount, 1465 R

"Even so every good tree bringeth forth good fruit; but a corrupt tree bringeth forth evil fruit. A good tree cannot bring forth evil fruit, neither can a corrupt tree bring forth good fruit" (Matthew 7:17–18).

If we say we are right with God, the world has a perfect right to watch our private life and see if we are so. If we say we are born again, we are put under scrutiny, and rightly so. If the performance of our life is to be steadily holy, the principle of our life must be holy, i.e., if we are going to bring forth good fruit, we must have a good root.

Studies in the Sermon on the Mount, 1469 L

(Continued)

BEHAVIOR (Continued)

Sincerity means that the appearance and the reality are exactly the same.

Studies in the Sermon on the Mount, 1449 L

Is the word of God tremendously keen to me as I hand it on to you, or does my life give the lie to the things I profess to teach? I may teach sanctification and yet exhibit the spirit of Satan, the spirit that persecutes Jesus Christ.

My Utmost for His Highest, January 28, 744 L

BELIEF / BELIEFS

It is absurd to tell a man he must believe this and that; in the meantime he can't! Scepticism is produced by telling men what to believe. We are in danger of putting the cart before the horse and saying a man must believe certain things before he can be a Christian; his beliefs are the effect of his being a Christian, not the cause of it.

Facing Reality, 25 L

The Deity of Jesus Christ does not come to a man's intellect first, but to his heart and life. Nowhere in the New Testament are you asked to believe these facts before you are a Christian. They are Christian doctrines, and the Bible is the illustration of the Christian faith. The New Testament is not written to prove that Jesus Christ was the Son of God, but written for those who believe He is.

Facing Reality, 26 L

To be a believer in Jesus Christ means that we realise that what Jesus said to Thomas is true—"I am the way, the truth, and the life," not the road we leave behind as we travel, but the Way itself.

Facing Reality, 34 L

"A believer in Jesus Christ" is a phrase that embraces the whole of Christianity. . . . To believe in Jesus means much more than the experience of salvation in any form; it entails a mental and moral commitment to our Lord Jesus Christ's view of God and man, of sin and the devil, and of the Scriptures.

Facing Reality, 33 L

Our Lord's word "believe" does not refer to an intellectual act, but to a moral act; with our Lord to believe means to commit. "Commit yourself to Me," and it takes a man all he is worth to believe in Jesus Christ.

Facing Reality, 37 L

Every now and again the Spirit of God calls on us to take a spiritual stock-taking in order to see what beliefs we can do without. The things our Lord asks us to believe are remarkably few, and John 14:1 seems to sum them up—"Ye believe in God, *believe also in Me.*"

Facing Reality, 39 L

We say "seeing is believing," but it is not; we must believe a thing is possible before we would believe it, even though we saw it. Belief must be the will to believe, and I can never will to believe without a violent effort on my part to dissociate myself from all my old ways of looking at things and putting myself right over on to God.

Conformed to His Image, 350 L

The only way traditional belief can be transformed into a personal possession is by suffering. Look at what you say you believe; not an atom of it is yours saving the bit you have proved by suffering and in no other way.

Conformed to His Image, 377 L

We never enter into the Kingdom of God by having our head questions answered, but only by commitment.

The Highest Good—Thy Great Redemption, 565 R

We begin our Christian life by believing what we are told to believe, then we have to go on to so assimilate our beliefs that they work out in a way that redounds to the glory of God. The danger is in multiplying the acceptation of beliefs we do not make our own.

Conformed to His Image, 381 L

The only noble sense in which we can claim to believe a thing is when we ourselves are living in the inner spirit of that thing.

Disciples Indeed, 385 L

I have no right to say I believe in God unless I order my life as under His all-seeing Eye.

Disciples Indeed, 385 L

Believe what you do believe and stick to it, but don't profess to believe more than you intend to stick to. If you say you believe God is love, stick to it, though all Providence becomes a pandemonium shouting that God is cruel to allow what He does.

Disciples Indeed, 388 R

Note the thing which makes you say, "I don't believe it"; it will prove where you are spiritually. What I resent reveals who governs me.

Disciples Indeed, 394 L

To believe in Jesus means retiring and letting God take the mastership inside. That is all God asks of us.

If Thou Wilt Be Perfect, 587 L

Never run away with the idea that it does not matter much what we believe or think; it does. What we think and believe, we are; not what we say we think and believe, but what we really do think and believe, we are; there is no divorce at all. To believe, in the sense our Lord used the word, is never an intellectual act but a moral act.

The Moral Foundations of Life, 718 L

Re-state to yourself what you believe, then do away with as much of it as possible, and get back to the bedrock of the Cross of Christ.

My Utmost for His Highest, November 25, 848 R

BIBLE

The mere reading of the Word of God has power to communicate the life of God to us mentally, morally and spiritually. God makes the words of the Bible a sacrament, i.e., the means whereby we partake of His life; it is one of His secret doors for the communication of His life to us.

Approved Unto God, 5 L

We have to learn to rely on the Holy Spirit because He alone gives the Word of God life. All our efforts to pump up faith in the Word of God is without quickening, without illumination. You reason to yourself and say, "Now God says this and I am going to believe it," and you believe it, and re-believe it, and re-re-believe it, and nothing happens, simply because the vital power that makes the words living is not there.

Biblical Ethics, 113 R

(Continued)

BIBLE (Continued)

Am I learning how to use my Bible? The way to become complete for the Master's service is to be well soaked in the Bible; some of us only exploit certain passages. Our Lord wants to give us continuous instruction out of His word; continuous instruction turns hearers into disciples.

Approved Unto God, 11 L

Beware of "spooned meat" spirituality, of using the Bible for the sake of getting messages; use it to nourish your own soul. Be a continuous learner, don't stop short, and the truth will open to you on the right hand and on the left until you find there is no problem in human life with which the Bible does not deal. But remember that there are certain points of truth Our Lord cannot reveal to us until our character is in a fit state to bear it. The discernment of God's truth and the development of character go together.

Approved Unto God, 11 L

If you are religious, it is easier to read some pious book than the Bible. The Bible treats you like human life does—roughly. There are two ways of dealing with facts—one is to shut your eyes and say that they are not there, the other is to open your eyes and look at them and let them mould you.

Facing Reality, 25 L

The Bible is a world of revelation facts, and when you explain the Bible, take into account all the record of it. The Bible nowhere says we have to believe it is the Word of God before we can be Christians. The Bible is not the Word of God to me unless I come at it through what Jesus Christ says; it is of no use to me unless I know Him.

Facing Reality, 25 R

The key to my understanding of the Bible is not my intelligence, but personal relationship to Jesus Christ. I begin my theories after I have got on the inside. You may believe the Bible is the Word of God from Genesis to Revelation and not be a Christian at all.

Facing Reality, 25 R

Jesus Christ says the message of the Bible is about Himself—we cannot interpret it according to any other key. " . . . no prophecy of the scripture is of any private interpretation." We can prove anything we choose from the Bible once we forget the message Jesus says it contains. "The test that you know the Bible is that you understand what it is driving at; it is expounding Me, giving the exposition of what I am after."

Facing Reality, 26 L

The Bible instructs us in righteousness, in the rightness of practical living; its meaning is to keep us living right. Most people like to use the Bible for anything other than that, for a kind of jugglery to prove special doctrines.

Facing Reality, 26 L

"And they are they which testify of Me"
(John 5:39).
"For had ye believed Moses, ye would have believed Me: for he wrote of Me" (John 5:46).
How much intellectual impertinence there is to-day among many Christians relative to the Scriptures, because they forget that to "believe also" in Jesus means that they are committed beforehand to His attitude to the Bible. He said that He was the context of the Scriptures, ". . . they are they which testify of Me." We hear much about "key words" to the Scriptures, but there is only one "key word" to the Scriptures for a believer, and that is our Lord Jesus Christ Himself.

Facing Reality, 33 R

The recovery of the Bible affirmation about sin is what is needed. The Bible distinctly states that sin is not the natural result of being a finite being, but a definite stepping aside from what that finite being knew to be right. How one wishes that people who read books about the Bible would read the Bible itself!

Biblical Ethics, 129 R

"For the word of God is quick, and powerful, and sharper than any two-edged sword, piercing even to the dividing asunder of soul and spirit, and of the joints and marrow, and is a discerner of the thoughts and intents of the heart" (Hebrews 4:12).

"Why should I believe a thing because it is in the Bible?" That is a perfectly legitimate question. There is no reason why you should believe it; it is only when the Spirit of God applies the Scriptures to the inward consciousness that a man begins to understand their living efficacy.

Biblical Ethics, 131 L

There is another dangerous tendency, that of closing all questions by saying, "Let us get back to the external authority of the Bible." That attitude lacks courage and the power of the Spirit of God; it is a literalism that does not produce "written epistles," but persons who are more or less incarnate dictionaries; it produces not saints but fossils, people without life, with none of the living reality of the Lord Jesus. There must be the Incarnate Word and the interpreting word, i.e., people whose lives back up what they preach, written epistles, "known and read of all men." Only when we receive the Holy Spirit and are lifted into a total readjustment to God do the words of God become "quick, and powerful" to us.

Biblical Ethics, 131 R

The Bible not only explains God, it explains the world in which we live; it explains not only things that are right, but things that are wrong. If we start out with the idea that everything is going well and all is bright and happy and then there is an earthquake, or someone is killed by lightning, or there are tremendous floods, or a shocking murder, or worse crime, the idea with which we started out will be flatly contradicted by the world outside, that is, by the facts we see and know. The Bible and the outside world agree, but both the Bible and the outside world are an absolute puzzle to us until we receive the Spirit of God.

Biblical Psychology, 207 R

The Bible does not reveal all truth; we have to find out scientific truth and common-sense truth for ourselves; but knowledge of the Truth, our Lord Himself, is only possible through the reception of the Holy Spirit.

Biblical Ethics, 132 L

Beware of reasoning about God's Word. Obey it.

Disciples Indeed, 387 R

The words of the Bible express the inner soul; the words we use to-day are nearly all technical, borrowed from somewhere else, and our most modern words do not express the spirit at all, but cunningly cloak it over and give no expression.

Biblical Psychology, 210 R

When a man's heart is right with God the mysterious utterances of the Bible are spirit and life to him. Spiritual truth is discernible only to a pure heart, not to a keen intellect. It is not a question of profundity of intellect, but of purity of heart.

Bringing Sons Unto Glory, 231 L

(Continued)

BIBLE *(Continued)*

The Bible is the Word of God only to those who are born from above and who walk in the light. Our Lord Jesus Christ, the *Word* of God, and the Bible, the *words* of God, stand or fall together; they can never be separated without fatal results. A man's attitude to our Lord determines his attitude to the Bible.

Christian Disciplines, Volume 1,
The Discipline of Divine Guidance, 271 L

Take the old-fashioned way of erecting a scaffolding and building the structure inside. The scaffolding may be so skilfully erected and admirably proportioned and be there for so long that we come to consider this the scheme in the mind of the architect. Then one day we see the loosening of ropes and planks and ladders, and the turmoil destroys for ever the skill and beautiful proportion of the scaffolding; all that is happening is but to clear the real building that it may stand nobly before all as a thing of beauty. There is something similar to the Bible revelation of the way God deals with the world's Ages.
    There have been prophets and students who handle the Bible like a child's box of bricks; they explain to us the design and structure and purpose; but as time goes on things do not work out in their way at all. They have mistaken the scaffolding for the structure, while all the time God is working out His purpose with a great and undeterred patience.

Christian Disciplines, Volume 2,
The Discipline of Patience, 335 L

People can dispute the words of the Bible as they like, but get a soul in whom the craving for God has come, and the words of the Bible create the new life in him. " . . . being born again, . . . by the word of God" (1 Peter 1:23).

Disciples Indeed, 386 L

The Epistles are not the cogitations of men of extraordinary spiritual genius, but the posthumous work of the Ascended Christ and they have therefore a peculiar signifi-cance in the programme of Redemption. The Holy Ghost used these men, with all their personal idiosyncrasies, to convey God's message of salvation to the world.

Conformed to His Image, 352 L

The main characteristic which is the proof of the indwelling Spirit is an amazing ten-derness in personal dealing, and a blazing truthfulness with regard to God's Word.

Disciples Indeed, 386 R

Beware of bartering the Word of God for a more suitable conception of your own.

Disciples Indeed, 386 R

The Bible does not thrill; the Bible nour-ishes. Give time to the reading of the Bible and the recreating effect is as real as that of fresh air physically.

Disciples Indeed, 387 R

If we understood what happens when we use the Word of God, we would use it oftener. The disablement of the devil's power by means of the Word of God con-veyed through the lips of a servant of His is inconceivable.

Disciples Indeed, 386 R

It is not the thing on which we spend most time that moulds us, but the thing that exerts the greatest power. Five minutes with God and His word is worth more than all the rest of the day.

Our Brilliant Heritage, 954 R

The reason some of us are not healthy spiritually is because we don't use the Bible as the Word of God but only as a text-book.

Disciples Indeed, 387 L

To read the Bible according to God's providential order in your circumstances is the only way to read it, viz., in the blood and passion of personal life.

Disciples Indeed, 387 R

Beware of interpreting Scripture in order to make it suit a pre-arranged doctrine of your own.

Disciples Indeed, 387 R

The revelation of God's will has been brought down to us in words. The Bible is not a book containing communications from God; it is God's revelation of Himself, in the interests of grace; God's giving of Himself in the limitation of words. The Bible is not a faery romance to beguile us for a while from the sordid realities of life; it is the Divine complement of the laws of Nature, of Conscience and of Humanity; it introduces us to a new universe of revelation facts not known to unregenerate commonsense. The only Exegete of these facts is the Holy Spirit, and in the degree of our reception, recognition, and reliance on the Holy Spirit will be our understanding.

God's Workmanship, 439 L

The mystery of the Bible is that its inspiration was direct from God (2 Peter 1:21). To believe our Lord's consciousness about Himself commits me to accept Him as God's last endless Word. That does not mean that God is not still speaking, but it does mean that God is saying nothing different from the Final Word, Jesus Christ; all God says expounds that Word.

The Moral Foundations of Life, 698 R

What is needed is a final court of appeal, and this we have in the Bible. It is not a question of the infallibility of the Bible—that is a side issue—but of the finality of the Bible. The Bible is a whole library of literature giving us the final interpretation of the Truth, and to take the Bible apart from that one supreme purpose is to have a book and nothing more; and further, to take our Lord Jesus Christ away from the revelation of Him given in the Bible is to be left with one who is open to all the irreverent slanders of unbelief.

God's Workmanship, 425 R

Our danger is to water down God's word to suit ourselves. God never fits His word to suit me; He fits me to suit His word.

Not Knowing Whither, 901 R

To people who are satisfied on too shallow a level the Bible is a book of impertinences; but whenever human nature is driven to the end of things, then the Bible becomes the only Book and God the only Being in the world.

The Philosophy of Sin, 1107 L

The Bible is the only Book that gives us any indication of the true nature of sin, and where it came from.

The Philosophy of Sin, 1107 R

We so continually run down the revelations of the New Testament to the level of our own experience. That is wrong; we must let God lift up our experience to the standard of His word.

The Psychology of Redemption, 1076 L

The Bible does not prove the existence of God, nor does it prove that Jesus Christ is the Son of God. The Bible was written to confirm the faith of those who already believe in God.

Shade of His Hand, 1195 L

(Continued)

BIBLE (Continued)

We are reverent over the Bible simply because our fathers and mothers taught us to be reverent; but we find no practical reason for reverence until we get to the last lap, until we are pressed out of the outer court into the inner; then we find there is no mind among men that has ever penned words that are sufficient for us there; we begin to find that the only Book there is the Bible.

The Philosophy of Sin, 1108 R

Exegesis is not torturing a text to agree with a theory of my own, but leading out its meaning.

Disciples Indeed, 387 R

The vital relationship which the Christian has to the Bible is not that he worships the letter, but that the Holy Spirit makes the words of the Bible spirit and life to him.

The Psychology of Redemption, 1066 L

We are all so scientifically orthodox nowadays, so materialistic and certain that rationalism is the basis of things, that we make the Bible out to be the most revolutionary, unorthodox and heretical of books.

Shade of His Hand, 1208 R

The Bible is a relation of facts, the truth of which must be tested. Life may go on all right for a while, when suddenly a bereavement comes, or some crisis; unrequited love or a new love, a disaster, a business collapse, or a shocking sin, and we turn up our Bibles again and God's word comes straight home, and we say, "Why, I never saw that there before."

Shade of His Hand, 1223 L

The Bible is neither obsolete nonsense nor poetic blether; it is a universe of revelation facts.

Shade of His Hand, 1210 R

BIOGRAPHY

An eminent difference is discernible between biographic studies in the Bible and outside the Bible. When men write studies of the servants of God, they are apt to drop out the uncouth and the unlovely, and out of their devotion state only the elements that idealise the servant. But the Bible reveals the blunderings and the sins and the uncouthness of the servants of God, and leaves only one idea dominant—that these men were for the glory of God.

Christian Disciplines, Volume 1,
The Discipline of Divine Guidance, 275 L

When we come to study the lives of the saints, the confusing thing is that from one standpoint they are a jumble of inconsistencies, whilst from another standpoint they are an exhibition of the boundless consistency of God. This needs to be heeded, because if we study the life of a saint in order to find out what God is like, we shall finish up in the dumps and say—It is enough; whereas if we study God Himself, we shall find that He manifests His amazing consistency in the weakest and feeblest saint.

Not Knowing Whither, 870 L

The study of biography is always inspiring, but it has this one drawback, that it is apt to leave the life more given to sentiment and thinking and perhaps less to endeavour than is usually supposed; but when we realise what the Psalmist is pointing out and what the New Testament so strongly insists on, viz., "*the Lord* is our help," we are able to understand such a mountain character as the Apostle Paul saying "Follow my ways which be in Christ." We have not been told to follow in all the footsteps of the mountain-like characters, but in the footsteps of their faith, because their faith is in a Person.

The Place of Help, 984 R

BLESSING

By "Blessing" we mean the great magnanimous overflowing of the heart of God to all people, whether they be good, bad, or indifferent. By "Beatitude" we mean the overflowing benediction of a life that is rightly related to God—character that lives within the frontiers where God makes Himself known. So many people think they must be right with God because He blesses them. This needs correcting. . . .

In the first place, God's blessings fall, like His rain, on evil and good alike. The great blessings of health, genius, prosperity, all come from His overflowing grace, and not from the condition of the character of the recipients. For instance, if health were a sign that a man is right with God, we should lose all distinction as to what a good character is, for many bad men enjoy good health.

God's Workmanship, 431 L

When we no longer seek God for His blessings, we have time to seek Him for Himself.

The Moral Foundations of Life, 728 L

If God makes no difference in His external blessings to men, who are we that we should? One of the chief stagnating influences on spiritual character is this reasoning—"Do they deserve it?" How much do any of us deserve the blessings of God? Let us ever remember that to enter into the experience of God's beatitudes is to find ourselves able to show to our fellow-men the same unmerited mercy, the same unselfish, unmerited love that God has shown to us. Jesus told His disciples that this is indeed the test: "For if ye forgive men their trespasses, your heavenly Father will also forgive you. But if ye forgive not men their trespasses, neither will your Father forgive your trespasses" (RV).

God's Workmanship, 431 R

"Seek ye Me, and ye shall live" (Amos 5:4).

It is the Lord Himself and not the places of blessing the children of God are to seek. The place of former victories for God, the place that was heaven on earth in days gone by, will be places of defeat and failure if you persist in going there as a means of reviving. The message of God is "Seek ye Me, and ye shall live."

God's Workmanship, 458 R

Remember God's blessing may mean God's blasting. If God is going to bless me, He must condemn and blast out of my being what He cannot bless. "Our God is a consuming fire." When we ask God to bless, we sometimes pray terrible havoc upon the things that are not of God. God will shake all that can be shaken, and He is doing it just now.

The Highest Good—The Pilgrim's Song Book, 529 R

Moral and spiritual integrity cannot be measured by God's blessings. God sends His favours on good and bad alike. The blessings of God are an indication that God is overflowing in grace and benediction irrespective of a man's relationship to Him. Men may partake of the blessings of God and yet never come into relationship with Him. (See Matthew 5:45–48.)

The Place of Help, 1007 R

The great difficulty spiritually is to concentrate on God, and it is His blessings that make it difficult. Troubles nearly always make us look to God; His blessings are apt to make us look elsewhere. The teaching of the Sermon on the Mount is, in effect—Narrow all your interests until the attitude of mind and heart and body is concentration on Jesus Christ. "Look unto Me."

My Utmost for His Highest, January 22, 741 R

BODY, PHYSICAL

Much of the misery in our Christian life comes not because the devil tackles us, but because we have never understood the simple laws of our make-up. We have to treat the body as the servant of Jesus Christ: when the body says "Sit," and He says "Go," go! When the body says "Eat," and He says "Fast," fast! When the body says "Yawn," and He says "Pray," pray!

Biblical Ethics, 107 R

In the Middle Ages the body was looked upon as a clog, a hindrance, an annoyance, something that kept us back and upset our higher calling; something which had sin in the very corpuscles of its blood, in the cells of its make-up. The Bible entirely disproves this view; it tells us that our body is "the temple of the Holy Ghost," not a thing to be despised. The Bible gives the body a very high place indeed.

Biblical Psychology, 187 L

Our spiritual life does not grow *in spite of* the body, but *because* of the body.

The Moral Foundations of Life, 703 R

"*I beseech you therefore, brethren, by the mercies of God, that ye present your bodies a living sacrifice*"*(Romans 12:1).*
    The Bible never says any thing so vague as "present your all," but "present your bodies." There is nothing ambiguous or indefinite about that statement; it is definite and clear. The body means only one thing to us all, viz., this flesh and blood body.

Biblical Psychology, 187 L

Our spirit goes no further than we bring our body. One of the best means of spiritual progress is to learn to deny the body in a great number of unnecessary ways (cf. 1 Corinthians 9:27).

Conformed to His Image, 353 R

We imagine that our bodies are a hindrance to our development, whereas it is only through our bodies that we develop. We cannot express a character without a body.

The Moral Foundations of Life, 711 L

The Bible makes much of man's body. The teaching of Christianity on this point has been twisted by the influence of Plato's teaching, which says that a man can only further his moral and spiritual life by despising his body. The Bible teaches that the body is the temple of the Holy Ghost; it was moulded by God of the dust of the ground and is man's chief glory, not his shame.

Shade of His Hand, 1216 R

Robert Browning of all the poets is the one who insists that we make headway not in spite of the flesh, but because of the flesh, and in no other way.

Shade of His Hand, 1213 L

BOOKS

With regard to other men's minds, take all you can get, whether those minds are in flesh-and-blood editions or in books; but remember, the best you get from another mind is not that mind's verdict, but its standpoint. Note the writers who provoke you to do your best mentally.

Disciples Indeed, 409 L

Always keep in contact with those books and those people that enlarge your horizon and make it possible for you to stretch yourself mentally.

The Moral Foundations of Life, 721 R

The books and the men who help us most are not those who teach us, but those who can express for us what we feel inarticulate about.

The Place of Help, 1032 R

It is a striking indication of the trend and shallowness of the modern reading public that George MacDonald's books have been so neglected.

Christian Disciplines, Volume 1,
The Discipline of Divine Guidance, 277 R

The things we listen to and read ought to be beyond our comprehension; they go into our minds like seed thoughts, and slowly and surely bring forth fruit. This is good counsel for boys and girls in their teens.

Shade of His Hand, 1215 R

We should always choose our books as God chooses our friends, just a bit beyond us, so that we have to do our level best to keep up with them.

Shade of His Hand, 1216 L

An elemental thing to remember is that we must never read into a man's words what we mean, but just try and find out what the author of the words means. As a rule we read into his words what we mean and consequently miss his meaning altogether.

Shade of His Hand, 1220 L

It is impossible to read too much, but always keep before you why you read. Remember that "the need to receive, recognise, and rely on the Holy Spirit" is before all else.

Approved Unto God, 11 L

Keep yourself full with reading. Reading gives you a vocabulary.

Disciples Indeed, 400 R

Don't read to remember; read to realise.

Disciples Indeed, 400 R

BROKEN BREAD / POURED-OUT WINE

Just as my Lord was made broken bread and poured-out wine for me, so I must be made broken bread and poured-out wine in His hands for others. What is meant by "in His hands" is seen in the kind of things that bruise me—tyrannic powers, misunderstanding people, things that ordinarily I would have resented and said, "No, I can't allow that." Is there being produced in me, through the crushing of His disguised feet, the wine that is a real quickening of other lives? A yielded life to God becomes a doormat for men. He leaves us here to be trampled on.

God's Workmanship, 423 L

God can never make me wine if I object to the fingers He uses to crush me with. If God would only crush me with His own fingers, and say, "Now, My son, I am going to make you broken bread and poured-out wine in a particular way and everyone will know what I am doing. . . ." But when He uses someone who is not a Christian, or someone I particularly dislike, or some set of circumstances which I said I would never submit to, and begins to make *these* the crushers, I object. I must never choose the scene of my own martyrdom, nor must I choose the things God will use in order to make me broken bread and poured-out wine.

So Send I You, 1291 L

You may be the mouthpiece for God's truth to the unsaved, but you cannot nourish the flock of God which is among you unless you are rightly related to the Shepherd, unless you are willing to let God use you as broken bread and poured-out wine to feed His sheep.

Workmen of God, 1361 L

(Continued)

BROKEN BREAD / POURED-OUT WINE
(Continued)

We are all too set on our own sanctification, forgetting that we are to be broken bread and poured-out wine for the lifting up of others who are not there yet.

God's Workmanship, 441 L

CALAMITY *(See DISASTER)*

CALL OF GOD

God can break or bend or mould, just as He chooses. You do not know why He is doing it; He is doing it for One purpose only, that He may be able to say, "This is My man, My woman." Never choose to be a worker, but when once God has put His call on you, woe be to you if you turn to the right hand or to the left. God will do with you what He never did with you before the call came; He will do with you what He is not doing with other people. Let Him have His way.

Approved Unto God, 3 R

Is He going to help Himself to your life, or are you taken up with your conception of what you are going to do? God is responsible for our lives, and the one great keynote is reckless reliance upon Him.

Approved Unto God, 10 R

If I hear the call of God and refuse to obey, I become the dullest, most common-place of Christians because I have seen and heard and refused to obey.

Disciples Indeed, 387 L

The call of God embarrasses us because of two things—it presents us with sealed orders, and urges us to a vast venture.

Not Knowing Whither, 864 L

One man or woman called of God is worth a hundred who have elected to work for God.

Disciples Indeed, 387 R

We need no call of God to help our fellow men; that is the natural call of humanity; but we do need the supernatural work of God's grace before we are fit for God to help Himself through us.

Disciples Indeed, 388 L

The first thing that impresses us about the call of God is that it comes to the whole man, not to one part of him. The majority of us are godly in streaks, spiritual in sections; it takes a long time to locate us altogether to the call of God. We have special days and religious moods, but when we get into contact with God we are brought in touch with Reality and made all of a piece. Our Lord's life was all one reality; you could never cut it into two—shallow here and profound there. My conception of God must embrace the whole of my life.

He Shall Glorify Me, 508 L

Many of us have heard Jesus Christ's first "Follow Me"—to a life of liberty and joy and gladness; how many of us have heard the second "Follow Me"—"deny your right to yourself and 'do to death' in yourself everything that never was in Me"?

If Thou Wilt Be Perfect, 585 R

We are all based on a conception of importance, either our own importance, or the importance of someone else; Jesus tells us to go and teach based on the revelation of His importance. "All power is given unto Me. . . . Go ye therefore. . . ."

So Send I You, 1325 R

Beware of the "seeking great things for yourself" idea—cold shivers down the back, visions of angels and visitations from God. "I can't decide in this plain, commonplace, ordinary evening as to whether I will serve Jesus or not." That is the only way Jesus Christ ever comes to us. He will never take us at a disadvantage, never terrify us out of our wits by some amazing manifestation of His power and then say "Follow Me." He wants us to decide when all our powers are in full working order, and He chooses the moment when the world, not Himself, is in the ascendant. If we chose Him when He was in the ascendant, in the time of religious emotion and excitement, we would leave Him when the moment of excitement passed, but if we choose Him with all our powers about us, the choice will abide.

If Thou Wilt Be Perfect, 603 L

The call of God is like the call of the sea, or of the mountains; no one hears these calls but the one who has the nature of the sea or of the mountains; and no one hears the call of God who has not the nature of God in him. It cannot be definitely stated what the call of God is to, because it is a call into comradeship with God Himself for His own purposes, and the test of faith is to believe that God knows what He is after.

Not Knowing Whither, 864 R

Most of us have no ear for anything but ourselves; anything that is not "me" we cannot hear. We are dead to, and without interest in the finest music; we can yawn in a picture gallery, and be uninspired by a sunrise or a sunset. That is true not only of the soul's denseness to natural beauties, or to music and art and literature, but true with regard to the awakening of the soul to the call of God. To be brought within the zone of God's voice is to be profoundly altered.

So Send I You, 1288 R

We have to beware of making the need the call; the Redemption is the call; the need is the opportunity, and the opportunity is in our own homes, in our work, just wherever we are, not simply in meetings. Naturally we always want to go somewhere else, but the love of God works just where we are, and His love works irrespective of persons.

Our Brilliant Heritage, 933 L

"Come unto Me" (Matthew 11:28).
    The questions that matter in life are remarkably few, and they are all answered by these words, "Come unto Me." Not— "Do this" and "Don't do that," but "Come."

Our Brilliant Heritage, 946 L

To study the teaching of our Lord in connection with the verb "to go" would amaze us. How often do you hear in meetings the word "go," and how often do you hear the word "get"? We emphasise "get"; the New Testament emphasises "go." If you have escaped the edge of the sword, go!

The Philosophy of Sin, 1114 L

The call of God is a call according to the nature of God; where we go in obedience to that call depends entirely on the providential circumstances which God engineers, and is not of any moment. The danger is to fit the call of God into the idea of our own discernment and say, "God called me *there*." If we say so and stick to it, then it is good-bye to the development of the life of God in us. We have deliberately shifted the ground of His call to fit our own conception of what He wants.

The Psychology of Redemption, 1073 L

We are apt to forget the mystic, supernatural touch of God which comes with His call. If a man can tell you how the call of God came to him and all about it, it is questionable whether he ever had the call.

So Send I You, 1289 L

(Continued)

CALL OF GOD *(Continued)*

If we have been getting hard and metallic, untouched spiritually—not backsliding, but getting out of touch with God, we shall find the reason is because we are allowing things to come in between us and the sense of God's call. At any minute God may bring the wind of His Spirit across our life, and we shall realise with a startled mind that the work we have been doing in the mean-time is so much rubbish (cf. 1 Corinthians 3:12–13).

So Send I You, 1290 L

We will readily give up sin and worldliness, but God calls us to give up the very clos-est, noblest and most right tie we have, if it enters into competition with His call.

So Send I You, 1301 R

It is easier to serve God without a vision, easier to work for God without a call, because then you are not bothered by what God requires; common sense is your guide, veneered over with Christian sentiment.

My Utmost for His Highest, March 4, 756 L

You will be more prosperous and successful, more leisure-hearted, if you never realise the call of God. But if once you receive a commission from Jesus Christ, the memory of what God wants will always come like a goad; you will no longer be able to work for Him on the commonsense basis.

My Utmost for His Highest, March 4, 756 L

"Come unto Me" (Matthew 11:28).

You say—"But God can never have called *me* to this, I am too unworthy, it can't mean *me*." It does mean you, and the weaker and feebler you are, the better. The one who has something to trust in is the last one to come anywhere near saying—"I will serve the Lord."

My Utmost for His Highest, July 9, 799 R

"I have chosen you" (John 15:16). Keep that note of greatness in your creed. It is not that you have got God, but that He has got you.

My Utmost for His Highest, October 25, 837 R

CHARACTER

It is not what a man does that is of final importance, but what he is in what he does. The atmosphere produced by a man, much more than his activities, has the lasting influence.

Baffled to Fight Better, 51 L

Discernment of God's truth and develop-ment in spiritual character go together.

Approved Unto God, 20 L

An intellectual conception of God may be found in a bad vicious character. The knowledge and vision of God is dependent entirely on a pure heart. Character deter-mines the revelation of God to the indi-vidual. The pure in heart see God.

Biblical Ethics, 125 R

God deals with the designs of our hearts, either for good or for bad. Character is the whole trend of a man's life, not isolated acts here and there, and God deals with us on the line of character building.

Biblical Psychology, 170 L

We bend the whole energy of our lives to machinery, and when an accident happens and the machinery breaks up we say, What a disaster. Probably it was the emancipa-tion of the man's life. We make nests here and there, competences here and there, but God has no respect for any of them; at any minute He may send a wind and over goes the whole thing. The one thing God is after is character.

The Highest Good, 548 L

You cannot judge a man by the good things he does at times; you must take all the times together, and if in the greater number of times he does bad things, he is a bad character, in spite of the noble things he does intermittently. You cannot judge your character by the one time you spoke kindly to your grandmother if the majority of other times you spoke unkindly. The fact that people say of a man, "Oh well, he does do good things occasionally," proves that he is a bad character; the very statement is a condemnation. Character in a saint means the disposition of Jesus Christ persistently manifested.

Biblical Psychology, 199 L

Crises reveal character. When we are put to the test the hidden resources of our character are revealed exactly.

Disciples Indeed, 393 R

It is an appalling fact that our features tell our moral character unmistakably to those who can read them, and we may be very thankful there are few who can; our safety is in other people's ignorance. In spite of the disguise of refinement, sensuality, selfishness and self-indulgence speak in our features as loud as a thunder-clap. Our inner spirit tells with an indelible mark on every feature, no matter how beautiful or how ugly the features may be. Let us remember that that is how God sees us.

Disciples Indeed, 394 R

We are apt to think that everything that happens to us is to be turned into useful teaching; it is to be turned into something better than teaching, viz. into character. We shall find that the spheres God brings us into are not meant to teach us something but to make us something.

The Love of God—The Ministry of the Unnoticed, 664 L

A man's character cannot be summed up by what he does in spots, but only by what he is in the main trend of his existence. When we describe a man we fix on the exceptional things, but it is the steady trend of a man's life that tells. Character is that which steadily prevails, not something that occasionally manifests itself. Character is made by things done steadily and persistently, not by the exceptional or spasmodic, that is something God mourns over—"your goodness is as a morning cloud," He says (Hosea 6:4). In Matthew 7 our Lord is dealing with the need to make character.

Studies in the Sermon on the Mount, 1460 L

We are only what we are in the dark; all the rest is reputation. What God looks at is what we are in the dark—the imaginations of our minds; the thoughts of our heart; the habits of our bodies; these are the things that mark us in God's sight.

The Love of God—The Ministry of the Unnoticed, 669 L

On the basis of the Redemption God expects us to erect characters worthy of the sons of God. He does not expect us to carry on "evangelical capers," but to manifest the life of the Son of God in our mortal flesh.

The Love of God—The Making of a Christian, 679 R

Character is the way we have grown to act with our hands and our feet, our eyes and our tongue; and the character we make always reveals the ruling disposition within. "If any man is in Christ, there is a new creation." Where is the new creation? If I am still the same miserable cross-patch, set on my own way, it is a lie to say that I am a new creature in Christ.

Our Brilliant Heritage, 939 R

(Continued)

CHARACTER (Continued)

Not what the disciple says in public prayer, not what he preaches from pulpit or platform, not what he writes on paper or in letters, but what he is in his heart which God alone knows, determines God's revelation of Himself to him. Character determines revelation (see Psalm 18:24–26).

The Place of Help, 987 R

We infect our surroundings with our own personal character.

Disciples Indeed, 405 L

Never run away with the idea that you can ever do a thing or have an attitude of mind before God which no one else need know anything about. A man is what he is in the dark. Remain loyal to God and to His saints in private and in public, and you will find that not only are you continually with God, but that God is counting on you.

The Place of Help, 1008 L

"A good name is better than precious ointment; and the day of death than the day of one's birth" (Ecclesiastes 7:1).

Solomon is speaking of character, not of reputation. Reputation is what other people think of you; "character is what you are in the dark," where no one sees but yourself. That is where the worth of a man's character lies, and Solomon says that the man who has attained a sagacious character during life is like a most refreshing, soothing, healing ointment.

Shade of His Hand, 1220 L

We remember the bad a man has done but not the good. It is possible to blast a man's reputation by raising your shoulders; but you can never blast a man's character. Character is what a man is; reputation is what other people think he is.

Shade of His Hand, 1239 L

CHARACTER OF GOD

Jesus Christ reveals, not an embarrassed God, not a confused God, not a God who stands apart from the problems, but One who stands in the thick of the whole thing with man.

Disciples Indeed, 388 L

Never accept an explanation that travesties God's character.

Disciples Indeed, 388 L

God is true to the laws of His own nature, not to my way of expounding how He works.

Disciples Indeed, 388 R

Am I becoming more and more in love with God as a holy God, or with the conception of an amiable Being who says, "Oh well, sin doesn't matter much"?

Disciples Indeed, 389 L

God never coerces, neither does He ever accommodate His demands to human compromise, and we are disloyal to Him if we do.

Disciples Indeed, 389 L

Never accept an explanation of any of God's ways which involves what you would scorn as false and unfair in a man.

Disciples Indeed, 389 R

Consider this revelation: the eternal fact that God is Love, not, God is loving. God and love are synonymous. Love is not an attribute of God; it is God; whatever God is, love is.

The Love of God, 656 L

We can understand the attributes of God in other ways, but we can only understand the Father's heart in the Cross of Christ.

The Highest Good—Thy Great Redemption, 558 L

Try and weave a conception of God out of Jesus Christ's presentation of Him and then look at life as it is, and you will find that God, as He is revealed in Jesus Christ, is flatly contradicted in the natural world. God is the only Being Who can afford to be misunderstood; He deliberately stands aside and lets Himself be slandered and misrepresented; He never vindicates Himself.

The Love of God, 659 L

Spiritual character is only made by standing loyal to God's character, no matter what distress the trial of faith brings. The distress and agony the prophets experienced was the agony of believing God when everything that was happening contradicted what they proclaimed Him to be; there was nothing to prove that God was just and true, but everything to prove the opposite.

Our Portrait in Genesis, 964 L

God is the only Being Who can stand the slander that arises because the devil and pain and sin are in the world.

The Place of Help, 1007 L

Faith is trust in a God Whose ways you cannot trace, but whose character you know, and the man of faith hangs on to the fact that He is a God of honour. Fatalism means "my number's up," I have to bow to the power whether I like it or not; I do not know the character of the power, but it is greater than I am and I must submit. In this dispensation we do know the character of God, although we do not know why His providential will should be as it is.

Shade of His Hand, 1234 R

If we will hang in to the fact that God is true and loving and just, every judgment He passes will find us in agreement with it finally.

Shade of His Hand, 1206 L

The test of true religion is the knowledge of the character of God. As long as you think of God in the quietness of a religious meeting you will never know God—what kind of God have you got when you are in touch with the wrong, bad, evil things? God's Book reveals that it is right in the midst of the very opposite of God that His blessings occur. The very things which seem to be making for destruction become the revealers of God.

Notes on Isaiah, 1380 L

The message of the prophets is that although they have forsaken God, it has not altered God. The Apostle Paul emphasizes the same truth, that God remains God even when we are unfaithful (see 2 Timothy 2:13). Never interpret God as changing with our changes. He never does; there is no variableness in Him.

Notes on Ezekiel, 1477 L

CHILD / CHILDREN

Luke 2:40–52
 A child's life has no dates; it is free, silent, dateless. A child's life ought to be a child's life, full of simplicity.

Bringing Sons Unto Glory, 221 L

The illustration Jesus gives to His disciples of a saintly life is a little child. Jesus did not put up a child as an ideal, but to show them that ambition has no place whatever in the disposition of a Christian. The life of a child is unconscious in its fullness of life, and the source of its life is implicit love.

If Thou Wilt Be Perfect, 581 L

(Continued)

CHILD / CHILDREN
(*Continued*)

A bad man's relation to his children is in God's hand; the child's relation to the badness of his father is in his own hand. Because we see children suffering physically for the sins of their parents, we say they are being punished; they are not; there is no element of punishment in their suffering; there are Divine compensations we know nothing about. The whole subject of heredity and what is transmitted by heredity, if taken out of its Bible setting, can be made the greatest slander against God, as well as the greatest exoneration of the bitterness of a man's spirit.

Conformed to His Image, 365 L

The Lord Jesus spoke and worked from the great big Child-heart of God. God Almighty became Incarnate as a little Child, and Jesus Christ's message is, You must "become as little children." God always keeps the minds of His children open with wonder, with open-eyed expectancy for Him to come in where He likes.

If Ye Shall Ask, 617 L

Awe is the condition of a man's spirit realising Who God is and what He has done for him personally. Our Lord emphasises the attitude of a child; no attitude can express such solemn awe and familiarity as that of a child.

Not Knowing Whither, 882 L

The reason that our prayers are not answered is that we are not stupid enough to believe what Jesus says. It is a child, and only a child who has prayer answered; a wise and prudent man does not (cf. Matthew 11:25). We have to be as natural as children in our relationship to Jesus Christ, and He does His work all the time.

So Send I You, 1323 R

If I never correct my child I am making a nice mess for other folks by and by.

Shade of His Hand, 1232 R

CHOICE / CHOOSING

The power of individual choice is the secret of human responsibility. I can choose which line I will go on, but I have no power to alter the destination of that line once I have taken it—yet I always have the power to get off one line on to the other.

Our Portrait in Genesis, 974 L

Every art, every healing, and every good can be used for an opposite purpose. Every possibility I have of producing a fine character in time, I can use to produce the opposite; I have that liberty from the Creator. God will not prevent my disobeying Him; if He did, my obedience would not be worth anything.

Shade of His Hand, 1202 L

It is in the middle that human choices are made; the beginning and the end remain with God. The decrees of God are birth and death, and in between those limits man makes his own distress or joy.

Shade of His Hand, 1223 L

There is always a point where I have the power to choose. I have no power to choose whether or not I will take the consequences of my choice; no power to say whether or not I will be born; no power to choose my "cage"; but within the cage I have power to choose which perch I will sit on.

Shade of His Hand, 1202 L

Unless a man relates his disposition to God in between birth and death, he will reap a heritage of distress for himself and for those who come after him.

Shade of His Hand, 1203 L

We can choose the way we take, but we have no control over where that way ends.

Notes on Ezekiel, 1483 R

If you try and define Divine omnipotence and human free will in intellectual terms, you find language fails because they contradict each other. Every choice a saint makes is a free, untrammeled choice of a human will, and yet in the final analysis it will be found to be in accord with the foreknowledge of God.

Notes on Ezekiel, 1483 R

CHRISTIANITY

The essence of Christianity is not a creed or a doctrine, but an illumination that emancipates me—"I see who Jesus Christ is." It is always a surprise, never an intellectual conception.

Facing Reality, 27 R

Christianity is not consistency to conscience or to convictions; Christianity is being true to Jesus Christ.

Biblical Ethics, 111 L

Both nations and individuals have tried Christianity and abandoned it, because it has been found too difficult; but no man has ever gone through the crisis of deliberately making Jesus Lord and found Him to be a failure.

The Love of God—The Making of a Christian, 680 R

For the past three hundred years men have been pointing out how similar Jesus Christ's teachings are to other good teachings. We have to remember that Christianity, if it is not a supernatural miracle, is a sham.

The Highest Good, 548 L

Wherever Christianity comes straight home to us, we ignore it; when it gets at others, we preach it for all we are worth. The general history of Christianity is that it has been tried and abandoned because it is found to be difficult; but wherever it has been tried and honourably gone on with, it has never failed.

Shade of His Hand, 1207 L

In every age it has always been the despised crowd that have been called Christians.

Christian Disciplines, Volume 2, The Discipline of Patience, 337 R

Wherever Christianity has ceased to be vigorous it is because it has become Christian *ethics* instead of the Christian *evangel*. People will listen more readily to an exposition of the Sermon on the Mount than they will to the meaning of the Cross; but they forget that to preach the Sermon on the Mount apart from the Cross is to preach an impossibility.

Biblical Ethics, 111 L

The essence of Christianity is that we give the Son of God a chance to live and move and have His being in us, and the meaning of all spiritual growth is that He has an increasing opportunity to manifest Himself in our mortal flesh.

The Place of Help, 994 R

CHRISTMAS (See INCARNATION)

CHURCH

Christianity is in its essence social. When once we begin to live from the otherworldly standpoint, as Jesus Christ wants us to live, we shall need all the fellowship with other Christians we can get. Some of us can do without Church fellowship because we are not Christians of the otherworldly order. Immediately a man dares to live on Jesus Christ's line, the world, the flesh and the devil are dead against him in every particular. "The only virtue you will have in the eyes of the world as My disciples," says Jesus, "is that you will be hated." That is why we need to be knit together with those of like faith; and that is the meaning of the Christian Church.

Approved Unto God, 6 L

When the world gets in a bad way, she refers to the Church; when she is prosperous, she hates it. If men could blot out the standard of the Christian Church they would do so; but in a crisis they find a need in their own heart.

Approved Unto God, 12 R

The Christian Church should not be a secret society of specialists, but a public manifestation of believers in Jesus.

Facing Reality, 34 R

The Church is a separated band of people who are united to God by the regenerating power of the Spirit, and the bedrock of membership in the Church is that we know who Jesus is by a personal revelation of Him. The indwelling Spirit is the supreme Guide, and He keeps us absorbed with our Lord.

Conformed to His Image, 357 R

The Church ceases to be a spiritual society when it is on the look-out for the development of its own organisation.

My Utmost for His Highest, July 12, 800 R

The emphasis to-day is placed on the furtherance of an organisation; the note is, "We must keep this thing going." If we are in God's order the thing will go; if we are not in His order, it won't.

Conformed to His Image, 357 R

When we are baptised with the Holy Ghost we are no longer isolated believers but part of the Mystical Body of Christ. Beware of attempting to live a holy life alone; it is impossible. Paul continually insists on the "together" aspect—"God . . . hath quickened us *together*, . . . and hath raised us up *together*, and made us sit *together* . . ." (Ephesians 2:4–6). The "together" aspect is always the work of the Holy Ghost.

He Shall Glorify Me, 477 R

There is only one thing as futile as the Roman Catholic Church and that is Protestantism. In Roman Catholicism the great dominating authority is Churchianity; the Church is vested with all authority. In Protestantism it is what the Book says that is the supreme authority, and a man gets rest when he decides for either. "I am going to give up all the turmoil and let my Church do my thinking for me." If you put your faith in a Church, it will solve your problems for you. Or you may stake your faith in Bibliolatry with the same result. "Ye search the scriptures, because ye think in them ye have eternal life; and these are they which bear witness of Me, and ye will not come to Me that ye may have life" (John 5:39–40 RV). Jesus Christ says neither the Church nor the Bible is the authority, but "I am the Way, the Truth, and the Life"; the Church and the Bible are secondary. The context of the Bible is Jesus Christ, and a personal relationship with Him interprets the Bible in a man's life.

The Shadow of an Agony, 1173 R

CIRCUMSTANCES

Think of the imperative haste in our spirit to wish we were somewhere else! That danger is always there, and we have to watch it. When I wish I was somewhere else I am not doing my duty to God where I am. If I am ill-tempered, set on some change of circumstances, I find God is not supporting me at all; I have worried myself outside the moral frontier where He works and my soul won't sing; there is no joy in God, no peace in believing.

The Highest Good—The Pilgrim's Song Book, 534 L

Have you got hold of this secret that if you are right with God, the very thing which is an affliction to you is working out an eternal weight of glory? The afflictions may come from good people or from bad people, but behind the whole thing is God.

The Love of God—The Message of Invincible Consolation, 671 L

Whenever Paul tries to state the unfathomable joy and glory which he has in the heavenlies in Christ Jesus, it is as if he cannot find words to express his meaning. In order to try to express it here* he balances his words—for instance, "affliction" is matched with "glory"; "light" is matched with "weight"; and "moment" is matched with "eternal." I wonder if we balance our words like that?

The Love of God—The Message of Invincible Consolation, 671 L
*See 2 Corinthians 4:17.

The fiery furnaces are there by God's direct permission. It is misleading to imagine that we are developed in spite of our circumstances; we are developed because of them. It is mastery *in* circumstances that is needed, not mastery over them.

The Love of God—The Message of Invincible Consolation, 674 R

Can I see Jesus in my present circumstances? Is it an obscure farther shore, with wild waves between? can I see Him walking on the waves? Is it a fiery furnace? can I see Him walking in the midst of the fire? Is it a placid, commonplace day? can I see Him there? If so, that is the perpetual mystery of the guidance of God, that is Eternal Life.

God's Workmanship, 426 R

We talk about "circumstances over which we have no control." None of us have control over our circumstances, but we are responsible for the way we pilot ourselves in the midst of things as they are. Two boats can sail in opposite directions in the same wind, according to the skill of the pilot. The pilot who conducts his vessel on to the rocks says he could not help it, the wind was in that direction; the one who took his vessel into the harbour had the same wind, but he knew how to trim his sails so that the wind conducted him in the direction he wanted. Never allow to yourself that you could not help this or that; and never say you reach anywhere *in spite of* circumstances; we all attain *because of* circumstances and no other way.

The Moral Foundations of Life, 722 L

There is a difference between circumstances and environment. We cannot control our circumstances, but we are the deciders of our own environment. . . . Our environment depends upon our personal reaction to circumstances.

Not Knowing Whither, 867 L

No matter how disagreeable things may be, say—"Lord, I am delighted to obey Thee in this matter," and instantly the Son of God presses to the front and in our human minds there is formed the way of reasoning that glorifies Jesus.

Our Brilliant Heritage, 938 R

(Continued)

CIRCUMSTANCES *(Continued)*

"Circumstances over which I have no control" is a perfectly true phrase, but it must never be made to mean that we cannot control ourselves in those circumstances. No matter into what perplexing circumstances God's providence may lead us or allow us to go, we have to see to it that in our reaction to those circumstances, which dance around us so perplexingly, we exhibit a personal relation to the highest we know. It is only by living in the presence of God that we cease to act in an ungodlike manner in perplexing circumstances.

Not Knowing Whither, 867 R

God does not further our spiritual life in spite of our circumstances, but in and by our circumstances.

Not Knowing Whither, 900 L

Are you saying to God, "I shall not accept these circumstances"? God will not punish you; but you will punish yourself when you realise that He was giving you a glorious opportunity of filling up that which is behind of the afflictions of Christ.

Our Brilliant Heritage, 940 R

It is a good thing to keep a note of the things you prayed about when you were in distress. We remain ignorant of ourselves because we do not keep a spiritual autobiography.

Our Portrait in Genesis, 976 R

Our Lord in His historic life came up against the providential order of tyranny, to which He submitted; He also met hatred and detestation and compromise; and He is born into the same kind of circumstances in our bodily lives. So beware of getting on the line of "Oh, well, if only I had better circumstances." The circumstances of our Lord were anything but ideal, they were full of difficulties. Perhaps ours are the same,

and we have to watch that we remain true to the life of the Son of God in us, not true to our own aims and ends. There is always a danger of mistaking our own aim and end for the aim of the life of God in us.

The Psychology of Redemption, 1072 R

We are inclined to ask God to do the magic business, to perform a miracle which will alter our external circumstances; but if we are ever going to understand what the God whom Jesus Christ presents is like, we have to remember that that is not His first job. The first thing God does is to alter a man's disposition on the inside, and then enable him to deal with the "mess" on the outside.

The Servant as His Lord, 1277 L

Tribulation describes a section of a man's life. Rightly or wrongly, we are exactly in the condition we are in. I am sorry for the Christian who has not some part of his circumstances he wishes was not there!

The Servant as His Lord, 1277 R

When you are joyful, *be* joyful; when you are sad, *be* sad. If God has given you a sweet cup, don't make it bitter; and if He has given you a bitter cup, don't try and make it sweet; take things as they come.

Shade of His Hand, 1226 L

It is in the actual circumstances of my life that I have to find out whether the wisdom of worshipping God can steer me.

Shade of His Hand, 1200 R

When we are rightly related to God we must let things have their way with us and not pretend things are not as they are. . . . Don't deal only with the section that is sad or with the section that is joyful; deal with them together. When we accept God's purpose for us in Christ Jesus, we know that "all things work together for good."

Shade of His Hand, 1225 R

Circumstances are the things that twist a man's thinking into contortions.

The Shadow of an Agony, 1174 R

We all have the trick of saying—If only I were not where I am!—If only I had not got the kind of people I have to live with! If our faith or our religion does not help us in the conditions we are in, we have either a further struggle to go through, or we had better abandon that faith and religion.

The Shadow of an Agony, 1178 L

To say "[military] camp life has made men worse" is not true; nothing can! Camp life strips the veneer of civilised life from a man, and he comes out with what he is; he has to reveal himself, but nothing can make a man either better or worse than he is.

The Shadow of an Agony, 1182 R

The surf that distresses the ordinary swimmer produces in the surf-rider the super joy of going clean through it. Apply that to our own circumstances; these very things—tribulation, distress, persecution—produce in us the super joy; they are not things to fight. We are more than conquerors through Him *in* all these things; not in spite of them, but in the midst of them.

My Utmost for His Highest, March 7, 757 L

If a man cannot prove his religion in the valley, it is not worth anything.

Shade of His Hand, 1200 L

Watch God's cyclones. The only way God sows His saints is by His whirlwind. Are you going to prove an empty pod? It will depend on whether or not you are actually living in the light of what you have seen. Let God fling you out, and do not go until He does. If you select your own spot, you will prove an empty pod. If God sows you, you will bring forth fruit.

My Utmost for His Highest, March 11, 758 L

The saint is hilarious when he is crushed with difficulties, because the thing is so ludicrously impossible to anyone but God.

My Utmost for His Highest, August 2, 808 L

CIRCUMSTANCES, ENGINEERED BY GOD

We have to maintain spiritual reality wherever we are placed by the engineering of our circumstances by God; as servants we are to be subject to our masters, to the froward master as well as to the good and gentle. That is where the shoe pinches, and whenever you feel the pinch it is time you went to the death of something.

Biblical Ethics, 95 L

We imagine that God must engineer special circumstances for us, peculiar sufferings; He never does, because that would feed our pride; He engineers things which from the standpoint of human pride are a humiliation.

Conformed to His Image, 381 R

We are not fundamentally free; external circumstances are not in our hands, they are in God's hands, the one thing in which we are free is in our personal relationship to God. We are not responsible for the circumstances we are in, but we are responsible for the way we allow those circumstances to affect us; we can either allow them to get on top of us, or we can allow them to transform us into what God wants us to be.

Conformed to His Image, 354 L

(Continued)

CIRCUMSTANCES, ENGINEERED BY GOD
(Continued)

If I recognise Jesus as my Lord, I have no business with where He engineers my circumstances. If He gives me the pictorial thrill of enabling me to do something ostensibly wonderful, and then suddenly alters my circumstances and puts me, so to speak, at the bottom of the ocean, what right have I to be afraid? If Jesus Christ can keep me walking on the top of the waves, He can keep me underneath them.

God's Workmanship, 434 L

> # Prayer is the battle; it is a matter of indifference where you are. Whichever way God engineers circumstances, the duty is to pray.

My Utmost for His Highest, October 17, 834 R

One of the last things we learn is that God engineers our circumstances; we do not believe He does; we say we do. Never look for second causes; if you do, you will go wrong. We blunder when we look at circumstances as secondary, "And we know that all things work together for good to them that love God, to them who are the called according to His purpose."

God's Workmanship, 434 R

The attitude of a Christian towards the providential order in which he is placed is to recognise that God is behind it for purposes of His own.

Biblical Ethics, 99 R

God engineers circumstances to see what we will do. Will we be the children of our Father in heaven, or will we go back again to the meaner, common-sense attitude? Will we stake all and stand true to Him? "Be thou faithful unto death, and I will give thee a crown of life." The crown of life means I shall see that my Lord has got the victory after all, even in me.

The Highest Good—The Pilgrim's Song Book, 530 L

The circumstances of a saint's life are ordained by God, and not by happy-go-lucky chance. There is no such thing as chance in the life of a saint, and we shall find that God by His providence brings our bodies into circumstances that we cannot understand a bit, but the Spirit of God understands; He is bringing us into places and among people and under conditions in order that the intercession of the Holy Spirit in us may take a particular line.

If Ye Shall Ask, 634 L

God engineers our circumstances as He did those of His Son; all we have to do is to follow where He places us. The majority of us are busy trying to place ourselves.

The Love of God—The Ministry of the Unnoticed, 667 L

The only place to prosecute our life in Christ is just where we are, in the din of things, and the only way in which we can prosecute our life in Christ is to remember that it is God Who engineers circumstances, and that the only place where we can be of use to Him is where we are, not where we are not. God is in the obvious things.

Our Brilliant Heritage, 950 R

Wherever the providence of God may dump us down, in a slum, in a shop, in the desert, we have to labour along the line of His direction. Never allow this thought— "I am of no use where I am," because you certainly can be of no use where you are not! Wherever He has engineered your circumstances, pray.

So Send I You, 1325 L

Ministering as opportunity surrounds does not mean selecting our surroundings, but being very selectly God's in any haphazard surroundings He may engineer for us. The characteristics we exhibit in our immediate surroundings are an indication of what we shall be like in other circumstances by and by.

So Send I You, 1310 R

We have no right to judge where we should be put, or to have preconceived notions as to what God is fitting us for. God engineers everything; wherever He puts us, our one great aim is to pour out a whole-hearted devotion to Him in that particular work. "Whatsoever thy hand findeth to do, do it with thy might."

My Utmost for His Highest, April 23, 773 L

CIVILISATION

Civilisation is the gloss over chaos and wrath; we are so sheltered that we are blinded to our need of God, and when calamity comes there is nothing to hold to. Over and over again in the history of the world man has made life into chaos. Men try to find their true life in everything but God, but they cannot.

Conformed to His Image, 345 R

Civilisation is based on principles which imply that the passing moment is permanent. The only permanent thing is God, and if I put anything else as permanent, I become atheistic. I must build only on God (John 14:6).

The Highest Good—Thy Great Redemption, 565 L

At the basis of trade and civilised life lie oppression and tyranny. Whether you are king or subject, says Solomon, you cannot find joy in any system of civilised life, or in trade and commerce; for underneath there is a rivalry that stings and bites, and the kindest man will put his heel on his greatest friend. These are not the blind statements of a disappointed man, but statements of facts discerned by the wisest man that ever lived.

Shade of His Hand, 1209 L

"The best thing to do is to be a Bohemian and have nothing to do with civilised life; to live from hand to mouth and not do a hand's turn." This has been a cult in every age of civilised life. We have seen it in our own day in Charles Wagner and his plea for a simple life, and in Walt Whitman and Thoreau, who advocated the simple life on a higher line. When a man is fed up with a certain line of things, he revolts and goes to the opposite extreme. To-day tyranny and oppression have eaten into men's sense of justice, and they have revolted and gone to the other extreme.

Shade of His Hand, 1209 L

No education, no culture, no sociology or government can touch the fathomless rot at the basis of human life in its deepest down storey. We live in the twenty-second storey up, and the tragedies we touch are only personal tragedies; only one in a million comes to understand the havoc that underlies everything. This line of thinking is absolutely important, not relatively important.

Shade of His Hand, 1228 L

The destruction of every civilisation there has ever been has come about through a force for which the civilisation had a contempt.

Notes on Isaiah, 1377 L

(Continued)

CIVILISATION (Continued)

The evidence of Christianity is not the good works that go on in the world; these are the outcome of the good there is in human nature, which still holds remnants of what God designed it to be. There is much that is admirable in the civilisation of the world, but there is no promise in it. The natural virtues exhaust themselves; they do not develop. Jesus Christ is not a social reformer; He came to alter *us* first, and if any social reform is to be done on earth, we will have to do it.

The Psychology of Redemption, 1080 L

CLOSED MIND

It is an easy thing to argue from precedent because it makes everything simple, but it is a risky thing to do. Give God "elbow room"; let Him come into His universe as He pleases. If we confine God in His working to religious people or to certain ways, we place ourselves on an equality with God.

Baffled to Fight Better, 51 L

[Job's friends] had the ban of finality about their views, which is always the result of theology being put before God. The friends suffered as well as Job, and the suffering which comes from having outgrown one's theological suit is of an acute order.

Baffled to Fight Better, 49 R

COMFORT

The "gospel of temperament" works very well if you are suffering only from psychical neuralgia, so to speak, and all you need is a cup of tea; but if you have a real deep complaint, the injunction to "Cheer up" is an insult. What is the use of telling a woman who has lost her husband and sons in the war to "Cheer up and look on the bright

side"? There *is* no bright side; it is absolute blackness, and if God cannot come to her help, truly she is in a pitiable condition. It is part of the role of a man to be honest enough to know when he is up against cases like this. A gospel based on preconceived notions is merely an irritant.

Baffled to Fight Better, 56 L

The place for the comforter is not that of one who preaches, but of the comrade who says nothing, but prays to God about the matter. The biggest thing you can do for those who are suffering is not to talk platitudes, not to ask questions, but to get into contact with God, and the "greater works" will be done by prayer (see John 14:12–13).

Baffled to Fight Better, 56 R

When we come to the real downright problems of life, which have no explicit answer saving by the Designer of life, we are exactly where Job was, and we can understand his petulance with those who tried to answer him. If Job's friends had remained dumb and reverent with what they did not understand, as they did during the first seven days, they would have been a great sustaining to him, and they too would have approached the place Job ultimately reached and would not have been rebuked by God. Job's friends never once prayed for him; all they did was to try and make coin for the enrichment of their own creed out of his sufferings.

Baffled to Fight Better, 55 R

The sympathy which is reverent with what it cannot understand is worth its weight in gold.

Baffled to Fight Better, 69 L

There is no reasonable hope for countless lives on account of this war, and it is shallow nonsense to tell them to "cheer up"; life to them is a hell of darkness of the most appalling order. The one who preaches at such a time is an impertinence, but the one who says "I don't know why you are going through this; it is black and desperate, but I will wait with you," is an unspeakable benediction and sustaining.

Baffled to Fight Better, 69 R

Some years ago the wife of a murdered missionary in China told me of the blank amazed agony of those days. . . . In those days of dull dreary reaction the people who nearly drove her wild with distress were those who knew chapter and verse, the "why" and "wherefore" of her suffering and grief. She said, "I used to beat a tattoo on the floor with my foot while they chattered, crying in my heart 'How long, O Lord, how long?'" One day as she lay prostrate on the sofa, the old minister who had known her husband in the glad other days entered the room softly; he did not speak but came gently over to her and kissed her on the forehead and went out without saying a word. "From that moment," she said, "my heart began to heal."

*Christian Disciplines, Volume 1,
The Discipline of Suffering, 281 L*

COMMANDMENTS OF GOD

There are teachers who argue that the Sermon on the Mount supersedes the Ten Commandments, and that, because "we are not under law, but under grace" (RV), it does not matter whether we honour our father and mother, whether we covet, *et cetera*. Beware of statements like this: *There is no need nowadays to observe giving the tenth either of money or of time; we are in a new dispensation and everything belongs to God.*

That, in practical application, is sentimental dust-throwing. The giving of the tenth is not a sign that all belongs to God, but a sign that the tenth belongs to God and the rest is ours, and we are held responsible for what we do with it.

Studies in the Sermon on the Mount, 1443 L

The moral law ordained by God does not make itself weak to the weak; it does not palliate our shortcomings; it takes no account of our heredity and our infirmities; it demands that we be absolutely moral. Not to recognise this is to be less than alive. God's laws are not watered down to suit anyone; if God did that He would cease to be God. The moral law never alters for the noblest or the weakest; it remains abidingly and eternally the same.

Biblical Ethics, 89 R

God's "oughts" never alter; we never grow out of them. Our difficulty is that we find in ourselves this attitude—"I ought to do this, but I won't"; "I ought to do that, but I don't want to." That puts out of court the idea that if you teach men what is right they will do it—they won't; what is needed is a power which will enable a man to do what he knows is right. Once we realise this we see why it was necessary for Jesus Christ to come. The Redemption is the Reality which alters inability into ability.

Biblical Ethics, 90 L

If the old commandments were difficult, our Lord's principles are unfathomably more difficult. Our Lord goes behind the old law to the disposition. Everything He teaches is impossible unless He can put into us His Spirit and remake us from within. The Sermon on the Mount is quite unlike the Ten Commandments in the sense of its being absolutely unworkable unless Jesus Christ can remake us.

Studies in the Sermon on the Mount, 1443 L

COMMONPLACE
(See DRUDGERY and ORDINARY)

COMMON SENSE

There is always a quarrel between our common sense and the revelations made in God's Book.

The Psychology of Redemption, 1095 L

We hear it said that Jesus Christ taught nothing contrary to common sense: everything Jesus Christ taught was contrary to common sense. Not one thing in the Sermon on the Mount is common sense. The basis of Christianity is neither common sense nor rationalism; it springs from another centre, viz. a personal relationship to God in Christ Jesus in which everything is ventured on from a basis that is not seen.

Shade of His Hand, 1241 L

The danger with us is that we want to water down the things that Jesus says and make them mean something in accordance with common sense; if it were only common sense, it was not worth while for Him to say it. The things Jesus says about prayer are supernatural revelations.

My Utmost for His Highest, May 26, 784 R

COMMUNITY
(See also SOLITARINESS)

"And not one of them said that aught of the things which he possessed was his own; but they had all things common" (Acts 4:32 RV).

"And let us consider one another to provoke unto love and good works; not forsaking the assembling of ourselves together. . . ." (Hebrews 10:24–25).

These two passages serve to indicate the main characteristic of Christianity, viz., the "together" aspect; false religions inculcate an isolated holy life. Try and develop a holy life in private, and you find it cannot be done. Individuals can only live the true life when they are dependent on one another.

Biblical Ethics, 97 L

Immediately you try to develop holiness alone and fix your eyes on your own whiteness, you lose the whole meaning of Christianity. The Holy Spirit makes a man fix his eyes on his Lord and on intense activity for others. In the early Middle Ages people had the idea that Christianity meant living a holy life apart from the world and its sociability, apart from its work and citizenship. That type of holiness is foreign to the New Testament; it cannot be reconciled with the records of the life of Jesus. The people of His day called Him "the friend of publicans and sinners" because He spent so much time with them.

Biblical Ethics, 97 R

Our Lord insists on the social aspect of our lives: He shows very distinctly that we cannot further ourselves alone.

Biblical Psychology, 186 L

How insistent God is that we keep together in fellowship! In the natural world it is only by mixing with other people that we get the corners rubbed off. It is the way we are made naturally, and God takes this principle and transfigures it. "Not forsaking the assembling of ourselves together" is a Scriptural injunction.

Biblical Psychology, 189 L

Beware of isolation; beware of the idea that you have to develop a holy life alone. It is impossible to develop a holy life alone; you will develop into an oddity and a peculiarism, into something utterly unlike what God wants you to be. The only way to develop spiritually is to go into the society of God's own children, and you will soon find how God alters your set. God does not contradict our social instincts; He alters them.

Biblical Psychology, 189 L

"*And who is my neighbour?*" (Luke 10:29). Jesus gives an amazing reply, viz., that the answer to the question, "Who is my neighbour?" is not to be found in the claim of the person to be loved, but in the heart of the one who loves. If my heart is right with God, every human being is my neighbour.

Conformed to His Image, 366 R

"I can't stand coming in contact with other people"—why? Because when you do you find the beautiful conceptions and thoughts you get when you are alone don't work. Separating myself from other people is the greatest means of producing deception because there is nothing to clash against me. Immediately people clash against me I know whether my beautiful thinking really expresses "me," or is a garment that disguises the real "me." If my actual life is not in agreement with my thinking, the danger is that I exclude myself from actualities which bring home to me the knowledge of what I am, in spite of what I think.

God's Workmanship, 418 L

To live a life alone with God does not mean that we live it apart from everyone else. The connection between godly men and women and those associated with them is continually revealed in the Bible, e.g., 1 Timothy 4:10.

Not Knowing Whither, 867 L

The next time you feel inclined to grouse over uncongenial companions, remember that Jesus Christ had a devil in His company for three years.

The Psychology of Redemption, 1073 L

We must keep ourselves in touch, not with theories, but with people, and never get out of touch with human beings, if we are going to use the word of God skilfully amongst them.

Workmen of God, 1341 L

If you are a worker, He will constantly surround you with different kinds of people, with different difficulties, and He will constantly put you to school amongst those facts. He will keep you in contact with human stuff, and human stuff is very sordid; in fact, human stuff is made of just the same stuff as you and I are made of; do not shut yourself away from it. Beware of the tendency to live a life apart and shut away. Get amongst men.

Workmen of God, 1341 L

COMPASSION

Remember, each life has a solitary way alone with God. Be reverent with His ways in dealing with other souls because you have no notion, any more than Job had, why things are as they are. Most of us are much too desirous of getting hold of a line which will vindicate us in our view of God.

Disciples Indeed, 388 R

We are in danger of being stern where God is tender, and of being tender where God is stern.

The Love of God—The Message of Invincible Consolation, 673 L

COMPETITION

"And he builded a city" (Genesis 4:17).

The first civilisation was founded by a murderer, and the whole basis of civilised life is a vast, complicated, more or less gilded-over system of murder. We find it more conducive to human welfare not to murder men outright; we do it by a system of competition.

Our Portrait in Genesis, 963 L

It is ingrained in our thinking that competition and rivalry are essential to the carrying on of civilised life; that is why Jesus Christ's statements seem wild and ridiculous. They are the statements either of a madman or of God Incarnate. To carry out the Sermon on the Mount is frankly impossible to anyone but a fool, and who is the fool? The man who has been born again and who dares to carry out in his individual life the teaching of Jesus. And what will happen? The inevitable result, not the success he would otherwise have. A hard saying, but true.

Our Portrait in Genesis, 963 R

COMPLAINING

A man who is on the grousing line has no brightness or joy, no time for other people; he is taken up with the diseases of his own mind.

He Shall Glorify Me, 496 R

We cannot look up if we are murmuring; we are like the child who does not want to do what he is told, and the father comes and says, "Now look up," but the child won't. We behave like that with God; our circumstances are hard, we are not making progress in life, and the Spirit of God says, "Look up," but we refuse and say, "I'm not going to play this game of faith any more."

The Highest Good—The Pilgrim's Song Book, 530 L

COMPROMISE

We must never compromise with the kingdoms of this world; the temptation the devil presents is that we should compromise. We recognise his temptation in the teaching which proclaims that there is no such being as the devil and no such place as hell; much that is called sin is a mere defect; men and women are like poor babes lost in the wood; just be kind and gentle with them; talk about the Fatherhood of God, about Universalism and Brotherhood, the kindness of Providence and the nobility of man. Our Lord's temptations reveal where the onslaught will come.

The Psychology of Redemption, 1081 R

CONCEIT

Conceit means my own point of view and I don't care what anyone else says. "Be not wise in your own conceits," says Paul. Conceit makes the way God deals with me personally the binding standard for others.

Approved Unto God, 13 R

CONCENTRATION

To concentrate is not to be absorbed or carried away with a subject; concentration is the sternest physical effort. There is nothing spiritual about the brain. Control over associated ideas must be acquired; it is not a natural gift. Never garrison an infirmity with indifference—"Oh, I can't." DO IT!

Approved Unto God, 6 L

God may be dealing with you on the line of considering the lilies; He is causing you to take deeper root and meanwhile you do not bear flowers. . . . Don't get impatient with yourself; your dominating interest is taking deeper root. In all probability in your time of active service you were living from hand to mouth on spooned meat, you nourished your life by the interesting details of religious life, you had no nutritious root, and your work proved to be an elaborate way of evading concentration on God. There are far more people interested in consecration than concentration. It is easier to fuss around at work than to worship; easier to pay attention to details, to say our prayers or conduct a meeting, than to concentrate on God.

Facing Reality, 28 L

'. . . *work out your own salvation"*
(Philippians 2:12).
'The normal course of all religious experience is expansion followed by concentration" (Forsyth).
When God gives a vision of what sanctification means or what the life of faith means, we have instantly to pay for the vision, and we pay for it by the inevitable law that "expansion must be followed by concentration." . . . Every expansion of brain and heart that God gives in meetings or in private reading of the Bible must be paid for inevitably and inexorably by concentration on our part, not by consecration. God will continually bring us into circumstances to make us prove whether we will work out with determined concentration what He has worked in.

Conformed to His Image, 358 R

Your mind can never be under your control unless you bring it there; there is no gift for control. You may pray till Doomsday but your brain will never concentrate if you don't make it concentrate.

Disciples Indeed, 404 R

Every expansion of heart or brain or spirit must be paid for in added concentration. . . . In our personal lives every expansion of heart, whether it is the awakening of human love, or bereavement, must be paid for by watchfulness; if it is not, looseness, the feeling of all-abroadness, ending in moral

collapse, is sure to result. It is because people do not understand the way they are made that all the havoc is produced in the lives of those who really have had times with God and experienced expansions of heart, but they have forgotten to concentrate, and the general feeling of looseness is a sure sign that God's presence has gone.

Our Portrait in Genesis, 979 L

The one message all through the Sermon on the Mount is—Concentrate on God, and be carefully careless about everything else. Today we are evading concentration on God and devoting ourselves to the cause of Christian work. The busy-ness of duties will knock us out of relationship to God more quickly than the devil.

The Place of Help, 1007 R

We may have a dead set about our lives, but it may be a dead set on comfort or on money, not a dead set on God and on the wonder and majesty of His dealings. The rich fool in our Lord's parable did not ask his soul to consider God, but to consider his possessions—"Soul, thou hast much goods laid up for many years; take thine ease, eat, drink, be merry." Be careful to concentrate on a worthy object.

The Place of Help, 1013 L

An artist or a musician must know how to brood on his conception. It is no use being the home of furtive ideas and having conceptions that come floating through like sunrise clouds. The artist has to go after the idea and stick to it until it is wrought into the character of his conception. It is not easy to maintain the conception of Jesus Christ as Master. Spiritual concentration is needed to do it.

The Place of Help, 1018 L

(Continued)

CONCENTRATION
(Continued)

You no more need a holiday from spiritual concentration than your heart needs a holiday from beating. You cannot have a moral holiday and remain moral, nor can you have a spiritual holiday and remain spiritual. God wants you to be entirely his, and this means that you have to watch to keep yourself fit. It takes a tremendous amount of time. Some of us expect to "clear the numberless ascensions"* in about two minutes.

> *My Utmost for His Highest, April 15, 770 R*
> *A quote from George MacDonald: "But think not thou, by one wild bound, to clear / The numberless ascensions, more and more, / Of starry stairs that must be climbed, before / Thou comest to the Father's likeness near. . . ."*

CONFESSION

There is never any shattering blow of God on the life that pays attention to the checks of the Spirit, but every time there is a spurning of the still small voice, the hardening of the life away from God goes on until destruction comes and shatters it. When I realise that there is something between God and me, it is at the peril of my soul I don't stop everything and get it put right. Immediately a thing makes itself conscious to me, it has no business there.

> *Conformed to His Image, 365 R*

"O my God, I lie in Thy fire burning and purifying—so much dross I seem to discover today, so little of Thy sweet and lovely grace in my dealing with others' faults. Lord, forgive me."

> *Knocking at God's Door, March 8, 639 R*

A false idea of confessing makes us tell secrets that should never be told; they are between God and the soul. There are affinities of heart and of life that are dealt with by God in secret and we must never say a word about them to others.

> *So Send I You, 1306 L*

CONFIDENCE IN GOD

In the Christian life the saint is ever young; amazingly and boisterously young, certain that everything is all right. A young Christian is remarkably full of impulse and delight, because he realises the salvation of God; but this is the real gaiety of knowing that we may cast all our cares on Him and that He careth for us. This is the greatest indication of our identification with Jesus Christ.

> *Facing Reality, 29 R*

The one thing Satan tries to shake is our confidence in God. It is not difficult for our confidence to be shaken if we build on our experience; but if we realise that all we experience is but the doorway leading to the knowledge of God, Satan may shake that as much as he likes, but he cannot shake the fact that God remains faithful (see 2 Timothy 2:13), and we must not cast away our confidence in Him.

> *The Highest Good—The Pilgrim's Song Book, 533 L*

"The Lord is *my* rock, and *my* fortress, and *my* deliverer; *my* God, *my* strong rock . . . *my* shield, and the horn of *my* salvation, *my* high tower" (Psalm 18:2 RV). Note the "my's" here, and laugh at everything in the nature of misgiving for ever after!

> *The Highest Good—Thy Great Redemption, 564 R*

"Above all, taking the shield of faith." Faith is unbreakable confidence in the Personality of God, not in His power. There are some things over which we may lose faith if we have confidence in God's power only. There is so much that looks like the mighty power of God that is not. We must have confidence in God over and above everything He may do, and stand in confidence that His character is unsullied. Faith stands under all tests—"Though He slay me, yet will I trust in Him."

If Ye Shall Ask, 615 L

So many of us limit our praying because we are not reckless in our confidence in God.

If Ye Shall Ask, 622 R

It seems so ridiculous and so conceited to say that God Almighty is our Father and that He is looking after our affairs; but looked at from the position in which Jesus places us, we find it is a marvellous revelation of truth.

The Moral Foundations of Life, 700 R

We forget that we have to build in absolute confidence on God. There is nothing more heroic than to have faith in God when you can see so many better things in which to have faith.

Not Knowing Whither, 875 R

Robert Browning wrote from the standpoint of Hebrew wisdom, viz. that of unshakeable confidence in God, but he also wrote with the mind of Solomon or Ibsen or Shakespeare for the actual facts of life. He blinks [deliberately ignores] nothing, yet underneath is the confidence that the basis of a right direction of things is not a man's reason but his strong faith that God is not unjust; and that the man who hangs in to the honour of God will come out all right.

Shade of His Hand, 1201 L

Every time your wits compete with the worship of God you had better take a strong dose of Isaiah 30:15–16—"In returning and rest shall ye be saved; in quietness and in confidence shall be your strength: and ye would not."

Our Portrait in Genesis, 966 R

Misgiving is the pathetic poem of the whole of human life in a word; it signifies the destruction of confidence. Many things will destroy confidence; as in the case of Jacob, cunning and sin will do it, or cowardice; but in every experience of misgiving there is an element which it is difficult to define, and the shallow element is the most difficult. "I can't understand why I have no confidence in God"; the reason may be a matter of digestion, not enough fresh air or sleep, too much tea—something slight. It is the shallow things that put us wrong much more quickly than the big things.

Our Portrait in Genesis, 976 L

The great object of the enemy of our souls is to make us fling away our confidence in God; to do this is nothing less than spiritual suicide. When we experience misgiving because we have sinned there is never any ambiguity as to its cause; the Holy Spirit brings conviction home like a lightning flash.

Our Portrait in Genesis, 976 L

God expects His children to be so confident in Him that in a crisis they are the ones upon whom He can rely. A great point is reached spiritually when we stop worrying God over personal matters or over any matter. God expects of us the one thing that glorifies Him—and that is to remain absolutely confident in Him, remembering what He has said beforehand, and sure that His purposes will be fulfilled.

The Place of Help, 996 L

(Continued)

CONFIDENCE IN GOD
(Continued)

In personal life, in Church life and in national life, we try Jesus Christ's teaching, but as soon as it becomes difficult we abandon it, or else we compromise. "Take no thought, saying, What shall we eat? or, What shall we drink? or, Wherewithal shall we be clothed?" Bank your faith in God, do the duty that lies nearest and "damn the consequences." Who is prepared to do this, prepared to stake his all on Jesus Christ and His word? We do it in preaching and in books, but not in practical life.

Shade of His Hand, 1218 R

Have I any confidence in the flesh? Or have I got beyond all confidence in myself and in men and women of God, in books and prayers and ecstasies; and is my confidence placed now in God Himself, not in His blessings? "I am the Almighty God"—El-Shaddai, the Father-Mother God. The one thing for which we are all being disciplined is to know that God is real. As soon as God becomes real, other people become shadows. Nothing that other saints do or say can ever perturb the one who is built on God.

My Utmost for His Highest, January 19, 741 L

Certainty is the mark of the commonsense life; gracious uncertainty is the mark of the spiritual life. To be certain of God means that we are uncertain in all our ways; we do not know what a day may bring forth. This is generally said with a sigh of sadness; it should be rather an expression of breathless expectation. We are uncertain of the next step, but we are certain of God. Immediately we abandon to God, and do the duty that lies nearest, He packs our life with surprises all the time.

My Utmost for His Highest, April 29, 775 L

Faith in God is a terrific venture in the dark; we have to believe that God is love in spite of all that contradicts it. Every soul represents some kind of battlefield. The great point for the Christian is to remain perfectly confident in God.

The Love of God, 661 L

CONSCIENCE

My conscience may be a competitor against Jesus Christ; I may be conscientious to the backbone, as Saul of Tarsus was, and be anti-Christ.

Biblical Ethics, 111 L

My conscience makes me know what I ought to do, but it does not empower me to do it. "For that which I do I allow not: for what I would, that do I not; but what I hate, that do I" (Romans 7:15).

Disciples Indeed, 392 L

The result of the idea that we are a bundle of separate faculties, the faculty of faith having nothing to do with the faculty of conscience, makes it possible for a man to do the most unrighteous things in his business all the week and the most devout things on Sunday.

God's Workmanship, 414 R

Conscience is that faculty in a man that attaches itself to the highest he knows and tells him what the highest he knows demands that he does. Never be caught away with the phrase that conscience is the voice of God. If it were, it would be the most contradictory voice human ears ever listened to. Conscience is the eye of the soul and it looks out either towards God or towards what it regards as the highest, and the way conscience records is dependent entirely upon the light thrown on God (cf. Acts 26:9 and 24:16).

The Moral Foundations of Life, 705 R

'Having their conscience seared with a hot iron"
(1 Timothy 4:2).

If I do a wrong thing often enough, I
cease to realise the wrong in it. A bad man
can be perfectly happy in his badness. That
is what a seared conscience means.

Our Brilliant Heritage, 936 L

Men living in sin don't know anything
about it. Sin destroys the capacity of knowing what sin is.

The Highest Good, 555 R

Our critical faculties are given us for the
purpose of self-examination, and the way
to examine ourselves under the control of
the Spirit of God is to ask ourselves—"Am
I less sensitive than I used to be to the
indications of God's will, less sensitive
regarding purity, uprightness, goodness,
honesty and truth?" If I realise that I am, I
may be perfectly certain that something
I have done (not something done to me)
has seared my conscience. It has given me,
so to speak, a bloodshot eye of the soul and
I cannot see aright.

Our Brilliant Heritage, 936 L

God will never allow any of us to rest in a
sleep of conscience; He will reason with
us and rouse us, and then He will give
us a "clearing house" for conscience. . . .
The "clearing house" which God grants
to us through the atoning blood of Jesus
Christ is intercession. We enter into a
roused relationship with God through the
Atonement, and then we are put in the
place where we can repair the damage we
have done to other lives. No matter what
our spiritual experiences may be, if we
are in danger of forgetting what we owe
in intercession to the lives we damaged
before we got right with God, the Holy
Spirit will bring it back to us—"Remember that person, that relationship."

Notes on Isaiah, 1371 L

How Jesus Christ does cleanse our conscience! It is freedom not only from sin and
the damage sin has done, but emancipa-
tion from the impairing left by sin, from all
the distortions left in mind and imagination. Then when our conscience has been
cleansed from dead works, Jesus Christ
gives us the marvellously healing ministry
of intercession as "a clearing-house for conscience." Not only is all sense of past guilt
removed, but we are given the very secret
heart of God for the purpose of vicarious
intercession (see Romans 8:26–27).

The Philosophy of Sin, 1112 L

That "Conscience is the voice of God" is
easily proved to be absurd. If conscience
were the voice of God, it would be the same
in everyone.

The Philosophy of Sin, 1127 L

CONSECRATION

A Christian is a sanctified man in his business, or legal or civic affairs, or artistic and
literary affairs. Consecration is not the
giving over of the calling in life to God, but
the separation from all other callings and
the giving over of ourselves to God, letting
His providence place us where He will—in
business, or law, or science; in workshop, in
politics, or in drudgery. We are to be there
working according to the laws and principles of the Kingdom of God.

Christian Disciplines, Volume 2,
The Discipline of Loneliness, 323 R

Consecration is the narrow, lonely way to
over-flooding love. We are not called upon
to live long on this planet, but we are called
upon to be holy at any and every cost. If
obedience costs you your life, then pay it.

Christian Disciplines, Volume 2,
The Discipline of Loneliness, 324 L

CONTROVERSY
(*See* ARGUE / ARGUMENT)

CONVICTION OF SIN

When you hear a man cry out, like the publican of old, "God be merciful to me a sinner," you have the problem of the whole universe. That man has reached the realisation of himself at last; he knows that he is a guilty, immoral type of man and needs saving.

Approved Unto God, 14 R

There is nothing attractive about the Gospel to the natural man; the only man who finds the Gospel attractive is the man who is convicted of sin. Conviction of sin and being guilty of sins are not the same thing. Conviction of sin is produced by the incoming of the Holy Spirit because conscience is promptly made to look at God's demands and the whole nature cries out, in some form or other, "What must I do to be saved?"

Biblical Ethics, 115 L

Romans 7 is the classic for all time of the conflict a man experiences whose mind is awakened by the incoming of the light of God. A lot of tawdry stuff has been written on this chapter simply because Christians so misunderstand what conviction of sin really is. Conviction of sin such as the apostle Paul is describing does not come when a man is born again, nor even when he is sanctified, but long after, and then only to a few. It came to Paul as an apostle and saint, and he could diagnose sin as no other.

Biblical Ethics, 115 R

The worst state a man could be in is never to have had a twinge of conviction of sin; everything happy and peaceful, but absolutely dead to the realm of things Jesus represents.

Bringing Sons Unto Glory, 233 L

Knowledge of what sin is is in inverse ratio to its presence; only as sin goes do you realise what it is; when it is present you do not realise what it is because the nature of sin is that it destroys the capacity to know you sin.

Biblical Ethics, 115 R

The sense of sin is in inverse ratio to its presence; that is, the higher up and the deeper down we are saved, the more pangingly terrible is our conviction of sin. The holiest person is not the one who is not conscious of sin, but the one who is most conscious of what sin is. The one who talked most about sin was our Lord Jesus Christ.

The Highest Good, 555 L

When once the real touch of conviction of sin comes, it is hell on earth—there is no other word for it. One second of realising ourselves in the light of God means unspeakable agony and distress; but the marvel is that when the conviction does come, there is God in the very centre of the whole thing to save us from it.

The Highest Good—Thy Great Redemption, 558 R

In the early days of Christianity men brooded on their sins; nowadays psychologists tell us the more wholesome way is to forget all about sin—fling yourself into the work of the world. Rushing into work in order to deaden conscience is characteristic of the life we live today. "Live the simple life; keep a healthy body; never let your conscience be disturbed; for any sake keep away from religious meetings; don't bring before us the morbid tendency of things." We shall find that the morbid tendency of things is the conviction of the Holy Ghost.

The Philosophy of Sin, 1128 L

If you have never faced the question yourself, face it now—you are not as bothered now as you once were, if you are bothered at all, about Jesus Christ's line of things, and you are to blame; there will come a time when you will not be bothered even as much as you are now. Once Herod heard John the Baptist gladly (Mark 6:20). If God has ever pointed out to you in the past the one thing that is wrong in your life, you are to blame if you did not listen. A time will come when all the tremendous presentation of the truth of God will become a farce.

Workmen of God, 1347 L

Before the Spirit of God can bring peace of mind He has to clear out the rubbish, and before He can do that He has to give us an idea of what rubbish there is.

The Servant as His Lord, 1260 R

CONVICTIONS

When Jesus Christ came He was found to be unresolvable by every set of religious principles; that was His "reproach." To "go forth therefore unto Him without the camp, bearing His reproach," does not mean going outside the worldly crowd; it means being put outside the religious crowd you belong to. One of the most poignant bits of suffering for a disciple comes along that line. If you remain true to Jesus Christ there are times when you will have to go through your convictions and out the other side, and most of us shrink from such a step because it means going alone. The "camp" means the religious set you belong to; the set you do not belong to does not matter to you.

Baffled to Fight Better, 71 R

Christianity is not walking in the light of our convictions but walking in the light of the Lord, a very different thing. Convictions are necessary, but only as stepping stones to all that God wants us to be.

Bringing Sons Unto Glory, 239 L

It is easier to be true to convictions formed in a vivid religious experience than to be true to Jesus Christ, because if we are going true to Jesus Christ our convictions have to be altered. Unless our experiences lead us on to a life, they will turn us into fossils; we will become mummified gramophones of convictions instead of "witnesses unto Me."

The Moral Foundations of Life, 731 L

We are not sent to specialise in doctrine, but to lift up Jesus, and He will do the work of saving and sanctifying souls. When we become doctrine-mongers, God's power is not known, only the passionateness of an individual appeal.

Disciples Indeed, 385 L

God has a way of bringing in facts which upset a man's doctrines if these stand in the way of God getting at his soul.

Disciples Indeed, 385 L

It would be a liberal education to go through the Bible unbiased by convictions. Stop exploiting the Bible to back up a particular doctrine and let the Bible bring you into its own atmosphere and you will find that instruction is clear and emphatic regarding every phase of life there is.

Notes on Isaiah, 1377 R

The further we get away from Jesus the more dogmatic we become over what we call our religious beliefs, while the nearer we live to Jesus the less we have of certitude and the more of confidence in Him.

Disciples Indeed, 385 L

(Continued)

CONVICTIONS (Continued)

The way our heart is hardened is by sticking to our convictions instead of to Christ. Look back at your life with God and you will find that He has made havoc of your convictions, and now the one thing that looms larger and larger is Jesus Christ and Him only, God and God only. "And this is life eternal, that they might know Thee the only true God." Convictions and creeds are always about God; eternal life is to know Him.

God's Workmanship, 426 R

Beware of making a fetish of consistency to your convictions instead of being devoted to God. "I shall never do that"—in all probability you will have to, if you are a saint. There never was a more inconsistent Being on this earth than Our Lord, but He was never inconsistent to His Father. The one consistency of the saint is not to a principle, but to the Divine life. It is easier to be a fanatic than a faithful soul, because there is something amazingly humbling, particularly to our religious conceit, in being loyal to God.

My Utmost for His Highest, November 14, 844 R

Doctrine is never the guide into Christian experience; doctrine is the exposition of Christian experience.

Disciples Indeed, 385 L

COURAGE

Spiritual courage is the high heart that sees the difficulty and faces it. That is the courage that is valuable to God.

Notes on Jeremiah, 1392 R

CREATION (See also NATURE)

The matter of God's creation is a satisfaction to God, and when we come to know God by His Spirit we are as delighted with His creation as He is Himself. A child enjoys all that God has created; everything is wonderful to him.

Our Portrait in Genesis, 959 R

Six days God laboured, *thinking* Creation, until, as He thought, so it was. On the seventh day God rested, not from fatigue, but because that work was finished which enabled Him to rest.

Our Portrait in Genesis, 960 L

Those who deal with the great secrets of the universe imply that our planet is such a tiny spot in the tremendous universe that it is a piece of stupid conceit on our part to think that God watches over us. And to make our planet the centre where God performed the marvellous drama of His own history of the Incarnation and Atonement is absurd, they say. But watch a simple-minded person, one who is right with God and is not terrified by the reasonings of men, as he looks at the stars and exclaims, "When I consider Thy heavens, the work of Thy fingers, the moon and the stars, which Thou hast ordained; what is man, that Thou are mindful of him?" It is said not in despair, but in adoring wonder.

The Servant as His Lord, 1256 L

Look at the world either through a telescope or a microscope and you will be dwarfed into terror by the infinitely great or the infinitely little. Naturalists tell us that there are no two blades of grass alike, and close inspection of a bee's wing under a microscope reveals how marvellously it is made. What do I read in the Bible? I read that the God of heaven counts the hairs of our heads. Jesus says so. I read that the mighty God watches the sparrows so intimately that not one of them falls on the ground without His notice. (Luke 12:6–7) I read that the God who holds the seas in the hollow of His hand and guides the stars in their courses, clothes the grass of the field. Through the love of God in Christ Jesus we are brought into a wonderful intimacy with the infinitely great and the infinitely little.

The Servant as His Lord, 1256 R

Nature to a saint is sacramental. If we are children of God, we have a tremendous treasure in Nature. In every wind that blows, in every night and day of the year, in every sign of the sky, in every blossoming and in every withering of the earth, there is a real coming of God to us if we will simply use our starved imagination to realise it.

My Utmost for His Highest, February 10, 748 L

Learn to associate ideas worthy of God with all that happens in Nature—the sunrises and the sunsets, the sun and the stars, the changing seasons, and your imagination will never be at the mercy of your impulses, but will always be at the service of God.

My Utmost for His Highest, February 11, 748 R

"Thus saith God . . . , He that created the heavens and stretched them out; . . . I the Lord have called thee in righteousness. . . ."
(Isaiah 42:5–6).

Naturally we never look to Nature for illustrations of the spiritual life, we look at the methods of business men, at man's handiwork. Our Lord drew all His illustrations from His Father's handiwork; He spoke of lilies and trees and grass and sparrows. As Christians we have to feast our souls on the things ignored by practical people. A false spirituality blots Nature right out. The way to keep your spiritual life un-panicky, free from hysterics and fuss, free from flagging and breaking, is to consider the bits of God's created universe you can see *where you are*. Foster your life on God and on His creation and you will find a new use for Nature.

Notes on Isaiah, 1385 R

CRISIS

If we do not fit ourselves by practice when there is no crisis, we shall find that our nature will fail us when the crisis comes. The grace of God never fails, but we may fail the grace of God.

Biblical Ethics, 94 L

This war has brought tension to countless lives and people are coming to see differently because of it. When a man goes through a crisis he fears he is losing God; but instead of that he is beginning to see Him for the first time, and he sees Him as a grander, more marvellous Being than ever he imagined.

He Shall Glorify Me, 508 L

It is essential to go through a crisis with God which costs you something, otherwise your devotional life is not worth anything. You cannot be profoundly moved by nothing, or by doctrine; you can only be profoundly moved by devotion.

Not Knowing Whither, 908 L

(Continued)

CRISIS *(Continued)*

In the whirlwind of nations, such as is on just now, many men have lost—not their faith in God (I never met a man who lost his faith in God), but their belief in their beliefs, and for a while they think they have lost their faith in God. They have lost the conception which has been presented to them as God, and are coming to God on a new line.

The Love of God, 660 L

"Say not thou, What is the cause that the former days were better than these? for thou dost not enquire wisely concerning this" (Ecclesiastes 7:10).

At the beginning of the war what was called the Christian religion was mainly a cult of reminiscence. Take any denomination you like, and the religious bodies that do not consider themselves denominations—was their main object the establishment of a family likeness to Jesus Christ? No, their main object was to establish the particular creed they upheld; consequently when the crisis struck us, the religious element of the country was powerless to grip the situation.

Shade of His Hand, 1224 L

In a crisis we are always in danger of standing true to something that is acclaimed by this world, rather than standing absolutely loyal to God.

The Highest Good—The Pilgrim's Song Book, 528 L

If our testimony is hard, it is because we have gone through no crisis with God; there is no heartbroken emotion behind it. If we have been through a crisis in which human feeling has been ploughed to its inner centre by the Lord, our testimony will convey all the weight of the greatness of God along with human greatness.

Not Knowing Whither, 908 L

All through, a personal crisis ought to serve as an occasion for revealing the fact that God reigns, as well as compelling us to know our own character. You may think yourself to be generous and noble until a crisis comes, and you suddenly find you are a cad and a coward; no one else finds it out, but you do. To be found out by yourself is a terrible thing.

Our Portrait in Genesis, 974 R

A crisis does not make character; a crisis reveals character . . . we all say—"If I had been in your place, I should have done so and so." You have no means of knowing what you would have done; the nature of a crisis is that it takes you unawares, it happens suddenly, and the line you take reveals your character . . . The crisis is always the judgment.

The Philosophy of Sin, 1120 L

Crises always reveal character. A great snare about crises is that we want to live for them. If we have had one great crisis in which the revelation has come of how wonderfully God has altered us, we will want another crisis. It is a risky business to live in crises. Most of our life is lived in ordinary human affairs, not in crises.

The Psychology of Redemption, 1072 R

We imagine we should be all right if a big crisis arose; but the crisis only reveals the stuff we are made of, it does not put anything into us. "If God gives the call, of course, I shall rise to the occasion." You will not, unless you have risen to the occasion in the workshop. If you are not the real article before God there, doing the duty that lies nearest, instead of being revealed as fit for God when the crisis comes, you will be revealed as unfit. Crises always reveal character, and we are all ignorant of our true character until it is revealed to us.

So Send I You, 1310 L

We can estimate our life on the spiritual line by our dominant interest. How do we know what is our dominant interest? It is not the thing that occupies most time. The dominating interest is a peculiarly personal one, viz., the thing that is really fundamentally ours in a crisis. In sorrow or joy we reveal our dominating interest.

Facing Reality, 27 R

Trust entirely in God, and when He brings you to the venture, see that you take it. We act like pagans in a crisis; only one out of a crowd is daring enough to bank his faith in the character of God.

My Utmost for His Highest, May 30, 785 R

Every now and again, not often, but sometimes, God brings us to a point of climax. That is the Great Divide in the life; from that point we either go towards a more and more dilatory and useless type of Christian life, or we become more and more ablaze for the glory of God—"My Utmost for His Highest."

My Utmost for His Highest, December 27, 860 L

It is not easy to find your way to God in a sudden crisis unless you have been in the habit of going to God about everything. The thing that rationalism ridicules is not a man praying to God when he is in distress, but a man praying to God when he is not in distress. To the rationalist it is ridiculous to pray to God about everything; behind the ridicule is the devil to keep us from knowing the road when the crisis comes.

Notes on Isaiah, 1382 L

CRITIC / CRITICISE / CRITICISM
(See also JUDGING OTHERS)

No human being dare criticise another human being, because immediately he does he puts himself in a superior position to the one he criticises. A critic must be removed from what he criticises. Before a man can criticise a work of art or a piece of music, his information must be complete; he must stand away from what he criticises as superior to it. No human being can ever take that attitude to another human being; if he does he puts himself in the wrong position and grieves the Holy Spirit.

Studies in the Sermon on the Mount, 1460 R

A man who is continually criticised becomes good for nothing; the effect of criticism knocks all the gumption and power out of him. Criticism is deadly in its effect because it divides a man's powers and prevents his being a force for anything. That is never the work of the Holy Ghost. The Holy Ghost alone is in the true position of a critic; He is able to show what is wrong without wounding and hurting.

Studies in the Sermon on the Mount, 1461 L

The temper of mind that makes us lynx-eyed in seeing where others are wrong does not do them any good, because the effect of our criticism is to paralyse their powers, which proves that the criticism was not of the Holy Ghost; we have put ourselves into the position of a superior person. Jesus says a disciple can never stand away from another life and criticise it, therefore He advocates an uncritical temper, "Judge not." Beware of anything that puts you in the place of the superior person.

Studies in the Sermon on the Mount, 1461 L

(Continued)

CRITIC / CRITICISE / CRITICISM (Continued)

Take to God the things that perturb your spirit. You notice that certain people are not going on spiritually and you begin to feel perturbed; if the discernment turns you to intercession, it is good; but if it turns to criticism it blocks you in your way to God. God never gives us discernment of what is wrong for us to criticise it, but that we might intercede.

The Highest Good—The Pilgrim's Song Book, 531 R

"Judge not, that ye be not judged" (Matthew 7:1).

Criticism is part of the ordinary faculty of a man; he has a sense of humour, i.e., a sense of proportion; he sees where things are wrong and pulls the other fellow to bits; but Jesus says, "As a disciple, cultivate the uncritical temper."

Studies in the Sermon on the Mount, 1460 R

In the spiritual domain, criticism is love turned sour. In a wholesome spiritual life there is no room for criticism. The critical faculty is an intellectual one, not a moral one. If criticism becomes a habit it will destroy the moral energy of the life and paralyse spiritual force. The only person who can criticise human beings is the Holy Spirit.

Studies in the Sermon on the Mount, 1460 R

Life serves back in the coin you pay; you are paid back not necessarily by the same person, but the law holds good—"with what judgment ye judge, ye shall be judged." And it is so with regard to good as well as evil. If you have been generous, you will meet with generosity again; if you mete out criticism and suspicion to others, that is the way you will be treated.

Studies in the Sermon on the Mount, 1461 R

If you are annoyed with someone, notice how uncomfortably conscious you are that there is an element in him you cannot reach, and rather than allow the recognition of that element you work yourself up into self-respecting indignation. . . . This trick of stirring up self-respecting indignation is a very common subterfuge when we are embarrassed by a problem involving our self-respect. The temptation comes to yield to the bombastic mood, and we use terms of righteous indignation to condemn the thing we are not guilty of, while all the time we may be guilty of tenfold worse.

Baffled to Fight Better, 60 L

Whenever you are in a critical temper, it is impossible to enter into communion with God. Criticism makes you hard and vindictive and cruel, and leaves you with the flattering unction that you are a superior person. It is impossible to develop the characteristics of a saint and maintain a critical attitude. The first thing the Holy Spirit does is to give us a spring-cleaning, and there is no possibility of pride being left in a man after that.

Studies in the Sermon on the Mount, 1461 R

"For with what judgment ye judge, ye shall be judged: and with what measure ye mete, it shall be measured to you again" (Matthew 7:2).

This statement of our Lord's is not a haphazard guess; it is an eternal law which works from God's throne right down (see Psalm 18:25–26). The measure you mete is measured to you again. Jesus speaks of it here in connection with criticism. If you have been shrewd in finding out the defects of others, that will be exactly the measure meted out to you; people will judge you in the same way.

Studies in the Sermon on the Mount, 1461 R

CROSS OF CHRIST

The Church confronts the world with a message the world craves for but resents because it comes through the Cross of Christ. The central keystone for all Time and Eternity on which the whole purpose of God depends is the Cross (see Galatians 6:14).

Approved Unto God, 12 R

Never confuse the Cross of Christ with the benefits that flow from it. For all Paul's doctrine, his one great passion was the Cross of Christ, not salvation, nor sanctification, but the great truth that God so loved the world that He gave His only begotten Son; consequently you never find him artificial, or making a feeble statement. Every doctrine Paul taught had the blood and the power of God in it. There is an amazing force of spirit in all he said because the great passion behind was not that he wanted men to be holy, that was secondary, but that he had come to understand what God meant by the Cross of Christ. If we have only the idea of personal holiness, of being put in God's show room, we shall never come anywhere near seeing what God wants; but when once we have come where Paul is and God is enabling us to understand what the Cross of Christ means, then nothing can ever turn us (see Romans 8:35–39).

Approved Unto God, 17 L

What direction does my preaching take? What direction do my letters take, my dreams? What direction does the whole trend of my life take? Paul says he is determined that his life shall take no other direction than this: the emphasis on and exposition of the Cross of Christ. That is the note that is being lost sight of in our preaching to-day. We hear any amount about our cross, about what it costs us to follow Christ; but who amongst us has any inkling of what the apostle Paul saw? He

had caught an understanding of the mind of God in the Cross of Christ and grasped it; consequently he could never be exhausted or turned aside.

Approved Unto God, 17 R

You cannot be profoundly moved by a sentiment or by an idea of holiness, but you can be moved by a passion; and the old writers used to speak of the Cross as the Passion of Our Lord. The Cross is the great opening through which all the blood of Christian service runs.

Approved Unto God, 18 L

The Cross of Christ is the Self-revelation of God, the way God has given Himself. In the preaching and writing of to-day there is much brilliant stuff that passes into thin air because it is not related to this tremendous fact of the Self-bestowal of God that lifts up humanity to be in accordance with Himself.

Approved Unto God, 19 R

God made His own Son to be sin that He might make the sinner a saint. The Bible reveals all through that Jesus Christ bore the sin of the world by *identification*, not by sympathy. He deliberately took upon Himself and bore in His own Person the whole massed sin of the human race, and by so doing He rehabilitated the human race, that is, put it back to where God designed it to be, and anyone can enter into union with God on the ground of what Our Lord did on the Cross.

Approved Unto God, 23 L

". . . *God was in Christ*, reconciling the world unto Himself." We do not worship an austere, remote God; He is here in the thick of it. The Cross is a Reality, not a symbol—at the wall of the world stands God with His arms outstretched.

Biblical Ethics, 109 L

(Continued)

CROSS OF CHRIST (Continued)

Put away the reverential blasphemy that what Jesus Christ feared in Gethsemane was death on the cross. There was no element of fear in His mind about it; He stated most emphatically that He came on purpose for the Cross (Matthew 16:21). His fear in Gethsemane was that He might not get through as Son of Man. Satan's onslaught was that although He would get through as Son of God, it would only be as an isolated Figure; and this would mean that He could be no Saviour.

The Psychology of Redemption, 1086 L

There is nothing more certain in Time or Eternity than what Jesus Christ did on the Cross: He switched the whole human race back into right relationship to God and made the basis of human life Redemptive; consequently any member of the human race can get into touch with God *now*. It means not simply that men are saved from hell and put right for heaven, but that they are freed from the wrong disposition and can have imparted to them the very disposition of the Son of God, viz., Holy Spirit. . . . On that basis I can be forgiven, and through the forgiveness I can be turned into another man.

Biblical Ethics, 109 L

All heaven is interested in the Cross of Christ, all hell terribly afraid of it, while men are the only beings who more or less ignore its meaning.

Biblical Ethics, 130 L

The death of Jesus was not the death of a martyr; it was the revelation of the Eternal heart of God. That is why the Cross is God's last word; that does not mean God is not speaking still; it means that He is saying nothing contrary to the Cross.

Conformed to His Image, 351 R

Bear in mind that our human life viewed from a moral standpoint is a tragedy, and that preaching precepts while we ignore the Cross of Jesus Christ is like giving "a pill to cure an earthquake," or a poultice for a cancer. Our attempts to face the problems of human life apart from Jesus Christ are futile.

The Highest Good, 542 L

The abominable "show business" is creeping into the very ranks of the saved and sanctified—"We must get the crowds." We must not; we must keep true to the Cross; let folks come and go as they will, let movements come and go, let ourselves be swept along or not, the one main thing is—true to the yoke of Christ, His Cross.

If Thou Wilt Be Perfect, 598 R

The cry on the Cross, "My God, My God, why hast Thou forsaken Me?" is unfathomable to us. The only ones—and I want to say this very deliberately—the only ones who come near the threshold of understanding the cry of Jesus . . . the only ones who come near the threshold of understanding the experience of God-forsakenness are men like Cain—"My punishment is greater than I can bear"; men like Esau, " . . . an exceeding bitter cry"; men like Judas. Jesus Christ knew and tasted to a fuller depth than any man could ever taste what it is to be separated from God by sin.

The Philosophy of Sin, 1110 R

The most devout among us are too flippant about this great subject of the death of Jesus Christ.

The Philosophy of Sin, 1110 R

At the back of the wall of the world stands God with His arms outstretched, and every man driven there is driven into the arms of God. The Cross of Jesus is the supreme evidence of the love of God (Romans 8:35–39).

The Place of Help, 1004 L

In the Cross God is revealed not as One reigning in calm disdain above all the squalors of earth, but as One Who suffers more keenly than the keenest sufferer—"a man of sorrows, and acquainted with grief."

The Place of Help, 1027 R

The Cross of Jesus Christ is not the cross of a martyr, but the door whereby God keeps open house for the universe. Anyone can go in through that door.

The Psychology of Redemption, 1067 L

If the cross of Jesus Christ is the expression of the secret heart of God, the lever by which God lifts back the human race to what it was designed to be, then there is a new attitude to things.

The Shadow of an Agony, 1158 L

To ten men who talk about the character of Jesus there is only one who will talk about His Cross.

The Shadow of an Agony, 1165 R

CURE OF SOULS
(See SPIRITUAL CARE)

CYNIC / CYNICAL

A cynic spiritually is one who cuts himself off from other people because the enchantment of service and association with others instead of producing reality has been engendering priggishness, the attitude of a superior person.

He Shall Glorify Me, 509 L

One of the cruellest experiences is the disappointment over what we find in other lives. The last thing we learn is not to glory in men. Jesus Christ never expected from human nature what it was not designed to give; consequently He was never bitter or cynical.

He Shall Glorify Me, 510 L

Never partake of the cynical view of life.

The Highest Good, 548 L

Our Lord never trusted any man, "for He knew what was in man"; but He was not a cynic for He had the profoundest confidence in what He could do for every man; consequently He was never in a moral or intellectual panic, as we are, because we will put our confidence in man and in the things that Jesus put no confidence in.

The Highest Good, 546 R

Bitterness and cynicism are born of broken gods; bitterness is an indication that somewhere in my life I have belittled the true God and made a god of human perfection.

Not Knowing Whither, 913 L

When we are hurt we are apt to become cynical; cynicism is a sign that the hurt is recent.

Shade of His Hand, 1201 L

DEATH

We must lay our account with the invincible portion of death; it will come every time. Remember that your friend will die and act accordingly, and many a mean thing will wither on your tongue.

Shade of His Hand, 1236 R

(Continued)

DEATH (Continued)

"Let not your heart be troubled: ye believe in God, believe also in Me" (John 14:1).

Jesus Christ is talking here about what no man knows but Himself, viz. the day after death, and He says, "Don't be troubled about it." We grow in this Great Life by making room for Jesus Christ in our outlook on everything. Before you seal your opinion on any matter, find out what He has said about it—about God, about life, about death. Men discuss matters of heaven and hell, of life and death, and leave Jesus Christ out altogether; He says, "Before you finally seal your mind, Believe *also* in Me."

Facing Reality, 37 R

"The hour is coming, in the which all that are in the graves shall hear His voice, and shall come forth; they that have done good, unto the resurrection of life; and they that have done evil, unto the resurrection of damnation" (John 5:28–29).

We know what the resurrection body for glorification will be like: it will be like "His glorious body"; but all we know about the resurrection of the bad is that Jesus Christ (Who ought to know what He is talking about) says that there will be a resurrection to damnation. The question of eternal punishment is a fearful one, but let no one say that Jesus Christ did not say anything about it, He did. He said it in language we cannot begin to understand and the least thing we can do is to be reverent with what we do not understand.

Biblical Psychology, 214 R

It is a farce to make nothing of death; the natural expressions of the heart are not suppressed, but tempered and transfigured. It is no part of faith to affect insensibility to sorrow; that is stoical humbug. In certain stages of religious experience we have the idea that we must not show sorrow when we are sorrowful. That idea is an enemy to the Spirit of Jesus Christ, because it leads to heartlessness and hypocrisy. Not to sorrow is not even human; it is diabolical. The Spirit of God hallows sorrow.

Not Knowing Whither, 907 L

"And the serpent said unto the woman, *Ye shall not surely die*" (Genesis 3:4). Eve finds that what Satan told her is true; death does not strike them all at once, but its possibility has come in. Death has secretly begun. We transgress a law of God and expect an experience akin to death, but exactly the opposite happens; we feel enlarged, more broad-minded, more tolerant of evil, but we are more powerless.

Our Portrait in Genesis, 961 L

Death to us has become natural, but the Bible reveals it to be abnormal.

The Psychology of Redemption, 1062 L

It is appalling to find spiritual people when they come into a crisis taking an ordinary common-sense standpoint as if Jesus Christ had never lived or died. It is a man's personal relationship that tells. When he dies he can take nothing he has done or made in his lifetime with him. The only thing he can take with him is what he *is*.

Shade of His Hand, 1215 R

There is no warrant in the Bible for the modern speculation of a second chance after death. There may be a second chance. There may be numbers of interesting things—but it is not taught in the Bible. The stage between birth and death is the probation stage.

Shade of His Hand, 1215 R

It is remembering the invincible portion of death that makes things different. Solomon says you cannot bank on insurance, or speculations, or on any kind of calculation; you can bank on only one thing, that your interim of life may at any second be cut short; therefore your only confidence is to remain true to God.

Shade of His Hand, 1236 R

Death transforms nothing. Every view of death outside the Bible view concludes that death is a great transformer. The Bible says that death is a confirmer. Instead of death being the introduction to a second chance, it is the confirmation of the first chance. In dealing with the Bible, bear in mind this point of view.

Shade of His Hand, 1241 R

Our Lord makes little of physical death, but He makes much of moral and spiritual death.

So Send I You, 1315 L

We must build our faith, not on the fading light, but on the light that never fails. When "big" men go we are sad, until we see that they are meant to go; the one thing that remains is looking in the face of God for ourselves.

My Utmost for His Highest, April 22, 772 R

In the year that king Uzziah died, I saw also the Lord" (Isaiah 6:1).

Our soul's history with God is frequently the history of the passing of the hero. Over and over again God has to remove our friends in order to bring Himself in their place, and that is where we faint and fail and get discouraged. Take it personally: In the year that the one who stood to me for all that God was, died—I gave up everything? I became ill? I got disheartened? or—I saw the Lord?

My Utmost for His Highest, July 13, 800 R

The Bible never allows us to waste time over the departed. It does not mean that the fact of human grief is ignored, but the worship of reminiscence is never allowed.

Shade of His Hand, 1236 L

DECEPTION

"Deliver my soul, O Lord, from lying lips, and from a deceitful tongue" (Psalm 120:2).

One of the hardest things on earth to bear is deception, especially when it comes through our friends. We do not need the grace of God to stand the deception or slander of an enemy; human pride will stand that; but to be wounded in the house of our friends takes us unawares.

The Highest Good—The Pilgrim's Song Book, 527 L

DECISION
(See also CHOICE / CHOOSING)

If when a clear emphatic vision of some truth is given you by God, not to your intellect but to your heart, and in spite of it all you decide to take another course, the vision will fade and may never come back . . . It has nothing to do with salvation, but with lost opportunities in service for God.

The Philosophy of Sin, 1122 L

Our choice is indelibly marked for time and eternity. What we decide makes our destiny; not what we have felt, nor what we have been moved to do, or inspired to see, but what we decide to do in a given crisis, it is that which makes or mars us. Sooner or later there comes to every life the question—Will I choose to side with God's verdict on sin in the Cross of Christ? I may say "I won't accept," or "I will put it off," but both are decisions, remember.

The Philosophy of Sin, 1121 L

(Continued)

DECISION (Continued)

It is a terrible thing in the spiritual career not to be apprehended by the light that has been given; it may have been at some midday or midnight, in childhood or in the early days of your Christian life, or as recently as last week; you know exactly when it was; it is between you and God; are you going to decide along that line—"My God, I don't know all that it means, but I decide for it"? Whenever any light is given you on any fundamental issue and you refuse to settle your soul on it and apprehend it, your doom is sealed along that particular line.

The Philosophy of Sin, 1121 R

Redemption is absolutely finished and complete, but its reference to individual men is a question of their individual action. The whole human race is condemned to salvation by the Cross of our Lord. God nowhere holds a man responsible for having the heredity of sin; the condemnation begins when a man sees and understands that God can deliver him from the heredity of sin and he refuses to let Him do it; at that moment he begins to get the seal of damnation. John 3:19 is the final word of condemnation—"This is the judgment," i.e., the critical moment, "that the light is come into the world, and men loved the darkness rather than the light; for their works were evil."

The Psychology of Redemption, 1075 L

Our Lord never once used signs and wonders to get a man off his guard and then say, "Now believe in Me." Jesus Christ never coerced anybody; He never used supernatural powers or the apparatus of revival; He refused to stagger human wits into submitting to Him; He always put the case to a man in cold blood, "Take time and consider what you are doing" (cf. Luke 9:57–62).

The Psychology of Redemption, 1080 R

A moral decision is not a decision that takes time, one second is sufficient; what takes time is my stubborn refusal to come to the point of morally deciding.

Conformed to His Image, 361 L

DEFINITIONS

We are not intended to understand Life. Life makes us what we are, but Life belongs to God. If I can understand a thing and can define it, I am its master. I cannot understand or define Life; I cannot understand or define God; consequently I am master of neither.

Baffled to Fight Better, 56 R

Avoid definitions as you would avoid the devil. Immediately your mind accepts a definition you will learn no more about that thing until the definition is smashed. Definition and human authority are the two things that kill faith; with Jesus Christ there are no definitions at all. Jesus Christ always taught vaguely; in the beginning of our Christian life we think He teaches definitely, and we get hold of trite definitions until we find the marvellous life of God is not there at all.

He Shall Glorify Me, 522 R

"Let us also . . . lay aside every weight, and the sin which doth so easily beset us, and let us run with patience the race that is set before us. . . ." (Hebrews 12:1 RV).

Run light—nothing clings to us more closely than trying to live up to the ideas we have got from saintly people. We have nothing to do with saintly people; we have only to do with "looking unto Jesus." How much "cargo" are you carrying in the upper storey? how many definitions to fit your teaching into? No wonder people have nervous breakdowns!

He Shall Glorify Me, 522 L

The tendency to stereotype Christian experience is an abiding danger; it leads to the amateur providence attitude—"I am not likely to go wrong, but you are." I become, as it were, god almighty over a particular doctrine and imagine that everyone else is off on a side track. For example, when I think I can define what sanctification is, I have done something God refuses to do. Books about sanctification are much clearer than the Bible. The Bible is uncommonly confusing; so is human life. There is only one thing that is simple, and that is our relationship to Jesus Christ.

The Place of Help, 1011 L

The rationalist demands an explanation of everything. The reason I won't have anything to do with God is because I cannot define Him. If I can define God, I am greater than the God I define. If I can define love and life, I am greater than they are. Solomon indicates that there is a great deal we do not know and cannot define (Ecclesiastes 11:5–6). We have to go on trust in a number of ways; therefore, he says, be careful that you are not too emphatic and dogmatic in your exposition of things.

Shade of His Hand, 1242 L

DELIVERANCE

It is perilously easy to conclude that God's honour is bound up with my deliverance; whereas my deliverance is in order to bring me into touch with Reality and not for God's honour at all.

Notes on Isaiah, 1382 R

DEMONS / DEMON POSSESSION

The modern attitude to demon possession is very instructive; so many take the attitude that there is no such thing as demon possession, and infer that Jesus Christ Himself knew quite well that there was no such thing, not seeing that by such an attitude they put themselves in the place of the superior person, and claim to know all the private opinions of the Almighty about iniquity. Jesus unquestionably did believe in the fact of demon possession. The New Testament is full of the supernatural; Jesus Christ continually looked on scenery we do not see, and saw supernatural forces at work.

Biblical Psychology, 164 R

DEPENDABLE / DEPENDABILITY

We can depend on the man or woman who has been disciplined in character, and we become strong in their strength. When we depend on someone who has had no discipline, we both degenerate. We are always in danger of depending on people who are undisciplined, and the consequence is that in the actual strain of life they break down and we do too. We have to be actually dependable.

Facing Reality, 40 R

When we are young, a hurricane or thunderstorm impresses us as being very powerful, yet the strength of a rock is infinitely greater than that of a hurricane. The same is true with regard to discipleship. The strength there is not the strength of activity but the strength of *being*. Activity may be a disease of weariness, or of degeneration; to be dependable means to be strong in the sense of disciplined reliability.

Facing Reality, 40 R

DEPRAVITY

Depravity must be taken to mean much more than going wrong; it means rather to be so established in the wrong that the result is a real pleasure in it.

Our Portrait in Genesis, 963 L

It is entire rightness with Jesus Christ alone that prevents elemental depravity working in the heart and out into deeds. If I trust Jesus Christ's diagnosis and hand over the keeping of my heart to Him, I need never know in conscious experience what depravity is; but if I trust in my innocent ignorance I am likely one of these days to turn a corner and find that what He said is true.

Our Portrait in Genesis, 963 R

Whenever any choice of ours is based on implicit disregard of God, we are depraved, and this possibility remains in every saint.

Our Portrait in Genesis, 963 R

DEPRESSION

If we were never depressed we should not be alive; it is the nature of a crystal never to be depressed. A human being is capable of depression; otherwise there would be no capacity for exaltation. There are things that are calculated to depress, things that are of the nature of death; and in taking an estimate of yourself, always take into account the capacity for depression.

My Utmost for His Highest, February 17, 750 R

When the Spirit of God comes He does not give us visions; He tells us to do the most ordinary things conceivable. Depression is apt to turn us away from the ordinary commonplace things of God's creation, but whenever God comes, the inspiration is to do the most natural simple things—the things we would never have imagined God

was in, and as we do them we find He is there. The inspiration which comes to us in this way is an initiative against depression; we have to do the next thing and to do it in the inspiration of God.

My Utmost for His Highest, February 17, 750 R

DESPAIR

Facing facts as they are produces despair, not frenzy, but real downright despair, and God never blames a man for despair. The man who thinks must be pessimistic; thinking can never produce optimism. The wisest man that ever lived said that "he that increaseth knowledge increaseth sorrow." The basis of things is not reasonable, but wild and tragic, and to face things as they are brings a man to the ordeal of despair.

When a man gets to despair he knows that all his thinking will never get him out; he will only get out by the sheer creative effort of God, consequently he is in the right attitude to receive from God that which he cannot gain for himself.

Baffled to Fight Better, 48 L

A man may get to the point of despair in a hundred and one different ways, but when he does get there, there is no horizon. In everything else there is hope that a dawn may come, but in despair there is no hope of anything brighter; it is the most hopeless frontier a human mind can enter without becoming insane. An insane person is never despairing; he is either immensely melancholy or immensely exalted. Despair is the hopelessness that overtakes a sane mind when it is pushed to the extreme in grief.

Baffled to Fight Better, 66 L

We said that the teaching of Jesus Christ apart from His Atonement leads to despair; but if it produces the pauper condition, it is the right kind of despair. "Blessed are the poor in spirit. . . ." Conviction of sin will bring a man there, and so will the realisation of God's demands. The best expression for us is the 139th Psalm, "Search me, O God"; I cannot make my heart pure, I cannot alter my heredity, I cannot alter the dreams of my mind; "Search me, O God, and know my heart." That is the poverty of spirit Jesus says is blessed; if you are in that condition, He says you can easily enter the kingdom of heaven. Why? Because God gives the almighty gift of salvation from sin to paupers; He gives the Holy Spirit to paupers (see Luke 11:13).

Biblical Ethics, 90 R

If this Book means anything it means that at the wall of the world stands God, and any man driven there by conviction of sin finds the arms of God outstretched to save him. God can forgive a man anything but despair that He can forgive him.

He Shall Glorify Me, 492 R

We can judge a nation by its songs. The minor note is indicative of a crushed, but unconquered people. In the Bible there is nothing altogether minor; nothing, that is, of the nature of despair. The Bible deals with terrors and upsets, with people who have got into despair—in fact, the Bible deals with all that the devil can do, and yet all through there is the uncrushable certainty that in the end everything will be all right.

The Highest Good—The Pilgrim's Song Book, 526 L

Despair is always the gateway of faith. "If Thou canst! All things are possible to him that believeth" (RV). So many of us get depressed about ourselves, but when we get to the point where we are not only sick of ourselves, but sick to death, then we shall understand what the Atonement of the Lord Jesus Christ means. It will mean that we come to Him without the slightest pre-

tence, without any hypocrisy, and say, "Lord, if You can make anything of me, do it," and He will do it.

The Highest Good, 550 R

The sense of the irreparable is apt to make us despair, and we say—"It is all up now; it is no use trying any more." If we imagine that this kind of despair is exceptional, we are mistaken; it is a very ordinary human experience. Whenever we realise that we have not done that which we had a magnificent opportunity of doing, then we are apt to sink in despair, and Jesus Christ comes and says—"Sleep on now, that opportunity is lost for ever, you cannot alter it, but arise and go to the next thing." Let the past sleep, but let it sleep on the bosom of Christ, and go out into the irresistible future with Him.

My Utmost for His Highest, February 18, 750 R

DETACHED / DISENTANGLED

Jesus never shut Himself away from things; the first place He took His disciples to was a marriage feast. But there was one characteristic of Jesus—He was fundamentally dead to the whole thing, it had no appeal to Him. The "hundredfold" which Jesus promised means that God can trust a man anywhere and with anything when he is fundamentally dead to things.

If Thou Wilt Be Perfect, 591 R

It is easy to fling away what you have, child's play to sell all you have got and have nothing left, the easiest piece of impulse, nothing heroic in it; the thing that is difficult is to remain detached from what you have so that when it goes you do not notice it. That is only possible by the power of the love of God in Christ Jesus.

The Servant as His Lord, 1278 R

(Continued)

DETACHED / DISENTANGLED (Continued)

A disciple of Jesus must know from what he is to be disentangled. The disentanglement is from things which would be right for us but for the fact that we have taken upon us the vows of God.

Approved Unto God, 21 L

There is a difference between disentanglement for our own soul's sake and disentanglement for God's sake. We are apt to think only about being disentangled from the things which would ensnare us—we give up this and that, not for Jesus Christ's sake, but for our own development. A worker has to disentangle himself from many things that would advantage and develop him but which would turn him aside from being broken bread and poured out wine in his Lord's hands. We are not here to develop our own spiritual life, but to be broken for Jesus Christ's sake.

Approved Unto God, 21 L

The detached life is the result of an intensely narrow moral purity, not of a narrow mind. The mental view of Jesus Christ was as big as God's view, consequently He went anywhere—to marriage feasts, into the social life of His time, because His morality was absolutely pure; and that is what God wants of us.

Approved Unto God, 21 R

In the beginning we are fanatical and we cut ourselves off from external things, until we learn that detachment is the outcome of an inner moral purity, inwrought by God and maintained by walking in the light. Then God can put us where He likes, in the foreign field or anywhere, and we will never be entangled—placed there, but detached.

Approved Unto God, 21 R

We are taken up with interesting details; Jesus Christ was not. His insulation was on the inside, not the outside; His dominating interest was hid with God. His kingdom was on the inside, consequently He took the ordinary social life of His time in a most unobtrusive way. His life externally was oblivious of details; He spent His time with publicans and sinners and did the things that were apparently unreligious. But one thing He never did—He never contaminated His inner kingdom.

Facing Reality, 28 L

Our Lord did not teach detachment from other things: He taught attachment to Himself. Jesus Christ was not a recluse. He did not cut Himself off from society; He was amazingly in and out among the ordinary things of life; but He was disconnected fundamentally from it all. He was not aloof, but He lived in another world. His life was so social that men called Him a glutton and a winebibber, a friend of publicans and sinners. His detachments were inside towards God. Our external detachments are often an indication of a secret vital attachment to the thing from which we keep away externally.

So Send I You, 1335 L

The real deep crisis of abandonment is reached internally, not externally. The giving up of external things may be an indication of being in total bondage.

My Utmost for His Highest, April 17, 771 L

DEVOTION TO CHRIST

There is a difference between devotion to principles and devotion to a person. Hundreds of people to-day are devoting themselves to phases of truth, to causes. Jesus Christ never asks us to devote ourselves to a cause or a creed; He asks us to devote ourselves to Him, to sign away the right to ourselves and yield to Him absolutely, and take up that cross daily. The cross Jesus asks us to take up cannot be suffering for conviction's sake, because a man will suffer for conviction's sake whether he is a Christian or not. Neither can it be suffering for conscience' sake, because a man will go to martyrdom for his principles without having one spark of the grace of God in his heart.

Facing Reality, 31 R

Occasionally we have to revise our ways of looking at God's Providence. The usual way of looking at it is that God presents us with a cup to drink, which is strangely mixed. But there is another aspect which is just as true, perhaps more vitally true, viz., that we present God with a cup to drink, full of a very strange mixture indeed. God will never reverse the cup. He will drink it. Beware of the ingredient of self-will, which ought to have been dissolved by identification with the Death of Jesus, being there when you hand the cup of your life back to God.

Disciples Indeed, 396 R

Our Lord never called anyone to work for Him because they realise a need, but only on the basis that He has done something for them. The only basis on which to work for God is an esteemed appreciation of His deliverance; that is, our personal history with God is so poignant that it constitutes our devotion to Him. God's deliverance makes us His absolute debtors.

The Highest Good—The Pilgrim's Song Book, 532 R

"Go, sell that thou hast, and give to the poor . . . and come, follow Me" (Luke 18:22 RV).

These words mean a voluntary abandoning of riches and a deliberate, devoted attachment to Jesus Christ. We are so desperately wise in our own conceit that we continually make out that Jesus did not mean what He said, and we spiritualise His meaning into thin air. Jesus saw that this

man depended on his riches. If He came to you or to me He might not say that, but He would say something that dealt with whatever He saw we were depending on. "Sell that thou hast," strip yourself of every possession, disengage yourself from all things until you are a naked soul; be a man merely and then give your manhood to God. Reduce yourself until nothing remains but your consciousness of yourself, and then cast that consciousness at the feet of Jesus Christ.

So Send I You, 1303 L

One life yielded to God at all costs is worth thousands only touched by God.

The Servant as His Lord, 1271 L

We start out with the notion that God is an almighty piece of ourselves, but God can never be on the side of any individual; the question to ask is—"Am I on God's side?"

Baffled to Fight Better, 62 L

Am I as spontaneously kind to God as I used to be, or am I only expecting God to be kind to me? Am I full of the little things that cheer His heart over me, or am I whimpering because things are going hardly with me? There is no joy in the soul that has forgotten what God prizes. It is a great thing to think that Jesus Christ has need of me—"Give Me to drink." How much kindness have I shown Him this past week? Have I been kind to His reputation in my life?

My Utmost for His Highest, January 21, 741 R

(Continued)

DEVOTION TO CHRIST
(Continued)

Am I as full of the extravagance of love to Jesus Christ as I was in the beginning, when I went out of my way to prove my devotion to Him? Does He find me recalling the time when I did not care for anything but Himself? Am I there now, or have I become wise over loving Him? Am I so in love with Him that I take no account of where I go? or am I watching for the respect due to me, weighing how much service I ought to give?

My Utmost for His Highest, January 21, 741 R

Beware of anything that competes with loyalty to Jesus Christ. The greatest competitor of devotion to Jesus is service for Him. It is easier to serve than to be drunk to the dregs. The one aim of the call of God is the satisfaction of God, not a call to do something for Him. We are not sent to battle for God, but to be used by God in His battlings. Are we being more devoted to service than to Jesus Christ?

My Utmost for His Highest, January 18, 740 R

DIFFICULTIES (See CIRCUMSTANCES)

DISASTER

There are people to-day who are going through an onslaught of destruction that paralyses all our platitudes and preaching; the only thing that will bring relief is the consolations of Christ. It is a good thing to feel our own powerlessness in the face of destruction; it makes us know how much we depend upon God.

Baffled to Fight Better, 47 R

The greatest demand God makes of us is to believe that He is righteous when everything that happens goes against that faith.

God's Workmanship, 428 L

Wrong things happen *actually* because things are wrong really. One of the dangers of fanaticism is to accept disaster as God's appointment, as part of His design. It is not God's design, but His permissive will. There is a vital moral difference between God's order and His permissive will. God's order is—no sin, no Satan, no sickness, no limitations. . . . Then comes the permissive will of God—sin, Satan, difficulty, wrong and evil, and when desolation and disaster strike a man there is a wicked sting at the heart of it, and if he does not allow for the real thing behind it all he is a fool. We have to grasp God's order through His permissive will.

Baffled to Fight Better, 48 R

The slander of men is against God when disasters occur. If you have never felt inclined to call God cruel and hard, it is a question whether you have ever faced any problems at all.

Conformed to His Image, 376 L

The greatest challenge to a Christian is to believe Matthew 28:18—"All power is given unto Me in heaven and in earth." How many of us get into a panic when we are faced by physical desolation, by death, or war, injustice, poverty, disease? All these in all their force will never turn to panic the one who believes in the absolute sovereignty of his Lord.

Disciples Indeed, 386 R

In a time of calamity God appears to pay scant courtesy to all our art and culture, He sweeps the whole thing aside till civilisation rages at Him. It is the babe and the fool who get through in the day of God's visitation.

Disciples Indeed, 389 R

There are disasters to be faced by the one who is in real fellowship with the Lord Jesus Christ. God has never promised to keep us immune from trouble; He says "I will be with him in trouble," which is a very different thing.

The Place of Help, 997 L

DISCIPLE / DISCIPLESHIP

Our Lord never pressed anyone to follow Him unconditionally; nor did He wish to be followed merely out of an impulse of enthusiasm. He never pleaded, He never entrapped; He made discipleship intensely narrow, and pointed out certain things which could never be in those who followed Him. To-day there is a tendency to take the harshness out of Our Lord's statements. What Jesus says *is* hard; it is only easy when it comes to those who are His disciples. Whenever Our Lord talked about discipleship He prefaced it with an "IF," never with an emphatic assertion, "You must." Discipleship carries an option with it.

Approved Unto God, 16 L

Our Lord never allows an allegiance which is the outcome of an impulse of enthusiasm that sweeps us off our feet, not knowing what we are doing. We must be at the balance of our wills when we choose.

Approved Unto God, 16 L

When Jesus Christ talked about discipleship He indicated that a disciple must be detached from property and possessions, for if a man's life is in what he possesses, when disaster comes to his possessions, his life goes too (cf. Luke 12:15).

Baffled to Fight Better, 47 R

If you have taken on you the vows of God, never be surprised at the misery and turmoil that come every time you turn aside. Other people may do a certain thing and prosper, but you cannot, and God will take care you do not. There is always one fact more known only to God.

Approved Unto God, 22 L

The Cross of Christ stands unique and alone; we are never called upon to carry His Cross. Our cross is something that comes only with the peculiar relationship of a disciple to Jesus Christ; it is the evidence that we have denied the right to ourselves. What the Cross was to Our Lord such also in measure was it to be to those who followed Him. The cross is the pain involved in doing the will of God.

Approved Unto God, 16 L

We are apt to think that Jesus Christ took all the bitterness and we get all the blessing. It is true that we get the blessing, but we must never forget that the wine of life is made out of crushed grapes; to follow Jesus will involve bruising in the lives of the disciples as the purpose of God did in His own life.

Approved Unto God, 16 R

If you want a good time in this world, do not become a disciple of Jesus.

Our Brilliant Heritage, 932 R

"Thou art My beloved Son; in Thee I am well pleased"; the Father's heart was thrilled with delight at the loyalty of His Son. Is Jesus Christ thrilled with delight at the way we are living a sacrificial life of holiness? The disciple has no programme, only a distinguished passion of devotion to his Lord.

Facing Reality, 35 R

Discipleship and salvation are two different things: a disciple is one who, realising the meaning of the Atonement, deliberately gives himself up to Jesus Christ in unspeakable gratitude.

Disciples Indeed, 395 L

(Continued)

DISCIPLE / DISCIPLESHIP
(Continued)

We don't go in for making disciples to-day, it takes too long; we are all for passionate evangelism—taken up with adding to the statistics of "saved souls," adding to denominational membership, taken up with the things which show splendid success. Jesus Christ took the long, long trail—"If any man will come after Me, let him deny himself"—"Take time to make up your mind." Men were not to be swept into the Kingdom on tidal waves of evangelism, not to have their wits paralysed by supernatural means; they were to come deliberately, knowing what they were doing. One life straight through to God on the ground of discipleship is more satisfactory in His sight than numbers who are saved but go no further.

Conformed to His Image, 346 R

Have I been able to reproduce my own kind spiritually? If so, in a time of difficulty I will be brought through magnificently victorious; but woe be to the spiritual man who has never produced his own kind; when the difficulties come there is none to assist; he is isolated and lonely.

The Highest Good—The Pilgrim's Song Book, 537 R

The one mark of discipleship is the mastership of Jesus—His right to me from the crown of my head to the sole of my foot.

Disciples Indeed, 395 L

"Go and sell that thou hast. . . ." "Do you mean to say that it is necessary for our soul's salvation to do that?" Our Lord is not talking about salvation; He is saying—"If thou wilt be perfect . . ." Do mark the ifs of Jesus. "If any man would be my disciple. . . ." Remember, the conditions of discipleship are not the conditions for salvation. We are perfectly at liberty to say, "No, thank you, I am much obliged for being delivered from hell, very thankful to escape the abominations of sin, but when it comes to these conditions it is rather too much; I have my own interests in life, my own possessions."

If Thou Wilt Be Perfect, 602 R

"I will make the place of My feet glorious" (Isaiah 60:13)—among the poor, the devil-possessed, the mean, the decrepit, the selfish, the sinful, the misunderstanding—that is where Jesus went, and that is exactly where He will take you if you are His disciple.

God's Workmanship, 449 R

We never become disciples in crowds or even in twos; discipleship is always a personal matter (see Luke 13:23–24; John 21:21–22).

He Shall Glorify Me, 514 L

Do you have to say, "Do as I say, but not as I do"? Before we can disciple all the nations, we ourselves must be where we want other people to be.

Workmen of God, 1361 R

By a "disciple" we mean one who continues to be concentrated on our Lord. Concentration is of much more value than consecration, because consecration is apt to end in mere religious sentiment. Concentration is the gist of the Sermon on the Mount—"Be carefully careless about everything saving your relationship to Me," our Lord says.

Facing Reality, 39 L

Saving souls is God's work; man's work is discipling those souls (see Matthew 28:18–20).

Biblical Ethics, 109 R

The Lord won't cajole, He won't caress, He won't go after you, He won't plead; He will simply repeat every time He meets you on that point, "If you mean what you say, these are the conditions . . . ."

God's Workmanship, 442 L

God saves men; we are sent out to present Jesus Christ and His Cross, and to disciple the souls He saves. The reason we do not make disciples is that we are not disciples ourselves; we are out for our own ends.

So Send I You, 1301 L

DISCIPLINE

The first requirement of the worker is discipline voluntarily entered into. It is easy to be passionate, easy to be thrilled by spiritual influences, but it takes a heart in love with Jesus Christ to put the feet in His footprints, and to square the life to a steady going "up to Jerusalem" with Him. Discipline is the one thing the modern Christian knows nothing of; we won't stand discipline nowadays.

Approved Unto God, 20 R

The discipline of a worker is not in order to develop his own life, but for the purposes of his Commander. The reason there is so much failure is because we forget that we are here for that one thing, loyalty to Jesus Christ; otherwise we have no business to have taken the vows of God upon us. If a soldier is not prepared to be killed, he has no business to have enlisted as a soldier. The only way to keep true to God is by a steady persistent refusal to be interested in Christian work and to be interested alone in Jesus Christ.

Approved Unto God, 21 L

A disciplined life means three things—a supreme aim incorporated into the life itself; an external law binding on the life from its

Commander; and absolute loyalty to God and His word as the ingrained attitude of heart and mind.

Approved Unto God, 21 L

Our life as disciples is not a dream, but a discipline which calls for the use of all our powers.

The Shadow of an Agony, 1178 R

Our Lord Himself is the example of a disciplined life. He lived a holy life by sacrificing Himself to His Father; His words and His thinking were holy because He submitted His intelligence to His Father's word, and He worked the works of God because He steadily submitted His will to His Father's will; and as is the Master, so is the disciple.

Approved Unto God, 21 L

People go wrong spiritually because they stubbornly refuse to discipline themselves physically, mentally, or in any way, and after a while they become that most contemptible and objectionable thing, a petted man or woman, and their own greatest cause of suffering. There is no suffering to equal the suffering of self-love arising from independent individuality which refuses to submit either to God or to its nobler self.

Not Knowing Whither, 896 L

The one thing for which we are all being disciplined is to know that God is real. As soon as God becomes real, other people become shadows. Nothing that other saints do or say can ever perturb the one who is built on the real God.

So Send I You, 1294 L

(Continued)

DISCIPLINE *(Continued)*

Beware of saying, "I haven't time to read the Bible, or to pray"; say rather, "I haven't disciplined myself to do these things."

Disciples Indeed, 405 R

Vision is an inspiration to stand us in good stead in the drudgery of discipline; the temptation is to despise the discipline.

Disciples Indeed, 405 R

DISCOURAGEMENT

Discouragement is "disenchanted egotism." "Things are not happening in the way I expected they would, therefore I am going to give it all up." To talk like that is a sure sign that we are not possessed by love for Him, but only by love for ourselves. Discouragement always comes when we insist on having our own way.

So Send I You, 1337 L

Discouragement comes when we say what God will do—that God will always keep me healthy, that He will always be bringing me into the land of Canaan where I will eat honey; well, He won't. God is concerned about only one thing, viz. getting me into a personal relationship with Himself. There is no possibility of discouragement if we will only remember that this is the relationship—not God's blessings, but Himself.

Notes on Isaiah, p. 1376 R

DOCTRINE *(See CONVICTIONS)*

DOUBT

Doubt is not always a sign that a man is wrong; it may be a sign that he is thinking.

Disciples Indeed, 409 R

The problems of Providence, the puzzles of Nature, the paradoxes of Christianity do not bother everybody; they are the problems of men who are good and upright, but distinctly individual, and their individuality causes them to misinterpret God's ways and repudiate Christianity.

Conformed to His Image, 377 R

"Jesus saith unto him, Thomas, because thou hast seen Me, thou hast believed: blessed are they that have not seen, and yet have believed" (John 20:29).

Thomas was not an intellectual doubter, he was a temperamental doubter; there was not a more loyal disciple than Thomas; he was a loyal, gloomy-hearted man. He had seen Jesus killed; he saw them drive the nails through His hands and His feet, and he says, "Except I shall see . . . , I will not," I dare not, "believe." This is a man with a passionate desire to believe something over which he dare not allow himself to be deceived.

He Shall Glorify Me, 494 R

Beware of restlessness and wits persuading you that God has made a blunder—"God would never allow me to fall sick after giving me such a blessing"; but He has! No matter what revelations God has made to you, there will be destitution so far as the physical apprehension of things is concerned—God gives you a revelation that He will provide; then He provides nothing and you begin to realise that there is a famine, of food, or of clothes, or money, and your commonsense as well as other people's says, "Abandon your faith in God, do this, and that." Do it at your peril. Watch where destitution comes; if it comes on the heels of a time of quiet confidence in God, then thank Him for it and stay starving and He will bring a glorious issue.

Our Portrait in Genesis, 966 R

When in doubt physically, dare; when in moral doubt, stop; when in spiritual doubt, pray; and when in personal doubt, be guided by your life with God.

Shade of His Hand, 1207 R

Beware of the pious fraud in you which says—"I have no misgivings about Jesus, only about myself." None of us ever had misgivings about ourselves; we know exactly what we cannot do; but we do have misgivings about Jesus. . . . My misgivings arise from the fact that I ransack my own person to find out how He will be able to do it.

My Utmost for His Highest, February 26, 753 R

DREAMING

Dreaming about a thing in order to do it properly is right; but dreaming about it when we should be doing it is wrong.

My Utmost for His Highest, February 20, 751 R

When we are getting into contact with God in order to find out what He wants, dreaming is right; but when we are inclined to spend our time in dreaming over what we have been told to do, it is a bad thing and God's blessing is never on it.

My Utmost for His Highest, February 20, 751 R

DRUDGERY (See also ORDINARY)

Drudgery is one of the finest touchstones of character there is. Drudgery is work that is very far removed from anything to do with the ideal—the utterly mean, grubby things; and when we come in contact with them we know instantly whether or not we are spiritually real.

My Utmost for His Highest, February 19, 751 L

"*Jesus . . . took a towel . . . , and began to wash the disciples' feet*" *(John 13:3–5).*

Are we refusing to enter the domain of drudgery? Drudgery is the touchstone of character. . . .

The greatest hindrance of our spiritual life lies in looking for big things to do; Jesus Christ "took a towel. . . ."

Our Brilliant Heritage, 947 L

The snare in Christian life is in looking for the gilt-edged moments, the thrilling times; there are times when there is no illumination and no thrill, when God's angel is the routine of drudgery on the level of towels and washing feet. Are we prepared to "get a move on" *there*? Routine is God's way of saving us between our times of inspiration. We are not to expect Him to give us His thrilling minutes always.

Our Brilliant Heritage, 947 R

Read John 13; we see there the Incarnate God doing the most desperate piece of drudgery, washing fishermen's feet, and He says—"If I then, your Lord and Master, have washed your feet, ye also ought to wash one another's feet." It requires the inspiration of God to go through drudgery with the light of God upon it. Some people do a certain thing, and the way in which they do it hallows that thing for ever afterwards. It may be the most commonplace thing, but after we have seen them do it, it becomes different.

My Utmost for His Highest, February 19, 751 L

Sometimes it is not difficulty that makes me think God will forsake me, but drudgery. There is no *Hill Difficulty* to climb, no vision given, nothing wonderful or beautiful, just the commonplace day in and day out—can I hear God's say-so in these things?

My Utmost for His Highest, June 4, 787 R

(Continued)

DRUDGERY (Continued)

"They that sow in tears shall reap in joy. He that goeth forth and weepeth, bearing precious seed, shall doubtless come again with rejoicing, bringing his sheaves with him" (Psalm 126:5–6).

We make the blunder of wanting to sow and plough and reap all at the same time. We forget what our Lord said, that "one soweth, and another reapeth." "They that sow in tears . . ." The seed is the word of God, and no word of God is ever fruitless. If I know that the sowing is going to bring forth fruit, I am blessed in the drudgery. Drudgery is never blessed, but drudgery can be enlightened. The Psalmist says, "Thou hast enlarged me . . . in distress"; the enlargement comes through knowing that God is looking after everything.

The Highest Good—The Pilgrim's Song Book, 536 L

DUTY

We have the idea that our duty must always be disagreeable, and we make any number of duties out of diseased sensibilities. If our duty is disagreeable, it is a sign that we are in a disjointed relationship to God. If God gave some people a fully sweet cup, they would go carefully into a churchyard and turn the cup upside down and empty it, and say, "No, that could never be meant for me." The idea has become incorporated into their make-up that their lot must always be miserable. Once we become rightly related to God, duty will never be a disagreeable thing of which we have to say with a sigh, "Oh, well, I must do my duty."

The Moral Foundations of Life, 720 L

The Sermon on the Mount is not, Do your duty; but, Do what is not your duty. It is never your duty to "resist not evil"; that is only possible to the Son of God in you.

Studies in the Sermon on the Mount, 1450 R

Duty is the daughter of God. Never take your estimate of duty after a sleepless night, or after a dose of indigestion; take your sense of duty from the Spirit of God and the word of Jesus.

The Moral Foundations of Life, 720 L

Always go the second mile with God. It is never our duty to do it; but if we make duty our god we cease to be Christians in that particular. It is never our duty to go the second mile, to turn the other cheek, but it is what we shall do if we are saints.

Our Brilliant Heritage, 940 R

There is something in human pride that can stand big troubles, but we need the supernatural grace and power of God to stand by us in the little things. The tiniest detail in which we obey has all the omnipotent power of the grace of God behind it. When we do our duty, not for duty's sake, but because we believe that God is engineering our circumstances in that way, then at the very point of our obedience the whole superb grace of God is ours.

Our Brilliant Heritage, 948 L

Have I been persecuting Jesus by a zealous determination to serve Him in my own way? If I feel I have done my duty and yet have hurt Him in doing it, I may be sure it was not my duty, because it has not fostered the meek and quiet spirit, but the spirit of self-satisfaction. We imagine that whatever is unpleasant is our duty! Is that anything like the spirit of our Lord—"I delight to do Thy will, O My God."

My Utmost for His Highest, January 29, 744 L

Never live for the rare moments; they are surprises. God will give us touches of inspiration when He sees we are not in danger of being led away by them. We must never make our moments of inspiration our standard; our standard is our duty.

My Utmost for His Highest, May 1, 776

EARNESTNESS

Earnestness is not everything; I may be an earnest lunatic. Solomon's warning is that earnestness may often cover up an evasion of concentration in a life. John McNeill* said about the student of Elisha who lost the axe-head—"If he had been of the modern school, Elisha would have said 'Whack awa wi' the stump, man; earnestness is everything.' " . . . earnestness may be the characteristic of a fool.

Shade of His Hand, 1239 R
Late-19th-century Scottish evangelist brought to faith in Christ through the preaching of D. L. Moody.

EARTH

The twenty-fifth chapter of Leviticus is the great classic on the rights of the land. The establishment of men's rights on the earth is limited by the rights of the earth itself. If you keep taking from the land, never giving it any rest, in time it will stop giving to you. We talk about the rights of the land, and make it mean our right to grab as much from it as we can. In God's sight the land has rights just as human beings have, and many of the theories which are being advanced to-day go back to God's original prescription for the land.

Biblical Ethics, 95 R

In the teaching of Jesus the earth is never confounded with the world. "Blessed are the meek: for they shall inherit the earth" (Matthew 5:5). The world is the system of things which man has erected on God's earth. He says that the meek, those who obey the laws of God, shall inherit the earth. The material earth is God's, and the way men treat it is a marvellous picture of the long-suffering of God.

Biblical Ethics, 95 R

This Eternal Paradise, entered now by those who walk alone with God, must not be spiritualised by a process of abstractions into a mere inward state of soul. This Mother Earth will yet be governed by the saints. "The kingdom of the world is become the kingdom of our Lord and of His Christ" (Rev. 11:15 RV). The saints, with a tested, heroic mastership of earth and air and sky, will reign in a very real concrete Paradise.

Christian Disciplines, Volume 2,
The Discipline of Loneliness, 333 R

Earth is man's domain, but the Bible talks about a "hereafter" without the sin and iniquity, "a new heaven and a new earth." We are going to be here, marvellously redeemed, in this wonderful place which God made very beautiful, and which has been played havoc with by sin.

The Love of God, 660 L

EDUCATION

It has been a favourite belief in all ages that if only men were taught what good is, everyone would choose it; but history and human experience prove that that is not so. To know what good *is* is not to *be* good.

Disciples Indeed, 392 L

The kingdom within must be adjusted first before education can have its true use. To educate an unregenerate man is but to increase the possibility of cultured degradation. No one would wish to belittle the lofty attainments of education and culture, but we must realise we have to put them in their high, mighty, second place.

The Place of Help, 985 L

ELECTION (See PREDESTINATION)

EMOTION(S)

Enthusiasm means, to use the phrase of a German mystic, "intoxicated with God"; the word has come down in the world and popularly means anything that enthuses. Christianity takes all the emotions, all the dangerous elements of human nature, the things which lead us astray, all feelings and excitabilities, and makes them into one great power for God. Other religions either cut out dangerous emotions altogether or base too much on them.

Biblical Ethics, 112 L

The tendency is in us all to say, "You must not trust in feelings"; perfectly true, but if your religion is without feeling, there is nothing in it. If you are living a life right with God, you will have feeling, most emphatically so, but you will never run the risk of basing your faith on feelings. The Christian is one who bases his whole confidence in God and His work of grace, then the emotions become the beautiful ornament of the life, not the source of it.

Biblical Ethics, 112 L

God holds the saints responsible for emotions they have not got and ought to have as well as for the emotions they have allowed which they ought not to have allowed. If we indulge in inordinate affection, anger, anxiety, God holds us responsible; but He also insists that we have to be passionately filled with the right emotions. The emotional life of a Christian is to be measured by the exalted energy exhibited in the life of our Lord.

Biblical Ethics, 114 L

In natural life people without any emotions are undesirable to have as friends, and a Christian life that is without the continual recurrence of Divine emotion is suffering from spiritual sleeping-sickness.

Biblical Ethics, 113 R

Remember, a bad man whose life is wrong has a hilariously happy time, and a good man whose life is right has a hilarious time. All in between are more or less diseased and sick; there is something wrong somewhere: the healthy pagan and the healthy saint are the only ones who are hilarious. The New Testament writers, especially the Apostle Paul, are intense on the hilarity of life. Enthusiasm is the idea, intoxicated with the life of God.

Biblical Psychology, 160 R

"When the Lord turned again the captivity of Zion, we were like them that dream" (Psalm 126:1).

Religion is never intellectual; it is always passionate and emotional; but the curious thing is that it is religion that leads to emotion, not emotion to religion. If religion does not make for passion and emotion, it is not the true kind. When you realise that you are saved, that God has forgiven your sins, given you the Holy Spirit, I defy you not to be carried away with emotion. Religion which makes for logic and reason is not religion, but to try to make religion out of emotion is to take a false step.

The Highest Good—The Pilgrim's Song Book, 535 L

A sentimentalist is one who delights to have high and devout emotions stirred whilst reading in an arm-chair, or in a prayer meeting, but he never translates his emotions into action. Consequently a sentimentalist is usually callous, self-centred and selfish, because the emotions he likes to have stirred do not cost him anything.

The Moral Foundations of Life, 694 R

The higher the emotion, the purer the desire, the viler is the revenge in the moral character unless the emotion is worked out on its right level.

The Moral Foundations of Life, 694 R

There are certain phases of the life of faith which look so much like cant and humbug that we are apt to grieve God's Spirit by our religious respectability in regard to them, and ecstasy is just one of those phases. An ecstasied man is one whose state of mind is marked by mental alienation from his surroundings, and his very consciousness is altered into excessive joy. These states are open gateways for God or for the devil. If they are worked up by thrills of our own seeking, they are of the devil; but when they come unsought in faithful performance of duties, they are the gateway into direct communication with God. Ecstasy is not a state in which to live; keep your ecstatic times dark. You have no business to show the depths to anyone but yourself and God.

Not Knowing Whither, 883 R

I have no business to allow false emotions before God, emotions that are not "me" at all, and that I have not the remotest intention of carrying out. Our Lord requires not only chastity of body; He requires chastity of thought.

Not Knowing Whither, 890 R

An unemotional love is inconceivable. Love for the good must involve displeasure and grief for the evil. God is not an almighty sultan reigning aloof; He is right in the throes of life, and it is there that emotion shows itself.

Our Portrait in Genesis, 964 L

Test every emotional affinity in this way—If I let this thing have its way, what will it mean? If you can see the end of it to be wrong, grip it on the threshold of your mind, and at the peril of your soul never let it encroach again upon your attention.

The Place of Help, 1008 L

ENDURANCE

We have to learn to go the second mile with God. Some of us get played out in the first ten yards because God compels us to go where we cannot see the way, and we think we will wait until we get nearer the big crisis. We can all see the big crisis—"Oh yes, I would like to do that for God"; but what about the obscure duty waiting to be done? If we do not do the walking, steadily and carefully, in the little matters, we shall do nothing when the big crisis comes.

So Send I You, 1320 L

Getting into the stride of God means nothing less than union with Himself. It takes a long time to get there, but keep at it. Don't give in because the pain is bad just now; get on with it, and before long you will find you have a new vision and a new purpose.

My Utmost for His Highest, October 12, 833 L

EPISTLES

Always view the Epistles as the posthumous work of the ascended Christ; don't say, "That is only what Paul says." In the Epistles we have not got Paul's ideas or Peter's ideas; we have the ideas of the Holy Ghost, and the "pens" happen to be Paul or Peter or John. ". . . holy men of God spake as they were moved by the Holy Ghost" (2 Peter 1:21).

He Shall Glorify Me, 474 L

The Epistles are the posthumous writings of the Ascended Lord; He sent the Holy Ghost, and the "pens" used were the apostles, and the expositions given are from the Holy Ghost. Our Lord's teachings and the expositions given in the Epistles stand or fall together.

The Psychology of Redemption, 1067 L

(Continued)

EPISTLES *(Continued)*

The Gospels always present truth in "nugget" form, and if we want to know the stages of evangelical experience, we must go to the Epistles which beat out into negotiable gold the nuggets of truth presented by our Lord. . . . We mean by the Evangelical Experience an experience based on the fact that the Cross of our Lord Jesus Christ—that is, His death—is the gateway for us into His life.

The Psychology of Redemption, 1066 R

The "nuggets of gold" spoken by our Lord in the Gospels are beaten out by the apostles in the Epistles.

Our Brilliant Heritage, 917 R

ETERNAL LIFE

Never confound eternal life with immortality. Eternal has reference to the quality of life, not to its duration. Eternal life is the life Jesus exhibited when He was here on earth, with neither time nor eternity in it, because it is the life *of* God Himself (see John 17:3).

If Thou Wilt Be Perfect, 601 L

A great and glorious fact—to believe in Jesus Christ is to receive God, Who is described to the believer as "eternal life." Eternal life is not a gift *from* God, but the gift *of* God, that is, God Himself (see John 6:47; 17:2–3; Romans 6:23).

Facing Reality, 34 R

"And this is life eternal, that they should know Thee the only true God, and Him whom Thou didst send, even Jesus Christ" (John 17:3 RV). This constitutes eternal life—an increasing knowledge of the unfathomable God and His only begotten Son. This is Eternal Pleasure—to know Him! How far removed it is from our conceptions of rewards and crowns and heaven.

Christian Disciplines, Volume 2,
The Discipline of Loneliness, 332 L

Eternal Life has nothing to do with Time; it is the life which Jesus lived when He was down here. The only source of Life is the Lord Jesus Christ.

My Utmost for His Highest, April 12, 769 R

"This is life eternal, that they might know Thee." The real meaning of eternal life is a life that can face anything it has to face without wavering. If we take this view, life becomes one great romance, a glorious opportunity for seeing marvellous things all the time. God is disciplining us to get us into this central place of power.

My Utmost for His Highest, May 8, 778 R

EVANGELISM

When Our Lord said to the disciples "Follow Me, and I will make you fishers of men," His reference was not to the skilled angler, but to those who use the drag-net—something which requires practically no skill; the point being that you have not to watch your "fish," but to do the simple thing and God will do the rest.

Baffled to Fight Better, 52 R

The pseudo-evangelical line is that you must be on the watch all the time and lose no opportunity of speaking to people, and this attitude is apt to produce the superior person. It may be a noble enough point of view, but it produces the wrong kind of character. It does not produce a disciple of Jesus, but too often the kind of person who smells of gunpowder and people are afraid of meeting him. . . . It was this form of pseudo-evangelism, so unlike the New Testament evangelism, that made Huxley say—"I object to Christians: they know too much about God."

Baffled to Fight Better, 52 R

We preach to men as if they were conscious of being dying sinners; they are not; they are having a good time, and all our talk about the need to be born again is from a domain they know nothing about; because some men try to drown unhappiness in worldly pleasures it does not follow all are like that.

Biblical Ethics, 115 L

Profoundly speaking, it is not sufficient to say, "Because God says it," or, "Because the Bible says it," unless you are talking to people who know God and know the Bible to be His Word. If you appeal from the authority of God or of the Bible to a man not born again, he will pay no attention to you because he does not stand on the same platform. You have to find a provisional platform on which he can stand with you, and in the majority of cases you will find that the platform is that of moral worth. If Jesus Christ is proved Worthy on the plane men are on, they will be ready to put Him as the Most Worthy One, and all the rest will follow.

Disciples Indeed, 387 L

If you are sufficiently strong-minded you can generate any number of intentions in people and make them think anything you like; if they are not in the habit of thinking for themselves you can always sway them. The power of an evangelist over men and women who do not think is a dangerous thing.

The Moral Foundations of Life, 697 R

Beware of the people who tell you how to fish! I know a good many people who have tried to learn how to fish from books, but they never did learn. The only way to learn how to fish is to fish! . . .

Beware of the books that tell you how to catch men. Go to Calvary, and let God Almighty deal with you until you understand the meaning of the tremendous cost to our Lord Jesus Christ, and then go out to catch men. God grant we may get away from the instructors on how to catch fish and get out into the fishing business!

Workmen of God, 1360 L

The presentation made by a false evangelism is that Jesus Christ taught a man must have his own soul saved, be delivered from hell and get a pass for heaven, and when one is taken and the other left, he must look out that he is the one taken. Could anything be more diametrically opposed to what Jesus Christ did teach, or more unlike the revelation of God given in the Bible? A man is not to serve God for the sake of gain, but to get to the place where the whole of his life is seen as a personal relationship to God.

Shade of His Hand, 1199 R

To terrorise a man into believing in God is never the work of God, but the work of human expediency. If we want to convince a congregation of a certain thing, we may use terror to frighten them into it; but never say that is God's way; it is our way. If we do not get conversions one way, then we preach hell fire and produce terror; we don't care what we preach as long as we dominate. To call that God's method is a travesty of the character of God. The methods God uses are indicated in Jesus Christ, and He never terrorised anyone.

Shade of His Hand, 1203 R

(Continued)

EVANGELISM *(Continued)*

One of the dangers in modern evangelism is that it lays the emphasis on decision for Christ instead of on surrender to Jesus Christ. That to me is a grave blunder. When a man decides for Christ he usually puts his confidence in his own honour, not in Christ at all.

Shade of His Hand, 1212 L

Pseudo-evangelism has gone wildly off the track in that it has made salvation a bag of tricks whereby if I believe a certain shibboleth, I am tricked out of hell and made right for heaven—a travesty of the most tremendous revelation of the Redemption of the human race by Jesus Christ. The New Testament's teaching about Christianity is that the Son of God is formed in me on the basis of His marvellous regeneration until, as Paul says, "the life which I now live in the flesh"—not the life I am going to live when I get to heaven, but the life I now live in this flesh, the life that all see and know— "I live by the faith of the Son of God who loved me, and gave Himself for me."

The Shadow of an Agony, 1186 L

Modern evangelism makes the mistake of thinking that a worker must plough his field, sow the seed, and reap the harvest in half-an-hour. Our Lord was never in a hurry with the disciples; He kept on sowing the seed and paid no attention to whether they understood Him or not. He spoke the truth of God, and by His own life produced the right atmosphere for it to grow, and then left it alone, because He knew well that the seed had in it all the germinating power of God and would bring forth fruit after its kind once it was put in the right soil. We are never the same after listening to the truth; we may forget it, but we will meet it again.

The Servant as His Lord, 1282 L

Both the fisherman's art and the shepherd's art sound poetical until you have tried them!

Workmen of God, 1360 R

EVOLUTION

The modern view is that man is continually evolving and developing, each phase being better than the last and the last gives us the best revelation of God; from this standpoint Jesus Christ is looked upon as the manifestation of all the best in the evolutionary processes of man. The evolutionary conception starts from something un-get-at-able, incalculable, with a power within itself to evolve endlessly. The great word we bow down and worship to-day is "progress"; we are progressing and developing, and the consequence is we are blind to the facts of history and blind to moral facts. The Bible revelation about man is that man, as he is, is not as God made him.

Biblical Ethics, 127 R

Evolution is simply a working way of explaining the growth and development of anything. When evolution is made a fetish and taken to mean God, then call it "bosh"; but evolution in a species, in an idea, in teaching, is exactly what our Lord taught: born of the Spirit and going on "till we all attain . . . unto the measure of the stature of the fulness of Christ" (RV).

The Highest Good, 540 L

According to modern thinking, man is a great being in the making; his attainments are looked on as a wonderful promise of what he is going to be; we are obsessed with the evolutionary idea. Jesus Christ talks about a revolution—"Ye must be born again."

Conformed to His Image, 347 L

The reason we do not see the need to be born from above is that we have a vast capacity for ignoring facts. People talk about the evolution of the race. The writers of to-day seem to be incapable of a profound understanding of history; they write glibly about the way the race is developing; where are their eyes and their reading of human life as it is? We are not evolving and developing in any sense to justify what is known as evolution. We have developed in certain domains but not in all. We are nowhere near the massive, profound intellectual grasp of the men who lived before Christ was born. What brain to-day can come near Plato, or Socrates? And yet people say we are developing and getting better, and we are laying the flattering unction to our souls that we have left Jesus Christ and His ideas twenty centuries behind. No wonder Jesus said that if we stand by Him and take His point of view, men will hate us as they hated Him.

The Highest Good, 546 L

EXCELLENCE

We have to realise that no effort can be too high, because Jesus says we are to be the children of our Father in heaven. It must be my utmost for His highest all the time and every time.

The Highest Good—The Pilgrim's Song Book, 531 L

EXPECTANCY
(See also SURPRISE)

As workers for God we have to learn to make room for God—to give God "elbow room." We calculate and estimate, and say that this and that will happen, and we forget to make room for God to come in as He chooses. Would we be surprised if God came into our meeting or into our preaching in a way we had never looked for Him to come? Do not look for God to come in any particular way, but *look for Him*. That is the way to make room for Him. Expect Him to come, but do not expect Him only in a certain way.

My Utmost for His Highest, January 25, 742 R

Keep your life so constant in its contact with God that His surprising power may break out on the right hand and on the left. Always be in a state of expectancy, and see that you leave room for God to come in as He likes.

My Utmost for His Highest, January 25, 743 L

EXPECTATIONS

God wants us to realise His sovereignty. We are apt to tie God up in His own laws and allow Him no free will. We say we know what God will do, and suddenly He upsets all our calculations by working in unprecedented ways; just when we expected He would do a certain thing, He did the opposite. There are unexpected issues in life; unexpected joys when we looked for sorrow, and sorrow when we expected joy, until we learn to say, all my expectations are from Thee.

The Place of Help, 1010 R

EXPERIENCE

The servant of God has to go through the experience of things before he is allowed to go through the study of them. When you have had the experience God will give you the line for study; the experience first, and then the explanation of the experience by the Spirit of God. Each one of us is an isolated person with God, and He will put us through experiences that are not meant for us at all, but meant to make us fit stuff to feed others.

Approved Unto God, 8 R

Experience is never your guide; experience is the doorway for you to know the Author of the experience. Get at the knowledge of God for yourself, be a continuous learner, and the truth will open on the right hand and on the left until you find there is not a problem in human life that Jesus Christ cannot deal with.

Approved Unto God, 20 R

If you go on the line of accepting whatever can be experienced, you will find you have to accept the wildest, vaguest, most indeterminate things. For example, a man may come and tell you that he has had communication with departed friends; well, he is no more likely to be untruthful than you are—how are you going to judge whether his experience is right or not? The only guide is your personal relationship to Jesus Christ. Jesus Christ prohibits it, and that shuts the door straight off for you from tampering with spiritualism; therefore you refuse to have anything to do with what He will not allow.

Bringing Sons Unto Glory, 240 R

Whenever ecstasies or visions of God unfit us for practical life they are danger signals that the life is on the wrong track.

Disciples Indeed, 389 R

Just now in this order of things we are confined in this bodily temple for a particular reason, but at any second, "in the twinkling of an eye," God can change this body into a glorified body.

All we are arguing for is the need to have an open mind about things we can know nothing of as yet. If when an experience is recorded, I say it is nonsense because I have never had it, I put myself in the place of the superior person, an attitude I have no business to take.

Biblical Psychology, 213 R

All ecstasies and experiences, all inner voices and revelations and dreams, must be tested by the pure outer light of Jesus Christ and His word.

Christian Disciplines, Volume 2,
The Discipline of Loneliness, 326 L

Subjective states must be tested and estimated and regulated by objective standards. This is the only safeguard against the irresponsible crowd of fanatics who live from hand to mouth in spiritual experience and get nowhere, and, by reason of their own shallowness, end in contemptible disasters.

Christian Disciplines, Volume 2,
The Discipline of Loneliness, 326 L

Experience as an end in itself is a disease; experience as a result of the life being based on God is health.

Disciples Indeed, 390 L

If my experience makes anyone wish to emulate me, I am decoying that one away from God.

Disciples Indeed, 390 L

Thank God for experiences, for the power to be enchanted, but this is the thing that tells—"Christ in you." I may be able to expound the Word of God, I may be an expert in a great many things, but unless my experience shows in expression a strong family likeness to Jesus, it is making me spiritually inefficient; . . . I may be expert in the knowledge of Scripture and expert in Christian work, but if all this is not turning me into an epistle in which men can read Jesus," it is making for spiritual inefficiency.

The Place of Help, 1038 R

The average preaching of the Gospel deals mainly with the scenic cases, with people who have gone through exceptional experiences. None of the early disciples had had these exceptional experiences; they saw in Jesus Christ what they had never seen before—a Man from another realm, and they began to long after what He stood for.

The Psychology of Redemption, 1062 R

If I have had a vivid religious experience and have power over people by means of that experience, the danger is that I usurp the place of God and say, "You must come my way; you must have this experience."

Shade of His Hand, 1233 L

Be ruthless with yourself if you are given to talking about the experiences you have had. Faith that is sure of itself is not faith; faith that is sure of God is the only faith there is.

My Utmost for His Highest, December 21, 858 L

EXPRESSION

An artist is one who not only sees but is prepared to pay the price of acquiring the technical knowledge to express what he sees. An artistic person is one who has not enough art in him to make him work at the technique of art whereby he can express

himself; he indulges in moods and tones and impressions; consequently there are more artistic people than there are artists. The same is true of poetry; there are many people with poetic notions, but very few poets. It is not enough for a man to feel the divine flame burning in him; unless he goes into the concentrated, slogging business of learning the technique of expression, his genius will be of no use to anyone.

The Moral Foundations of Life, 717 L

The value of a spiritual teacher is that he expresses for us what we have been trying to express for ourselves but could not. Whenever a person or a book expresses for us what we have been trying to express for ourselves, we feel unspeakably grateful, and in this way we learn how to express for ourselves.

Biblical Psychology, 210 R

No thought is ours until it can be expressed in words.

The Moral Foundations of Life, 707 L

When a man has the vision of a poet or an artist, he has to learn to express himself, to become his own medium. There are more artistic people than artists because folks refuse to do this. Artistic people have art like a severe headache; they never work it out; they spurt out artistic ability, which is of no use to anyone. That is artistic disease, not art.

Shade of His Hand, 1243 R

EXTRAVAGANCE
(*See also* GENEROSITY)

It is possible to be so economical that you venture nothing. We have deified economy, placed insurance and economy on the throne, consequently we will do nothing on the line of adventure or extravagance.

Shade of His Hand, 1242 L

(Continued)

EXTRAVAGANCE (Continued)

To use the word "economy" in connection with God is to belittle and misunderstand Him. Where is the economy of God in His sunsets and sunrises, in the grass and flowers and trees? God has made a superabounding number of things that are of no use to anyone. How many of us bother our heads about the sunrises and sunsets? Yet they go on just the same. Lavish extravagance to an extraordinary degree is the characteristic of God, never economy. Grace is the overflowing favour of God.

Shade of His Hand, 1242 L

The very nature of God is extravagance. How many sunrises and sunsets does God make?
Gloriously wasteful, O my Lord, art Thou!
Sunset faints after sunset into the night. . . .
How many flowers and birds, how many ineffable beauties all over the world, lavish desert blossoms, that only His eye sees?

The Place of Help, 1028 L

Our attitude is that if we are extravagant, a rainy day will come for which we have not laid up. You cannot lay up for a rainy day and justify it in the light of Jesus Christ's teaching. We are not Christians at heart; we don't believe in the wisdom of God, but only in our own. We go in for insurance and economy and speculation, everything that makes us secure in our own wisdom.

Shade of His Hand, 1242 L

FACTS (See also REALITY)

You cannot deal with facts as you like; you may object to them, but a fact is a fact, whether a commonsense fact or a revelation fact.

Disciples Indeed, 390 R

One man's experience is as valuable as another's, but experience has nothing to do with facts. Facts pay no attention to us; facts have to be accepted; they are the real autocrats in life.

Disciples Indeed, 390 R

We must base our thinking on the rugged facts of life according to God's Book, and not according to the finesse of modern civilisation. Let us not be so careful as to how we offend or please human ears, but let us never offend God's ears.

The Highest Good—The Pilgrim's Song Book, 537 R

Christian experience must be applied to the facts of life as they are, not to our fancies. We can live beautifully inside our own particular religious compartment as long as God does not disturb us; but God has a most uncomfortable way of stirring up our nests and of bringing in facts that have to be faced.

Our Brilliant Heritage, 944 L

Remember, whatever happens, God is there. It is easy to fix your *mind* on God in a lecture, but a different matter to fix your mind on Him when there is a war on. You never get at God by blinking [deliberately ignoring] facts, but only by naming Him in the facts; whether they are devilish or not, say, "Lord, I thank Thee that Thou art here."

Our Portrait in Genesis, 969 R

We have to learn to interpret the mysteries of life in the light of our knowledge of God. Unless we can look the darkest, blackest fact full in the face without damaging God's character, we do not yet know Him.

My Utmost for His Highest, July 29, 806 L

FAILURE

No man ever gets beside God who has not first been beside himself and knocked out of his wits with worry and anxiety about the mess he has made of things.

So Send I You, 1294 R

Never let the sense of failure corrupt your new action.

My Utmost for His Highest, February 18, 751 L

FAITH

"*Be ready always to give an answer to every man that asketh you a reason of the hope that is in you with meekness and fear*" (1 Peter 3:15).

Peter does not say "give an explanation," but "a reason of the hope that is in you"—be ready to say what you base your hope on. Faith is deliberate confidence in the character of God Whose ways you cannot understand at the time. "I don't know why God allows what He does, but I will stick to my faith in His character no matter how contradictory things look." Faith is not a conscious thing; it springs from a personal relationship and is the unconscious result of believing someone.

Facing Reality, 27 R

The Great Life is to believe that Jesus Christ is not a fraud. The biggest fear a man has is never fear for himself but fear that his Hero won't get through; that He won't be able to explain things satisfactorily; for instance, why there should be war and disease. The problems of life get hold of a man and make it difficult for him to know whether in the face of these things he really is confident in Jesus Christ. The attitude of a believer must

be, "Things do look black, but I believe Him; and when the whole thing is told I am confident my belief will be justified and God will be revealed as a God of love and justice." It does not mean that we won't have problems, but it does mean that our problems will never come in between us and our faith in Him. "Lord, I don't understand this, but I am certain that there will be an explanation, and in the meantime I put it on one side." Our faith is in a Person Who is not deceived in anything He says or in the way He looks at things. Christianity is personal, passionate devotion to Jesus Christ as God manifest in the flesh.

Facing Reality, 37 L

Faith in God is a terrific venture in the dark; I have to believe that God is good in spite of all that contradicts it in my experience. It is not easy to say that God is love when everything that happens actually gives the lie to it. Everyone's soul represents some kind of battlefield. The point for each one is whether we will hang in, as Job did, and say, "Though things look black, I will trust in God."

Baffled to Fight Better, 82 L

Faith is the indefinable certainty of God behind every thing, and is the one thing the Spirit of God makes clearer and clearer as we go on.

He Shall Glorify Me, 522 L

There is a great difference between Christian experience and Christian faith. The danger of experience is that our faith is made to rest in it, instead of seeing that our experience is simply a doorway to God Himself. The reason many of us refuse to think and discover the basis of true religion is because evangelical Christianity has been stated in such a flimsy way.

Baffled to Fight Better, 82 R

(Continued)

FAITH (Continued)

It is not easy to have faith in God, and it is not meant to be easy because we have to make character. God will shield us from no requirements of His sons and daughters any more than He shielded His own Son. It is an easy business to sit in an armchair and say, "Oh yes, I believe God will do this and that"; that is credulity, not faith. But let me say, "I believe God will supply all my needs," and then let me "run dry," no money, no outlook, and see whether I will go through the trial of my faith, or sink back and put my trust in something else. It is the trial of our faith that is precious. If we go through the trial, there is so much wealth laid up in our heavenly banking account to draw upon when the next test comes.

The Highest Good—The Pilgrim's Song Book, 530 L

"When the Son of man cometh, shall He find faith on the earth?" We all have faith in good principles, in good management, in good common sense, but who amongst us has faith in Jesus Christ? Physical courage is grand, moral courage is grander, but the man who trusts Jesus Christ in the face of the terrific problems of life is worth a whole crowd of heroes.

The Highest Good, 544 R

Our Lord did not rebuke His disciples for making mistakes, but for not having faith. The two things that astonished Him were "little faith" and "great faith." Faith is not in what Jesus Christ can do, but in Himself, and anything He can do is less than Himself.

The Love of God—Now Is It Possible, 685 R

Seeing is never believing: we interpret what we see in the light of what we believe. Faith is confidence in God before you see God emerging; therefore the nature of faith is that it must be tried.

He Shall Glorify Me, 494 R

Faith is not a bargain with God—I will trust You if You give me money, but not if You don't. We have to trust in God whether He sends us money or not, whether He gives us health or not. We must have faith in God, not in His gifts. Let us walk before God and be perfect, you in your circumstances and I in mine; then we will prove ourselves true children of Abraham.

Not Knowing Whither, 881 R

If there is only one strand of faith amongst all the corruption within us, God will take hold of that one strand.

Not Knowing Whither, 888 L

The thing for us to examine is: Are we really living the Great Life, or are we living in a bandbox with a priggish notion that Jesus Christ is tied up in some formula? Jesus Christ is God manifest in the flesh, and He says, "This is the work of God that you believe in Me."

Facing Reality, 38 R

Beware of pronouncing any verdict on the life of faith if you are not living it.

Not Knowing Whither, 900 R

Faith never knows where it is being led, but it loves and knows the One Who is leading.

My Utmost for His Highest, March 19, 761 L

The life of faith is not a life of mounting up with wings, but a life of walking and not fainting.

My Utmost for His Highest, March 19, 761 L

Beware of the "yes-but," of putting your prudence-crutch under the purpose of God when you find His engineering of things has nearly unearthed your own little bag of tricks.

Our Portrait in Genesis, 976 L

Unless you bank your faith in God, you will not only be wrongly related in practical life and have your heart broken, but you will break other things you touch. (Cf. Matthew 18:6–7.)

Shade of His Hand, 1196 L

Fatalism means I am the sport of a force about which I know nothing; faith is trust in a God Whose ways I do not know, but Whose character I do know.

Shade of His Hand, 1201 R

The root of faith is the knowledge of a Person, and one of the biggest snares is the idea that God is sure to lead us to success.

My Utmost for His Highest, March 19, 761 L

Faith is the heroic effort of your life; you fling yourself in reckless confidence on God. God has ventured all in Jesus Christ to save us; now He wants us to venture our all in abandoned confidence in Him.

My Utmost for His Highest, May 8, 778 L

The great thing about faith in God is that it keeps a man undisturbed in the midst of disturbance.

Notes on Isaiah, 1376 R

FALL, THE

God created man to be master of the life in the earth and sea and sky, and the reason he is not is because he took the law into his own hands, and became master of himself, but of nothing else.

The Shadow of an Agony, 1163 L

Until Adam fell, he was not *interested in* God, he was *one with* God in communion—a man is never interested in that which he is; when Adam fell, he became so appallingly interested in God that he was afraid of Him—"and the man and his wife hid themselves from the presence of the Lord God amongst the trees of the garden" (RV).

Our Portrait in Genesis, 960 L

Adam disobeyed, and there entered in the disposition of sin, the disposition of self-realisation—I am my own God. This disposition may work out in a hundred and one different ways, in decorous morality or in indecorous immorality, but it has the one basis—my claim to my right to myself. That disposition was never in our Lord. Self-will, self-assertiveness, self-seeking were never in Him.

The Psychology of Redemption, 1083 L

FAMILY

The things we cannot touch are not things for us to pout over, but things for us to accept as God's providential order for us. As natural men, we are not inclined to like the things God makes. At certain stages of our life we much prefer the friends we make to our God-made relations, because we can be noble with our friends, we have no past history with them. We cannot be noble with our relations, because they knew us when we were mean, and now when we are with them we cannot put on the pretence; it won't work.

The Psychology of Redemption, 1071 R

No one could have had a more sensitive love in human relationship than Jesus; and yet He says there are times when love to father and mother must be hatred in comparison to our love for Him.

So Send I You, 1301 L

(Continued)

FAMILY (Continued)

We say, "Oh, but the Lord must have had a sweet and delightful home life." But we are wrong. He had an exceedingly difficult home life. Jesus Christ's intimates were brothers and sisters who did not believe in Him, and He says that the disciple is not above his Master (Luke 6:40).

The Psychology of Redemption, 1073 L

Our Lord preached His first public sermon in the place where He was brought up, where He was most intimately known, and they smashed up His service and tried to kill Him. "Oh, but," we say, "I expected that when I was saved and sanctified, my father and mother and brothers and sisters would be made right, but instead they seem to be all wrong." If the mother of our Lord misunderstood Him, and His brethren did not believe in Him, the same things will happen to His life in us, and we must not think it strange concerning the misunderstandings of others. The life of the Son of God in us is brought into the same kind of circumstances that the historic life of Jesus Christ was brought into, and what was true of Him will be true also of His life in us.

The Psychology of Redemption, 1073 R

It never cost a disciple anything to follow Jesus; to talk about cost when you are in love with anyone is an insult. The point of suffering is that it costs other people— fathers, mothers, households; consequently we decline to go on; consideration for others causes us to hold back. If we go on with it, then others will suffer.

The Servant as His Lord, 1280 R

FANATIC / FANATICISM

A fanatic is one who entrenches himself in invincible ignorance.

Baffled to Fight Better, 59 R

The theological view ought to be constantly examined. If we put it in the place of God we become invincibly ignorant; that is, we won't accept any other point of view, and the invincible ignorance of fanaticism leads to delusions for which we alone are to blame. The fundamental things are not the things which can be proved logically in practical life.

Baffled to Fight Better, 62 R

Fanaticism is sticking true to my interpretation of my destiny instead of waiting for God to make it clear. The fanatical line is—*Do* something; the test of faith lies in *not* doing. Fanaticism is always based on the highest I believe; a sordid being is never fanatical.

Not Knowing Whither, 877 L

A fanatic is concerned not about God but about proving his own little fanatical ideas. It is a danger peculiar to us all. It is easier to be a fanatic than a faithful soul, because there is something amazingly humbling, particularly to our religious conceit, in being loyal to God.

Not Knowing Whither, 911 L

There is always the danger of becoming a fanatical adherent to what God has said instead of adhering to God who said it.

Our Portrait in Genesis, 966 L

FATE / FATALISM

If I view anything as inevitable with regard to any human being I am [an] unbeliever. I have no right to have anything less than the hope and the belief of Jesus Christ with regard to the worst and most hopeless of men.

Notes on Isaiah, 1370 R

There is no such thing as fate; a human being always has the power to do the incalculable thing. There are fatal issues, but not fate.

Notes on Isaiah, 1370 R

Until we get through all the shivering wisdom that will not venture out on God, we will never know all that is involved in the life of faith. Fate means stoical resignation to an unknown force. Faith is not resignation to a power we do not know; faith is committal to One Whose character we do know because it has been revealed to us in Jesus Christ.

Not Knowing Whither, 865 L

Faith is the process by which our confidence is built up in a Person Whose character we know, however perplexing the present things may be that He is doing. Fate is superstitious yielding to a person whose character we do not know and have not the slightest confidence in but have succumbed to. A stoic is a fatalist; he succumbs to an unknown ruling; a saint is one who lives amongst earth's troubles and trials with a passionate joy the stoic knows nothing about.

Notes on Jeremiah, 1402 L

FATHERHOOD OF GOD

When we talk about the Fatherhood of God, let us remember that the Lord Jesus is the exclusive way to the Father. That is not an idea to be inferred, but to be received: "No man cometh unto the Father, but by Me" (John 14:6). We can get to God as Creator apart from Jesus Christ (see Romans 1:20), but never to God as our Father saving through Him.

Christian Disciplines, Volume 2,
The Discipline of Prayer, 309 R

FEAR

The truth is we have nothing to fear and nothing to overcome because He is all in all and we are more than conquerors through Him. The recognition of this truth is not flattering to the worker's sense of heroics, but it is amazingly glorifying to the work of Christ.

Approved Unto God, 4 R

The greatest fear a man has is not that he will be damned, but that Jesus Christ will be worsted, that the things He stood for—love and justice and forgiveness and kindness among men—will not win out in the end; the things He stands for look like will-o'-the-wisps. Then comes the call to spiritual tenacity, not to hang on and do nothing, but to work deliberately on the certainty that God is not going to be worsted.

My Utmost for His Highest, February 22, 752 L

The greatest fear in life is not personal fear for myself, but fear that after all God will be worsted. . . . the fear that in the end Jesus Christ will not come out triumphant, that evil and wrong will triumph. We reveal our fear by intense assertions that of course He will win through. That is the curious way we are built; we speak as intensely of a position about which we are fearful as we do of a position we are sure of.

He Shall Glorify Me, 493 L

"Blessed is every one that feareth the Lord; that walketh in His ways" (Psalm 128:1).
    The remarkable thing about fearing God is that when you fear God you fear nothing else, whereas if you do not fear God you fear everything else. "Blessed is every one that feareth the Lord"; the writer to the Hebrews tells us to fear, lest haply there should be any promise of God's of which we come short (Hebrews 4:1).

The Highest Good—The Pilgrim's Song Book, 537 L

FEELINGS (See EMOTION(S))

FELLOWSHIP WITH GOD

The measure of the worth of our public activity for God is the private profound communion we have with Him. . . . We have to pitch our tents where we shall always have quiet times with God, however noisy our times with the world may be.

My Utmost for His Highest, January 6, 736 R

It is impossible for a saint, no matter what his experience, to keep right with God if he will not take the trouble to spend time with God. In order to keep the mind and heart awake to God's high ideals you have to keep coming back again and again to the primal source. If you do not, you will be crushed into degeneracy.

Not Knowing Whither, 908 R

Just as a poet or an artist must keep his soul brooding on the right lines, so a Christian must keep the sense of God's call always awake. Spend plenty of time with God; let other things go, but don't neglect Him. And beware of practical work. We are not here to do work *for* God; we are here to be workers *with* Him, those through whom He can do His work.

Not Knowing Whither, 908 R

FORGET / FORGETTING
(See also MEMORY)

There are other passages which refer to the marvellous power of God to blot certain things out of His memory. Forgetting with us is a defect; forgetting with God is an attribute. "I have blotted out, as a thick cloud, thy transgressions, and, as a cloud, thy sins" (Isaiah 44:22).

Biblical Psychology, 174 R

The surest test of maturity is the power to look back without blinking [deliberately ignoring] anything. When we look back we get either hopelessly despairing or hopelessly conceited. The difference between the natural backward look and the spiritual backward look is in what we forget. Forgetting in the natural domain is the outcome of vanity—the only things I intend to remember are those in which I figure as being a very fine person! Forgetting in the spiritual domain is the gift of God. The Spirit of God never allows us to forget what we have been but He does make us forget what we have attained to, which is quite unnatural.

Conformed to His Image, 369 R

FORGIVENESS

Forgiveness is the Divine miracle of grace. Have we ever contemplated the amazing fact that God through the Death of Jesus Christ forgives us for every wrong we have ever done, not because we are sorry, but out of His sheer mercy? God's forgiveness is only natural in the supernatural domain.

Approved Unto God, 15 L

If I am forgiven without being altered, forgiveness is not only damaging to me, but a sign of unmitigated weakness in God. Unless it is possible for God's forgiveness to establish an order of holiness and rectitude, forgiveness is a mean and abominable thing.

Baffled to Fight Better, 59 R

I have no right to say that I believe in forgiveness as an attribute of God if in my own heart I cherish an unforgiving temper. The forgiveness of God is the test by which I myself am judged.

Disciples Indeed, 385 L

Think what God's forgiveness means: it means that He forgets away every sin. Forgetting in the Divine mind is an attribute; in the human mind it is a defect; consequently God never illustrates His Divine forgetfulness by human pictures, but by pictures taken from His own creation—"As far as east is from the west, so far hath He removed our transgressions from us" (Psalm 103:12); "I have blotted out, as a thick cloud, thy transgressions . . ." (Isaiah 44:22).

God's Workmanship, 415 R

Jesus Christ did not come to fling forgiveness broadcast; He did not come to the Pharisees, who withstood Him and said He was possessed with a devil, and say "I forgive you": He said, "How can ye escape the damnation of hell?" We may talk as much as we like about forgiveness, but it will never make any difference to us unless we realise that we need it. God can never forgive the man who does not want to be forgiven.

He Shall Glorify Me, 505 R

The revelation of forgiveness in the Bible is not that God puts snow over a rubbish heap, but that He turns a man into the standard of Himself, the Forgiver.

He Shall Glorify Me, 506 L

God exhausts metaphors to show what His forgiveness means—"I, even I, am He that blotteth out thy transgressions for Mine own sake, and will not remember thy sins" (Isaiah 43:25); "I have blotted out, as a thick cloud, thy transgressions, and, as a cloud, thy sins" (Isaiah 44:22); "As far as the east is from the west, so far hath He removed our transgressions from us" (Psalm 103:12); "For Thou hast cast all my sins behind Thy back" (Isaiah 38:17); "For I will forgive their iniquity, and I will remember their sin no more" (Jeremiah 31:34).

He Shall Glorify Me, 506 R

"Then after three years I went up to Jerusalem to visit Cephas, and tarried with him fifteen days" (Galatians 1:18 RV).

Think of Paul after three years in Arabia, where he was altogether broken and then remade by the grace of God, coming to Peter and being with him for fifteen days—can you imagine what happened? How Peter would go over the whole story, beginning with the scenes on the lake right on to the Garden of Gethsemane and the Cross; and Peter would take Paul to the Communion service, and they would see widows there, made so by Paul. Think what a memory like that would mean to a man of acute sensitiveness. It takes great courage for a forgiven man to come in contact with those whom he has wronged.

The Place of Help, 1006 L

John 15:13 has reference to human love, which lays down its life for its friends. Romans 5:8 has reference to the Divine love, which lays down its life for its enemies, a thing human nature can never do. This does not mean that human beings cannot forgive; they can and do forgive; but forgiveness is not human; it belongs entirely to the Divine nature, and is a miracle when exhibited in the human.

The Psychology of Redemption, 1098 R

FREEDOM *(See also LIBERTY)*

"Oh, I can give that habit up when I like." You cannot; you will find that the habit absolutely dominates you because you yielded to it willingly. It is easy to sing— "He will break every fetter," and at the same time be living a life of obvious slavery to yourself. Yielding to Jesus will break every form of slavery in any human life.

My Utmost for His Highest, March 14, 759 L

(Continued)

FREEDOM (Continued)

"If the Son . . . shall make you free, ye shall be free indeed," said Jesus—free from the inside, free in essence; there will be no pretence, no putting yourself on a pedestal and saying "This is what God has done for me"; you will be free; the thing will be there ostensibly.

Biblical Ethics, 121 R

"If the Son therefore shall make you free, ye shall be free indeed" (John 8:36).
 "Free indeed," i.e., free from the inside. The freedom of Jesus is never license; it is always liberty, and liberty means ability to fulfil the law of God.

The Love of God—The Ministry of the Unnoticed, 668 L

Worldly people imagine that the saints must find it difficult to live with so many restrictions, but the bondage is with the world, not with the saints. There is no such thing as freedom in the world, and the higher we go in the social life the more bondage there is. True liberty exists only where the soul has the holy scorn of the Holy Ghost—I will bow my neck to no yoke but the yoke of the Lord Jesus Christ; there is only one law, and that is the law of God.

The Moral Foundations of Life, 732 L

It is rarely the big compellings of God that get hold of us in our prayers; instead we tell God what He should do; we tell Him that men are being lost and that He ought to save them. This is a terrific charge against God; it means that He must be asleep. When God gets me to realise that I am being taken up into *His* enterprises, then I get rest of soul; I am free for my twenty-four hours.

The Place of Help, 1039 R

The thing that interferes with the life with God is our abominable seriousness which chokes the freedom and simplicity which ought to mark the life. The freedom and simplicity spring from one point only, a heart at rest with God and at leisure from itself.

Approved Unto God, 22 R

FRIENDSHIP

There is always an intangible something which makes a friend; it is not what he does, but what he is. You feel the better for being in the presence of some men.

Baffled to Fight Better, 68 R

What is the sign of a friend? That he tells you secret sorrows? No, that he tells you secret joys. Many will confide to you their secret sorrows, but the last mark of intimacy is to confide secret joys. Have we ever let God tell us any of His joys, or are we telling God our secrets so continually that we leave no room for Him to talk to us?

My Utmost for His Highest, June 3, 787 L

FUTURE

"The best is yet to be" is really true from Jesus Christ's standpoint. There is nothing noble the human mind has ever hoped for or dreamed of that will not be fulfilled, and a great deal more.

He Shall Glorify Me, 479 L

"And God shall wipe away all tears from their eyes." There will come one day a personal and direct touch from God when every tear and perplexity, every oppression and distress, every suffering and pain, and wrong and injustice will have a complete and ample and overwhelming explanation.

Shade of His Hand, 1208 R

Immediately you begin to forecast and plan for yourself, God will break up your programme; He delights to do it, until we learn to live like children based on the knowledge that God is ruling and reigning and rejoicing, and His joy is our strength.

Biblical Ethics, 119 L

Jesus Christ and He alone is able to satisfy the craving of the human heart to know the "whence" and "whither" of life. He enables men to understand that they have come into this life from a deep purpose in the heart of God; that the one thing they are here for is to get readjusted to God and become His lovers. And whither are we going? We are going to where the Book of Life is opened, and we enter into an effulgence of glory we can only conceive of now at rare moments.

Conformed to His Image, 379 R

At the end of the year we turn with eagerness to all that God has for the future, and yet anxiety is apt to arise from remembering the yesterdays. Our present enjoyment of God's grace is apt to be checked by the memory of yesterday's sins and blunders. But God is the God of our yesterdays, and He allows the memory of them in order to turn the past into a ministry of spiritual culture for the future. God reminds us of the past lest we get into a shallow security in the present.

My Utmost for His Highest, December 31, 861 R

GENEROSITY / GIVING
(See also EXTRAVAGANCE)

As sorrowful, yet alway rejoicing; as poor, yet making many rich; as having nothing, and yet possessing all things" (2 Corinthians 6:10).

As we draw on the grace of God He increases voluntary poverty all along the line. Always give the best you have got every time; never think about who you are giving it to; let other people take it or leave it as they choose. Pour out the best you have, and always be poor. Never reserve anything; never be diplomatic and careful about the treasure God gives.

Facing Reality, 155 L

We never get credit spiritually for impulsive giving. If suddenly we feel we should give a shilling to a poor man, we get no credit from God for giving it; there is no virtue in it whatever. As a rule, that sort of giving is a relief to our feelings; it is not an indication of a generous character, but rather an indication of a lack of generosity. God never estimates what we give from impulse. We are given credit for what we determine in our hearts to give; for the giving that is governed by a fixed determination. The Spirit of God revolutionises our philanthropic instincts. Much of our philanthropy is simply the impulse to save ourselves an uncomfortable feeling. The Spirit of God alters all that. As saints our attitude towards giving is that we give for Jesus Christ's sake, and from no other motive. God holds us responsible for the way we use this power of voluntary choice.

Biblical Psychology, 169 R

When we have had a good dinner and feel remarkably generous, we say, "If only I had a thousand pounds, what I would do with it!" We do not get credit for that until what we do with what we have is considered. The proof that the design for the thousand pounds would be worked out is what we do with the twopence-halfpenny* we have.

Biblical Psychology, 170 L
*A colloquial expression meaning next to nothing.

(Continued)

GENEROSITY / GIVING
(Continued)

"And the second is like, namely this, Thou shalt love thy neighbour as thyself."

Everything our Lord taught about the duty of man to man might be summed up in the one law of giving. It is as if He set Himself to contradict the natural counsel of the human heart, which is to acquire and keep.

Conformed to His Image, 366 L

A child will say of a gift, "Is it my own?" When a man is born again that instinct is replaced by another, the instinct of giving. The law of the life of a disciple is Give, Give, Give (e.g., Luke 6:38). As Christians our giving is to be proportionate to all we have received of the infinite giving of God. "Freely ye have received, freely give." Not how much we give, but what we do not give, is the test of our Christianity.

Conformed to His Image, 366 L

When we speak of giving we nearly always think only of money. Money is the life-blood of most of us. We have a remarkable trick—when we give money we don't give sympathy; and when we give sympathy we don't give money. The only way to get insight into the meaning for ourselves of what Jesus taught is by being indwelt by the Holy Spirit, because He enables us first of all to understand our Lord's life; unless we do that, we will exploit His teaching, take out of it only what we agree with.

Conformed to His Image, 366 L

There is one aspect of giving we think little about, but which had a prominent place in our Lord's life, viz., that of social intercourse. He accepted hospitality on the right hand and on the left, from publicans and from the Pharisees, so much so that they said He was "a gluttonous man, and a winebibber, a friend of publicans and sinners!" He spent Himself with one lodestar all the time, to

seek and to save that which was lost; and Paul says, "I am become all things to all men, that I may by all means save some" (RV). How few of us ever think of giving socially! We are so parsimonious that we won't spend a thing in conversation unless it is on a line that helps us!

Conformed to His Image, 366 R

We are measured by what we do according to what we have. Some people only give to the deserving, because they imagine they deserve all they have. Our Lord says, Give, not because they deserve it, but because I tell you to.

The Highest Good, 553 L

The teaching of Jesus revolutionises our modern conception of charity.

Conformed to His Image, 378 L

We are economically drunk nowadays; everybody is an economist, consequently we imagine that God is economical. Think of God in Creation! Think of the number of trees and blades of grass and flowers, the extravagant wealth of beauty no one ever sees! Think of the sunrises and sunsets we never look at! God is lavish in every degree. For God's sake, don't be economical; be God's child.

Our Portrait in Genesis, 975 R

"Be ye therefore perfect, even as your Father which is in heaven is perfect," and the connection of this perfection with its context must be observed. Its context is Matthew 5:45, "that ye may be sons of your Father which is in heaven: for He maketh His sun to rise on the evil and the good, and sendeth rain on the just and the unjust." Our Lord means by being perfect then obviously that we exhibit in our actual relationships to men, as they are, the hospitality and generosity our Heavenly Father has exhibited to us. In 2 Corinthians 4:7–11 Paul makes it plain that there are no ideal conditions of life, but "My Utmost for His Highest" has to be carried out in the actual conditions of human life.

The Place of Help, 993 L

To-day we enthrone insurance and economy, but it is striking to recall that the one thing Jesus Christ commended was extravagance. Our Lord only called one work "good," and that was the act of Mary of Bethany when she broke the alabaster box of ointment. It was neither useful nor her duty; it sprang from her devotion to Jesus, and He said of it—"Wheresoever this gospel shall be preached throughout the whole world, this also that she hath done shall be spoken of for a memorial of her."

Shade of His Hand, 1218 L

All through the Old and New Testaments the counsel is on the line of hospitality. As long as we have something to give, we must give. How does civilisation argue? "Does this man deserve that I should give to him?" "If I give that man money, I know what he will do with it." Jesus Christ says, *"Give to him that asketh thee,"* not because he deserves it, but *because I tell you to* (see Matthew 5:42).

Shade of His Hand, 1241 R

"Having nothing. . . ." Never reserve anything. Pour out the best you have, and always be poor. Never be diplomatic and careful about the treasure God gives. This is poverty triumphant.

My Utmost for His Highest, June 26, 795 L

The counsel of extravagance comes out all through the Bible. We are apt to ignore it by the timidity of our reasoning. The one thing Jesus Christ commended was Mary of Bethany's extravagant act. . . . The dis-

ciples, who were perfectly reasonable, said, What a waste! Jesus Christ said, "She hath wrought a good work on Me." The true nature of devotion to Jesus Christ must be extravagance.

Shade of His Hand, 1241 R

Don't be careful whether men receive what you give in the right way or the wrong way; see to it that you don't withhold your hand. As long as you have something to give, give, let the consequences be what they may.

Shade of His Hand, 1242 R

Verse 42 is an arena for theological acrobats: "Give to him that asketh thee, and from him that would borrow of thee turn not thou away" (Matthew 5:42). That is the statement either of a madman, or of God Incarnate. We always say we do not know what Jesus Christ means, when we know perfectly well He means something which is a blunt impossibility unless He can remake us and make it possible.

Studies in the Sermon on the Mount, 1451 L

Much of our modern philanthropy is based on the motive of giving to the poor man because he deserves it, or because we are distressed at seeing him poor. Jesus never taught charity from those motives: He said, "Give to him that asketh thee, not because he deserves it, but because I tell you to." The great motive in all giving is Jesus Christ's command.

Studies in the Sermon on the Mount, 1451 L

We enthrone commonsense as God and say, "It is absurd; if I give to every one that asks, every beggar in the place will be at my door." Try it. I have yet to find the man who obeyed Jesus Christ's command and did not realise that God restrains those who beg.

Studies in the Sermon on the Mount, 1451 R

GIFTS / GIFTEDNESS

Another danger in work for God is to make natural temperament the line of service. The gifts of the Spirit are built on God's sovereignty, not on our temperament. We are apt to limit God by saying, "Oh, I'm not built like that"; or, "I have not been well educated." Never limit God by those paralysing thoughts; it is the outcome of unbelief.

Approved Unto God, 8 L

What does it matter to the Lord Almighty of heaven and earth what your early training was like! What does matter to Him is that you don't lean to your own understanding, but acknowledge Him in all your ways. So crush on the threshold of your mind any of those lame, limping "I can'ts,"—"you see I am not gifted." The great stumbling-block that prevents some people being simple disciples of Jesus is that they *are* gifted—so gifted that they won't trust in the Lord with all their hearts. You have to learn to break by the power of the Holy Spirit the fuss and the lethargy which alternate in your life, and remember that it is a crime to be weak in His strength.

Approved Unto God, 8 L

We have a way of saying—"What a wonderful power that man or woman would be in God's service." Reasoning on man's broken virtues makes us fix on the wrong thing. The only way any man or woman can ever be of service to God is when he or she is willing to renounce all their natural excellencies and determine to be weak in Him— "I am here for one thing only, for Jesus Christ to manifest Himself in me." That is to be the steadfast habit of a Christian's life.

The Moral Foundations of Life, 725 R

GIFTS, CONSECRATION OF

Consecrating natural gifts is popular but a snare. "I have the gift of a voice and I will consecrate it to God and sing 'Always, only, for my King.'" If a man or woman is devoted to God, they can sing anything with the blessing of God; but if they are not right they may sing "Take my life," and serve the devil in doing it. It is not the external things that tell, but the ruling disposition. There is no indication in God's Word that we should consecrate natural gifts, although we find many such indications in hymns. The only thing we can consecrate is our bodies. If we consecrate them to God, He takes them.

Facing Reality, 29 R

There is a theory abroad to-day that we have to consecrate our gifts to God. We cannot; they are not ours to consecrate; every gift we have has been given to us. Jesus Christ does not take my gifts and use them; He takes me and turns me right about face, and realises Himself in me for His glory.

Facing Reality, 32 R

As long as the artist or musician imagines he can consecrate his artistic gifts to God, he is deluded. Abandonment of ourselves is the kernel of consecration; not presenting our gifts, but presenting ourselves without reserve.

Christian Disciplines, Volume 2, The Discipline of Loneliness, 324 L

GOOD VS. BEST

Whenever *right* is made the guidance in the life, it will blunt the spiritual insight. The great enemy of the life of faith in God is not sin, but the good which is not good enough. The good is always the enemy of the best.

My Utmost for His Highest, May 25, 784 L

Anyone will give up wrong things if he knows how to, but will I give up the best I have for Jesus Christ? If I am only willing to give up wrong things, never let me talk about being in love with Him! We say, "Why shouldn't I do it; there is no harm in it?" For pity's sake, go and do it, but remember that the construction of a spiritual character is doomed once you take that line.

Biblical Ethics, 104 R

One of the greatest snares is the number of good things we might do. Jesus Christ never did the good things He might have done; He did everything He ought to do because He had His eye fixed on His Father's will and He sacrificed Himself for His Father.

Bringing Sons Unto Glory, 223 R

The mark of the saint is the good right things he has the privilege of not doing. There are a hundred and one right and good things which, if you are a disciple of Jesus, you must avoid as you would the devil although there is no devil in them. If our Lord's words in Matthew 5:29–30 were read more often we would have a healthier young manhood and womanhood.

Disciples Indeed, 395 R

There can be no such thing as God's second best. We can perversely put ourselves out of God's order into His permissive will, but that is a different matter.

Not Knowing Whither, 876 L

In seeking the Best we soon find that our enemy is our good things, not our bad. The things that keep us back from God's best are not sin and imperfection, but the things that are right and good and noble from the natural standpoint. To discern that the natural virtues antagonise surrender to God is to bring our soul at once into the centre of our greatest battlefield.

Not Knowing Whither, 876 R

It is not sin that keeps us away from Jesus, but our own goodness. "I am not come to call the righteous," Jesus said, "but sinners to repentance." We don't seem to need God until we come up against things.

Conformed to His Image, 356 L

Sanctification means not only that we are delivered from sin, but that we start on a life of stern discipline. It is not a question of praying but of performing, of deliberately disciplining ourselves. There is no royal road there; we each have it entirely in our own hands. It is not wrong things that have to be sacrificed, but right things. "The good is the enemy of the best"; not the bad, but the good that is not good enough.

Biblical Ethics, 104 R

GOSPEL, COMMUNICATION OF

We preach to men as if they were conscious of being dying sinners; they are not; they are having a good time, and our talk about being born again is from a domain of which they know nothing. The natural man does not want to be born again.

The Psychology of Redemption, 1062 R

There must be a sense of need before your message is of any use. Thousands of people are happy without God in this world.

My Utmost for His Highest, December 19, 857 L

(Continued)

GOSPEL, COMMUNICATION OF
(Continued)

Another danger is to imagine that it is my particular presentation of things that will attract people. It may attract them, but never to God. The line of attraction is always an indication of the goal of the attracted; if you attract by personal impressiveness, the attracted will get no further than you. Our Lord said—"I, if I be lifted up, will draw all men unto Me."

Not Knowing Whither, 868 R

What is needed to-day is not a new gospel, but live men and women who can re-state the gospel of the Son of God in terms that will reach the very heart of our problems. To-day men are flinging the truth overboard as well as the terms. Why should we not become workmen who need not to be ashamed, rightly dividing the word of truth to our own people? The majority of orthodox ministers are hopelessly useless, and the unorthodox seem to be the only ones who are used. We need men and women saturated with the truth of God who can re-state the old truth in terms that appeal to our day.

Approved Unto God, 5 R

We do not need a new Gospel; what we need is the old truths re-stated to hit the things that are wrong to-day. If you use the terms of a bygone age and apply them to the sins of bygone days, you don't hit the things that are wrong to-day.

Notes on Jeremiah, 1394 L

We have to be stern in proclaiming God's word; let it come out in all its rugged bluntness, unwatered down and unrefined; but when we deal with others we have to remember that we are sinners saved by grace. The tendency to-day is to do exactly the opposite: we make all kinds of excuses for God's word—"Oh God does not expect us to be perfect," and when we deal with people personally we are amazingly hard.

All these things lead us back to Jesus Christ—He is the Truth; He is the Honourable One; He is the just One; He is the Pure One; He is the altogether Lovely One: He is the only One of Good Report. No matter where we start from, we will always come back to Jesus Christ.

The Moral Foundations of Life, 720 R

The gospel of Jesus awakens a tremendous craving but also a tremendous resentment. People want the blessing of God, but they will not stand the probing and the humiliation. As workers, our one method is merciless insistence on the one line, cutting down to the very root; otherwise there will be no healing.

Approved Unto God, 7 L

GOSPEL OF CHRIST

The ministry is the "glorious gospel of the blessed God, which was committed to my trust." If I am going to be loyal to that trust, it will mean I must never allow any impertinent sensitiveness to hinder my keeping the trust. My trust is the glorious gospel for myself and through me to others, and it is realised in two ways: in the perfect certainty that God has redeemed the world, and in the imperative necessity of working on that basis with everyone with whom I come in contact (cf. Colossians 1:28–29).

Approved Unto God , 4 R

We have no right to preach unless we present the Gospel; we have not to advocate a cause or a creed or an experience, but to present the Gospel, and we cannot do that unless we have a personal testimony based on the Gospel.

Approved Unto God, 12 L

The Gospel of Jesus Christ awakens an intense craving and an equally intense resentment.

Approved Unto God, 14 R

The Gospel comes in with a backing of Divine authority and an arrestment which men resent. There is something in every man that resents the interference of God. Before a man can be saved, the central citadel of his being has to be stormed and taken possession of by the Holy Spirit.

Approved Unto God, 12 L

Our Lord taught that men could only be right with each other as they are right with Him, and Jesus Christ can take any man and place him in right relationship with God.

Approved Unto God, 12 R

Never water down or minimise the mighty Gospel of God by considering that people may be misled by certain statements. Present the Gospel in all its fullness and God will guard His own truth.

Approved Unto God, 12 R

Our Lord did not scathe sin; He came to save from it. We are apt to put the superb blessings of the Gospel as something for a special few; they are for sinners saved by grace.

Disciples Indeed, 403 R

In the teaching of Jesus the term "The Greatest Good" is embodied in its most comprehensive sense in His use of the word 'Gospel." Our Lord in no way means what we commonly mean when we say "Gospel," viz. salvation by faith in Jesus. The Bible never gives definitions; the Bible states facts, and the Gospel that Jesus brought of good news about God is the most astounding thing the world ever heard, but it must be the Gospel that Jesus brought. Whenever the Gospel of Jesus loses the note of unutterable gladness, it is like salt that has lost its savour.

The Highest Good, 541 L

God or sin must die in me. The one elementary Bible truth we are in danger of forgetting is that the Gospel of God is addressed to men as sinners, and nothing else.

Facing Reality, 32 L

The temptation to win and woo men is the most subtle of all, and it is a line that commends itself to us naturally. But you cannot win and woo a mutiny; it is absolutely impossible. You cannot win and woo the man who, when he recognises the rule of God, detests it. The Gospel of Jesus Christ always marks the line of demarcation; His attitude all through is one of sternness; there must be no compromise. The only way in which the Kingdom of God can be established is by the love of God as revealed in the Cross of Jesus Christ, not by the lovingkindness of a backboneless being without justice or righteousness or truth. The background of God's love is holiness. His is not a compromising love, and the Kingdom of our Lord can only be brought in by means of His love at work in regeneration.

The Psychology of Redemption, 1081 R

GOSPEL OF TEMPERAMENT

. . . preaching the gospel of temperament, the gospel of "cheer up," when a person cannot cheer up; telling him to look on the bright side of things when there is no bright side. It is as ridiculous as telling a jelly-fish to listen to one of Handel's Oratorios; it would have to be made over again first. It is just as futile to tell a man convicted of sin to cheer up; what he needs is the grace of God to alter him and put in him the well-spring of joy.

Biblical Psychology, 172 L

If our religion is only a religion of cheerfulness for the healthy-minded, it is no good for London, because more than half the people . . . a great deal more than half, are not able to be cheerful; their minds and consciences and bodies are so twisted and tortured that exactly the opposite seems to be their portion. All the talking and preaching about healthy-mindedness, about cheering up and living in the sunshine, will never touch that crowd. If all Jesus Christ can do is to tell a man he has to cheer up when he is miserable; if all the worker for God can do is to tell a man he has no business to have the "blues"—I say if that is all Jesus Christ's religion can do, then it is a failure.

Workmen of God, 1353 L

GOVERNMENT

The ordinance of government, whether it is a bad or good government, does not lie with men, but is entirely in God's hands; the king or the government will have to answer to God (cf. 1 Peter 2:13–14). The conservative attitude—my king, right or wrong—is a degeneration from the one great central point of the government of man by man.

Shade of His Hand, 1231 R

God has ordained that man is to govern man, whether he wants to or not . . . [but] we must never think of men and women in the mass . . . there is no such thing; the mass is made up of separate individuals. The danger of thinking of people in the mass is that you forget they are human beings, each one an absolutely solitary life. Everyone has something or someone to govern—the most ignominious slave has an influence somewhere—and God is going to hold us responsible for the way we govern.

Biblical Ethics, 93 L

Another thing to be borne in mind is the incalculable element in every life. In the government of man by man you are not dealing with a mathematical problem, but with human beings, and you can never be sure how they will act, any more than you can always be sure how you yourself will act.

Biblical Ethics, 93 R

"Submit yourselves to every ordinance of man for the Lord's sake . . ." (1 Peter 2:13; see 2 Peter 2:13–18).

Peter's statements in these verses are remarkable, and they are statements the modern Christian does not like. He is outlining what is to be the conduct of saints in relation to the moral institutions based on the government of man by man. No matter, he says, what may be the condition of the community to which you belong, behave yourself as a saint in it. Many people are righteous as individuals, but they ignore the need to be righteous in connection with human institutions. Paul continually dealt with insubordination in spiritual people. Degeneration in the Christian life comes in because of this refusal to recognise the insistence God places on obedience to human institutions.

Biblical Ethics, 95 L

GRACE

"In stripes, in imprisonments, in tumults, in labours, in watchings, in fastings" (2 Corinthians 6:5).

These verses are Paul's spiritual diary; they describe the outward hardships which proved the hotbed for the graces of the Spirit—the working together of outward hardships and inward grace. Imprisonments, tumults, labours—these are all things in the external life. "In tumults"—watch a porridge pot boiling and you will know what tumult means; in that condition draw on the grace of God now. Don't say "I will endure it till I can get away and pray"; draw now; it is the most practical thing on earth. Whenever you are going through any tribulation that tears, don't pray about it, but draw on the grace of God now. The exercise of prayer is the work of drawing now.

Facing Reality, 41 L

"I know both how to be abased, and I know how to abound: every where and in all things I am instructed both to be full and to be hungry, both to abound and to suffer need" (Philippians 4:12)—drawing on the grace of God in every conceivable condition. One of the greatest proofs that we are drawing on the grace of God is that we can be humiliated without the slightest trace of anything but the grace of God in us. Draw on the grace of God now, not presently. The one word in the spiritual vocabulary is "NOW."

Facing Reality, 42 R

'For ye know the grace of our Lord Jesus Christ, that, though He was rich, yet for your sakes He became poor, that ye through His poverty might become rich" (2 Corinthians 8:9 RV).

"Grace" means the overflowing nature of God; we see it in Nature; we have no words to describe the lavishness of God. "The grace of our Lord Jesus Christ" is the overflowing of God's nature in entire and absolute forgiveness through His own sacrifice. Do we discern that grace? We talk about the sacrifice of the Son of God and forget that it was the sacrifice of God Himself. "God was in Christ, reconciling the world unto Himself."

Bringing Sons Unto Glory, 233 R

We have the sneaking idea that we earn things and get into God's favour by what we do—by our praying, by our repentance: the only way we get into God's favour is by the sheer gift of His grace.

God's Workmanship, 415 L

"God is able to make all grace abound unto you . . ." (2 Corinthians 9:8 RV).

In talking to people you will be amazed to find that they much more readily listen if you talk on the line of suffering, of the attacks of the devil; but get on the triumphant line of the Apostle Paul, talk about the super-conquering life, about God making all His Divine grace to abound, and they lose interest—"That is all in the clouds," a sheer indication that they have never begun to taste the unfathomable joy that is awaiting them if they will only take it.

God's Workmanship, 416 L

The overflowing grace of God has no limits, and we have to set no limits to it, but "grow in grace, and in the knowledge of our Lord and Saviour Jesus Christ."

God's Workmanship, 416 R

"Lord, swamp me with Thy grace and glory that the ample tide of Thyself may be all in all."

Knocking at God's Door, September 2, 647 L

The grace we had yesterday won't do for to-day.

Facing Reality, 40 L

(Continued)

GRACE (Continued)

Our Lord trusted no man (see John 2:24–25), yet He was never suspicious, never bitter; His confidence in what God's grace could do for any man was so perfect that He never despaired of anyone. If our trust is placed in human beings, we will end in despairing of every one. But when we limit our thinking to the things of purity we shall think only of what God's grace has done in others, and put our confidence in that and in nothing else.

The Moral Foundations of Life, 719 R

God can turn cunning, crafty people into simple, guileless people. The marvel of His grace is such that He can take out the strands of evil and twistedness from a person's mind and imagination, and make him single-minded and simple towards God so that his life becomes radiantly beautiful by the miracle of His grace.

The Shadow of an Agony, 1170 L

God's grace turns out men and women with a strong family likeness to Jesus Christ.

My Utmost for His Highest, July 7, 799 L

It is a matter of indifference to God's grace how abominable I am if I come to the light; but woe be to me if I refuse the light (see John 3:19–21).

My Utmost for His Highest, July 18, 802 R

"Unto me . . . is this grace given, that I should preach . . . the unsearchable riches of Christ." . . . We have the idea that it is a sign of modesty to say at the close of the day—"Well, I have got through, but it has

been a severe tussle!" And all the grace of God is ours without let or hindrance* through the Lord Jesus, and He is ready to tax the last grain of sand and the remotest star to bless us. What does it matter if circumstances are hard? Why shouldn't they be! We are the ones who ought to be able to stand them.

Our Brilliant Heritage, 941 R
"Without let or hindrance" is a legal phrase meaning "without obstacle or impediment."

GRATITUDE

When we ask "grace before meat" let us remember that it is not to be a mere pious custom, but a real reception of the idea of Jesus that God enables us to receive our daily bread from Him. I sometimes wonder if there would be as much chronic indigestion as there is if we received our ideas from God as Jesus would have us do.

Christian Disciplines, Volume 2,
The Discipline of Prayer, 310 L

GUIDANCE

How much time have you given to wondering what God is doing with you? It is not your business. Your part is to acknowledge God in all your ways, and He will blend the active and the spiritual until they are inseparable and you learn to live in activities knowing that your life is hid with Christ in God.

Approved Unto God, 8 R

We have to get out of the old pagan way of guiding ourselves by our heads and get into the Christian way of being guided by faith in a personal God, whose methods are a perpetual contradiction to our every preconceived notion.

Disciples Indeed, 388 R

"O Lord, be such a disposer of the lot that is cast into the lap that our mouths shall be filled with laughter at what Thou wilt bring to pass!"

Knocking at God's Door, March 29, 640 R

One of the greatest difficulties in Christian work is that everyone says—"Now what do you expect to do?" Of course you do not know what you are going to do. The only thing you know is that God knows what He is about.

The Love of God—Now Is It Possible, 684 L

Whenever the conviction of God's Spirit comes there is the softening of the whole nature to obey; but if the obedience is not instant there will come a metallic hardening and a corrupting of the guidance of God.

The Moral Foundations of Life, 695 L

If we have been storing our minds with the word of God, we are never taken unawares in new circumstances because the Holy Spirit brings back these things to our remembrance and we know what we should do; but the Holy Spirit cannot bring back to our minds what we have never troubled to put there.

The Moral Foundations of Life, 708 R

Faith never knows where it is being led; it knows and loves the One Who is leading. It is a life of *faith*, not of intelligence and reason, but a life of knowing Who is making me "go."

Not Knowing Whither, 864 R

The path *to* God is never the same as the path *of* God. When I am going on with God in His path, I do not understand, but God does; therefore I understand God, not His path.

Not Knowing Whither, 903 L

When we come to a crisis it is easy to get direction, but it is a different matter to live in such perfect oneness with God that in the ordinary occurrences of life we always do the right thing.

Our Brilliant Heritage, 935 R

We give credit to human wisdom when we should give credit to the Divine guidance of God through childlike people who were foolish enough in the eyes of the world to trust God's wisdom and supernatural equipment, while watching carefully their own steadfast relationship to Him.

So Send I You, 1308 L

Have you been asking God what He is going to do? He will never tell you. God does not tell you what He is going to do; He reveals to you Who He is. Do you believe in a miracle-working God, and will you go out in surrender to Him until you are not surprised an atom at anything He does?

My Utmost for His Highest, January 2, 735 R

God never tells us what He is going to do. He reveals Who He is.

Not Knowing Whither, 903 L

There are times when you cannot understand why you cannot do what you want to do. When God brings the blank space, see that you do not fill it in, but wait. The blank space may come in order to teach you what sanctification means; or it may come after sanctification to teach you what service means. Never run before God's guidance. If there is the slightest doubt, then He is not guiding. Whenever there is doubt—*don't.*

My Utmost for His Highest, January 4, 736 L

GUILT

The guilty man is the one who wants to be alone; the man who is right with God does not; neither does a child. The final curse of a disobedient soul is that it becomes a separate, self-conscious individual.

Biblical Ethics, 117 L

HABITS

Habits are built up, not by theory, but by practice. The one great problem in spiritual life is whether we are going to put God's grace into practice. God won't do the mechanical; He created us to do that; but we can only do it while we draw on the mysterious realm of His divine grace.

Biblical Ethics, 107 L

The way to examine whether we are doing what Jesus Christ wants us to do is to look at the habits of our life in three domains—physical, emotional, and intellectual. The best scrutiny we can give ourselves is along this line: Are my bodily habits chaste? Is my emotional nature inordinate? Is my intellectual life insubordinate?

Biblical Ethics, 107 R

When we begin to work out what God has worked in, we are faced with the problem that this physical body, this mechanism, has been used by habit to obeying another rule called sin; when Jesus Christ delivers us from that rule, He does not give us a new body; He gives us power to break and then re-mould every habit formed while we were under the dominion of sin.

Biblical Ethics, 107 R

Habit is a mechanical process of which we have ceased to become conscious. The basis of habit is always physical. A habit forms a pathway in the material stuff of the brain, and as we persist in thinking along a certain line we hand over a tremendous amount to the machine and do things without thinking. Habit becomes second nature.

The Moral Foundations of Life, 696 L

We do not sufficiently realise the power we have to infect the places in which we live and work by our prevailing habits in those places.

The Moral Foundations of Life, 723 R

Spiritually we have to learn to form habits on the basis of the grace of God. What happens at new birth is that the incoming of a totally new life breaks all the old habits; they are completely dislodged by the "expulsive power of a new affection." Most of us do not realise this and we continue to obey habits when there is no need to.

The Moral Foundations of Life, 715 R

Your god may be your little Christian habit, the habit of prayer at stated times, or the habit of Bible reading. Watch how your Father will upset those times if you begin to worship your habit instead of what the habit symbolises—"I can't do that just now, I am praying; it is my hour with God." No, it is your hour with your habit.

My Utmost for His Highest, May 12, 779 R

HAPHAZARD

According to the wisdom of this world, God seems to be haphazard. He is not calculable in His providence; He works in ways we cannot estimate. If we try to work things out in logical ways, we are apt to find that suddenly in the providence of God a great upheaval comes we had never calculated on.

God's Workmanship, 443 L

If you try to forecast the way God will work you will get into a muddle; live the life of a child and you will find that every haphazard occasion fits into God's order.

Our Portrait in Genesis, 972 L

One great essential lesson in Christianity is that God's order comes to us in the haphazard. We are men and women, we have appetites, we have to live on this earth, and things do happen by chance; what is the use of saying they do not? "One of the most immutable things on earth is mutability."

Shade of His Hand, 1199 R

One great thing to notice is that God's order comes to us in the haphazard. We try to plan our ways and work things out for ourselves, but they go wrong because there are more facts than we know; whereas if we just go on with the days as they come, we find that God's order comes to us in that apparently haphazard way. The man who does not know God depends entirely on his own wits and forecasting. If instead of arranging our own programmes we will trust to the wisdom of God and concentrate all our efforts on the duty that lies nearest, we shall find that we meet God in that way and in no other.

He Shall Glorify Me, 480 L

It is easy to see God in exceptional things or in a crisis, but it requires the culture of spiritual discipline to see God in every detail. Never allow that the haphazard is anything less than God's appointed order.

Not Knowing Whither, 911 R

Your life and mine is a bundle of chance. It is absurd to say it is fore-ordained for you to have so many buttons on your tunic, and if

that is not fore-ordained, then nothing is. If things were fore-ordained, there would be no sense of responsibility at all. A false spirituality makes us look to God to perform a miracle instead of doing our duty. We have to see that we do our duty in faith in God. Jesus Christ undertakes to do everything a man cannot do, but not what a man can do. Things do happen by chance, and if we know God, we recognise that His order comes to us in that way. We live in this haphazard order of things, and we have to maintain the abiding order of God in it.

Shade of His Hand, 1199 R

How haphazard God seems, not sometimes but always. God's ways turn man's thinking upside down.

Not Knowing Whither, 895 R

Nothing happens by chance to a saint, no matter how haphazard it seems.

The Psychology of Redemption, 1069 R

Life is immensely precarious, haphazard. A Christian does not believe that everything that happens is ordained by God; what he believes is that he has to get hold of God's order no matter what happens in the haphazard. "And we know that to them that love God all things work together for good, even to them that are called according to His purpose" (Romans 8:28 RV). All things are permitted by God, but all things are not appointed by God; they appoint themselves; but God's order abides, and if I maintain my relationship to Him, He will make everything that happens work for my good.

Shade of His Hand, 1237 L

HAPPINESS

The Bible nowhere speaks about a "happy" Christian; it talks plentifully of joy. Happiness depends on things that happen, and may sometimes be an insult; joyfulness is never touched by external conditions, and a joyful heart is never an insult. . . . Happiness is the characteristic of a child's life, and God condemns us for taking happiness out of a child's life, but we should have done with happiness long ago; we should be men and women facing the stern issues of life, knowing that the grace of God is sufficient for every problem the devil can present.

The Shadow of an Agony, 1183 L

Read the Seventy-third Psalm; it is the description of the man who has made happiness his aim—he is not in trouble as other men, neither is he plagued like other men; he has more than heart could wish; but once let his moral equilibrium be upset by conviction of sin and all his happiness is destroyed. The end and aim of human life is not happiness, but "to glorify God and enjoy Him for ever."

Biblical Ethics, 92 L

Holiness of character, chastity of life, living communion with God—that is the end of a man's life, whether he is happy or not is a matter of moonshine. Happiness is no standard for men and women because happiness depends on my being determinedly ignorant of God and His demands.

Biblical Ethics, 92 L

"These things have I spoken unto you, that My joy might remain in you, and that your joy might be full" (John 15:11).
   You can never use the word "happiness" in connection with Jesus or His disciples. It is an insult to God and to human nature to have as our ideal a happy life. Happiness is a thing that comes and goes; it can never be an end in itself; holiness, not happiness, is

the end of man. The great design of God in the creation of man is that he might "glorify God and enjoy Him forever." A man never knows joy until he gets rightly related to God. Satan's claim is that he can make a man satisfied without God, but all he succeeds in doing is to give happiness and pleasure, never joy.

Bringing Sons Unto Glory, 235 R

Happiness is not a sign that we are right with God; happiness is a sign of satisfaction, that is all, and the majority of us can be satisfied on too low a level. Jesus Christ disturbs every kind of satisfaction that is less than delight in God.

If Thou Wilt Be Perfect, 599 R

Happiness would be all right if things were reasonable; it would be ideal if there were no self-interest, but everyone of us is cunning enough to take advantage somewhere, and after a while my inclination is to get my happiness at your cost.

The Shadow of an Agony, 1183 L

HEALING

To the broken in heart, to the bound in hereditary prisons, and to the wounded and weak, Jesus our Saviour draws near.

Christian Disciplines, Volume 2,
The Discipline of Loneliness, 320 L

If we could see the floor of God's immediate presence, we would find it strewn with the "toys" of God's children who have said— This is broken, I can't play with it any more, please give me another present. Only one in a thousand sits down in the midst of it all and says—I will watch my Father mend this. God must not be treated as a hospital for our broken "toys," but as our Father.

Not Knowing Whither, 887 L

HEALTH

We become side-tracked if we make physical health our aim and imagine that because we are children of God we shall always be perfectly well; that there will be great manifestations of God's power, thousands saved, etc.

The Highest Good—The Pilgrim's Song Book, 527 L

Satan takes occasion of the frailty of the bodily temple and says, "Now you know you cannot do that; you are so infirm, you cannot concentrate your mind," etc. Never allow bodily infirmities to hinder you obeying the commands of Jesus.

If Thou Wilt Be Perfect, 583 L

"For which cause we faint not [the word 'faint' is used in the sense of cowardly surrender]; *but though our outward man perish, yet the inward man is renewed day by day"* (2 Corinthians 4:16).

The perishing of the outward man is not always indicative of old age. Look at your own life; you have had the experience of sanctification and have been lifted into the heavenly places in Christ Jesus, and yet God's hand has been laid upon you. He has allowed the finger of decay to come to your body and lay you completely aside, and you begin to see what a slight hold you have on life, and the thought comes—"Well, I expect I will have to 'cave in'; I have not the strength I once had; I can never do the things I thought I would for God." This message is for *you—"though* our outward man perish, yet *the inward man is renewed day by day."*

The experience may not come with years but in the ordinary circumstances of life. It may come in a hundred and one ways and you realise that the outward man is wasting, that you have not the might you once had . . . . The great craze to-day is—Be healthy, be sane; "a sound mind in a sound body." Very often the soundest minds have not been in sound bodies, but in very shaky tabernacles, and the word comes—*"though our outward man perish*, yet the inward man is renewed day by day."

The Love of God—The Message of Invincible Consolation, 670 L

How many of us succumb to flesh and blood circumstances—"I did not sleep well"; or, "I have indigestion"; or, "I did not do quite the right thing there." Never allow any of these things to be the reason to yourself why you are not prevailing in prayer. There are hundreds of people with impaired bodies who know what it is to pray in the Holy Ghost.

If Ye Shall Ask, 622 R

Our bodies are to be entirely at God's disposal, and not God at our disposal. God does give Divine health, but not in order to show what a wonderful being a divinely healed person is. If God has healed us and keeps us in health, it is not that we might parade it, but that we might follow the life of God for His purposes.

The Love of God—The Ministry of the Unnoticed, 667 R

The attitude to sickness in the Bible is totally different from the attitude of people who believe in faith-healing. The Bible attitude is not that God sends sickness or that sickness is of the devil, but that sickness is a fact usable by both God and the devil.

The Philosophy of Sin, 1133 L

God's Book deals with facts. Health and sickness are facts, not fancies. There are cases recorded in the Bible, and in our own day, of people who have been marvellously healed, for what purpose? For us to imitate them? Never, but in order that we might discern what lies behind, viz., the individual relationship to a personal God.

The Philosophy of Sin, 1133 R

(Continued)

HEALTH (Continued)

If we put the body and the concerns of the body before the eternal weight of glory, we will never have any inner winging at all; we will always be asking God to patch up this old tabernacle and keep it in repair. But when the heart sees what God wants, and knows that the body must be willing to spend and be spent for that cause and that cause alone, then the inner man gets wings.

The Love of God—The Message of Invincible Consolation, 670 L

The peace arising from fact is unintelligent and dangerous, e.g., people who base on the fact of health are at peace, but it is often a peace which makes them callous. On the other hand, people who accept the fact of being sick are inclined to have a jaundiced eye for everything healthy.

I am purposely leaving the subject vague and without an answer; there can be no answer. The great difficulty is that people find answers which they say came from God. You cannot prove facts; you have to swallow them. The fact of health and the fact of sickness are there; we have nothing to do with choosing them; they come and go.

The Philosophy of Sin, 1133 R

HEART

The New Testament teaches that no man or woman is safe apart from Jesus Christ because there is treachery on the inside. "Out of the heart of men, proceed . . . ." The majority of us are grossly ignorant about the possibilities of evil in the heart. Never trust your common sense when the statements of Jesus contradict it, and when you preach see that you base your preaching on the revelation of Jesus Christ, not on the sweet innocence of human nature.

Approved Unto God, 14 R

Never take anyone to be good, and above all never take yourself to be good. Natural goodness will always break, always disappoint, why? Because the Bible tells us that "the heart is deceitful above all things, and desperately wicked: who can know it?"

Approved Unto God, 14 R

The heart is the centre of all physical life and of all the imaginations of the mind. Anything that keeps the physical blood in good condition and the heart working properly benefits the soul life and spirit life as well. That is why Jesus Christ said, "Take heed to yourselves, lest at any time your hearts be overcharged with surfeiting . . . ."

Biblical Psychology, 167 L

If people knew that the circulation of the blood and quickening of the heart life would remove distempers from the body, there would be a great deal less medicine taken and a great deal more walking done.

Biblical Psychology, 167 L

The characteristic of the hardened heart is familiar in the Bible but not anywhere else. For instance, we read in Exodus that God hardened Pharaoh's heart (Exodus 4:21ff.). This must not be interpreted to mean that God hardened a man's heart and then condemned him for being hard. It means rather that God's laws, being God's laws, do not alter, and that if any man refuses to obey God's law he will be hardened away from God, and that by God's own decree. No man's destiny is made for him, he makes his own; but the imperative necessity that a man must make his own destiny is of God.

Biblical Psychology, 179 L

The Bible never deals with proportionate sin; according to the Bible an impure thought is as bad as adultery; a covetous thought is as bad as a theft. It takes a long education in the things of God before we believe that is true. Never trust innocence when it is contradicted by the word of God. The tiniest bit of sin is an indication of the vast corruption that is in the human heart.

Conformed to His Image, 364 R

Heart is the centre of all the vital activities of body, soul, and spirit. Never think of the heart in the way the old psychology thought of the will, viz., as a compartment, a kind of hat-box into which you put all your convictions and dole them out occasionally when you lift the lid. The heart is the centre of a man's personality.

The Moral Foundations of Life, 693 R

'Heart' is simply another term for "personality." The Bible never speaks of the heart as the seat of the affections. "Heart" is best understood if we simply say "me" (cf. Romans 10:10). When once expectation is killed out of the heart, we can scarcely walk, the feet become as lead, the very life and power goes, the nerves and everything begin to fall into decay.

The Moral Foundations of Life, 706 L

The true nature of a man's heart according to the Bible is that of expectation and hope. It is the heart that is strengthened by God (cf. Psalm 73:26), and Jesus Christ said that He came to "bind up the broken hearted." The marvel of the indwelling Spirit of God is that He can give heart to a despairing man.

The Moral Foundations of Life, 707 L

"For where your treasure is, there will your heart be also . . . " The Bible term "heart" is best understood if we simply say "me"; it is the central citadel of a man's personality. The heart is the altar of which the physical body is the outer court, and whatever is offered on the altar of the heart will tell ultimately through the extremities of the body. "Keep thy heart with all diligence; for out of it are the issues of life."

The Moral Foundations of Life, 727 R

The majority of us prefer to trust our innocence rather than the statements of Jesus. It is always risky to trust your innocence when the statements of Jesus are contrary to it. Jesus says that "from within, out of the heart of men, proceed . . . "; then comes the awful catalogue. You say, "Why, that is nonsense; I never had any of those things in my heart; I am innocent." Some day you will come up against a set of circumstances which will prove that your innocence was a figment, and that what Jesus said about the human heart was perfectly true.

The Philosophy of Sin, 1109 L

It is possible to be first in suffering for the Truth and in reputation for saintliness, and last in the judgment of the great Searcher of hearts. The whole question is one of heart-relationship to Jesus.

Disciples Indeed, 395 R

HEAVEN

Nowadays people have got tired of the preaching about a future heaven and they have gone to the other extreme and deal only with what is called the practical; consequently they rob themselves of the unfathomable joy of knowing that everything God has said will come to pass.

Biblical Ethics, 100 L

So many of us are caught up in the shows of things; not in the way of property and possessions, but of blessings, and all our efforts to persuade ourselves that our treasure is in heaven is a sure sign that it is not. If our treasure is in heaven we do not need to persuade ourselves that it is; we prove it is by the way we deal with matters of earth.

The Moral Foundations of Life, 727 R

(Continued)

HEAVEN *(Continued)*

"Unto an inheritance incorruptible, and unde-filed, and that fadeth not away, reserved in heaven for you" (*1 Peter 1:4 RV*).

We are so much taken up with what God wants us to be here that we have forgotten heaven. . . . Peter is reminding every Christian that there is an undefiled inheritance awaiting us which has never yet been realised, and that it has in it all we have ever hoped or dreamed or imag-ined, and a good deal more. It is always *Better to come* in the Christian life until the *Best of all* comes.

The Place of Help, 1046 L

HELL

Hell is the place of angelic condemna-tion. It has nothing to do primarily with man. God's Book never says that hell was made for man, although it is true that it is the only place for the man who rejects God's salvation. Hell was the result of a distinct condemnation passed by God on celestial beings, and is as eternal as those celestial anarchists.

Biblical Psychology, 137 L

All we know about eternal life, about hell and damnation, the Bible alone tells us.

Biblical Psychology, 165 R

HEREDITY

Breeding counts for nothing in the value of a man in God's sight; it is the heart relation-ship that counts, and one man cannot judge another. When Jesus Christ came He paid no attention to breeding.

Shade of His Hand, 1240 L

HEROD

Herod is a rare type of pagan; he is obscene; he was bad, unmentionably bad, and you will find that when he saw Jesus Christ face to face he was not the slightest bit troubled. Why? He had heard the voice of God before through John the Baptist, and he had ordered that voice to be silent.

Workmen of God, 1346 R

Herod decided to silence the voice of God in his life, and when the Son of God stood before him, he saw nothing in Him; there was no more compunction of conscience. Whenever a man makes the decision that Herod made—"I don't want to hear any more about the matter," it is the beginning of the silence of God in his soul. To silence the voice of God is damnation in time; eter-nal damnation is that for ever . . . . Divine silence is the ultimate destiny of the man who refuses to come to the light and obey it.

The Philosophy of Sin, 1121 R

Herod is the presentation of the awful pos-sibility of a fixed character, absolutely fixed in immorality. Jesus Christ did not awaken one tremor of conscience in him; he had signed his own death-warrant. When the voice of God came to him in repeated warn-ings through John the Baptist about the thing that was wrong in his life, he would not listen; he persisted in his badness until he killed all his affinity for God, and when Jesus Christ stood before him, he was not an atom troubled.

Workmen of God, 1346 R

HOLINESS

Never say God's holiness does not mean what it does mean. It means every part of the life under the scrutiny of God, knowing that the grace of God is sufficient for every detail. The temptation comes along the line of compromise: "Don't be so unbendingly holy; so fiercely pure and uprightly chaste." Never tolerate by sympathy with yourself or with others any practice that is not in keeping with a holy God.

Approved Unto God, 19 R

God is not making hot-house plants, but sons and daughters of God, men and women with a strong family likeness to Jesus Christ.

The Psychology of Redemption, 1097 L

Always carry out the significance of your text with as many details as possible. To the majority of men, holiness is all in the clouds; but take this message, "Holiness, without which no man shall see the Lord," and drive it home on every line until there is no refuge from the terrific application. Holy not only in my religious aspirations, but holy in my soul life, in my imagination and thinking; holy in every detail of my bodily life.

Approved Unto God, 7 L

"As He is, so are we in this world." Our Lord's own life proved that in the midst of the world where we are placed we can be holy men and women, not only talking rightly, but living rightly.

Biblical Ethics, 99 R

It is a wonderful point of illumination that Our Lord's soul was in a body like ours, and that for thirty silent years He exhibited a holy life through all the stages of development that our life goes through.

Bringing Sons Unto Glory, 222 R

A holy man is not one who has his eyes set on his own whiteness, but one who is personally and passionately devoted to the Lord who saved him—one whom the Holy Ghost takes care shall never forget that God has made him what he is by sheer sovereign grace. Accept as the tender touch of God, not as a snare of the devil, every memory

of sin the Holy Ghost brings home to you, keeping you in the place where you remember what you once were and what you now are by His grace.

Conformed to His Image, 380 R

Holiness in character is the only thing that will remain. Some of us will have a spiritual character so microscopic that it will take the archangels to find it!

Notes on Isaiah, 1377 R

Personal holiness brings the attention to bear on my own whiteness; I dare not be indiscreet or unreserved, I dare not do anything in case I incur a speck. God can't bless that sort of thing; it is as unlike His own character as could be. The holiness produced through the indwelling of His Son in me is a holiness which is never conscious of itself. There are some people in whom you cannot find a speck and yet they are not abundantly blessed of God, while others make grave indiscretions and get marvellously blessed; the reason being that the former have become devotees of personal holiness, conscientious to a degree; the latter are marked by abandonment to God.

Our Portrait in Genesis, 967 R

Holiness can only be worked out in and through the din of things as they are. God does not slide holiness into our hearts like a treasure box from heaven and we open the lid and out it comes; holiness works out in us as it worked out in our Lord.

The Love of God—The Message of Invincible Consolation, 673 R

Jesus Christ's holiness has to do with human life as it is. It is not a mystical, aesthetic thing that cannot work in the ordinary things of life; it is a holiness which "can be achieved with an ordinary diet and a wife and five children."

The Shadow of an Agony, 1176 R

(Continued)

HOLINESS (Continued)

"Ye shall be holy; for I am holy"
(1 Peter 1:16 RV).

Holiness means unsullied walking with the feet, unsullied talking with the tongue, unsullied thinking with the mind—every detail of the life under the scrutiny of God. Holiness is not only what God gives me, but what I manifest that God has given me.

My Utmost for His Highest, September 1, 818 R

HOLY COMMUNION
(See LORD'S SUPPER)

HOLY SPIRIT

The touchstone of the Holy Spirit's work in us is the answer to our Lord's question: "Who do men say that the Son of Man is?" Our Lord makes human destiny depend on that one thing, Who men say He is, because the revelation of Who Jesus is is only given by the Holy Spirit.

Bringing Sons Unto Glory, 226 R

When a man receives the Holy Spirit, his problems are not altered, but he has a Refuge from which he can deal with them; before, he was out in the world being battered; now the centre of his life is at rest and he can begin, bit by bit, to get things uncovered and rightly related.

Baffled to Fight Better, 60 R

Religious enterprise that has not learned to rely on the Holy Spirit makes everything depend on the human intellect— "God has said so-and-so, now believe it and it will be all right"—but it won't. The basis of Jesus Christ's religion is the acceptance of a new Spirit, not a new creed, and the first thing the Holy Spirit does is to awaken us out of sleep.

Biblical Ethics, 113 L

The Spirit of God always comes in surprising ways—"The wind bloweth where it listeth, . . . so is every one that is born of the Spirit." No creed or school of thought or experience can monopolise the Spirit of God. The great snare of some aspects of presenting the Gospel is that everything is put in the head, everything must be rational and logical, no room is left for the great power of life which shows itself in surprising ways.

Biblical Ethics, 113 R

The Spirit is the first power we practically experience but the last power we come to understand.

Biblical Psychology, 200 L

When the Holy Spirit is in me, He will bring to my remembrance what Jesus has said and make His Words live. The Spirit within me enables me to assimilate the words of Jesus. The Holy Spirit exercises a remarkable power in that He will frequently take a text out of its Bible context and put it into the context of our life. We have all had the experience of a verse coming to us right out of its Bible setting and becoming alive in the setting of our own life, and that word becomes a precious, secret possession. See that you keep it a secret possession; don't "cast your pearls before swine"—those are the strong words of our Lord.

Biblical Psychology, 206 R

The deep and engrossing need of those of us who name the Name of Christ is reliance on the Holy Spirit.

Disciples Indeed, 391 L

There is nothing so still and gentle as the checks of the Holy Spirit; if they are yielded to, emancipation is the result; but let them be trifled with, and there will come a hardening of the life away from God. Don't quench the Spirit.

Disciples Indeed, 391 L

If I have the right mental attitude to Jesus Christ the next step is easy: I will necessarily be led to accept what He says, and when He says, "If ye then, being evil, know how to give good gifts unto your children: how much more shall your heavenly Father give the Holy Spirit to them that ask Him?" then I will ask and receive.

Facing Reality, 36 L

This Holy Comforter represents the ineffable Motherhood of God. Protestantism has lost for many generations this aspect of the Divine revelation because of its violent antipathy to Mariolatry as practised by the Roman Catholic Church; and it behoves us to remember that Protestantism is not the whole Gospel of God, but an expression of a view of the Gospel of God specially adapted to the crying needs of a particular time.

Christian Disciplines, Volume 1,
The Discipline of Divine Guidance, 277 R

A great many people do not pray because they do not feel any sense of need. The sign that the Holy Ghost is in us is that we realise, not that we are full, but that we are empty; there is a sense of absolute need.

If Ye Shall Ask, 621 R

There is no authentic impulse of the Holy Spirit that is not wedded to the words of the Bible. To recognise this is the only way to be safe from dangerous delusions.

He Shall Glorify Me, 473 L

The Holy Spirit is absolutely honest; He indicates the things that are right and the things that are wrong.

The Love of God—The Making of a Christian,
679 L

I do not live the Christian life by adherence to principles; I live the Christian life as a child lives its life. You never can calculate what a child will do, neither can you calculate what the Spirit of God will do in you. When you are born from above, the Spirit of God in you works in spontaneous moral originality.

The Shadow of an Agony, 1170 R

HOLY SPIRIT: BAPTISM OF

There are plenty of Christians to-day who are not appealed to on the "bread" line, but the "signs and wonders" line does appeal to them. What is the cunning thing that is rending the Church to-day? Where it is not socialism, it is supernaturalism.—"Ask God for manifestations to prove you are a child of His." Satan's one aim is to thwart God's purpose, and he can easily do it if he succeeds in making us take this line—"Now that I am baptised with the Holy Ghost, there must be marvellous manifestations so that people will be amazed at what God has done for me." Jesus said, when the Holy Ghost is come, "He shall glorify Me," not glorify you. The error of the "signs and wonders" movement is that the eye is fixed not on Jesus, but on our own whiteness, or on the amazing of those around us because of what God has done. Jesus Christ never went on that line, and the unobtrusive kind of life He lived is exactly the type of life the saints are to live. There was no "show business" with the Son of God, and there is to be no "show business" with the saints.

Bringing Sons Unto Glory, 227 R

(Continued)

HOLY SPIRIT: BAPTISM OF (Continued)

The proof that we are baptised with the Holy Ghost is that we bear a strong family likeness to Jesus, and men take knowledge of us, as they did of the disciples after Pentecost, that we have been with Jesus; they recognise the family likeness at once.

Conformed to His Image, 360 L

Beware of the "show business"—"I want to be baptised with the Holy Ghost so that I may do wonderful works." God never allows anyone to do wonderful works: *He* does them, and the baptism of the Holy Ghost prevents my seeing them in order to glory in them.

Disciples Indeed, 391 R

The preacher must be part of his message; he must be incorporated in it. That is what the baptism of the Holy Ghost did for the disciples. When the Holy Ghost came at Pentecost He made these men living epistles of the teaching of Jesus, not human gramophones recording the facts of His life

Disciples Indeed, 397 L

People come piously together and ask God to baptise them with the Holy Ghost, but they forget that the first thing the Holy Ghost does is to illuminate the Cross of Christ. The emphasis in the New Testament is always on the Cross. The Cross is the secret of the heart of God, the secret of the Person of the Son of God, the secret of the Holy Ghost's work. It is the Cross alone that made it possible for God to give us the gift of eternal life, and to usher in the great era in which we live—the dispensation of the Holy Ghost.

He Shall Glorify Me, 476 R

For thirty years Jesus had remained unknown; then He was baptised and had a wonderful manifestation of the Father's approval, and the next thing we read is

that He is "led up of the Spirit into the wilderness to be tempted of the devil." The same thing puzzles us in our own spiritual experience; we have been born from above, or have had the wonderful experience of the baptism of the Holy Ghost—surely we are fit now to do something for God; and God deliberately puts us on the shelf, amongst the dust and the cobwebs, in an utterly unaccountable way.

The Place of Help, 1015 L

HOLY SPIRIT: FILLING OF

There is one thing we cannot imitate: we cannot imitate being full of the Holy Ghost.

Disciples Indeed, 392 L

The mark of the Holy Spirit in a man's life is that he has gone to his own funeral and the thought of himself never enters.

Disciples Indeed, 392 L

". . . *but tarry ye in the city, until ye be clothed with power from on high*" *(Luke 24:49 RV)*.

"Power from on high"—the words have a fascinating sound in the ears of men; but this power is not a magical power, not the power to work miracles; it is the power that transforms character, that sanctifies faculties. "But ye shall receive power, when the Holy Ghost is come upon you" (RV), said Jesus to the disciples, and they did—the power that made them like their Lord. (Cf. Acts 4:13.)

He Shall Glorify Me, 476 R

Anything that partakes of the nature of swamping our personality out of our control is never of God. Do we ever find a time in the life of the Lord Jesus Christ when He was carried beyond His own control? Never once. Do we ever find Him in a spiritual panic, crediting God with it? Never once. And the one great marvel of the work of the Holy Ghost is that the sanity of Jesus Christ is stamped on every bit of it. Jesus said we should know the work of the Holy Ghost by these signs—"He shall glorify Me"; "He shall teach you all things, and bring to your remembrance all that I said unto you" (RV), and, "He will guide you into all truth." The Spirit of God does not dazzle and startle and amaze us into worshipping God; that is why He takes such a long while; it is bit by bit, process by process, with every power slowly realising and comprehending "with all saints. . . ."

If Thou Wilt Be Perfect, 593 R

'. . . be filled with the Spirit" (Ephesians 5:18).
There are two ways of inspiration pos-sible—being drunk with wine, and being filled with the Spirit. We have no business to be nondescript, drunk neither one way nor the other. A man may be sober and incapable as well as drunk and incapable.

The Moral Foundations of Life, 717 R

It is as impossible to be filled with the Spirit and be free from emotion as it is for a man to be filled with wine and not show it. The reason some of us are so amazingly dull and get sleeping-sickness is that we have never once thought of paying attention to the stirring up the Spirit of God gives the mind and our emotional nature.

Biblical Ethics, 114 L

HOLY SPIRIT: FRUIT OF

It is possible for an aeroplane to imitate a bird, and it is possible for a human being to imitate the fruit of the Spirit. The vital dif-ference is the same in each: there is no prin-ciple of life behind. The aeroplane cannot

persist, it can only fly spasmodically; and our imitation of the Spirit requires certain conditions that keep us from the public gaze, then we can get on fairly well. Before we can have the right performance in our life, the inside principle must be right—we must know what it is to be born from above, to be sanctified and filled with the Holy Ghost; then our lives will bring forth the fruit.

Studies in the Sermon on the Mount, 1469 L

Jesus Christ is infinitely bigger than any of my experiences, but if in my experiences I am coming to know Him better, then the expression will come out in the life, and its sign is the fruit of the Spirit—"love, joy, peace . . . ." The fruit of the Spirit is the exact expression of the disposition of Jesus. We cannot pretend to have the fruit of the Spirit if we have not; we cannot be hypo-critical over it.

The Place of Help, 1038 L

We are one with God only in the manner and measure we have allowed the Holy Spirit to have way with us. The fruit of the Spirit is the fruit of a totally new disposition, the disposition of Christ-realisation. Instead now of self-realisation, self-consciousness and sin, there is sanctity and spiritual reality, bringing forth "fruit unto holiness."

Biblical Ethics, 118 R

HOLY SPIRIT: GIFTS OF

"When He ascended on high . . . He gave gifts unto men" (Ephesians 4:8 RV; cf. Acts 2:33).
The only sign that a particular gift is from the Ascended Christ is that it edifies the Church. Much of our Christian work to-day is built on what the Apostle pleads it should not be built on, viz., the excellencies of the natural virtues.

Disciples Indeed, 391 R

(Continued)

HOLY SPIRIT: GIFTS OF
(*Continued*)

The gifts of the Spirit are not for individual exaltation, but for the good of the whole Body of Christ.

He Shall Glorify Me, 472 L

HOME

Home is God's institution, and He says, "Honour thy father and thy mother"; are we fulfilling our duty to our parents as laid down in God's Book? Guard well the central institutions ordained by God, and there will be fewer problems in civilised life.

Biblical Ethics, 95 L

The description the Bible gives of home is that it is a place of discipline. Naturally we do not like what God makes; we prefer our friends to our God-made relations. We are undressed morally in our home life and are apt to be meaner there than anywhere else. If we have been captious and mean with our relations, we will always exhibit that spirit until we become new creatures in Christ Jesus. That is why it is easier to go somewhere else, much easier often to go as a missionary than to stay at home. God alters the thing that matters.

The Highest Good—The Pilgrim's Song Book, 527 R

The light is to be shown in all the trifling ways of home life. The average evangelical presentation is apt to produce a contempt for the trifling ways. A preacher of the Gospel may be a most objectionable being at home instead of giving light in the ordinary ways. Our Lord tells us to judge the preacher or the teacher "by his fruits." Fruit is not the salvation of souls; that is God's work; fruit is "the fruit of the Spirit," love, joy, peace, etc. We get much more concerned about not offending other people than about offending Our Lord. Our Lord often offended people, but He never put a stumbling-block in anyone's way.

The Love of God—The Ministry of the Unnoticed, 663 R

The greatest benefits God has conferred on human life, e.g., fatherhood, motherhood, childhood, home, become the greatest curse if Jesus Christ is not the Head. A home that does not acknowledge Jesus Christ as the Head will become exclusive on the line of its own affinities; related to Jesus Christ, the home becomes a centre for all the benedictions of motherhood and sonhood to be expressed to everyone—"an open house for the universe."

The Place of Help, 995 L

HONOUR

We have not sufficiently emphasised the fact that we have to live as saints, and that in our lives the honour at stake is not our personal honour, but the honour of Jesus Christ.

The Place of Help, 1034 L

God will bring across our path people who embody the characteristics that we have shown to Him—stubbornness, pride, conceit, opinionativeness, sensuality, a hundred little meannesses. "Now," He says, "love them as I have loved you." It works in this way: we see that someone is going to get the better of us, and every logical power in us says—"Resent it." Morally speaking, we should, but Jesus Christ says, "When you are insulted, not only do not resent it, but exhibit the Son of God." The disciple realises that his Lord's honour is at stake in his life, not his own honour.

The Psychology of Redemption, 1093 R

HOPE

The hope of the saint is the expectation and certainty of human nature transfigured by faith. . . . Hope without faith loses itself in vague speculation, but the hope of the saints transfigured by faith grows not faint, but endures "as seeing Him Who is invisible."

Christian Disciplines, Volume 2,
The Discipline of Patience, 339 L

When once a man has been "undressed" by the Holy Ghost, he will never be able to despair of anyone else.

The Place of Help, 1001 L

HOSPITALITY

The point is that we are to be "given to hospitality" from God's standpoint; not because other people deserve it, but because God commands it. This principle runs all through our Lord's teaching . . . my home is to be given to hospitality. Have you ever noticed how God's grace comes to those who are given to hospitality, if they are His children? Prosperity in home, in business, and in every way comes from following God's instructions in each detail.

Biblical Psychology, 188 R

Our Lord teaches that we have to receive those He sends as Himself (Matthew 10:40). When therefore we receive hospitality from others in His name, we have to remember that it is being offered to our Master, not to us. It is easier to receive the rebuffs and the spurnings than to receive the hospitality and welcome really offered to Our Lord. We say—"But I cannot accept this"; if we are identified with our Lord we will have to go

through the humiliation of accepting things of which we feel ourselves unworthy.

Not Knowing Whither, 886 L

If you have a house, the next thing the Bible counsels is hospitality—"given to hospitality" (Romans 12:13); "pursuing hospitality"; give your whole mind to it. "Be not forgetful to entertain strangers: for thereby some have entertained angels unawares" (Hebrews 13:2). That is the way the blessing comes. When we begin to try to economise, God puts dry rot in us instantly. I don't care what line the economy takes, it produces dry rot. When we have the lavish hand, there is munificence at once. "There is that scattereth, and increaseth yet more; and there is that withholdeth more than is meet, but it tendeth only to want" (Proverbs 11:24 RV).

The Highest Good—The Pilgrim's Song Book, 537 L

The reality of God being our Guest is the most awful joy in the discipline of fellowship. The spirit of hospitality consists in this, that in or with the stranger, we receive the Lord Himself.

Not Knowing Whither, 885 R

"Distributing to the necessity of saints; given to hospitality" (Romans 12:13).
   The Bible has a great deal to say about "hospitality" and "entertaining strangers." God recognises the enormous importance of our immediate circle. The term "blessings" includes my home and my property, all that I distinctly look upon as mine, and I have to use it with this outlook of hospitality, and immediately I do, I find how personal it is. My home is guarded in exactly the same way as my body is guarded. It is mine, therefore it is part of the very make-up of my personality, and God will not allow me to be exclusive over it; I must keep it open, be "given to hospitality."

Biblical Psychology, 188 L

HUMAN NATURE

There is a potential hero in every man—and a potential skunk.

Conformed to His Image, 372 L

We are held responsible by God for the way we deal with the great mass of things that come into our lives. We all have susceptibilities in every direction; everyone is made in the same way as everyone else; consequently it is not true to say we cannot understand why some people like to devote themselves to pleasure, to races and dancing, etc. If we do not understand it, it is because part of our nature has become atrophied. Whatever one human being can do, either in the way of good or bad, any human being can do.

The Moral Foundations of Life, 721 R

Love, more than any other experience in life, reveals the shallowness and the profundity, the hypocrisy and the nobility, of human nature.

Our Portrait in Genesis, 971 L

Jacob's character exhibits human nature as it is better than any other Bible character— the high mountain peaks and the cesspools, they all come out. No man is so bad but that he is good enough to know he is bad.

Our Portrait in Genesis, 974 L

The Bible reveals that human nature possesses an incurable suspicion of God. Its origin is explained in the Bible; two great primal creatures of God, the angel who became Satan, and Adam, negotiated a relationship which God never sanctioned. That was how sin was introduced into the world.

The Philosophy of Sin, 1108 R

In laying your account with men, whether it be with a government or with a drill-sergeant, remember there is no such being as a perfect man. You are bound to find shortcomings; and beware of the snare of remembering only the bad things a man does. We are all built that way.

Shade of His Hand, 1239 L

HUMANITY

The reason our Lord tells us to beware of men is that the human heart is "deceitful above all things, and desperately wicked," and if we put our trust in men we shall go under, because men are just like ourselves, and none of us in our wits before God would ever think of trusting ourselves; if we do it is a sign that we are ignorant of ourselves.

The Highest Good—The Pilgrim's Song Book, 532 L

Jesus Christ belonged to the order of things God originally intended for mankind; He was easily Master of the life of the sea and air and earth. If we want to know what the human race will be like on the basis of Redemption, we shall find it mirrored in Jesus Christ, a perfect oneness between God and man. In the meantime there is a gap, and the universe is wild.

The Love of God, 659 L

HUMILIATION

If you are without something that is a humiliation to you, I question whether you have ever come into a personal relationship with Jesus Christ. We are called to fellowship with His sufferings, and some of the greatest suffering lies in remaining powerless where He remained powerless.

The Love of God—The Ministry of the Unnoticed, 665 R

The sphere of humiliation is always the place of more satisfaction to Jesus Christ, and it is in our power to refuse to be humiliated, to say, "No, thank you, I much prefer to be on the mountaintop with God." Do I believe that God engineers my circumstances, that it is He who brings me each day into contact with the people I meet? Am I faithful enough to Him to know that all I meet with in the ordinary machinery of every day by chance or haphazard is absolutely under His dominance and rule? Do I face the humiliation which sometimes comes in my contact with people with a perfect knowledge that God is working out His own will?

The Love of God—The Ministry of the Unnoticed, 666 L

A coward does not hit back because he is afraid to; a strong man refuses to hit back because he is strong; but in appearance they are both the same, and that is where the intense humiliation of being a Christian comes in. The Lord is asking us to go the second mile with Him, and if we take the blow, we will save Him. We can always avoid letting Jesus Christ get the blow by taking it ourselves. Be absolutely abandoned to God; it is only your own reputation that is at stake. People will not discredit God; they will only think you are a fool.

The Psychology of Redemption, 1093 R

HUMILITY

Humility is not an ideal; it is the unconscious result of the life being rightly related to God and centred in Him.

Biblical Psychology, 193 L

There is nothing more awful than conscious humility; it is the most Satanic type of pride. To consciously serve is to be worse than the Pharisee who is eaten up with conceit.

Biblical Psychology, 193 L

The greatest philosophy ever produced does not come within a thousand leagues of the fathomless profundity of our Lord's statements, e.g., "Learn of Me; for I am meek and lowly in heart" (Matthew 11:29). If Jesus Christ cannot produce a meekness and lowliness of heart like His own, Christianity is nonsense from beginning to end, and His teaching had better be blotted out.

The Highest Good, 544 R

HUMOUR

The grace of God makes us honest with ourselves. We must be humorous enough to see the shallow tricks we all have, no matter what our profession of Christianity. We are so altogether perverse that God Almighty had to come and save us!

Not Knowing Whither, 891 L

Many of us are supernaturally solemn about our religion because it is not real. Immediately our religion becomes real, it is possible to have humour in connection with it. There are occasions, nevertheless, when there is not only no humour, but when humour is unfit; there is a dread sense of detachment from our ordinary attitude to things which fills us with awe.

The Place of Help, 1051 L

HURRY

The measure of the worth of our public activity to God is the private, profound communion we have with Him. Rush is always wrong; there is plenty of time to worship God.

Not Knowing Whither, 867 R

(Continued)

HURRY *(Continued)*

In personal life despise these two things—dumps and hurry; they are worse than the devil, and are both excessively culpable. Dumps is an absolute slur against God—I won't look up, I have done all I could but it is all up, and I am in despair. Hurry is the same mood expressed in an opposite way—I have no time to pray, no time to look to God or to consider anything; I must do the thing. Perspiration is mistaken for Inspiration. Consequently I drive my miserable little wagon in a rut instead of hitching it to a star and pulling according to God's plan.

Not Knowing Whither, 876 L

Our Lord's maxims
*Consider the lilies of the field, how
they grow.
Behold the fowls of the air.
Become as little children.*
Our Lord did not point out wonderful sights to His disciples all the time; He pointed out things that were apparently insignificant—lilies and grass and sparrows. God does not deal with the things that interest us naturally and compel our attention; He deals with things which we have to will to observe. The illustrations Jesus Christ used were all taken from His Father's handiwork because they express exactly how the life of God will develop in us. We draw our illustrations from the works of men, consequently we get into a hustling condition and forget our Lord's maxims.

The Moral Foundations of Life, 712 L

Our Lord always took His illustrations from His Father's handiwork. In illustrating the spiritual life, our tendency is to catch the tricks of the world, to watch the energy of the business man, and to apply these methods to God's work. Jesus Christ tells us to take the lessons of our lives from the things men never look at—"Consider the lilies"; "Behold the fowls of the air." How often do we look at clouds, or grass, at sparrows, or flowers? Why, we have no time to look at them, we are in the rush of things—it is absurd to sit dreaming about sparrows and trees and clouds! Thank God, when He raises us to the heavenly places, He manifests in us the very mind that was in Christ Jesus, unhasting and unresting, calm, steady and strong.

Our Brilliant Heritage, 924 L

HYPOCRISY / HYPOCRITE

The expression of our lips must correspond with our communion with God. It is easy to say good and true things without troubling to live up to them; consequently the Christian talker is more likely to be a hypocrite than any other kind of worker.

Approved Unto God, 9 L

You can't indulge in pious pretence when you come to the atmosphere of the Bible. If there is one thing the Spirit of God does it is to purge us from all sanctimonious humbug; there is no room for it.

Biblical Ethics, 95 L

No one preaches more earnestly, talks more earnestly, than we do; we are absolutely sincere, but we are not real because we have never acted when the opportunity occurred along the line Jesus Christ wants us to. The thing the world is sick of to-day is sincerity that is not real.

Biblical Ethics, 108 R

When Jesus brings a thing home by His word, don't shirk it. If you do, you will become a religious humbug. Watch the things you shrug your shoulders over, and you will know why you do not go on spiritually.

My Utmost for His Highest, July 27, 805 R

Our modern speech is a great aid to inner hypocrisy, and it becomes a snare because it is easy to talk piously and live iniquitously.

Biblical Psychology, 175 R

Beware of hypocrisy with God, especially if you are in no danger of hypocrisy among men.

Disciples Indeed, 398 L

If you have known Me, says Jesus, and pretend to be abiding in Me and yet are not bringing forth fruit, either My Father will remove you, or if you persist in masquerading, men will gather you and burn you in the fire. The exposing of hypocrisy is never a shock to the cause of God. Judgement begins at the house of God.

The Place of Help, 1055 L

"But there are so many humbugs." There is no counterfeit without the reality. Is Jesus Christ a fraud? We are to be judged by Him.

The Place of Help, 1021 L

We can always see sin in another because we are sinners. The reason we see hypocrisy and fraud and unreality in others is because they are all in our own hearts. The great danger is lest we call carnal suspicion the conviction of the Holy Ghost. When the Holy Ghost convicts men, He convicts for conversion, that men might be converted and manifest other characteristics. We have no right to put ourselves in the place of the superior person and tell others what we see is wrong; that is the work of the Holy Ghost.

Studies in the Sermon on the Mount, 1462 L

Always state things to yourself in order to realise whether you ruggedly are what you sentimentally think you ought to be, and you will soon know the kind of humbug you are.

The Psychology of Redemption, 1093 L

The last curse in our lives as Christians is the person who becomes a providence to us; he is quite certain we cannot do anything without his advice, and if we do not heed it, we are sure to go wrong. Jesus Christ ridiculed that notion with terrific power: "Thou hypocrite, first cast out the beam out of thine own eye; and then shalt thou see clearly to cast out the mote out of thy brother's eye" (Matthew 7:5). "Thou hypocrite," literally, "play-actor," one whose reality is not in keeping with his sincerity. A hypocrite is one who plays two parts consciously for his own ends. When we find fault with other people we may be quite sincere, and yet Jesus says in reality we are frauds.

Studies in the Sermon on the Mount, 1462 L

If you want to know how it was possible for a mighty man of God like David to have sinned the most wicked sin possible—I do not refer to adultery or to murder, but to something infinitely worse, a deep, subtle, inward hypocrisy, tremendous and profound; David lived it for a year and administered justice while all the time he was a "whited sepulchre"—you must first allow God to examine deep down into the possibilities of your own nature.

Workmen of God, 1351 R

God's Book is merciless on sham and pretence, anything that obscures the one real relationship—"In all the world there is none but Thee, my God there is none but Thee." God first, second, and third; not refinement, but holiness—a holy God and a holy people, and Isaiah cares for nothing else.

Notes on Isaiah, 1381 R

(Continued)

HYPOCRISY / HYPOCRITE (Continued)

"That the ministry be not blamed . . ."
(2 Corinthians 6:3).

The world is glad of an excuse not to listen to the Gospel message, and the inconsistencies of Christians is made the excuse. "Woe unto the world because of offences!" said our Lord. "For it must needs be that offences come; but woe to that man by whom the offence cometh!" Offence means something to strike up against, and the world is on the watch for that kind of thing. If a worker is tripped in private life, the world strikes against that at once and makes it the excuse for not accepting the Gospel. The perilous possibility of being an occasion of stumbling is always there. Paul never forgot the possibility of it in his own life—". . . lest that by any means, when I have preached to others, I myself should be a castaway." The only safeguard is living the life hid with Christ in God, and a steady watchfulness that we walk in the light as God is in the light.

> *The Love of God—The Message of Invincible Consolation, 673 R*

IBSEN, HENRIK

"Guilt remains guilt; you cannot bully God into any such blessing as turns guilt to merit, or penalty to rewards." —Ibsen

Ibsen* saw sin, but not Calvary; not the Son of God as Redeemer. If it cost God Calvary to deal with sin, we have no business to make light of it.

> *Conformed to His Image, 346 L*
> *Henrik Ibsen (1828–1906), Norwegian poet and dramatist.*

An appalling thing is that men who ignore Jesus Christ have their eyes open in a way many a preacher of the Gospel has not. Ibsen, for instance, saw things clearly: he saw the inexorable results of sin but without any deliverance or forgiveness, because he saw things apart from the Atonement.

> *Disciples Indeed, 409 L*

Ibsen saw very clearly the desolating desert of life, i.e., the terrific penalty of sin, and he also saw God as He appears to a man awakened to the facts of existence. We are apt to say that Ibsen was pessimistic, but every man whose thinking has not been interfered with by his temperament is a pessimist. To think fair and square is not to see goodness and purity everywhere, but to see something that produces despair. When a man sees life as it really is, there are only two alternatives—the Cross of Jesus Christ as something to accept, or suicide. We are shielded by a merciful density, by a curious temperament of hopefulness that keeps us blind to the desolating desert.

> *He Shall Glorify Me, 490 L*

To look at things as they are, with the superb wisdom and understanding and disillusioned eye of Solomon, takes a Solomon to do it. Another man did it with the knowledge and understanding of Solomon, and he was Ibsen. He saw facts as they are clearly; without losing his head, and without any faith in God he summed it all up—no forgiveness, no escape from penalty or retribution; it is absolutely and inexorably certain that the end of things is disaster.

> *Shade of His Hand, 1195 R*

IDENTITY

Never forget who you are, what you have been, and what you may be by the grace of God.

> *Approved Unto God, 13 R*

IDOL / IDOLATRY

The evolutionary idea that men develop from worshipping idols to worshipping God is absurd; it was the opposite with the people of God—they began with God and ended with idols. That accounts for the mercilessly scathing denunciation of idolatry by all the prophets.

Notes on Ezekiel, 1478 R

Let me become impatient, let me fix my heart on gain, and I do not see God. If I enthrone anything other than God in my life, God retires and lets the other god do what it can.

The Highest Good—The Pilgrim's Song Book, 533 R

IMAGINATION

There is a domain of our nature which we as Christians do not cultivate much, viz., the domain of the imagination. Almost the only way we use our imagination is in crossing bridges before we come to them. The religion of Jesus embraces every part of our make-up, the intellectual part, the emotional part; no part must be allowed to atrophy, all must be welded into one by the Holy Spirit.

Disciples Indeed, 394 R

"Thou wilt keep him in perfect peace, whose mind [imagination] is stayed on Thee: because he trusteth in Thee" (Isaiah 26:3).

Undisciplined imagination is the greatest disturber not only of growth in grace, but of spiritual sanity.

Notes on Isaiah, 1378 R

IMITATION

The embarrassing thing about Christian graces is that immediately you imitate them they become nauseating, because conscious imitation implies an affected preference for certain qualities, and we produce frauds by a spurious piety. All the qualities of a godly life are characteristic of the life of God; you cannot imitate the life of God unless you have it; then the imitation is not conscious, but the unconscious manifestation of the real thing.

Our Portrait in Genesis, 967 L

Many a one who has started the imitation of Christ has had to abandon it as hopeless because a strain is put on human nature that human nature cannot begin to live up to. To have attitudes of life without the life itself is a fraud; to have the life itself imitating the best Pattern of that life is normal and right (see 1 Peter 2:21–23). The teaching of Jesus Christ applies only to the life He puts in, and the marvel of His Redemption is that He gives the power of His own disposition to carry any man through who is willing to obey Him.

Approved Unto God, 20 R

"Pi"* people try to produce the life of God by sheer imitation; they pretend to be sweet when really they are bitter. The life of God has no pretence, and when His life is in you, you do not pretend to feel sweet, you *are* sweet.

Our Portrait in Genesis, 967 R
"Pi" is short for "pious." Chambers uses it to mean people who are self-focused pretenders who try to act like what they are really not.

IMMORALITY

Immorality has its seat in every one of us, not in some of us. If a man is not holy, he is immoral, no matter how good he may seem. Immorality is at the basis of the whole thing; if it does not show itself outwardly, it will show itself before God.

Approved Unto God, 14 R

IMPOSSIBLE / IMPOSSIBILITY

"Make thee an ark" (Genesis 6:14).

The ark stands as a reminder that nothing *is* until it is. Whenever we say a thing is impossible the reason is twofold—either our prejudices don't wish it to be, or we say it is too wonderful to be possible. From the building of the ark on, just make quite sure a thing is impossible, and God does it. God can only do the impossible. In the realm of our human possible we don't need God; common-sense is our God; we don't pray to God, we pray to an erection of our common-sense.

Our Portrait in Genesis, 965 L

IMPULSE

We must check all impulses by this test— Does this glorify Jesus, or does it only glorify ourselves? Does it bring to our remembrance something Jesus said—that is, does it connect itself with the word of God—or is it beginning to turn us aside and make us seek great things for ourselves? That is where the snare comes.

If Thou Wilt Be Perfect, 594 L

"Howbeit when He, the Spirit of truth, is come . . . He shall glorify Me" (John 16:13–14).

There is abroad to-day a vague, fanatical movement which bases everything on spiritual impulse—"God gave me an impulse to do this, and that," and there are the strangest outcomes to such impulses. Any impulse which does not lead to the glorification of Jesus Christ has the snare of Satan behind it. . . . Beware of any religious experience which glorifies you and not Jesus Christ.

Biblical Ethics, 127 L

Beware of all those things that run off on a tangent spiritually. They begin by saying, "God gave me an impulse to do this"; God never gave anyone any impulse. Watch Jesus Christ; the first thing He checked in the training of the twelve was impulse. Impulse may be all right morally and physically, but it is never right spiritually. Wherever spiritual impulse has been allowed to have its way it has led the soul astray.

If Thou Wilt Be Perfect, 594 L

INCARNATION

In Isaiah 7:14, the word comes—"Therefore the Lord Himself shall give you a sign; Behold, a virgin shall conceive, and bear a son, and shall call His name Immanuel." How much attention, think you, could the mighty Roman Empire, the tramp of whose legions shook the world and whose laws girdle it till now, pay to that little Babe born of a Jewish peasant girl and laid in a cow's trough! It was beneath the possibility of that gigantic world-power's notice.

Christian Disciplines, Volume 2, The Discipline of Patience, 337 L

Jesus Christ was born *into* this world, not *from* it. He came into history from the outside of history; He did not evolve out of history. Our Lord's birth was an advent; He did not come from the human race, He came into it from above. Jesus Christ is not the best human being; He is a Being Who cannot be accounted for by the human race at all. He is God Incarnate; not man becoming God, but God coming into human flesh, coming into it from the outside. His Life is the Highest and the Holiest entering in at the lowliest door. Our Lord entered history by the Virgin Mary.

The Psychology of Redemption, 1068 L

The tremendous revelation of Christianity is not the Fatherhood of God, but the Babyhood of God—God became the weakest thing in His own creation, and in flesh and blood He levered it back to where it was intended to be. No one helped Him; it was done absolutely by God manifest in human flesh. God has undertaken not only to repair the damage, but in Jesus Christ the human race is put in a better condition than when it was originally designed.

The Shadow of an Agony, 1162 R

Just as our Lord came into human history from the outside, so He must come into us from the outside. Have we allowed our personal human lives to become a "Bethlehem" for the Son of God?

The Psychology of Redemption, 1068 R

Beware of posing as a profound person; God became a Baby.

My Utmost for His Highest, November 22, 847 R

The essential nature of Deity is holiness, and the power of God is proved in His becoming a Baby. That is the staggering proposition the Bible gives—God became the weakest thing we know.

Facing Reality, 26 R

INDEPENDENCE
(See also FREEDOM and LIBERTY)

When natural independence of one another is wedded with independence of God it becomes sin, and sin isolates and destroys, and ultimately damns the life.

Biblical Ethics, 96 R

There is no such thing as a gift of freedom; freedom must be earned. The counterfeit of freedom is independence. When the Spirit of God deals with sin, it is independence that He touches; that is why the preaching

of the Gospel awakens resentment as well as craving. Independence must be blasted right out of a Christian; there must be only liberty, which is a very different thing. Spiritually, liberty means the ability to fulfil the law of God, and it establishes the rights of other people.

Biblical Ethics, 96 L

The characteristics of individuality are independence and self-assertiveness. There is nothing dearer to the heart of the natural man than independence, and as long as I live in the outskirts of my prideful independence, Jesus Christ is nothing to me.

Biblical Ethics, 96 L

Independence is not strength but unrealised weakness, and is the very essence of sin. There was no independence in our Lord; the great characteristic of His life was submission to His Father

The Moral Foundations of Life, 714 L

INDIFFERENCE

Never be afraid of the man who seems to you to talk blasphemously; he is up against problems you may never have met with; instead of being wrathful, be patient with him. The man to be afraid of is the one who is indifferent; what morality he has got is well within his own grasp, and Jesus Christ is of no account at all.

Biblical Ethics, 121 R

INDIVIDUALITY

Individuality is natural, but when individuality is indwelt by sin it destroys personal communion and isolates individuals, like so many crystals, and all possibility of fellowship is destroyed.

Biblical Ethics, 96 L

(Continued)

INDIVIDUALITY (Continued)

Positive* individuality in any form is not only anti-Christian, but antihuman, because it instantly says, "I care for neither God nor man; I live for myself."

> Biblical Ethics, 96 R
>
> *"Positive" here means independent; unrelated to anything else.

Personality is the characteristic of the spiritual man as individuality is the characteristic of the natural man. When the Holy Spirit comes in, He emancipates our personal spirit into union with God, and individuality ultimately becomes so interdependent that it loses all its self-assertiveness.

> Biblical Ethics, 98 R

When Jesus Christ emancipates the personality, individuality is not destroyed, it is transfigured, and the transfiguring, incalculable element is love, personal passionate devotion to Himself, and to others for His sake.

> Biblical Ethics, 98 R

We have to learn the first great stride of God—"I AM THAT I AM . . . hath sent thee." We have to learn that our individual effort for God is an impertinence; our individuality must be rendered incandescent by a personal relationship to God, and that is not learned easily.

> The Place of Help, 1055 R

INFLUENCE

Let the lowliest soul whose influence apparently amounts to nothing get rightly related to God, and out of him will flow rivers of living water which he does not see; but one day we shall find that it is those lives which have been spreading the lasting benediction.

> God's Workmanship, 427 R

The people who influence us most are not those who buttonhole us and talk to us, but those who live their lives like the stars in heaven and the lilies in the field, perfectly simply and unaffectedly. Those are the lives that mould us.

> My Utmost for His Highest, May 18, 781 R

Our Lord told the disciples not to rejoice in successful service, but to rejoice because they were rightly related to Him (see Luke 10:18–20). The danger in all these things is that we are apt to make the effect the cause. Who are the people who have influenced us most? Certainly not the priggish men and women, but our mothers, our fathers, our sisters—the ones who had not the remotest idea that they were influencing us.

> The Love of God—The Ministry of the Unnoticed, 662 L

Whatever Our Lord touched became wonderful. Some people do a certain thing and the way in which they do it hallows that thing to us for ever afterwards. When Our Lord does anything, He always transfigures it.

> The Love of God—The Ministry of the Unnoticed, 662 R

We infect the places we live in by our ruling habit.

> The Moral Foundations of Life, 1696 R

The way Jesus dealt with the disciples is the way He deals with us. He surrounded the disciples with an atmosphere of His own life and put in seed thoughts; that is, He stated His truth, and left it to come to fruition.

> The Love of God—The Making of a Christian, 680 R

A child always admires anyone with skill, and the teacher who says, "Do this and that," has no influence over a child compared with the one who says, "Come and do this with me." When a child has seen his teacher do a thing and is asked to do it, instantly the instinct of emulation is at work.

The Moral Foundations of Life, 714 L

Everyone who comes across a good nature is made better by it, unless he is determined to be bad. The test of a nature is the atmosphere it produces. When we are in contact with a good nature we are uplifted by it. We do not get anything we can state articulately, but the horizon is enlarged, the pressure is removed from the mind and heart, and we see things differently.

Shade of His Hand, 1220 L

The influence of one man of integrity over men is incalculable . . . and it is a terrible condemnation if a man's influence is without that characteristic.

Shade of His Hand, 1240 R

Think of the men and women you know who have made it easier for you to believe in God. You go to them with your problems, and things get different, the atmosphere of your mind alters; you have come in contact with a man or woman who in his actual life is working out his vision.

The Shadow of an Agony, 1181 R

You can never give another person that which you have found, but you can make him homesick for what you have.

My Utmost for His Highest, June 10, 789 R

The best way you and I can help our fellow-men is to work out the thing in our own lives first. Unless it is backed up by our life, talking is of no use. We may talk a donkey's hind leg off, but we are powerless to do any lifting. If we look after the vision in our own life, we shall be a benediction to other people.

The Shadow of an Agony, 1181 R

"*Making yourselves ensamples to the flock,*" says Peter (1 Peter 5:3).

What does that mean? Be a walking, talking, living example of what you preach, in every silent moment of your life, known and unknown; bear the scrutiny of God, until you prove that you are indeed an example of what He can do, and then "make disciples of all the nations."

Workmen of God, 1361 R

The people who influence us are those who have stood unconsciously for the right thing; they are like the stars and the lilies, and the joy of God flows through them all the time.

He Shall Glorify Me, 486 R

When anyone is right with God, there is the fascination of the power and Spirit of God through them that is attractive; it is a beautiful, a fascinating, winsome, wonderful thing, and gets hold of men, good, bad and indifferent, and the devil alike; but if once the individual saint forgets the source from whence it comes, God will curse the beauty. Beware that God's beauty, which He puts on you His saint, is not prostituted to a flirtation with God's antagonists.

Notes on Jeremiah, 1400 L

(Continued)

INFLUENCE (Continued)

One individual life may be of priceless value to God's purpose, and yours may be that life.

My Utmost for His Highest, November 30, 850 R

Has it ever dawned on you that you are responsible for other souls spiritually before God? For instance, if I allow any private deflection from God in my life, everyone about me suffers. We "sit together in heavenly places." "Whether one member suffer, all the members suffer with it." When once you allow physical selfishness, mental slovenliness, moral obtuseness, spiritual density, everyone belonging to your crowd will suffer.

My Utmost for His Highest, February 15, 750 L

INITIATIVE

"Be ye therefore followers of God . . ." (Ephesians 5:1).

The one striking thing about following is we must not find our own way, for when we take the initiative we cease to follow. In the natural world everything depends upon our taking the initiative, but if we are followers of God, we cannot take the initiative; we cannot choose our own work or say what we will do; we have not to find out at all, we have just to follow.

The Love of God—The Ministry of the Unnoticed, 666 L

INNOCENCE (See PURITY)

INSANITY

Insanity simply means that a man is differently related to affairs from the majority of other men and is sometimes dangerous. Paul was charged with madness (Acts 26:24–25), and the same charge was brought against Jesus Christ—"For they said, He is beside himself." Have you ever noticed the wisdom of the charge? . . . When we are imbued with Jesus Christ's Spirit and are related to life as He was, we shall find that we are considered just as mad according to the standard of this world.

Biblical Psychology, 185 L

We say that a lunatic is a man who has lost his reason; a lunatic is a man who has lost everything but his reason. A madman's explanation of things is always complete.

Not Knowing Whither, 912 R

INSIGHT

Spiritual insight does not so much enable us to understand God as to understand that He is at work in the ordinary things of life, in the ordinary stuff human nature is made of.

Disciples Indeed, 389 L

Insight into the instruction of Jesus depends upon our intention to obey what we know to be the will of God. If we have some doctrine or some end of our own to serve, we shall always find difficulty.

The Moral Foundations of Life, 698 L

The insight that relates us to God arises from purity of heart, not from clearness of intellect. Education and scholarship may enable a man to put things well, but they will never give him insight. Insight only comes from a pure-heartedness in working out the will of God.

The Moral Foundations of Life, 697 R

There is only one golden rule for spiritual discernment, and that is obedience. We learn more by five minutes' obedience than by ten years' study.

The Psychology of Redemption, 1066 L

INSPIRATION

When a person does extraordinary things and says, "God told me to do them," it may have been an inspiration, but its denomination* had not the characteristic of Jesus Christ. The character of Jesus Christ is the inspiration of the Holy Spirit, and holiness is transfigured morality. People are inspired to do the wildest things and have no control over the inspiration. The inspiration of the Spirit of God denominates itself at once. If you are impulsively led to do a thing, examine it and see what it means. Has it the characteristics of Jesus Christ? "For as many as are led by the Spirit of God, they are the sons of God."

> *Facing Reality, 28 R*
> *"Denominate" is "to give a specified name to; to call." In the case of an inspiration, it is a revealing of its origin or source.*

If you make a god of your best moments, you will find that God will fade out of your life and never come back until you do the duty that lies nearest, and have learned not to make a fetish of your rare moments.

My Utmost for His Highest, April 25, 773 R

'Be instant in season, out of season," whether we feel like it or not. If we do only what we feel inclined to do, some of us would do nothing for ever and ever. There are unemployables in the spiritual domain, spiritually decrepit people, who refuse to do anything unless they are supernaturally inspired. The proof that we are rightly related to God is that we do our best whether we feel inspired or not.

My Utmost for His Highest, April 25, 773 R

The demand for inspiration is the measure of our laziness. Do the things that don't come by inspiration.

Disciples Indeed, 404 R

INSTITUTIONS
(*See ORGANISATIONS*)

INSTRUMENT OF GOD
(*See SERVANT OF GOD*)

INTENTION

Jesus Christ demands of His disciples that they live in conformity to the right standard in intention. We say, "Though I didn't do well, I meant well'; then it is absolutely certain you did not mean well. Jesus Christ makes no allowance for heroic moods; He judges us by the diligently applied bent of our disposition.

Biblical Ethics, 94 L

INTERFERENCE (*See MEDDLING*)

INTROSPECTION

The only way we can be of use to God is to let Him take us through the crooks and crannies of our own characters. It is astounding how ignorant we are about ourselves! We do not know envy when we see it, or laziness, or pride. Jesus reveals to us all that this body has been harbouring before His grace began to work. How many of us have learned to look in with courage? We have to get rid of the idea that we understand ourselves; it is the last conceit to go. The only One Who understands us is God.

My Utmost for His Highest, January 12, 738 R

(Continued)

INTROSPECTION (Continued)

The most dangerous stage in a soul's development is the "No one understands me" stage—of course they don't! "I don't understand myself"—of course you don't! . . . It is well to remember that our examination of ourselves can never be unbiased, so that we are only safe in taking our estimate of ourselves from our Creator instead of from our own introspection which makes us either depressed or conceited.

Biblical Ethics, 97 L

It is never safe to do much introspection, but it is ruinous to do none.

The Highest Good—Thy Great Redemption, 561 L

"*O Lord, Thou hast searched me, and known me . . .*" (*Psalm 139:1*).

The 139th Psalm ought to be the personal experience of every Christian. My own introspection, or exploration of myself, will lead me astray, but when I realise not only that God knows me, but that He is the only One who does, I see the vital importance of intercessory introspection.

Biblical Ethics, 118 L

Every man is too big for himself; thank God for everyone who realises it and, like the Psalmist, hands himself over to be searched out by God. We only know ourselves as God searches us. "God knows me" is different from "God is omniscient"; the latter is a mere theological statement; the former is a child of God's most precious possession—"O Lord, Thou hast searched me, and known me" (Psalm 139:1).

Biblical Ethics, 118 L

If you examine yourself too much, you unfit yourself for life. There is a stage in life when introspection is necessary, but if it is pushed too far a man becomes abnormally hypersensitive, either in conceit or grovelling.

Shade of His Hand, 1226 R

"*Thou compassest my path and my lying down, and art acquainted with all my ways. For there is not a word in my tongue, but, lo, O Lord, Thou knowest it altogether*" (*Psalm 139:3–4*).

To say "Of course God is omniscient and knows everything" makes no effect on me; I don't care whether God is "omni" anything; but when by the reception of the Holy Spirit I begin to realise that God knows all the deepest possibilities there are in me, knows all the eccentricities of my being, I find that the mystery of myself is solved by this besetting God.

Biblical Ethics, 118 L

The great mystical work of the Holy Spirit is in the dim regions of our personality which we cannot get at. Read the 139th Psalm; the Psalmist implies—"Thou art the God of the early mornings, the God of the late at nights, the God of the mountain peaks, and the God of the sea; but, my God, my soul has further horizons than the early mornings, deeper darkness than the nights of earth, higher peaks than any mountain peaks, greater depths than any sea in nature—Thou Who art the God of all these, be my God. I cannot reach to the heights or to the depths; there are motives I cannot trace, dreams I cannot get at—my God, search me out."

My Utmost for His Highest, January 9, 737 R

The curse of much modern religion is that it makes us so desperately interested in ourselves, so overweeningly concerned about our own whiteness.

The Psychology of Redemption, 1073 L

ISOLATION

The intellectualist or dreamer who by his dreams or isolation is not made fitter to deal with actual life, proves that his dreams are mere hysterical drivel. If his dreams only succeed in making him hold aloof from his fellow-men, a visionary who deals only with things belonging to the mountaintop, he is self-indulgent to a degree. No man has any right to be a spectator of his fellow-men; he ceases to be in touch with reality.

The Shadow of an Agony, 1180 L

When we describe the isolation and loneliness of the prophets we are apt to imagine that that is what God expects of us today, but it is not; the isolation of those lonely mighty men of God of Old Testament days belongs to a different order. We are not called upon to live the life of the prophet in this dispensation; the life of the prophet is descriptive of the Church, not of individual Christians. Just as the Old Testament prophets stood alone for God, so the church of Christ in this dispensation is to stand alone for God. There is no room for the idea that I am a peculiarly isolated individual—"I . . . only am left." Nothing could be more foreign to the New Testament conception.

Notes on Ezekiel, 1475 L

Learn to distinguish between what isolates you and what insulates you. God insulates; sin isolates—a gloomy, sardonic standing off from everything, the disdain of superiority; only when you are closest to God do you understand that that is its nature.

Disciples Indeed, 394 R

ISRAEL

Jacob's dream was a vision of the purpose of God for all the families of the earth. The destiny of the people known as "Israel" is forecast in this one lonely man. God did not *select* this people, He *elected* them. God created them from Abraham to be His servants until through them every nation came to know who Jehovah was. They mistook the election of God's purpose to be the election of God's favouritism, and the story of their distress is due to their determination to use themselves for purposes other than God's. To this day they survive miraculously; the reason for their survival is the purpose of God to be fulfilled through them.

Our Portrait in Genesis, 970 R

In secular history Israel is disregarded as being merely a miserable horde of slaves, and justly so from the standpoint of the historian. The nations to which the Bible pays little attention are much finer to read about, but they have no importance in the Redemptive purpose of God. His purpose was the creation of a nation to be His bondslave, that through that nation all the other nations should come to know Him. The idea that Israel was a magnificently developed type of nation is a mistaken one. Israel was a despised and a despisable nation, continually turning away from God into idolatry; but nothing ever altered the purpose of God for the nation.

So Send I You, 1317 L

JACOB

Jacob is the man who represents life as it is. The world is not made up of saints or of devils, but of people like you and me, and our real home is at the foot of the ladder with Jacob.

Our Portrait in Genesis, 971 L

(Continued)

JACOB (Continued)

When we come to consider it, the phrase, "the God of Jacob," is the greatest possible inspiration; it has in it the whole meaning of the Gospel of Jesus Christ, who said " . . . for I came not to call the righteous, but sinners." Had we been left with such phrases as "the God of Joseph," or "the God of Daniel," it would have spelt hopeless despair for most of us; but "the God of Jacob" means "God is *my* God," the God not only of the noble character, but of the sneak. From the sneak to entire sanctification is the miracle of the grace of God.

Our Portrait in Genesis, 971 R

We have the notion that it is only when we are pure and holy that God will appear to us; that God's blessing is a sign that we are right with Him. Neither notion is true. Our Lord took care to say that God makes His sun to rise on the evil and on the good, and sends His rain on the just and on the unjust. God's blessings are not to be taken as an indication of the integrity of the character blessed . . . Jacob's undeservedness, and the fact that God continually blesses him, are brought out very clearly all through his life.

Our Portrait in Genesis, 975 L

A good many of us are "Jacobs," as mean and subtle as can be; yet Jacob is the man who had the vision, and he is taken as the type of the ancient people of God. Jacob was the man to whom God appeared, and whom God altered. "Jacob I loved" (RV). Esau is the home of all the natural vices and virtues. Perfectly contented with being once born, he does not need God; he is happy and healthy and a delight to meet; Jacob was the opposite. God loves the man who needs Him.

The Place of Help, 1036 L

Of all the Bible characters Jacob ever remains the best example of the recipient of God's life and power, simply because of the appalling mixture of the good and the bad, the noble and the ignoble in him.

Our Portrait in Genesis, 975 L

JESUS CHRIST

Jesus Christ became Man for one purpose, that He might put away sin and bring the whole human race back into the oneness of identification. Jesus Christ is not an individual iota of a man; He is the whole of the human race centred before God in one Person: He is God and Man in one. Man is lifted up to God in Christ, and God is brought down to man in Christ.

Approved Unto God, 22 R

No man was ever created to be his own god, and no man was ever created to be the god of another man, and no system of ideas was ever made to dominate man as god. There is "one God," and that God was Incarnate in the Lord Jesus Christ.

Biblical Ethics, 126 R

Paul puts everything down to the words of Jesus Christ: if He is not what He claims, there is nothing in religion; it is pure fiction. If, however, Jesus Christ is not a humbug, and not a dreamer, but what He claims to be, then Christianity is the grandest fact that ever was introduced to any man.

Facing Reality, 27 R

The character of Jesus Christ is exhibited in the New Testament, and it appeals to us all. He lived His life straight down in the ordinary amalgam of human life, and He claims that the character He manifested is possible for any man if he will come in by the door He provides (see Luke 11:13).

Facing Reality, 26 R

In presenting Jesus Christ, never present Him as a miraculous Being Who came down from heaven and worked miracles and Who was not related to life as we are; that is not the Gospel Christ. The Gospel Christ is the Being Who came down to earth and lived our life and was possessed of a frame like ours. He became Man in order to show the relationship man was to hold to God, and by His death and resurrection He can put any man into that relationship. Jesus Christ is the last word in human nature.

Approved Unto God, 14 L

There is nothing for which Jesus Christ is not amply sufficient and over which He cannot make us more than conquerors. The New Testament does not represent Jesus Christ as coming to us in the character of a celestial lecturer; He is here to re-create us, to presence us with Divinity in such a way that He can re-make us according to God's original plan, eternal lovers of God Himself, not absorbed into God, but part of the great Spirit-baptised humanity.

Biblical Ethics, 128 R

"In Him was life; and the life was the light of men" (John 1:4). Why did Jesus live thirty-three years if all He came to do was to die for sin? He lived thirty-three years because He had to show what a normal man after God's pattern was like. He died that through His death we might have the source of life that was in Him (see Romans 5:17). That is why it is so absurd to say, "I accept Jesus as a Teacher only." Try to apply the teachings of Jesus to your life without an understanding of His Death and you will find it cannot be done; it would either make you commit suicide or take you to the Cross and give you an understanding of why it was necessary for Him to die.

Bringing Sons Unto Glory, 220 R

We like to hear about the life of Jesus, about His teaching and His words, about His sympathy and tenderness, but when we stand face to face with Him in the light of God and He convicts us of sin, we resent it. Men crave for what the Gospel presents but they resent the way it is presented by Jesus.

Bringing Sons Unto Glory, 220 R

What weakness! Our Lord lived thirty years in Nazareth with His brethren who did not believe on Him (John 7:5); He lived three years of popularity, scandal, and hatred; fascinated a dozen illiterate men who at the end of three years all forsook Him and fled (Mark 14:50); and finally He was taken by the powers that be and crucified outside the city wall. Judged from every standpoint save the standpoint of the Spirit of God, His life was a most manifest expression of weakness, and the idea would be strong to those in the pagan world who thought anything about Him that surely now He and His crazy tale were stamped out.

Christian Disciplines, Volume 2,
The Discipline of Patience, 337 L

The only Being who ever walked this earth as God designed man should was Jesus Christ. He was easily Master of all created things because He maintained a steadfast obedience to the word and the will of His Father. "What manner of man is this, that even the winds and the sea obey Him?" (Matthew 8:27 RV).

Conformed to His Image, 345 L

The Carpenter, who offended so many, is the disguised Son of God, full of majestic power and condescension. We marvel, not that He performed miracles, but rather that He performed so few. He who could have stormed the citadels of men with mighty battalions of angels, let men spit upon Him and crucify Him.

God's Workmanship, 457 R

(Continued)

JESUS CHRIST *(Continued)*

I command what I can explain, and immediately I bring the natural desire to explain into the spiritual domain, I am in danger of explaining Jesus away; I "dissolve Him by analysis" (see 1 John 4:3 RV mg).

God's Workmanship, 418 R

The greatest annoyance to Satan and to humanity is Jesus Christ.

The Philosophy of Sin, 1132 L

Jesus Christ is a Fact; He is the most honourable and the holiest Man, and two things necessarily follow—first, He is the least likely to be deceived about Himself; second, He is least likely to deceive anyone else.

Facing Reality, 26 R

In some ages, as with some people, the tendency is strong to make an essential out of what is a mere accompaniment. In our day this tendency is marked in the emphasising of our Lord as a sympathiser, and the direct practical effect of this is to turn spirituality into sentimentality, and to make our Lord simply a kind brother-man. . . . He does come to the broken-hearted, to the captives bound by a cursed hereditary tendency, to the blind who grope for light, to the man bruised and crushed by his surroundings, but He does not come as a sympathiser—He binds up the broken-hearted, gives release to the captives, recovering of sight to the blind; He sets at liberty them that are bruised. Jesus Christ is not a mere sympathiser, He is a Saviour, and the only One, "for neither is there any other name under heaven, that is given among men, wherein we must be saved."

God's Workmanship, 439 L

The spirit of antichrist is that spirit which "dissolves by analysis" the person of Jesus— "someone unique, but not what the New Testament claims." To preach the Jesus of the Gospels at the expense of the Christ of the Epistles is a false thing, such a false thing that it is antichrist to the very core, because it is a blow direct at what Jesus said the Holy Spirit would do, viz., expound Him to the disciples, and "through their word" to innumerable lives to the end of Time.

Conformed to His Image, 353 L

Watch the tendency abroad to-day; people want to get rid of Jesus Christ; they cannot prove that He did not live, or that He was not a remarkable Man, but they set to work to dissolve Him by analysis, to say He was not really God Incarnate.

The Philosophy of Sin, 1132 L

Jesus Christ always upsets the calculations of humanity; that is what made Voltaire say "Crucify the wretch, stamp Him and His crazy tale out," because He was the stumbling-block to all the reasonings of men. You cannot work Jesus Christ into any system of thinking. If you could keep Him out, everything could be explained. The world could be explained by evolution, but you cannot fit Jesus Christ into the theory of evolution.

The Philosophy of Sin, 1132 L

To-day we have all kinds of Christs in our midst: the Christ of Labour and of Socialism; the Mind-cure Christ and the Christ of Christian Science and of Theosophy; but they are all abstract Christs. The one great sign of Christ is not with them—there are no marks of the Atonement about these Christs. Jesus Christ is the only one with the marks of atonement on Him, the wounded hands and feet, a symbol of the Redeemer Who is to come again. There will be signs and wonders wrought by these other Christs, and great problems may be solved, but the greatest problem of all, the problem of sin, will not be touched.

The Shadow of an Agony, 1171 R

JOB

It must be remembered what Job's creed was. Job believed that God prospered and blessed the upright man who trusted in Him, and that the man who was not upright was not prospered. Then came calamity after calamity; everything Job believed about God was contradicted and his creed went to the winds. . . . Most of us get touchy with God and desert Him when He does not back up our creed (cf. John 6:60, 66).

Baffled to Fight Better, 46 R

If there is no tragedy at the back of human life, no gap between God and man, then the Redemption of Jesus Christ is "much ado about nothing." Job is seeing things exactly as they are. A healthy-minded man bases his life on actual conditions, but let him be hit by bereavement, and when he has got beyond the noisy bit and the blasphemous bit, he will find, as Job found, that despair is the basis of human life unless a man accepts a revelation from God and enters into the Kingdom of Jesus Christ.

Baffled to Fight Better, 49 L

The explanation of the whole thing lies in the fact that God and Satan had made a battleground of Job's soul without Job's permission. Without any warning, Job's life is suddenly turned into desperate havoc and God keeps out of sight and never gives any sign whatever to Job that He *is*. . . . Will I trust the revelation given of God by Jesus Christ when everything in my personal experience flatly contradicts it?

Baffled to Fight Better, 47 R

God never once makes His way clear to Job. Job struggles with problem after problem, and Providence brings more problems all the time, and in the end Job says, " . . . now mine eye seeth Thee." He saw that all he had hung in to in the darkness was true, and that God was all he had believed Him to be, loving and just and honourable.

Baffled to Fight Better, 47 R

JOHN THE BAPTIST

John the Baptist must not be regarded as a mere individual; Jesus said of him that he was the greatest prophet that had been born of woman, and he is the last of the line of prophets. After four hundred years of absolute silence there came this lonely, mighty voice, "Prepare . . . ."

He Shall Glorify Me, 471 L

John the Baptist came straight from God and talked straight for God. Do you talk straight for God? When the message you have to deliver, brother preacher, strikes straight home, don't water it down just a little. Go straight for God if you come from Him. Neither for fear nor favour alter the message. What happened to John the Baptist? He went straight back to God, minus his head. That was the result of his message.

Workmen of God, 1353 L

JOY

A great thinker has said, "The seal and end of true conscious life is joy," not pleasure, nor happiness. Jesus Christ said to His disciples, "These things have I spoken unto you, that My joy might remain in you, and that your joy might be full"—identity with Jesus Christ and with His joy.

Facing Reality, 36 R

(Continued)

JOY *(Continued)*

Joy is the great note all through the Bible. We have the notion of joy that arises from good spirits or good health, but the miracle of the joy of God has nothing to do with a man's life or his circumstances or the condition he is in. Jesus does not come to a man and say "Cheer up"; He plants within a man the miracle of the joy of God's own nature.

He Shall Glorify Me, 486 L

In every phase of human experience apart from Jesus, there is something that hinders our getting full joy. We may have the fulfilment of our ambitions, we may have love and money, yet there is the sense of something unfulfilled, something not finished, not right. A man is only joyful when he fulfils the design of God's creation of him, and that is a joy that can never be quenched.

He Shall Glorify Me, 486 L

"In my distress . . ." There are elements in our circumstances if we are children of God that can only be described by the word *"distress"*; it would be untruthful to say it was otherwise. "Then will I go unto . . . God," says the Psalmist, not "with joy," but "unto God [Who is] my exceeding joy." We go to God when we have no joy in ourselves and find that His joy is our strength. Are our hearts resting in the certainty that God is full of joy although with us it is "clouds and darkness" because we are pilgrims?

The Highest Good—The Pilgrim's Song Book, 527 L

Joy means the perfect fulfilment of that for which I was created and regenerated, not the successful doing of a thing. The joy Our Lord had lay in doing what the Father sent Him to do, and He says—"As My Father hath sent Me, even so am I sending you."

My Utmost for His Highest, March 5, 756 L

What was the joy of the Lord Jesus Christ? His joy was in having completely finished the work His Father gave Him to do; and the same type of joy will be granted to every man and woman who is born of God the Holy Ghost and sanctified, when they fulfil the work God has given them to do. What is that work? To be a saint, a walking, talking, living, practical epistle of what God Almighty can do through the Atonement of the Lord Jesus Christ.

Facing Reality, 36 R

The Bible talks plentifully about joy, but it nowhere speaks about a "happy" Christian. Happiness depends on what happens; joy does not. Remember, Jesus Christ had joy, and He prays "that they might have My joy fulfilled in themselves."

Biblical Psychology, 171 R

The word "blessed" is sometimes translated "happy," but it is a much deeper word; it includes all that we mean by joy in its full fruition. Happiness is the characteristic of a child, and God condemns us for taking happiness out of a child's life; but as men and women we should have done with happiness long ago; we should be facing the stern issues of life, knowing that the grace of God is sufficient for every problem the devil can present.

Biblical Psychology, 172 L

If my religion is not based on a personal history with Jesus it becomes something I suffer from; not a joyous thing, but something that keeps me from doing what I want to do.

Disciples Indeed, 396 R

Joy is different from happiness, because happiness depends on what happens. There are elements in our circumstances we cannot help; joy is independent of them all.

He Shall Glorify Me, 486 L

JUDGEMENT OF GOD

The Standard for the Heathen (Matthew 25:31–46; John 1:9; Romans 2:11–16)

The first thing to ask in regard to this standard is—what about the people who have never heard of Jesus Christ, and may never hear of Him; how are they judged? The passages given all refer to God's standard of judgement for the heathen, viz., the light they have, not the light they have never had and could not get. Conscience is the standard by which men and women are to be judged until they have been brought into contact with the Lord Jesus Christ. The call to preach the Gospel to the heathen is not the frenzied doctrine that the heathen who have never known Jesus Christ, and never had the chance of knowing Him, are going to be eternally lost, but the command of Jesus Christ—"Go ye into all the world, and preach the gospel to every creature."

The Philosophy of Sin, 1120 R

The Standard for Christendom (John 3:18)

"He that believeth on Him is not judged: he that believeth not hath been judged already, because he hath not believed on the name of the only begotten Son of God." The standard for the judgement of Christendom is not the light it has received but the light it ought to have received. Every country in Christendom has had plenty of opportunity of knowing about Christ, and the doom of a soul begins the moment it consciously neglects to know Jesus Christ or consciously rejects Him when He is known. Beware of applying Our Lord's words in Matthew 25 to Christians; Matthew 25 is not the standard for the judgement of Christians, but the standard for the judgement of the nations that do not know Christ. The standard for the judgement of Christians is Our Lord.

The Philosophy of Sin, 1120 R

The judgements of God are a consuming fire whereby He destroys in order to deliver; the time to be alarmed in life is when all things are undisturbed. The knowledge that God is a consuming fire is the greatest comfort to the saint; it is His love at work on those characteristics that are not true to godliness. The saint who is near to God knows no burning, but the farther away from God the sinner gets, the more the fire of God burns him.

Conformed to His Image, 362 R

The judgements of God leave scars, and the scars remain until I humbly and joyfully recognise that the judgements are deserved and that God is justified in them. The last delusion God delivers us from is the idea that we don't deserve what we get.

Conformed to His Image, 364 L

As long as things are kept covered up we think God's judgement is severe, but let the Holy Ghost reveal the secret vileness of sin till it blazes out in a conspicuous glare, and we realise that His judgement is right.

Disciples Indeed, 403 R

One of the most remarkable things about Jesus Christ is that although He was full of love and gentleness, yet in His presence every one not only felt benefited, but ashamed. It is His presence that judges us; we long to meet Him, and yet we dread to. We have all known people like that; to meet them is to feel judged, not by anything they say—we are rarely judged by what people say, but by their character.

He Shall Glorify Me, 483 R

I am not judged by the light I have, but by the light I have refused to accept . . . . *This* is the condemnation, that the Light, Jesus Christ, has come into the world, and I prefer darkness, i.e., my own point of view.

The Shadow of an Agony, 1169 R

(Continued)

JUDGEMENT OF GOD
(Continued)

People realised His judgement in His words, not in His pronouncements such as Matthew 23, but in His casual language, judgement came straight home. So with our friends, some casual word, a word not necessarily addressed to us at all, judges us and we feel our meanness, that we have missed the mark. Jesus did not stand as a prophet and utter judgements; wherever He went the unerring directness of His presence located men. We are judged too by children; we often feel ashamed in their presence; they are much more our judges than we theirs; their simplicity and attitude to things illustrates our Lord's judgements.

He Shall Glorify Me, 484 L

The modern Christian laughs at the idea of a final judgement. That shows how far we can stray away if we imbibe the idea that the modern mind is infallible and not our Lord. To His mind at least the finality of moral decision is reached in this life. There is no aspect of our Lord's mind that the modern mind detests so fundamentally as this one. It does not suit us in any shape or form. The average modern mind reads such passages as Luke 16:23–24 and says our Lord was only using figurative language. If the picture is so dreadful figuratively, what must the reality be like? The things our Lord talks about are either arrant nonsense or they are a revelation of things that the common sense of man can never guess.

The Highest Good, 549 R

The parables in the 25th chapter of St. Matthew are three aspects of the Divine estimate of life. Beware of being an ingenious interpreter. You will always find at the basis of our Lord's parables and illustrations a fundamental consistency to His revelation.

The parable of the ten virgins reveals that it is fatal from our Lord's standpoint to live this life without preparation for the life to come. That is not the exegesis; it is the obvious underlying principle.

The parable of the talents is our Lord's statement with regard to the danger of leaving undone the work of a lifetime.

And the description of the last judgement is the picture of genuine astonishment on the part of both the losers and the gainers of what they had never once thought about.

The Highest Good, 549 R

"While ye have the light, believe on the light," said Jesus—do not believe what you see when you are not in the light. God is going to judge us by the times when we have been in living communion with Him, not by what we feel like to-day. . . . We are judged by our immortal moments, the moments in which we have seen the light of God.

The Place of Help, 1021 L

The 51st chapter of Jeremiah almost burns the page, it is so full of strong and intense destruction; but it gives the keynote to the purpose of God in destruction, viz., the deliverance of the good. You will never find in the Bible that things are destroyed for the sake of destruction. Human beings destroy for the sake of destruction, and so does the devil; God never does. He destroys the wrong and the evil for one purpose only, the deliverance of the good.

The Philosophy of Sin, 1112 R

The pronouncement of coming doom is a combining of judgement and deliverance. When God's limit is reached He destroys the unsaveable and liberates the saveable; consequently judgement days are the great mercy of God because they separate between good and evil, between right and wrong.

Our Portrait in Genesis, 965 L

The judgements of God are for another purpose than the vindictive spirit of man would like to make out. It was this that gave Jonah the sulks with the Almighty, and the same spirit is seen in the elder brother—jealous of God's generosity to others. You never find that spirit in the prophets.

Notes on Isaiah, 1379 L

One of the things we have to unlearn is the idea of judgement which never came from God's Book, viz., the idea that God is vindictive. Our Lord never spoke from personal vindictiveness, He spoke from a knowledge of the eternal principles of God, which are inexorable.

Notes on Isaiah, 1381 L

No man can stand before God unless God be in him. The final judgement in individual life is at the Cross of Jesus Christ.

Notes on Jeremiah, 1397 L

The servants of God have to be careful that they do not introduce any personal vindictiveness into the wrath of God, and here though Jeremiah stands with the people who are being swept away by God, he does not slander God by taking the people's point of view. When standing as God's mouthpiece, we must never do what Dante did: put our pet enemies in the hottest places. And when we stand with the people, we must not accept their slander against God. A prophet stands mid-way, not as a mediator, but as a director.

Notes on Jeremiah, 1402 R

Solomon says that God's judgement is right and true and that a man can rest his heart there. It is a great thing to notice the things we cannot answer just now, and to waive our judgement about them. Because you cannot explain a thing, don't say there is nothing in it. There are dark and mysterious and perplexing things in life, but the prevailing authority at the back of all is a righteous authority, and a man does not need to be unduly concerned. When we do find out the judgement of God, we shall be absolutely satisfied with it to the last degree; we won't have another word to say—"that Thou mightest be justified when Thou speakest, and be clear when Thou judgest."

Shade of His Hand, 1206 L

JUDGING OTHERS

There is always a twist about everyone of us until we get the dominating inspiration of the Spirit of God. It makes us condemn the sins we are not inclined to while we make any amount of excuses for those we have a mind to, and they may be ten times worse.

Facing Reality, 142 R

We say that a man is not right with God unless he acts on the line of the precedent we have established. We must drop our measuring-rods for God and for our fellow men. All we can know about God is that His character is what Jesus Christ has manifested; and all we know about our fellow men presents an enigma which precludes the possibility of the final judgement being with us.

Baffled to Fight Better, 51 R

No "excusing the sins we're most inclined to while condemning those we've no mind to"; there must be no moral partiality in the saint.

God's Workmanship, 466 L

(Continued)

JUDGING OTHERS (Continued)

In every life there is one place where God must have "elbow room." We must not pass judgement on others, nor must we make a principle of judging out of our own experience. It is impossible for a man to know the views of Almighty God.

Baffled to Fight Better, 52 L

When somebody has trespassed against me, I instantly impute to him every mean motive of which I would have been guilty had I been in his circumstances. "Wherefore thou art without excuse, O man, whosoever thou art that judgest: for wherein thou judgest another, thou condemnest thyself" (Romans 2:1 RV).

Biblical Psychology, 194 L

Whenever a truth comes home to me my first reaction is to fling it back on you, but the Spirit of God brings it straight home, "Thou art the man." We always want to lash others when we are sick with our own disobedience.

Disciples Indeed, 406 R

If I see meanness and wrong and evil in others, let me take the self-judgement at once—that is what I would be guilty of if I were in their circumstances. The searching light of the Scriptures comes over and over again on this line, and we come to find that there is no room in a Christian for cynicism.

Biblical Psychology, 194 L

We pronounce judgements, not by our character or our goodness, but by the intolerant ban of finality in our views, which awakens resentment and has none of the Spirit of Jesus in it. Jesus never judged like that. It was His presence, His inherent holiness that judged. Whenever we see Him we are judged instantly. We have to practise the presence of Jesus and work on the basis of His disposition. When we have experienced the unfathomable forgiveness of God for all our wrong, we must exhibit that same forgiveness to others.

He Shall Glorify Me, 485 R

We cannot judge ourselves by ourselves or by anyone else; there is always one fact more in everyone's life that we do not know.

Shade of His Hand, 1206 L

There is no room for harsh judgement on the part of a child of God. Harsh judgement is based not on the sternness of the Holy Ghost, but on my refusal to bear someone else's burden.

Disciples Indeed, 391 L

The scrutiny we give other people should be for ourselves. You will never be able to cast out the mote in your brother's eye unless you have had a beam removed, or to be removed, from your own eye (Matthew 7:3–4).

Disciples Indeed, 406 R

If I cannot see God in others, it is because He is not in me. If I get on my moral high horse and say it is they who are wrong, I become that last of all spiritual iniquities, a suspicious person, a spiritual devil dressed up as a Christian. Beware of mistaking suspicion for discernment; it is the biggest misunderstanding that ever twisted Christian humility into Pharisaism.

Not Knowing Whither, 888 R

Beware of looking to see where other people come short. God expects us to be exactly what we know the other person should be—when we realise that, we will stop criticising and having a measuring rod for other people.

The Place of Help, 1005 L

It is easy to condemn a state of things we know nothing about while we make excuses for the condition of things we ourselves live in.

Shade of His Hand, 1232 R

There is always one fact more in every life of which we know nothing; therefore Jesus says, "Judge not." We cannot do it once and for all; we have to remember always that this is our Lord's rule of conduct.

Studies in the Sermon on the Mount, 1461 R

It is a great education to try and put yourself into the circumstances of others before passing judgement on them.

Shade of His Hand, 1231 L

The average Christian is the most penetratingly critical individual; there is nothing of the likeness of Jesus Christ about him. A critical temper is a contradiction to all our Lord's teaching. Jesus says of criticism, "Apply it to yourself, never to anyone else." "Why dost thou judge thy brother? . . . for we shall all stand before the judgement seat of Christ."

Studies in the Sermon on the Mount, 1461 R

Jesus says regarding judging, "*Don't.* Be uncritical in your temper, because in the spiritual domain you can accomplish nothing by criticism." One of the severest lessons to learn to is leave the cases we do not understand to God.

Studies in the Sermon on the Mount, 1461 R

The danger is lest we make the little bit of truth we do know a pinnacle on which we set ourselves to judge everyone else. It is perilously easy to make our conception of God like molten lead and pour it into our specially designed mould and then when it is cold and hard, fling it at the heads of the religious people who don't agree with us.

Notes on Isaiah, 1386 R

JUSTICE

The thing that makes us whimper is that we will look for justice. If you look for justice in your Christian work you will soon put yourself in a bandage and give way to self-pity and discouragement. Never look for justice, but never cease to give it; and never allow anything you meet with to sour your relationship to men through Jesus Christ. "Love . . . as I have loved you."

Approved Unto God, 16 R

The teaching of the Sermon on the Mount is never to look for justice but never to cease to give it. We waste our time looking for justice; we have to see that we always give it to others. "If you are My disciple," Jesus says, "people won't play you fair; but never mind that; see that you play fair."

The Highest Good—The Pilgrim's Song Book, 527 R

(Continued)

JUSTICE (Continued)

One of the great stirring truths of the Bible is that the man who looks for justice from others is a fool. . . . Never waste your time looking for justice; if you do you will soon put yourself in bandages and give way to self-pity. Our business is to see that no one suffers from our injustice.

Shade of His Hand, 1205 R

KNOWING GOD

When once we get intimate with Jesus we are never lonely, we never need sympathy, we can pour out all the time without being pathetic. The saint who is intimate with Jesus will never leave impressions of himself, but only the impression that Jesus is having unhindered way, because the last abyss of his nature has been satisfied by Him. The only impression left by such a life is that of the strong calm sanity that Our Lord gives to those who are intimate with Him.

My Utmost for His Highest, January 7, 737 L

How unhesitatingly the language of Scripture mentions human relationships as the only means of suggesting the unspeakable pleasure of this eternal fellowship with God. Just as the language of lovers is inexplicable to an unloving nature, so the language of the heart in its aloneness with God is inexplicable to those not in a like relationship.

Christian Disciplines, Volume 2,
The Discipline of Loneliness, 331 R

"He calleth . . . by name" (John 10:3).
It is possible to know all about doctrine and yet not know Jesus. The soul is in danger when knowledge of doctrine outsteps intimate touch with Jesus. . . . Any Pharisee could have made a fool of Mary doctrinally, but one thing they could not ridicule out of her was the fact that Jesus had cast seven demons out of her; yet His blessings were

nothing in comparison to Himself. . . . Have I a personal history with Jesus Christ? The one sign of discipleship is intimate connection with Him, a knowledge of Jesus Christ which nothing can shake.

My Utmost for His Highest, August 16, 812 R

Friendship is rare on earth. It means identity in thought and heart and spirit. The whole discipline of life is to enable us to enter into this closest relationship with Jesus Christ. We receive His blessings and know His word, but do we know Him?

My Utmost for His Highest, January 7, 737 L

Joseph did not lose God; God was with Joseph in Egypt as in Canaan; with him in the prison as in the house of his master. If I simply delight in a godly atmosphere and refuse to appropriate God for myself, when I have to leave the godly atmosphere I will find myself God-less; then my natural adaptability becomes the adaptability to degenerate.

Our Portrait in Genesis, 980 R

We slander God by our very eagerness to work for Him without knowing Him.

My Utmost for His Highest, October 3, 829 R

Ever remember that "eternal life" is to know God, therefore you cannot expect to know Him in five minutes or forty years. Measure your ultimate delight in God's truth and joy in God by the little bit that is clear to you. There are whole tracts of God's character unrevealed to us as yet, and we have to bow in patience until God is able to reveal the things which look so dark.

Notes on Isaiah, 1386 L

KNOWLEDGE

It is a great boon to know there are deep things to know. The curse of the majority of spiritual Christians is that they are too cocksure and certain there is nothing more to know than they know. That is spiritual insanity. The more we go on with God the more amazed we are at what there is to find out, until we begin to use the power God gives us to forget earthly things, to be carefully careless about them, but never careless about our relationship to God.

If Thou Wilt Be Perfect, 590 L

Beware of knowing what you don't practise.

Approved Unto God, 11 L

LAUGHTER

Laughter and weeping are the two intensest forms of human emotion, and these profound wells of human emotion are to be consecrated to God. The devil is never said to laugh. Laughter that is not the laughter of a heart right with God, a child heart, is terrible; the laughter of sin is as the crackling of burning thorns. Whenever the angels come to this earth they come bursting with a joy which instantly has to be stayed (cf. Luke 2:13). This earth is like a sick chamber, and when God sends His angels here He has to say—"Now be quiet; they are so sick with sin that they cannot understand your hilarity." Whenever the veil is lifted there is laughter and joy. These are the characteristics that belong to God and God's order of things; sombreness and oppression and depression are the characteristics of all that does not belong to God.

Not Knowing Whither, 884 R

The man who sets himself to make others laugh has often an immensely sad life of his own behind [him].

Shade of His Hand, 1221 R

LAW (See COMMANDMENTS OF GOD)

LAZINESS

Spiritual sloth must be the greatest grief to the Holy Ghost. Sloth has always a moral reason, not a physical one; the self-indulgent nature must be slothful.

Disciples Indeed, 400 R

The discipline of our mind is the one domain God has put in our keeping. It is impossible to be of any use to God if we are lazy. God won't cure laziness; we have to cure it.

Disciples Indeed, 404 L

Jesus said, "I am come that they might have life," not laziness. Whenever we are in danger of nestling in spiritual armchairs, the clarion voice of the Lord comes and bids us neither "sit nor stand but go!"

The Philosophy of Sin, 1115 R

LEADERSHIP

One of the outstanding miracles of God's grace is to make us able to take any kind of leadership at all without losing spiritual power. There is no more searching test in the whole of Christian life than that.

The Love of God—The Message of Invincible Consolation, 672 R

LIBERTY

We have to present the liberty of Christ, and we cannot do it if we are not free ourselves. There is only one liberty, the liberty of Jesus Christ at work in my conscience enabling me to do what is right. If we are free with the liberty wherewith Christ makes us free, slowly and surely those whom we influence will begin to be free with the same freedom.

Approved Unto God, 19 R

We call liberty allowing the other fellow to please himself to the same extent as we please ourselves. True liberty is the ability earned by practice to do the right thing.

Biblical Ethics, 96 L

Paul continually dealt with people who under the guise of religion were libertines; they talked about liberty when what they really meant was, "I insist on doing what it is my right to do, and I don't care a jot about anyone else." That is not liberty; that is lawlessness.

Biblical Ethics, 96 R

The only liberty a saint has is the liberty not to use his liberty. There is nothing more searching than what the New Testament has to say about the use of liberty. It is never your duty to go the second mile, to give up your possessions or property to someone else, but Jesus says if we are His disciples, that is what we will do.

Biblical Ethics, 96 R

Licence simply means—"I will not be bound by any laws but my own." This spirit resents God's law and will not have anything to do with it—"I shall rule my body as I choose, I shall rule my social relationships and my religious life as I like, and I will not allow God or any creed or doctrine to rule me." That is the way licence begins to work.

Biblical Psychology, 178 L

Liberty means ability not to violate the law; license means personal insistence on doing what I like.

Disciples Indeed, 393 L

Watch how often the Apostle Paul warns us not to use our liberty "for an occasion to the flesh," i.e., don't use your liberty for licence. What is the difference between liberty and licence? Liberty is the ability to perform the law, perfect freedom to fulfil all the demands of the law.

Biblical Psychology, 178 L

When we are lifted up to where Jesus is . . . God lifts us up to a totally new plane where there is plenty of room to live and to grow, and to understand things from His stand-point and we see life as a whole; we see not only the glory which now is, but the glory which is yet to be.

The Love of God—The Message of Invincible Consolation, 671 R

In our spiritual life God does not provide pinnacles on which we stand like spiritual acrobats; He provides tablelands of easy and delightful security.

The Moral Foundations of Life, 701 L

It takes God a long time to get us out of the way of thinking that unless everyone sees as we do, they must be wrong. That is never God's view. There is only one liberty, the liberty of Jesus at work in our conscience enabling us to do what is right.

My Utmost for His Highest, May 6, 777 R

The Spirit of God is always the spirit of liberty; the spirit that is not of God is the spirit of bondage, the spirit of oppression and depression. The Spirit of God convicts vividly and tensely, but He is always the Spirit of liberty. God Who made the birds never made bird-cages; it is men who make bird-cages, and after a while we become cramped and can do nothing but chirp and stand on one leg. When we get out into God's great free life, we discover that that is the way God means us to live "the glorious liberty of the children of God."

The Moral Foundations of Life, 721 R

We are called to present liberty of conscience, not liberty of view. If we are free with the liberty of Christ, others will be brought into that same liberty—the liberty of realising the dominance of Jesus Christ.

My Utmost for His Highest, May 6, 777 L

LISTENING

Get into the habit of saying, "Speak, Lord," and life will become a romance. Every time circumstances press, say, "Speak, Lord"; make time to listen. Chastening is more than a means of discipline; it is meant to get me to the place of saying, "Speak, Lord." Recall the time when God did speak to you. Have you forgotten what He said? Was it Luke 11:13, or was it 1 Thessalonians 5:23? As we listen, our ear gets acute, and, like Jesus, we shall hear God all the time.

My Utmost for His Highest, January 30, 744 R

Why are we so terrified lest God should speak to us? Because we know that if God does speak, either the thing must be done or we must tell God we will not obey Him. If it is only the servant's voice we hear, we feel it is not imperative; we can say, "Well, that is simply your own idea, though I don't deny it is probably God's truth."

My Utmost for His Highest, February 12, 749 L

If I am united with Jesus Christ, I hear God by the devotion of hearing all the time. A lily, or a tree, or a servant of God may convey God's message to me. What hinders me from hearing is that I am taken up with other things. It is not that I will not hear God, but that I am not devoted in the right place. I am devoted to things, to service, to convictions, and God may say what He likes but I do not hear Him. The child attitude is always "Speak, Lord, for Thy servant heareth." If I have not cultivated this devotion of hearing, I can only hear God's voice at certain times; at other times I am taken up with things—things which I say I must do—and I become deaf to Him; I am not living the life of a child. Have I heard God's voice to-day?

My Utmost For His Highest, February 13, 749 R

Are you learning to say things after listening to God, or are you saying things and trying to make God's word fit in?

My Utmost for His Highest, June 5, 787 R

LORD'S SUPPER

The ordinance of the Lord's Supper is a symbol of what we should be doing all the time. It is not a memorial of One Who has gone, but of One Who is always here. "This do in remembrance of Me"—be in such fellowship with Me that you show My death until I manifest Myself again. It is in the common things of life that evidence of the discipline of fellowship is given.

Not Knowing Whither, 886 L

LOVE

Love for the Lord is not an ethereal, intellectual, dream-like thing; it is the intensest,
the most vital, the most passionate love of
which the human heart is capable.

Biblical Psychology, 187 R

How has God loved me? God has loved me
to the end of all my sinfulness, the end of all
my self-will, all my selfishness, all my stiff-
neckedness, all my pride, all my self-interest;
now He says—"love one another, as I have
loved you." I am to show to my fellow-men
the same love that God showed to me. That
is Christianity in practical working order.

Biblical Psychology, 195 L

The saint has one striking characteristic,
and that is in loving with a Divine love. Its
thirst is not so much to be loved as to be
loveable. The characteristics in the life of
the saint are the characteristics of our Lord's
life. The saint bears a strong family likeness
to Jesus Christ.

Christian Disciplines, Volume 2,
The Discipline of Patience, 331 R

Jesus knew God, and He makes Him known:
"He that hath seen Me hath seen the Father."
Get into the habit of recalling to your mind
what Jesus was like when He was here, picture what He did and what He said, recall
His gentleness and tenderness as well as His
strength and sternness, and then say, "That
is what God is like." I do not think it would
be difficult for us to love Jesus if He went in
and out among us as in the days of His flesh,
healing the sick and diseased, restoring the
distracted, putting right those who were
wrong, reclaiming backsliders—I do not
think it would be difficult for us to love Him.
That is to love God.

Conformed to His Image, 366 L

The love which springs from self-conceit
or self-interest ends in being cruel because
it demands an infinite satisfaction from
another human being which it will never
get. The love which has God as its centre
makes no demands.

God's Workmanship, 427 L

When I am rightly related to God, the more
I love the more blessing does He pour out
on other lives. The reward of love is the
capacity to pour out more love all the time,
"hoping for nothing again." That is the
essential nature of perfect love.

God's Workmanship, 427 R

If my love for God is so faint and poor that
I will only do what is absolutely essential
and not what it is my privilege to do, it is
then that I deserve not only to be "least in
the kingdom of heaven," but not to be in it
at all.

He Shall Glorify Me, 519 R

Love is not blind; love sees a great deal
more than the actual; it sees the ideal in the
actual, consequently the actual is transfigured by the ideal. That is a different thing
from "halo-slinging," which means you
have your own idea about other people and
expect them to live up to it, and then when
they don't, you blame them.

Our Portrait in Genesis, 972 R

"Having loved His own which were in the
world, He loved them unto the end." The
revelation comes home to me that God has
loved me to the end of all my meanness
and my sin, my self-seeking and my wrong
motives; and now this is the corresponding
revelation—that I have to love others as
God has loved me. God will bring around
us any number of people we cannot respect,
and we have to exhibit the love of God to
them as He has exhibited it to us.

Our Brilliant Heritage, 932 L

O Lord, I would crave more and more to put on love like a garment, that in my contact with men that is what they will most lastingly recognise.

Knocking at God's Door, February 13, 638 R

If your conception of love does not agree with justice and judgement and purity and holiness, then your idea of love is wrong. It is not love you conceive of in your mind, but some vague infinite foolishness, all tears and softness and of infinite weakness.

The Love of God, 656 L

We have to dedicate ourselves to love, which means identifying ourselves with God's interests in other people, and God is interested in some funny people, viz., in you and in me!

Our Brilliant Heritage, 951 R

First Corinthians 13 is sentiment transfigured into character. Love springs spontaneously; that is, it is not premeditated; but love does not develop like that. Both naturally and spiritually love requires careful developing; love won't stay if it is not sedulously cultivated. If I am not careful to keep the atmosphere of my love right by cultivation, it will turn to lust—"I must have this thing for myself."

He Shall Glorify Me, 518 R

We must beware of letting natural affinities hinder our walking in love. One of the most cruel ways of killing love is by disdain built on natural affinities. To be guided by our affinities is a natural tendency, but spiritually this tendency must be denied,

and as we deny it we find that God gives us affinity with those for whom we have no natural affinity. Is there anyone in your life who would not be there if you were not a Christian?

Our Brilliant Heritage, 951 R

"Love never faileth" (1 Corinthians 13:8 RV).
"Love never faileth"! What a wonderful phrase that is! But what a still more wonderful thing the reality of that love must be; greater than prophecy—that vast forth-telling of the mind and purpose of God; greater than the practical faith that can remove mountains; greater than philanthropic self-sacrifice; greater than the extraordinary gifts of emotions and ecstasies and all eloquence; and it is this love that is shed abroad in our hearts by the Holy Ghost which is given unto us.

The Place of Help, 991 L

"As He sat at meat, there came a woman having an alabaster cruse of ointment of spikenard very costly; and she brake the cruse, and poured it over His head" (Mark 14:3 RV).
The characteristic of love is that it is spontaneous, it bursts up in extraordinary ways; it is never premeditated. The reason Jesus called Mary's act "a good work" was because it was wrought out of spontaneous love to Himself. It was neither useful nor her duty; it was an extravagant act for which no one else saw any occasion.

The Place of Help, 1028 L

No love of the natural heart is safe unless the human heart has been satisfied by God first. The tragedies of human lives can only be solved by an understanding of the one great fundamental truth that Jesus Christ alone can satisfy the last aching abyss of the human heart.

He Shall Glorify Me, 518 R

(Continued)

LOVE (Continued)

Natural love does not grow if we do not do anything at it. It is the most ordinary business to fall in love; it is the most extraordinary business to abide there. The same thing with regard to the love of our Lord. The Holy Ghost gives us the great power to love Jesus Christ. That is not a rare experience at all; the rare experience is to get into the conception of loving Him in such a way that the whole heart and mind and soul are taken up with Him.

The Place of Help, 1018 L

If human love does not carry a man beyond himself, it is not love. If love is always discreet, always wise, always sensible and calculating, never carried beyond itself, it is not love at all. It may be affection, it may be warmth of feeling, but it has not the true nature of love in it.

My Utmost for His Highest, February 21, 751 L

LOVE, GOD'S

Abandon to the love of Christ is the one thing that bears fruit. Personal holiness may easily step over into sanctified Pharisaism, but abandon to the love of God will always leave the impression of the holiness and the power of God.

Approved Unto God, 10 L

The Bible says that "God so loved the world . . ."—and the unfathomable depth of His love is in that word "so"—yet it also says that "whosoever would be *a friend of the world* maketh himself an enemy of God" (James 4:4). The apparent contradiction can be explained like this—God's love for the world is the kind of love that makes Him go all lengths in order to remove the sin and evil from it. Love to be anything at all must be personal; to love without hating is

an impossibility, and the stronger and more emphatic the love, the more intense is its obverse, hatred. God loves the world so much that He hates with a perfect hatred the thing that switched men wrong; and Calvary is the measure of His hatred.

Biblical Ethics, 98 L

The Spirit of Jesus is expressed in John 3:16, "God so loved the world . . . ." God keeps open house for the universe.

He Shall Glorify Me, 479 L

There is nothing on earth like the love of God when once it breaks on the soul; it may break at a midnight or a dawn, but always as a great surprise, and we begin to experience the uniting of our whole being with the nature of God.

Conformed to His Image, 369 R

Just as human nature is put to the test in the actual circumstances of life, so the love of God in us is put to the test. "Keep yourselves in the love of God," says Jude; that is keep your soul open not only to the fact that God loves you, but that He is *in* you, in you sufficiently to manifest His perfect love in every condition in which you can find yourself as you rely upon Him.

Conformed to His Image, 370 L

A false idea of God's honour ends in misinterpreting His ways. It is the orthodox type of Christian who, by sticking to a crude idea of God's character, presents the teaching which says, "God loves you when you are good, but not when you are bad." God loves us whether we are good or bad. That is the marvel of His love. "I came not to call the righteous, but sinners to repentance"—whether there are any righteous is open to question. "The righteous have no need of Me; I came for the sinful, the ungodly, the weak." If I am not sinful and ungodly and weak, I don't need Him at all.

Conformed to His Image, 378 L

The presentation Jesus gives of the father is that he makes no conditions when the prodigal returns, neither does he bring home to him any remembrance of the far country—the elder brother does that. It is the revelation of the unfathomable, unalterable, amazing love of God. We would feel much happier in our backslidden condition if only we knew it had altered God towards us, but we know that immediately we do come back we will find Him the same, and this is one of the things that keeps men from coming back. If God would only be angry and demand an apology, it would be a gratification to our pride. When we have done wrong we like to be lashed for it. God never lashes. Jesus does not represent the father as saying, "You have been so wicked that I cannot take you back as my son, I will make you a servant"; but as saying,

"Bring forth quickly the best robe, and put it on him; and put a ring on his hand, and shoes on his feet: and bring the fatted calf, and kill it, and let us eat, and make merry: for this My son was dead, and is alive again; he was lost, and is found."

Conformed to His Image, 378 R

Look back over your own history as revealed to you by grace, and you will see one central fact growing large—God is love. . . . In the future, when trial and difficulties await you, do not be fearful; whatever and whoever you may lose faith in, let not this faith slip from you—God is Love.

The Love of God, 655 R

Nothing is too hard for God, no sin too difficult for His love to overcome, not a failure but He can make it a success.

The Love of God, 657 R

The curious thing about the love of God is that it is the cruellest thing on earth to everything that is not of Him. God hurts desperately when I am far away from Him; but when I am close to Him, He is unutterably tender.

Our Brilliant Heritage, 932 L

The Self-expenditure of God for His enemies in the life and death of our Lord Jesus Christ becomes the great bridge over the gulf of sin whereby human love may cross over and be embraced by the Divine love, the love that never fails.

The Place of Help, 992 R

"Feed My sheep." And Jesus has some extraordinarily funny sheep, some bedraggled, dirty sheep, some awkward butting sheep, some sheep that have gone astray! It is impossible to weary God's love, and it is impossible to weary that love in me if it springs from the one centre.

My Utmost for His Highest, March 3, 755 R

The most painful and most crushing thing to a man or woman is unrequited love. In summing up the attitude of men to Himself, God says that that is the way men treat Him; they "un-requite" His love.

Shade of His Hand, 1203 L

(Continued)

LOVE, GOD'S (Continued)

It is easy to say "God is love" when there is no war and when everything is going well; but it is not so easy to say when everything that happens actually gives the lie to it. For instance, when a man realises he has an incurable disease, or a severe handicap in life, or when all that is dear has been taken from a man, for that man to say, as he faces these things, "God is love," means he has got hold of something the average man has missed.

The Love of God, 658 L

Paul says he is overruled, overmastered, held as in a vice, by the love of Christ. Very few of us know what it means to be held in a grip by the love of God; we are held by the constraint of our experience only. The one thing that held Paul, until there was nothing else on his horizon, was the love of God. "The love of Christ constraineth us"—when you hear that note in a man or woman, you can never mistake it. You know that the Spirit of God is getting unhindered way in that life.

My Utmost for His Highest, February 4, 746 L

The love of God pays no attention to the distinctions made by natural individuality. If I love my Lord I have no business to be guided by natural temperament; I have to feed His sheep. There is no relief and no release from this commission. Beware of counterfeiting the love of God by working along the line of natural human sympathy, because that will end in blaspheming the love of God.

My Utmost for His Highest, March 3, 755 R

When we preach the love of God there is a danger of forgetting that the Bible reveals not first the love of God but the intense, blazing holiness of God, with His love as the centre of that holiness.

The Philosophy of Sin, 1111 L

Undaunted radiance is not built on anything passing, but on the love of God that nothing can alter. The experiences of life, terrible or monotonous, are impotent to touch the love of God, which is in Christ Jesus our Lord.

My Utmost for His Highest, March 7, 757 L

LOYALTY

Whenever you meet with difficulties, whether they are intellectual or circumstantial or physical, remain loyal to God. Don't compromise. If you do, everyone around you will suffer from your faithlessness, because you are disloyal to Jesus Christ and His way of looking at things.

The Place of Help, 1008 L

Many of us are loyal to our notions of Jesus Christ, but how many of us are loyal to Him? Loyalty to Jesus means I have to step out where I do not see anything (cf. Matthew 14:29); loyalty to my notions means that I clear the ground first by my intelligence. Faith is not intelligent understanding; faith is deliberate commitment to a Person where I see no way.

My Utmost for His Highest, March 28, 764 L

Loyalty to Jesus Christ is the thing that we "stick at" to-day. We will be loyal to work, to service, to anything, but do not ask us to be loyal to Jesus Christ. Many Christians are intensely impatient of talking about loyalty to Jesus. . . . Our Lord is dethroned more emphatically by Christian workers than by the world. God is made a machine for blessing men, and Jesus Christ is made a Worker among workers.

My Utmost for His Highest, December 18, 856 R

LUST

Lust means, I will satisfy myself; whether I satisfy myself on a high or a low level makes no difference, the principle is the same. It is the exercise of my claim to my right to myself, and that has to go; in the final wind-up of the human race there won't be a strand of it left.

Biblical Ethics, 112 L

"Wherefore God also gave them up to uncleanness through the lusts of their own hearts" (Romans 1:24).

What is lust? "I must have it at once!" That is lust. Jesus said that lust would destroy the work of grace He has begun in us; "the lusts of other things entering in, choke the word" (Mark 4:19).

Biblical Psychology, 180 L

Lust and covetousness are summed up in the phrase, "I must have it at once and for myself." It is an absolute flood in the nature of man, it overtakes his spirit, it overtakes his soul and body.

If Thou Wilt Be Perfect, 574 R

When once God's mighty grace gets my heart wholly absorbed in Him, every other love of my life is safe; but if my love to God is not dominant, my love may prove to be lust. Nearly all the cruelty in the world springs from not understanding this. Lust in its highest and lowest form simply means I seek for a creature to give me what God alone can give, and I become cruel and vindictive and jealous and spiteful to the one from whom I demand what God alone can give.

If Thou Wilt Be Perfect, 594 L

We use the word lust for the gross abominable sins of the flesh only, but the Bible uses it for a great deal more than that. Lust simply means, "I must have this at once"; it may be a bodily appetite or a spiritual possession.

The principle lust works on is, "I must have it at once, I cannot wait for God's time, God is too indifferent"; that is the way lust works.

The Philosophy of Sin, 1109 L

MARRIAGE

"Wives, submit yourselves unto your own husbands, as unto the Lord" (Ephesians 5:22).

With a sudden abruptness Paul mentions the closest practical relationships in life, and immediately it becomes clear why he does so. If the expansive character of the Holy Spirit is at work in us as saints, it will transfigure the life in all these relationships. The Holy Spirit keeps us on the line of the transfiguration of self-hood and the thought of good to ourselves never enters in, unless it is introduced by someone else.

Biblical Ethics, 114 R

Two *individuals* can never merge; two *persons* can become one without losing their identity.

Biblical Ethics, 98 R
(See also INDIVIDUALITY)

The two things around which our Lord centred His most scathing teaching were money and marriage, because they are the two things that make men and women devils or saints. Covetousness is the root of all evil, whether it shows itself in money matters or in any way.

The Highest Good, 547 L (See also MONEY)

(Continued)

MARRIAGE (Continued)

Drink deep and full of the love of God and you will not demand the impossible from earth's loves, and the love of wife and child, of husband and friend, will grow holier and healthier and simpler and grander.

The Love of God, 657 L

Think of the average married life after, say, five or ten years; too often it sinks down into the most commonplace drudgery. The reason is that the husband and wife have not known God rightly; they have not gone through the transfiguration of love, nor entered through the discipline of disillusionment into satisfaction in God, and consequently they have begun to endure one another instead of having one another for enjoyment in God. The human heart must have satisfaction, but there is only one Being Who can satisfy the last aching abyss of the human heart, and that is our Lord Jesus Christ.

The Place of Help, 1000 L

If Christianity does not affect my money and my marriage relationships, it is not worth anything.

The Place of Help, 1003 R

In the natural life when two people fall in love with one another, the individuality is transfigured because the personalities are merged. Identity is not domination, but oneness between two distinct persons in which neither dominates, but the oneness dominates both.

The Psychology of Redemption, 1100 R

"For the husband is the head of the wife, even as Christ is the head of the church." If Christ is the Head of the husband, he is easily the head of the wife, not by effort, but because of the nature of the essentially feminine. But if Jesus Christ is not the Head of the husband, the husband is not the head of the wife. Our Lord always touches the most sacred human relationships, and He says—You must be right with Me first before those relationships can be right.

Shade of His Hand, 1230 R

According to New Testament wisdom and to Hebrew wisdom, until we are rightly related to God we will always be cruel to other men. Take it in the matter of love: if I am not related to God first my love becomes cruel, because I demand infinite satisfaction from the one I love; I demand from a human being what he or she can never give. There is only one Being Who can satisfy the last aching abyss of the human heart, and that is the Lord Jesus Christ.

Shade of His Hand, 1238 R

MATERIALISM

One thing we are realising to-day is that to the majority of us, civilised life is an elaborate way of doing without God. We have not been living a life hid with Christ in God; we have been living the abundance of the things which we possess.

Christian Disciplines, Volume 1,
The Discipline of Peril, 297 L

If a man lives in order to hoard up the means of living, he does not live at all; he has no time to; he is taken up with one form of drudgery or another to keep things going.

Shade of His Hand, 1213 L

MEANING IN LIFE

Solomon sums up the whole thing as follows: If you try to find enjoyment in this
order of things, you will end in vexation
and disaster. If you try to find enjoyment in
knowledge, you only increase your capacity
for sorrow and agony and distress. The only
way you can find relief and the right interpretation of things as they are is by basing
your faith in God, and by remembering that
man's chief end is to glorify God and enjoy
Him for ever. Jesus Christ is the One Who
can transmute everything we come across.

Shade of His Hand, 1197 R

What is the real design of man's creation?
Solomon deals with every possible phase
of life—metaphysics, philosophy, religion,
commercial prosperity, moral integrity—not
as guesswork, he had been through it all, no
one has the wisdom of Solomon, and his
verdict is that it all ends in disaster. That is
the summing up of it all unless a man sees
that his "chief end is to glorify God and
enjoy Him for ever," and it takes a long
while to get there. To put things on any
other basis will end in disaster.

Shade of His Hand, 1205 R

*Then I looked on all the works that my hands
had wrought, and on the labour that I had
laboured to do: and, behold, all was vanity and
vexation of spirit, and there was no profit under
the sun" (Ecclesiastes 2:11).*

This is deep, profound pessimism. All
the books of Wisdom in the Bible prove
that the only result of sheer thinking on the
basis of rationalism is pessimism, fathom-
essly profound. The reason most of us are
not pessimistic is either that we are religious
or we have a temperament that is optimis-
tic. The basis of life is tragic, and the only
way out is by a personal relationship to God
on the ground of Redemption. Solomon
deliberately revolted against everything and

found there was no satisfaction in anything
he tried.

Shade of His Hand, 1198 R

MEDDLING

The suffering which springs from being
"a meddler in other men's matters" ("a
busybody") is humiliating to the last degree.
A free translation of 1 Thessalonians 4:11
might well read: "Study to shut up and mind
your own business," and among all the texts
we hang on our walls, let this be one.

*Christian Disciplines, Volume 1,
The Discipline of Suffering, 282 L*

I want you to beware of a mistake I have
made over and over again in days gone by, of
trying to interpret God's plan for other lives
along the way He has led me. Never! Keep
open-eyed in wonder.

If Ye Shall Ask, 617 R

> Never interfere with
> God's providential
> dealings with other
> souls. Be true to God
> yourself and watch.

Disciples Indeed, 410 R

Individual responsibility for others without
becoming an amateur providence is one of
the accomplishments of the Holy Spirit in
a saint.

Disciples Indeed, 410 R

(Continued)

MEDDLING (Continued)

"It is vain for you that ye rise up early, and so late take rest, and eat the bread of toil: for so He giveth unto His beloved sleep" (Psalm 127:2 RV).

This verse describes an amateur providence. We are all amateur providences, until we learn better; we are most impertinent toward God, we tell Him there are certain things we will never allow to happen in other lives, and God comes and says, "Don't interfere with that life any more." Are you rising up early and sitting up late to try and unravel difficulties? You cannot do it. It is a great thing to get to the place where you countenance God and know He rules. It is not done by impulse but by a settled and abiding conviction based on God's truth and the discipline of life. I know that God rules; and He gives me power to perceive His rule. There is no use sitting up late or rising up early; I must do the work that lies before me, and avoid worry as I would the devil.

The Highest Good—The Pilgrim's Song Book, 536 R

It is not only sin that produces the havoc in life, but the natural determination to "boss the show" for God and everyone else.

Not Knowing Whither, 877 R

The duty of every Christian (and it is the last lesson we learn) is to make room for God to deal with other people direct as He deals with us; we will limit them and try to make everyone in our mould. We have to keep in unbroken touch with God and give every soul the same freedom and liberty before God as God gives us.

Notes on Jeremiah, 1434 L

MEDITATION

Meditation means getting to the middle of a thing; not being like a pebble in a brook letting the water of thought go over us; that is reverie, not meditation. Meditation is an intense spiritual activity; it means bringing every bit of the mind into harness and concentrating its powers; it includes both deliberation and reflection.

Biblical Psychology, 171 L

"Meditate upon these things . . ." (1 Timothy 4:15).

Meditation means getting to the middle of a thing, pinning yourself down to a certain thing and concentratedly brooding upon it. The majority of us attend only to the "muddle" of things, consequently we get spiritual indigestion, the counterpart of physical indigestion, a desperately gloomy state of affairs.

The Moral Foundations of Life, 711 R

MEMORY
(See also FORGET / FORGETTING)

When you are in difficult circumstances, remember the time when they were not so trying. God has given us this power to turn ourselves by remembrance; if we lose the power, we punish ourselves and it will lead on to melancholia and the peril of fixed ideas.

Biblical Psychology, 174 L

People say God helps us to forget our past, but is that true? Every now and again the Spirit of God brings us back to remember who we are, and the pit from whence we were digged, so that we understand that all we are is by the sovereign grace of God, not by our own work, otherwise we would be uplifted and proud.

Biblical Psychology, 174 R

" . . . for that He counted me faithful, putting me into the ministry; who was before a blasphemer, and a persecutor, and injurious" (1 Timothy 1:12–13).

" . . . and such were some of you" (1 Corinthians 6:11).

No aspect of Christian life and service is in more need of revision than our attitude to the memory of sin in the saint. When the Apostle Paul said "forgetting those things which are behind," he was talking not about sin, but about his spiritual attainment. Paul never forgot what he had been; it comes out repeatedly in the Epistles—"For I am the least of the apostles, that am not meet to be called an apostle" (1 Corinthians 15:9); "unto me who am less than the least of all saints, is this grace given" (Ephesians 3:8); "sinners, of whom I am chief" (1 Timothy 1:15). And these are the utterances of a ripe, glorious servant of God.

Conformed to His Image, 380 L

"The Lord hath done great things for us; whereof we are glad. Turn again our captivity, O Lord, as the streams in the south" (Psalm 126:3–4).

Whenever God brings His deliverances they are so supernatural that we are staggered with amazement. It is one of the most helpful spiritual exercises to reckon what God has done for us already. When God wanted to make His ancient people realise what manner of God He was, He said, "Remember the crossing of the Red Sea," and in the New Testament Paul says, "Remember, it is the God Who raised Jesus from the dead. . . ." These two things are the unit of measurement of God's power. If I want to know what God can do, He is the God Who made a way through the sea; if it is a question of power for my life, the measurement of that is the Resurrection of Jesus.

The Highest Good—The Pilgrim's Song Book, 535 R

MERCY

Belief in God's mercy will always be inclined to wobble between sleepy satisfaction that God is indulgent and fretful impatience that He is indifferent.

Notes on Isaiah, 1380 R

MIND *(See also THINKING and THOUGHTS / THOUGHT LIFE)*

It is possible to have a saved and sanctified experience and a stagnant mind. Learn how to make your mind awake and fervid, and when once your mind is awake never let it go to sleep. The brain does not need rest; it only needs change of work. The intellect works with the greatest intensity when it works continuously; the more you do, the more you can do. We must work hard to keep in trim for God. Clean off the rust and keep bright by use.

Approved Unto God, 11 R

When people say, "Preach us the simple Gospel," what they mean is, "Preach us the thing we have always heard, the thing that keeps us sound asleep; we don't want to see things differently"; then the sooner the Spirit of God sends a thrust through their stagnant minds the better. Continual renewal of mind is the only healthy state for a Christian. Beware of the ban of finality about your present views.

Biblical Ethics, 101 R

Obedience to the Holy Spirit will mean that we have power to direct our ideas. It is astonishing how we sit down under the dominance of an idea, whether a right or wrong idea; and saints have sat down under this idea more than any other—that they cannot help thoughts of evil. Thank God that's a lie; we can.

Biblical Ethics, 113 L

(Continued)

MIND *(Continued)*

Note two things about your intelligence: first, when your intelligence feels numb, quit at once, and play or sleep; for the time being the brain must recuperate; second, when you feel a fidget of associated ideas, take yourself sternly in hand and say, "You shall study, so it's no use whining."

Disciples Indeed, 405 R

Mental stodge is different. Mental stodge is the result of one of three forms of over-feeding—too much dinner, too much reading, or too much meetings.

Disciples Indeed, 405 R

If a man lets his garden alone, it pretty soon ceases to be a garden; and if a saint lets his mind alone, it will soon become a garbage patch for Satan's scarecrows. Read the terrible things that Paul says will grow in the mind of a saint unless he looks after it (e.g., Colossians 3:5). . . . See to it by the careful watching of your mind that only those thoughts come in that are worthy of God.

The Philosophy of Sin, 1115 R

One of the best things for your spiritual welfare is to keep recounting the wonders God has done for you: record them in a book, mark the passage in your Bible and continually refer to it, keep it fresh in your mind.

The Place of Help, 998 R

MIND OF CHRIST

We have to lose our own way of thinking and form Jesus Christ's way. "Acquire your soul with patience." It takes time and discipline. When we are regenerated and have the life of the Son of God in us, God engineers our circumstances in order that we may form the mind of Christ.

So Send I You, 1314 L

MIRACLES

The miracles which our Lord performed (a miracle simply means the public power of God) transcend human reason, but not one of them contradicts human reason. For example, our Lord turned water into wine, but the same thing is done every year all over the world in process of time: water is sucked up through the stem of the vine and turned into grapes. Why, should it be considered more of a miracle when it is done suddenly by the same Being Who does it gradually? When Jesus Christ raised a man from the dead, He simply did suddenly what we all believe implicitly He is going to do by and by.

Biblical Psychology, 214 L

Indiscernible—you cannot discern exactly why the power should take the turn it does. The old divines spoke of a miracle as "the public power of God." God emerges suddenly and does something beyond human power. Our Lord's miracles were cinematograph shows to His disciples of what His Father was always doing (see John 2:1–11). Our Lord never worked a miracle in order to show what He could do; He was not a wonder worker, and when people sought Him on that line, He did nothing (cf. Luke 23:8–9).

Shade of His Hand, 1235 L

MISSIONARY / MISSIONS

In Acts 1:8 our Lord said this striking thing—"Ye shall be witnesses *unto* Me." When Christ is formed in us, we are a satisfaction to our Lord and Master wherever He places us. The point of importance is to know that we are just exactly where He has engineered our circumstances. There is no "foreign field" to our Lord.

The Psychology of Redemption, 1069 R

Watch how subtly the missionary call has changed. It is not now the watchword of the Moravian call, which saw behind every suffering heathen the Face of Christ: the need has come to be the call. It is not that Jesus Christ said "Go," but that the heathen will not be saved if we do not go. It is a subtle change that is sagacious, but not spiritual. The need is never the call: the need is the opportunity.

The Servant as His Lord, 1276 L

Missionary enterprise, to be Christian, must be based on the passion of obedience, not on the pathos of pity. The thing that moves us to-day is pity for the multitude; the thing that makes a missionary is the sight of what Jesus did on the Cross, and to have heard Him say "Go."

So Send I You, 1300 L

According to Our Lord, there is not a home church and a foreign church; it is all one great work, beginning at home and then going elsewhere, "beginning from Jerusalem." Jerusalem was not the home of the disciples; Jerusalem was the place where Our Lord was rejected. "Begin there," said Jesus.

So Send I You, 1309 L

There is no room for the specialist or the crank or the fanatic in missionary work. A fanatic is one who has forgotten he is a human being. Our Lord never sent out cranks and fanatics; He sent out those who were loyal to His domination. He sent out ordinary men and women, plus dominating devotion to Himself by the indwelling Holy Ghost.

So Send I You, 1335 L

There is not the slightest use in going to the foreign field to work for God if we are not true to His ideal at home. We should be a disgrace to Him there.

So Send I You, 1323 L

The great Author and Originator of all missionary enterprise is God, and we must keep in touch with His line. The call to the missionary does not arise out of the discernment of his own mind, or from the sympathy of his own heart, but because behind the face of every distorted, downtrodden heathen, he sees the face of Jesus Christ, and hears His command—"Go ye therefore, and make disciples of all the nations."

So Send I You, 1321 L

"And that repentance and remission of sins should be preached in His name. . . ." (Luke 24:47).

It is easy to forget that the first duty of the missionary is not to uplift the heathen, not to heal the sick, not to civilise savage races, because all that sounds so rational and so human, and it is easy to arouse interest in it and get funds for it. The primary duty of the missionary is to preach "repentance and remission of sins . . . in His name." The key to the missionary message, whether the missionary is a doctor, a teacher, an industrial worker, or a nurse—the key is the remissionary purpose of Our Lord Jesus Christ's death.

So Send I You, 1328 L

There is no more wholesome training for the foreign field than doing our duty in the home field. The foreign field is apt to have a glamour over it because it is away somewhere else. There is an inspiration and a sense of the heroic about going to the foreign field—until we get there. . . .

So Send I You, 1332 R

Unless the life of a missionary is hid with Christ in God before he begins his work, that life will become exclusive and narrow; it will never become the servant of all men; it will never wash the feet of others.

So Send I You, 1332 R

MONEY

The two things around which our Lord centred His most scathing teaching were money and marriage, because they are the two things that make men and women devils or saints. Covetousness is the root of all evil, whether it shows itself in money matters or in any way.

The Highest Good, 547 L

The measure of a man's want is seen in the nature of the power that awakened it. No man can stand in front of Jesus Christ and say, "I want to make money."

The Moral Foundations of Life, 693 R

Money is one of the touchstones in our Lord's teaching. Nowadays we are taken up with our ideas of economy and thrift, and never see that those ideas are not God's ideas.

The Place of Help, 1028 L

"Oh, I can't afford it," we say—one of the worst lies is tucked up in that phrase. It is ungovernably bad taste to talk about money in the natural domain, and so it is spiritually, and yet we talk as if our Heavenly Father had cut us off with a shilling!

My Utmost for His Highest, May 16, 781 L

The test of true religion is when it touches these four things—food, money, sex, and mother earth. . . . A man needs to hold a right attitude to all these things by means of his personal relationship to God.

Shade of His Hand, p. 1227 L

"Give to him that asketh thee."
    Why do we always make this mean money? Our Lord makes no mention of money. The blood of most of us seems to run in gold. The reason we make it mean money is because that is where our heart is.

Studies in the Sermon on the Mount, 1451 R

Jesus saw in money a much more formidable enemy of the Kingdom of God than we are apt to recognise it to be. Money is one of the touchstones of reality. People say, "We must lay up for a rainy day." We must, if we do not know God. How many of us are willing to go the length of Jesus Christ's teaching? Ask yourself, how does the advocacy of insurance agree with the Sermon on the Mount, and you will soon see how un-Christian we are in spite of all our Christian jargon. The more we try to reconcile modern principles of economy with the teachings of Jesus, the more we shall have to disregard Jesus.

The Highest Good, 554 L

MOOD

You do not gather the vindictive mood from the Holy Ghost; you do not gather the passionately irritable mood from the patience of God; you do not gather the self-indulgent mood and the lust of the flesh in private life from the Spirit of God. God never allows room for any of these moods.

Studies in the Sermon on the Mount, 1468 L

MORALITY

Nominal Christians are often without the ordinary moral integrity of the man who does not care a bit about Jesus Christ; not because they are hypocrites, but because we have been taught for generations to think on one aspect only of Jesus Christ's salvation, viz., the revelation that salvation is not merited by us, but is the sheer sovereign act of God's grace in Christ Jesus. A grand marvellous revelation fact, but Jesus says we have got to say "Thank you" for our salvation, and the "Thank you" is that our righteousness is to exceed the righteousness of the most moral man on earth.

The Highest Good, 544 L

In the moral realm if you don't do things quickly you will never do them. Never postpone a moral decision.

Disciples Indeed, 393 R

If you make a moral struggle and gain a moral victory, you will be a benefit to all you come across, whereas if you do not struggle, you act as a moral miasma. Gain a moral victory in chastity or in your emotional life, it may be known to no one but yourself, and you are an untold benefit to everyone else; but if you refuse to struggle everyone else is enervated.

The Place of Help, 1008 R

The reward for doing right is not that I get an insurance ticket for heaven, but that I do the right because it is right. Honesty ceases to be the best policy if I am honest for a reason.

Shade of His Hand, 1233 R

The reason you are not so zealous for the glory of God as you used to be, not so keen about the habits of your spiritual life, is because you have imperceptibly begun to surrender morally.

The Place of Help, 998 L

The characteristic of a moral hell is satisfaction, no end in view, perfectly satisfied. Moral sickness is a perilous time; it is the condition to which sin brings us, and it accounts for the unutterable disappointments in life; there is no lure, no aim, no quest, no end in view.

The Moral Foundations of Life, 700 L

The natural pagan, a man whose word is as good as his bond, a moral and upright man, is more delightful to meet than the Christian who has enough of the Spirit of God to spoil his sin but not enough to deliver him from it.

The Place of Help, 1036 R

The first thing "the fool" does is to get rid of God ("The fool hath said in his heart, There is no God." Psalm 14:1); then he gets rid of heaven and hell; then he gets rid of all moral consequences—no such thing as right and wrong.

Biblical Ethics, 119 L

Second thoughts on moral matters are always deflections.

Disciples Indeed, 393 R

MORNING

It is not a haphazard thing, but in the constitution of God, that there are certain times of the day when it not only seems easier, but it *is* easier, to meet God. If you have ever prayed in the dawn you will ask yourself why you were so foolish as not to do it always: it is difficult to get into communion with God in the midst of the hurly-burly of the day. George MacDonald said that if he did not open wide the door of his mind to God in the early morning he worked on the finite all the rest of the day—"stand on the finite, act upon the wrong." It is not sentiment but an implicit reality that the conditions of dawn and communion with God go together.

He Shall Glorify Me, 500 R

MOSES

Moses was learned in all the wisdom of the Egyptians; he was a mighty man and a great statesman, and when he saw the oppression of his people he felt that God had called him out to deliver them, and in the righteous indignation of his own spirit he started to right their wrongs. God is never in a hurry. After the first big strike for God and for the right thing, God allowed Moses, the only man who could deliver his own people, to be driven into the desert to feed sheep—forty years of blank discouragement. Then when God appeared and told him to go and bring forth the people, Moses said—"Who am I, that I should go?" The big "I am" had gone, and the little "I am" had taken its place.

The Place of Help, 1055 L

At first, Moses was certain he was the man, and so he was, but he was not fit yet. He set out to deliver the people in a way that had nothing of the stride of God about it. Moses was right in the individual aspect, but he was not the man for the work until he had learned communion with God, and it took forty years in the desert while God worked through him in ways of terrific personal enlargement before he recognised this.

The Place of Help, 1055 R

MOTIVE / MOTIVATION

We have any number of instincts, but very few desires. Desire is what you determine in your mind and settle in your heart and set yourself towards as good, and that is the thing God will fulfil if you delight in Him—that is the condition. God deals with us on the line of character building—"Ye shall ask what ye *will*," said Jesus; not what you like, but what your will is in; and we *ask* very few things.

Biblical Ethics, 104 R

Remember, then, that we have the power to fix the form of our choice. "Delight thyself also in the Lord; and He shall give thee the desires of thine heart." Desire embraces both determination and design. Some people, when they read this verse, behave before God as people do over a wishing-bone at a Christmas dinner. They say, "Now I have read this verse, I wonder what shall I wish for?" That is not desire. Desire is what we determine in outline in our minds and plan and settle in our hearts; that is the desire which God will fulfil as we delight ourselves in Him.

Biblical Psychology, 170 L

You perhaps have not noticed before that you always take care to tell those to whom it matters how early you rise in the morning to pray, how many all nights of prayer you spend; you have great zealousness in proclaiming your protracted meetings. This is all pious play-acting. Jesus says, "Don't do it." Our Lord did not say it was wrong to pray in the corners of the street, but He did say it was wrong to have the motive to be "seen of men." It is not wrong to pray in the early morning, but it is wrong to have the motive that it should be known.

Christian Disciplines, Volume 2,
The Discipline of Prayer, 308 R

Earnestness is not by any means everything; it is very often a subtle form of pious self-idolatry, because it is obsessed with the method and not with the Master.

Christian Disciplines, Volume 2,
The Discipline of Prayer, 309 L

If we work on the idea that it is better physically and prosperously to be good, that is the wrong motive; the right motive is devotion to God, remaining absolutely true to God, no matter what it costs.

The Highest Good—The Pilgrim's Song Book,
534 R

The thing that tells is not that the actual life is lived rightly, but that the motive underneath is right. The characteristic of the Redemption when it works out subjectively in accordance with Scripture is that act of devotion of Mary of Bethany. It was not useful, nor was it her duty; it was an extravagant waste, but the motive of it was the spontaneous originality which sprang from a personal passionate devotion to Jesus Christ.

The Highest Good—Thy Great Redemption, 558 L

When I see Jesus Christ I simply want to be what He wants me to be.

The Moral Foundations of Life, 694 L

"The expulsive power of a new affection"—that is what Christianity supplies. The Spirit of God on the basis of Redemption gives us something else to think about. Are we going to think about it?

The Moral Foundations of Life, 711 L

If you are the servant of men for their sake you will soon be heartbroken; but if you serve men for the sake of Jesus Christ, nothing can ever discourage you (cf. 2 Corinthians 4:5).

Shade of His Hand, 1239 R

When the realisation comes home that Jesus Christ has served me to the end of all my meanness, my selfishness and sin, then nothing I meet with from others can exhaust my determination to serve men for His sake.

So Send I You, 1292 L

It needs more courage to face God with our motive in work for Him than it does to face an audience with our message. We have continually to face our own personal sanctification, and our motive for service, with the Lord Himself, to let His searchlight come, and to see that we remain true to Him.

So Send I You, 1322 L

Many of us are subtly serving our own ends, and Jesus Christ cannot help Himself to our lives; if I am abandoned to Jesus, I have no ends of my own to serve.

So Send I You, 1292 R

Our audience is God; not God's people, but God Himself. The saint who realises that can never be discouraged, no matter where he goes. The audience of the ready saint is God; He is the arena of all his actions.

So Send I You, 1296 R

Prayer, says Jesus, is to be looked at in the same way as philanthropy, viz., your eyes on God, not on men. Watch your motive before God; have no other motive in prayer than to know Him. The statements of Jesus about prayer which are so familiar to us are revolutionary.* Call a halt one moment and ask yourself—"Why do I pray? What is my motive? Is it because I have a personal secret relationship to God known to no one but myself?"

Studies in the Sermon on the Mount, 1455 L
*Matthew 6:5–15

MOUNTAINTOP EXPERIENCES

Mounting up with wings as eagles, running and not being weary, are indications that something more than usual is at work. Walking and not fainting is the life that glorifies God and satisfies the heart of Jesus to the full—the plain daylight life, unmarked, unknown; only occasionally, if ever, does the marvel of it break on other people.

The Philosophy of Sin, 1118 R

(Continued)

MOUNTAINTOP EXPERIENCES *(Continued)*

"And behold, there talked with Him two men . . . who . . . spake of His decease which He was about to accomplish at Jerusalem." They spake not of His glory, but of His death. . . . Here on the Mount Our Lord Jesus Christ was back in His pre-Incarnate glory, and what did He do? He turned His back on the glory and came down from the Mount into the demon-possessed valley to be identified with sin on the Cross.

Bringing Sons Unto Glory, 230 R

"And there was a cloud that overshadowed them: and a voice came out of the cloud, saying, This is My beloved Son: hear Him"—not, "This is My beloved Son: now spend halcyon days with Him on the Mount." Beware of celestial sensuality. No matter what your experience, you may be trapped by sensuality any time. Sensuality is not sin; it is the way the body works in connection with circumstances whereby I begin to satisfy myself.

Conformed to His Image, 381 L

The test of spiritual life is the power to descend; if we have power to rise only, there is something wrong. We all have had times on the mount when we have seen things from God's standpoint and we wanted to stay there; but if we are disciples of Jesus Christ, He will never allow us to stay there. Spiritual selfishness makes us want to stay on the mount; we feel so good, as if we could do anything—talk like angels and live like angels, if only we could stay there. But there must be the power to descend; the mountain is not the place for us to live; we were built for the valleys. This is one of the hardest things to learn because spiritual selfishness always wants repeated moments on the mount.

The Love of God—The Ministry of the Unnoticed, 664 L

The mountaintop is an exceptional type of experience; we have to live down in the valley. After every time of exaltation we are brought down with a sudden rush into things as they are, where things are neither beautiful nor poetic nor spiritual nor thrilling. The height of the mountaintop is measured by the drab drudgery of the valley. We never live for the glory of God on the mount; we *see* His glory there, but we do not live for His glory there; it is in the valley that we live for the glory of God.

The Love of God—The Ministry of the Unnoticed, 665 L

Our Lord came down from the Mount into the valley and went on to the Cross where He was glorified; and we have to come down from the mount of exaltation into the drab life of the valley. It is in the sphere of humiliation that we find our true worth to God, and that is where our faithfulness has to be manifested. Most of us can do things if we are always at the heroic pitch; but God wants us at the drab, commonplace pitch, where we live in the valley according to our personal relationship to Him.

The Love of God—The Ministry of the Unnoticed, 665 L

The real life of the saint on this earth, and the life that is most glorifying to Jesus, is the life that steadfastly goes on through common days and common ways, with no mountain-top experiences.

The Philosophy of Sin, 1118 R

The test of mountain-top experiences, of mysticism, of visions of God and of solitariness is when you are "in the soup" of actual circumstances. It is not a question of living a blind life in the brain, away from actuality; not of living in dawns or on mountain tops, but of bringing what you see there straight down to the valley where things are sordid, and living out the vision there.

Shade of His Hand, 1195 L

We are not built for mountains and dawns and artistic affinities; they are for moments of inspiration, that is all. We are built for the valley, for the ordinary stuff of life, and this is where we have to prove our mettle. A false Christianity takes us up on the mount and we want to stay there. But what about the devil-possessed world? Oh, let it go to hell! We are having a great time up here.

The Shadow of an Agony, 1180 L

It is a great thing to be on the mount with God, and the mountains are meant for inspiration and meditation; but a man is taken there only in order that he may go down afterwards among the devil-possessed and lift them up. Our Christianity has been as powerless as dish-water with regard to things as they are; consequently the net result of Christianity is judged to be a failure.

The Shadow of an Agony, 1180 R

We are not made for brilliant moments, but we have to walk in the light of them in ordinary ways. There was only one brilliant moment in the life of Jesus, and that was on the Mount of Transfiguration; then He emptied Himself the second time of His glory, and came down into the demon-possessed valley. For thirty-three years Jesus laid out His life to do the will of His Father, and, John says, "we ought to lay down our lives for the brethren." It is contrary to human nature to do it.

My Utmost for His Highest, June 16, 791 R

MURDER

"And He said, What hast thou done? the voice of thy brother's blood crieth unto Me from the ground" (Genesis 4:10). Murder may be done in a hundred and one ways; think of the number of voices that cry unto God to-day from men who have been murdered in civilised life. The cry of every murdered innocence, every

perverted right, is in the ear of God, and in this sense the blood of Abel still speaks and will never be silenced.

Our Portrait in Genesis, 962 L

MYSTERIOUS / MYSTERY

It is not possible to define life, or love, or suffering, for the words are but names for incalculable elements in human experience, the very essence of which is implicit, not explicit.

Christian Disciplines, Volume 1,
The Discipline of Suffering, 287 L

We all say what is obvious until we are plunged into the deeps; but when a man is profoundly moved he instantly finds himself beyond the reach of help or comfort from the obvious. The obvious becomes trivial; it is not what his heart wants. What he needs is something that can minister to the incalculable element.

The Moral Foundations of Life, 704 R

The Psalmist realised that God knew all about the vast universe outside him, but there was some thing more mysterious to him than the universe outside, and that was the mystery of his own heart, and he asks the great Creator to come and search him. God does not search a man without he knows it, and it is a marvellous moment in a man's life when he is explored by the Spirit of God. The great mystic work of the Holy Spirit is in the dim regions of a man's personality where he cannot go. God Himself is the explorer of man's will, and this is how He searches us.

The Moral Foundations of Life, 705 L

The sense of mystery must always be, for mystery means being guided by obedience to Someone Who knows more than I do.

The Place of Help, 987 L

NATIONS

We talk about a Christian nation—there never has been such a thing. There are Christians in the nations, but not Christian nations.

The Love of God, 660 L

According to the Bible, nations as we know them are the outcome of what ought never to have been. Civilisation was founded on murder, and the basis of our civilised life is competition. There are grand ingredients in civilisation, it is full of shelter and protection, but its basis is not good. We each belong to a nation, and each nation imagines that God is an Almighty representative of that nation. If nations are right, which is the right one?

The Love of God, 660 L

There is a lot of cheap-jack talk just now regarding the British Empire, viz., that God is punishing us for our sins—a hopeless misrepresentation. The Cross of Calvary and the Redemption have to do with the sins of the world. If God began to punish the nations for their sins there would be no nation left on the face of the earth. Job takes the right line, that the difficulties are produced by a conflict of wills.

Baffled to Fight Better, 74 R

We say, Why does God allow these things? Why does He allow a despot to rule? In this dispensation it is the patient long-suffering of God that is being manifested. God allows men to say what they like and do what they like (see 2 Peter 3:14). Peter says that God is long-suffering, and He is giving us ample opportunity to try whatever line we like both in individual and national life. . . . God is leaving us to prove to the hilt that it cannot be done in any other way than Jesus Christ's way, or the human race would not be satisfied.

Shade of His Hand, 1233 R

"Behold, the nations are as a drop of a bucket, and are counted as the small dust of the balance" (Isaiah 40:15).

Another demand God makes of His children is that they believe not only that He is not bewildered by the confused hubbub of the nations, but that He is the abiding Factor in the hubbub.

God's Workmanship, 429 L

The kingdoms of this world are founded on strong men, consequently they go. Jesus Christ founds His Kingdom on the weakest link, a Baby. God made His own Son a Babe.

The Highest Good—The Pilgrim's Song Book, 537 R

NATURAL ABILITY

The only way I can begin to fulfil the call of God is by keeping my convictions out of the way, my convictions as to what I imagine I am fitted for. The fitting goes much deeper down than the natural equipment of a man.

So Send I You, 1290 L

Our Lord pays not the remotest attention to natural abilities or natural virtues; He heeds only one thing—Does that man discern Who I am? Does he know the meaning of My Cross? The men and women Jesus Christ is going to use in His enterprises are those in whom He has done everything.

So Send I You, 1300 R

Our Lord's making of a disciple is supernatural. He does not build on any natural capacity at all. God does not ask us to do the things that are easy to us naturally; He only asks us to do the things we are perfectly fitted to do by His grace, and the cross will come along that line always.

My Utmost for His Highest, September 25, 827 L

When God gives a man work to do, it is seldom work that seems at all proportionate to his natural ability. Paul, lion-hearted genius though he was, spent his time teaching the most ignorant people.

The Psychology of Redemption, 1093 R

NATURE / NATURAL WORLD *(See also CREATION)*

There is a wildness all through Nature and we are suddenly struck with its brutality and ask, "Why, if God is a beneficent Creator, does He allow such diabolical things to happen?" Has the Bible anything to say about this, any revelation that explains it? The Bible explanation is that Nature is in a disorganised condition, that it is out of gear with God's purposes, and will only become organised when God and man are one (see Romans 8:19).

God's Workmanship, 463 L

NATURE OF GOD

How we limit ourselves and our conceptions of God by ignoring the side of the Divine Nature best symbolised by womanhood, and the Comforter, be it reverently said, surely represents this side of the Divine Nature.

Christian Disciplines, Volume 1,
The Discipline of Divine Guidance, 278 L

"I am God Almighty"—El Shaddai, the Father-Mother God, God proved as sufficient for everything. The wonder of El Shaddai (the power to create new things in the old world) runs through the whole kingdom of grace. Remember, Isaac was born of dead parents (Romans 4:19).

Not Knowing Whither, 880 R

NEW BIRTH

People say they are tired of life; no man was ever tired of life; the truth is that we are tired of being half dead while we are alive. What we need is to be transfigured by the incoming of a great and new life.

God's Workmanship, 438 R

"Marvel not that I said unto thee, Ye must be born again," that is, you must be invaded by the Spirit of God by means of a supernatural recreation. Being born again of the Spirit is an unmistakable work of God, as mysterious as the wind. Beware of the tendency to water down the supernatural in religion.

Approved Unto God, 15 L

When a man fails in Christian experience it is nearly always because he has never received anything. There are books which set out to give the psychology of new birth by saying that suddenly something bursts up from a man's unconscious personality and alters him: a man is never born again by a subliminal uprush, but only by receiving something that was never there before, viz., the Holy Spirit.

Biblical Ethics, 100 L

When the facts of life have humbled us, when introspection has stripped us of our own miserable self-interest and we receive a startling diagnosis of ourselves by the Holy Spirit, we are by that painful experience brought to the place where we can hear the marvellous message—profounder than the profoundest philosophies earth ever wove— "Come unto Me, all ye that labour and are heavy laden, and I will give you rest." Until this experience comes, men may patronise Jesus Christ, but they do not come to Him for salvation. The only solution is the one given by Jesus Christ Himself to a good upright man of His day: "Marvel not that I say unto thee, ye must be born from above."

Biblical Ethics, 126 R

(Continued)

NEW BIRTH *(Continued)*

I don't know what your natural heart was like before God saved you, but I know what mine was like. I was misunderstood and misrepresented; everybody else was wrong and I was right. Then when God came and gave me a spring-cleaning, dealt with my sin, and filled me with the Holy Spirit, I began to find an extraordinary alteration in myself. I still think the great marvel of the experience of salvation is not the alteration others see in you, but the alteration you find in yourself.

Conformed to His Image, 370 R

If we cannot be made all over again on the inside and indwelt by the Spirit of God, and made according to the teaching of the Sermon on the Mount, then fling your New Testament away, for it will put before you an ideal you cannot reach.

The Highest Good, 544 R

An artist does not tell us what he sees, he enables us to see; he communicates the unutterable identity of what he sees. It is a great thing to see *with* anyone. Jesus never tells us what to see, but when His touch is upon our eyes, we know that we see what He is seeing; He restores this pristine innocence of sight. "Except a man be born again, he cannot see the kingdom of God."

So Send I You, 1312 R

A skilled artist does not need to use more than two or three colours; an amateur requires all the tubes in his box squirted out like a condensed rainbow. The Master Artist used strange things to open blind eyes, e.g., spittle, clay, and water from a pool—but remember *He* used them, and He produced the miracle of sight. The missionary may easily be looked on as one of the despised things, but if Jesus uses him, he will produce sight in men.

So Send I You, 1313 L

In new birth God does three impossible things; impossible, that is, from the rational standpoint. The first is to make a man's past as though it had never been; the second, to make a man all over again; and the third, to make a man as certain of God as God is of Himself. New birth does not mean merely salvation from hell, but something more radical, something which tells in a man's actual life.

The Place of Help, 1041 L

When we are born from above the realisation dawns that we are built for God, not for ourselves: "He hath made me." We are brought, by means of new birth, into the individual realisation of God's great purpose for the human race, and all our small, miserable, parochial notions disappear.

So Send I You, 1316 R

There are three facts of our personal life that are restored by Jesus Christ to their pristine vigour. We get into real definite communion with God through Jesus Christ; we get to right relationship with our fellow-men and with the world outside; and we get into a right relationship with ourselves. We become Christ-centred instead of self-centred.

The Shadow of an Agony, 1168 R

OBEDIENCE

The reason we have no "open vision" is that in some domain we have disobeyed God. Immediately we obey, the word is opened up. The atmosphere of the Christian is God Himself, and in ordinary times as well as exceptional times He brings words to us. When He does not, never deceive yourself, something is wrong and needs curing, just as there would be something wrong if you could not get your breath.

Approved Unto God, 13 R

The doctrines of the New Testament as applied to personal life are moral doctrines; that is, they are understood by a pure heart, not by the intellect. "I want to know God's will in this matter" you say, and your next step is into a fog; because the only way to understand the will of God is to obey from the heart; it is a moral discernment (see Romans 12:2). My spiritual character determines the revelation of God to me.

Approved Unto God, 14 L

See that you do not use the trick of prayer to cover up what you know you ought to do.

Disciples Indeed, 397 R

Beware of any spiritual emotion that you do not work out mechanically; whenever in devotion before God His Spirit gives a clear indication of what He wants you to do, *do it.*

Biblical Ethics, 107 L

If you feel remarkably generous, then be generous at once, act it out; if you don't, it will react and make you mean. If you have a time of real devotion before God and see what God wants you to do and you do not work it out in your practical life, it will react in secret immorality. That is not an exceptional law, it is an eternal law, and I wish it could be blazed in letters of fire into the mind of every Christian.

Biblical Ethics, 113 R

Many a powerless, fruitless Christian life is the result of a refusal to obey in some insignificant thing—"first go."

Conformed to His Image, 348 L

Live in the reality of the Truth while you preach it.

Disciples Indeed, 398 L

If I am going to know who Jesus is, I must obey Him. The majority of us don't know Jesus because we have not the remotest intention of obeying Him.

Disciples Indeed, 383 R

If I pray that someone else may be, or do, something which I am not, and don't intend to do, my praying is paralysed.

Disciples Indeed, 397 L

Weighing the *pros and cons* for and against a statement of Jesus Christ's means that for the time being I refuse to obey Him.

Disciples Indeed, 406 L

The thing in you and in me that other people like and esteem and laud is the very thing that makes us unable to do what Jesus says.

God's Workmanship, 442 R

"*Greater love hath no man than this, that a man lay down his life for his friends. Ye are My friends, if ye do whatsoever I command you*" (*John 15:13–14*).

For a man to lay down his life is not to lay it down in a sudden crisis, such as death, but to lay it down in deliberate expenditure as one would lay out a pound note. Not—"Here it is, take it out in one huge martyrdom and be done with it." It is a continual substitution whereby we realise that we have another day to spend out for Jesus Christ, another opportunity to prove ourselves His friends.

The Love of God—The Ministry of the Unnoticed, 664 R

(Continued)

OBEDIENCE (Continued)

"To do our best is one part, but to wash our hands smilingly of the consequences is the next part of any sensible virtue."
—*Robert Louis Stevenson*

When Jesus Christ says "Follow Me," He never says to where; the consequences must be left entirely to Him. We come in with our "buts," and "supposings," and "what will happen if I do?" (cf. Luke 9:57–62). We have nothing to do with what will happen if we obey; we have to abandon to God's call in unconditional surrender and smilingly wash our hands of the consequences.

Not Knowing Whither, 865 L

If we are going to obey God there must be a concession made on our part; we have deliberately to trust the character of God as it has been revealed to us in the face of all obstacles.

Not Knowing Whither, 866 R

We have nothing to do with the afterwards of obedience.

Not Knowing Whither, 865 R

The spirit of obedience gives more joy to God than anything else on earth. . . . When the love of God is shed abroad in my heart by the Holy Ghost (Romans 5:5), I am possessed by the nature of God, and I know by my obedience that I love Him. The best measure of a spiritual life is not its ecstasies, but its obedience. "To obey is better than sacrifice."

Not Knowing Whither, 904 L

In order to maintain friendship and loyalty to Christ, be much more careful of your moral and vital relationship to Him than any other thing, even obedience. Sometimes there is nothing to obey; the only thing to do is to maintain your vital connection with Jesus Christ, to see that nothing interferes with your relationship to Him.

The Place of Help, 991 R

It is only by way of obedience that we understand the teaching of God. Bring it straight down to the commonplace things: have I done the duty that lies nearest? have I obeyed God there? If not, I shall never fathom the mysteries of God, however much I may try. When once I obey there, I receive a revelation of the meaning of God's teaching for me. How many of us have obeyed the bit of God's truth we do know?

The Place of Help, 1010 L

The most remarkable thing about the mastership of Jesus Christ is that He never insists on being Master. We often feel that if only He would insist, we would obey Him. Obedience to Jesus Christ is essential, but never compulsory; He will never take means to make me obey Him. Jesus Christ will always make up for my deficiencies; He always forgives my disobedience; but if I am going to be a disciple, it is essential for me to obey Him.

The Place of Help, 1018 L

There is a tendency in all of us to appreciate the sayings of Jesus Christ with our intellects while we refuse to *do* them.

Studies in the Sermon on the Mount, 1471 R

Our obedience to Jesus Christ is going to cost other people a great deal, and if we refuse to go on because of the cost to them, or because of the stab and the jeer, we may find that we have prevented the call of God coming to other lives; whereas if we will go through with God, all these natural relationships will be given to our credit spiritually in the final wind-up.

The Psychology of Redemption, 1064 R

How many of us really live up to all the light we have?

So Send I You, 1323 L

If for one whole day, quietly and determinedly, we were to give ourselves up to the ownership of Jesus and to obeying His orders, we should be amazed at its close to realise all He had packed into that one day.

So Send I You, 1324 R

It is easy to build *with* the sayings of Jesus, to sling texts of Scripture together and build them into any kind of fabric. But Jesus brings the disciple to the test, "You hear My sayings and quote them, but do you *do* them—in your office, in your home life, in your private life?"

Studies in the Sermon on the Mount, 1471 R

Stagnation in spiritual life comes when we say we will bear the whole thing ourselves. We cannot. We are so involved in the universal purposes of God that immediately we obey God, others are affected. Are we going to remain loyal in our obedience to God and go through the humiliation of refusing to be independent, or are we going to take the other line and say—"I will not cost other people suffering"? We can disobey God if we choose, and it will bring immediate relief to the situation, but we shall be a grief to our Lord. Whereas if we obey God, He will look after those who have been pressed into the consequences of our obedience. We have simply to obey and to leave all consequences with Him.

My Utmost for His Highest, January 11, 738 L

The tiniest detail in which I obey has all the omnipotent power of the grace of God behind it. If I do my duty, not for duty's sake, but because I believe God is engineering my circumstances, then at the very point of my obedience the whole superb grace of God is mine through the Atonement.

My Utmost for His Highest, June 15, 791 R

When we do anything from a sense of duty, we can back it up by argument; when we do anything in obedience to the Lord, there is no argument possible; that is why a saint can be easily ridiculed.

My Utmost for His Highest, February 28, 754 R

Right feeling is produced by obedience, never vice versa.

Not Knowing Whither, 873 R

Obey God in the thing He shows you, and instantly the next thing is opened up. We read tomes on the work of the Holy Spirit, when one five minutes of drastic obedience would make things as clear as a sunbeam.

My Utmost for His Highest, October 10, 832 R

OBSCURITY

God buries His men in the midst of paltry things; no monuments are erected to them, they are ignored, not because they are unworthy but because they are in the place where they cannot be seen.* Who could see Paul in Corinth? Paul only became marvellous after he had gone. All God's men are ordinary men made extraordinary by the matter He has given them. God puts His workers where He puts His Son. This is the age of the humiliation of the saints.

Approved Unto God, 3 R
*See 1 Corinthians 9:18–19.

(Continued)

OBSCURITY (Continued)

The curse in Christian work is that we want to preserve ourselves in God's museum; what God wants is to see where Jesus Christ's men and women are. The saints are always amongst the unofficial crowd, the crowd that is not noticed, and their one dominant note is Jesus Christ.

Approved Unto God, 21 R

The extraordinary conversions and phenomenal experiences are magnificent specimen studies of what happens in the life of everyone, but not one in a million has an experience such as the Apostle Paul had. The majority of us are unnoticed and unnoticeable people. If we take the extraordinary experience as a model for the Christian life, we erect a wrong standard without knowing it, and in the passing of the years we produce that worst abortion, the spiritual prig—an intolerant un-likeness to Jesus Christ.

The Love of God—The Ministry of the Unnoticed, 661 L

It takes Almighty God Incarnate in you to peel potatoes properly, and to wash heathen children for the glory of God. *Anyone* cannot do these things; anybody can do the shining in the sun and the sporting in the footlights, but it takes God's incarnated Spirit to make you so absolutely humanly His that you are utterly unnoticeable.

Not Knowing Whither, 906 L

It is one thing to go on the lonely way with dignified heroism, but quite another thing if the line mapped out for you by God means being a door-mat under other people's feet. Suppose God wants to teach you to say, "I know how to be abased"—are you ready to be offered up like that? Are you ready to be not so much as a drop in a bucket—to be so hopelessly insignificant that you are never thought of again in connection with the life you served? Are you willing to spend and be spent; not seeking to be ministered unto, but to minister? Some saints cannot do menial work and remain saints because it is beneath their dignity.

My Utmost for His Highest, February 5, 746 R

Remain true to God in your obscurity, and remember you are not the designer of your destiny. You hear the call of God and realise what He wants, then you begin to find reasons why you should not obey Him. Well, obey Him, because away in some other part of the world there are other circumstances being worked by God, and if you say—"I shan't, I wasn't made for this," you get out of touch with God. Your "goings" are not according to your mind, but according to God's mind. Remain true at all costs to what God is doing with you and don't ask why He is doing it.

Not Knowing Whither, 907 L

Jesus warned His disciples that they would be treated as nobodies; He never said they would be brilliant or marvellous. We all have a lurking desire to be exhibitions for God, to be put, as it were, in His show room. Jesus does not want us to be specimens; He wants us to be so taken up with Him that we never think about ourselves, and the only impression left on others by our life is that Jesus Christ is having unhindered way.

So Send I You, 1306 L

For a time we are conscious of God's attentions; then, when God begins to use us in His enterprises, we take on a pathetic look and talk of the trials and the difficulties, and all the time God is trying to make us do our duty as obscure people. None of us would be obscure spiritually if we could help it.

My Utmost for His Highest, May 1, 775 R

"The water that I shall give him shall be in him a well of water" (John 4:14).

Never look at yourself from the standpoint of—"Who am I?" In the history of God's work you will nearly always find that it has started from the obscure, the unknown, the ignored, but the steadfastly true to Jesus Christ.

My Utmost for His Highest, September 7, 820 R

It takes Almighty grace to take the next step when there is no vision and no spectator—the next step in devotion, the next step in your study, in your reading, in your kitchen; the next step in your duty, when there is no vision from God, no enthusiasm and no spectator. It takes far more of the grace of God, far more conscious drawing upon God to take that step, than it does to preach the Gospel.

My Utmost for His Highest, March 6, 756 R

OBSTINACY

It is easy to be determined, and the curious thing is that the more small-minded a man is the more easily he makes up his mind. If he cannot see the various sides of a question, he decides by the ox-like quality of obstinacy. Obstinacy simply means—"I will not allow any discernment in this matter; I refuse to be enlightened."

Facing Reality, 153 L

The one great enemy of discipleship to Jesus Christ is spiritual obstinacy, the emphatic "I won't" which runs all through. Jesus says, "If you are to be My disciple this and that must go"; we are at liberty to say, "No, thank you," and to go away, like the rich young ruler, with fallen countenances and sorrowful because we have great possessions, we are somebodies, we have opinions of our own, we know exactly what we intend to do.

The Highest Good, 541 R

From the moment that God uncovers a point of obstinacy in us and we refuse to let Him deal with it, we begin to be sceptical, to sneer and watch for defects in the lives of others. But when once we yield to Him entirely, He makes us blameless in our personal life, in our practical life, and in our profound life.

The Love of God—Now Is It Possible, 683 R

Like a theological buzzard, he [Eliphaz] sits on the perch of massive tradition and preens his ruffled feathers and croaks his eloquent platitudes.* There is no trace of the fraud in Eliphaz; he vigorously believes his beliefs, but he is at a total loss to know God. Eliphaz represents the kind of humbug that results from remaining true to conviction instead of to facts which dispute the conviction. The difference between an obstinate man and a strong-minded man lies just here: an obstinate man refuses to use his intelligence when a matter is in dispute, while a strong-minded man makes his decision after having deliberately looked at it from all standpoints, and when opposed, he is willing to give reasons for his decision.

Baffled to Fight Better, 64 L
*See Job 15.

When we come to the New Testament there is the quiet and grandly-easy certainty that we *can* attain. All God's commands are enablings. Never sympathise with a soul who cannot get through to God on Jesus Christ's lines. The Lord is never hard nor cruel; He is the essence of tender compassion and gentleness. The reason any soul cannot get through is that there is something in him that won't budge; immediately it does, Jesus Christ's marvellous life will have its way.

The Philosophy of Sin, 1124 R

(Continued)

OBSTINACY (Continued)

[Jesus Christ] says "Come unto Me," and there is no profounder word in human language than that. The one thing that keeps us from coming to Jesus Christ is obstinacy; we will do anything rather than come. It is not God's will that a man should be smashed before he is saved; it is the man's obstinacy that does it.

The Psychology of Redemption, 1066 L

There is any amount of weakness in us all, but deep down there is red-handed rebellion against the authority of Jesus Christ—"I'll be damned before I yield." Don't take a poetical view of things that go beyond science. At bottom, sin is red-handed mutiny that requires to be dealt with by the surgery of God—and He dealt with it on Calvary.

The Servant as His Lord, 1278 L

Obstinacy and strength of will are often confounded, but they are very different. An obstinate man is unintelligent; a strong-minded man is one who has made up his mind on a matter but is prepared to listen to your arguments and deal with them, and show to your satisfaction that his decision is right. A stubborn man is always a "small potato." We may make up our minds easily, but to make up a mind of any breadth takes time, there are so many sides to every matter.

Shade of His Hand, 1223 R

You were looking for a great big thing to do, and God is telling you of some tiny thing; but at the back of the tiny thing is the central citadel of obstinacy.

So Send I You, 1299 L

OCCUPATION (See WORK)

OPPORTUNITY

"For man also knoweth not his time." You never know when your opportunity is going to come. Every man has to go out to sea to break from his moorings, whether by a storm or by a big lifting tide.

Shade of His Hand, 1237 R

ORDINARY (See also DRUDGERY)

The thing we have to guard against is wanting to be somewhere else. Have I sufficient of the grace of God to behave myself as His child where I am? It is one thing to feel the sufficiency of God in a prayer meeting and in times of delight and excitement, but another thing to realise His sufficiency in whatever setting we may be—in a thunderstorm or on a calm summer day, in a cottage or a College, in an antique shop or on a moor.

The Highest Good—The Pilgrim's Song Book, 538 L

It is easy to stand fast in the big things, but very difficult in the small things.

Facing Reality, 153 L

It is in ordinary surroundings and among commonplace things that the blessing of God is to dwell and reveal itself. . . . The test is not the success of a revival meeting—that may be questionable—but the success of living in the commonplace things that make life what it is, letting God carry out His purposes as He will.

The Highest Good—The Pilgrim's Song Book, 538 R

After a time of rapt contemplation when your mind has been absorbing the truth of God, watch the kind of people God will bring round you; not people dressed in the "castoff nimbus" of some saint, but ordinary commonplace people just like yourself.

Conformed to His Image, 381 R

The greatest test of Christianity is the wear and tear of daily life; it is like the shining of silver: the more it is rubbed the brighter it grows.

Disciples Indeed, 393 L

Don't insult God by despising His ordinary ways in your life by saying, "Those things are beneath me." God has no special line; anything that is ordinary and human is His line.

Disciples Indeed, 411 L

Do you regard yourself as a highly respectable, dignified Christian? Are you religiously self-important, placing yourself where you fancy you ought to be placed, in stately surroundings? If so, you are not following Jesus Christ's example. If you cannot do ordinary things and live as nobody anywhere, you are not a saint. Jesus left heaven and lived nowhere of any importance all His earthly life.

God's Workmanship, 448 R

"He riseth from supper, and laid aside His garments; and took a towel, and girded Himself. After that He poureth water into a basin, and began to wash the disciples' feet" (John 13:4–5). Could anything be more sordid and commonplace? But it takes God Incarnate to do the most menial task properly.

The Love of God—The Ministry of the Unnoticed, 662 R

"Consider the lilies of the field," said Jesus; we consider motor-cars and aeroplanes, things full of energy. Jesus never drew His illustrations from these things, but always from His Father's handiwork. A lily grows where it is put and does not fuss; we are always inclined to say, "I would be all right if only I were somewhere else." If our spiritual life does not grow where we are, it will grow nowhere.

He Shall Glorify Me, 480 L

Our Lord did not say to His disciples: "I have had a most successful time on Earth; I have addressed thousands of people and been the means of their salvation; now you go and do the same kind of thing." He said: "If I then, your Lord and Master, have washed your feet, ye also ought to wash one another's feet." We try to get out of it by washing the feet of those who are not of our own set. We will wash the heathen's feet, the feet in the slums; but fancy washing my brother's feet! my wife's! my husband's! the feet of the minister of my church! Our Lord said "one another's feet." It is in the ordinary commonplace circumstances that the unconscious light of God is seen.

The Love of God—The Ministry of the Unnoticed, 663 L

All our relationships in life, all the joys and all the miseries, all the hells and all the heavens, are based on bodies; and the reality of Jesus Christ's salvation brings us down to the Mother Earth we live on, and makes us see by the regenerating power of God's grace how amazingly precious are the ordinary things that are always with us. Master that, and you have mastered everything.

The Moral Foundations of Life, 711 L

It is the attitude of a spiritual prig to go about with a countenance that is a rebuke to others because you have the idea that they are shallower than you. Live the surface commonsense life in a commonsense way, and remember that the shallow concerns of life are as much of God as the profound concerns.

Not Knowing Whither, 884 L

(Continued)

ORDINARY (Continued)

What the natural reason would call an anti-climax is the very climax of God's super-natural grace whereby a man, having gone through the most wonderful experience, emerges and lives an unwonderful, ordinary life. That is the difference between the fanatic and the faithful soul.

Not Knowing Whither, 906 L

Some of us can only hear God in the thunder of revivals or in public worship; we have to learn to listen to God's voice in the ordinary circumstances of life.

Our Brilliant Heritage, 952 R

A life with presence, i.e., an uncommon spirit, redeems any situation from the commonplace. It may be cleaning boots, doing house work, walking in the street, any ordinary thing at all, but immediately it is touched by a man or woman with presence it ceases to be commonplace.

Our Portrait in Genesis, 980 R

The test of a man's religious life and character is not what he does in the exceptional moments of his life, but what he does in the ordinary times when he is not before the footlights, when there is nothing tremendous or exciting on.

The Place of Help, 1055 L

The way I eat and drink will show who I regard as my master.

Shade of His Hand, 1200 L

The "show business," which is so incorporated into our view of Christian work to-day, has caused us to drift far from Our Lord's conception of discipleship. It is instilled in us to think that we have to do exceptional things for God; we have not. We have to be exceptional in ordinary things, to be holy in mean streets, among mean people, surrounded by sordid sinners. That is not learned in five minutes.

So Send I You, 1306 L

It was in the hour when Jesus knew "that the Father had given all things into His hands, and that He came forth from God, and goeth unto God" that He began to wash the disciples' feet; and it is when we realise our union with Jesus Christ as our Lord and Master that we shall follow His example. It takes God Incarnate to do the meanest duty as it ought to be done. When Jesus touched things that were sordid and ordinary, He transfigured them.

So Send I You, 1314 R

It is much easier to follow in the track of the heroic than to remain true to Jesus in drab, mean streets. Human nature unaided by God can do the heroic business; human pride unaided by God can do the self-sacrificing (cf. 1 Corinthians 13:1–3); but it takes the supernatural power of God to keep us as saints in the drab commonplace days.

So Send I You, 1334 L

We look for visions from heaven, for earth-quakes and thunders of God's power (the fact that we are dejected proves that we do), and we never dream that all the time God is in the commonplace things and people around us. If we will do the duty that lies nearest, we shall see Him. One of the most amazing revelations of God comes when we learn that it is in the commonplace things that the Deity of Jesus Christ is realised.

My Utmost for His Highest, February 7, 747 L

We flag when there is no vision, no uplift, but just the common round, the trivial task. The thing that tells in the long run for God and for men is the steady persevering work in the unseen, and the only way to keep the life uncrushed is to live looking to God.

My Utmost for His Highest, March 6, 756 R

It is the dull, bald, dreary, commonplace day, with commonplace duties and people, that kills the burning heart unless we have learned the secret of abiding in Jesus.

My Utmost for His Highest, March 22, 761 R

We have the idea that God is going to do some exceptional thing, that He is preparing and fitting us for some extraordinary thing by and by, but as we go on in grace we find that God is glorifying Himself here and now, in the present minute. If we have God's say-so behind us, the most amazing strength comes, and we learn to sing in the ordinary days and ways.

My Utmost for His Highest, June 4, 787 R

We always know when Jesus is at work because He produces in the commonplace something that is inspiring.

My Utmost for His Highest, August 21, 814 R

Discipleship is built entirely on the supernatural grace of God. Walking on the water is easy to impulsive pluck, but walking on dry land as a disciple of Jesus Christ is a different thing. Peter walked on the water to go to Jesus, but he followed Him afar off on the land. We do not need the grace of God to stand crises; human nature and pride are sufficient; we can face the strain magnificently; but it does require the supernatural grace of God to live twenty-four hours in every day as a saint, to go through drudgery as a disciple, to live an ordinary, unobserved, ignored existence as a disciple of Jesus.

My Utmost for His Highest, October 21, 836 L

The tendency in early Christian experience is to look for the marvellous. We are apt to mistake the sense of the heroic for being heroes. It is one thing to go through a crisis grandly, but a different thing to go through

every day glorifying God when there is no witness, no limelight, and no one paying the remotest attention to you. If we don't want medieval haloes, we want something that will make people say—What a wonderful man of prayer he is! What a pious, devoted woman she is! If anyone says that of you, you have not been loyal to God. If you are rightly devoted to Jesus Christ, you have reached the sublime height where no one thinks of noticing you; all that is noticed is that the power of God comes through all the time.

Not Knowing Whither, 906 L

ORGANISATION(S)

The institutions of Churchianity are not Christianity. An institution is a good thing if it is second; immediately an institution recognises itself it becomes the dominating factor.

Facing Reality, 27 L

Overmuch organisation in Christian work is always in danger of killing God-born originality; it keeps us conservative, makes our hands feeble. A false artificial flow of progress swamps true devotion to Jesus.

Disciples Indeed, 395 R

Whenever a spiritual movement has been true to Jesus Christ it has brought forth fruit in a hundred and one ways the originator of the movement never dreamed of.

Disciples Indeed, 395 R

God's idea is that individual Christians should become identified with His purpose for the world. When Christianity becomes over-organised and denominational it is incapable of fulfilling our Lord's commission; it doesn't "feed His sheep"; it can't. (See John 21:15–17.)

Disciples Indeed, 395 R

(Continued)

ORGANISATION(S)
(Continued)

Whenever a religious community begins to get organised it ceases to "draw [its] breath in the fear of the Lord"; the old way of talking is kept up, but the life is not there, and men who used to be keen on proclaiming the Gospel are keen now only on the success of the organisation.

Biblical Ethics, 103 R

Thank God for all the marvellous organisation there is in Christian work, for medical missions and finely educated missionaries, for aggressive work in every shape and form; but these are, so to speak, but wards to the lock; the key is not in any of our organisations; the key lies exactly to our hand by our Lord's instruction, "Pray ye therefore."

If Ye Shall Ask, 630 L

Churchianity is an organisation; Christianity is an organism. Organisation is an enormous benefit until it is mistaken for the life. God has no concern about our organisations. When their purpose is finished He allows them to be swept aside, and if we are attached to the organisation, we shall go with it. Organisation is a great necessity, but not an end in itself, and to live for any organisation is a spiritual disaster.

The Shadow of an Agony, 1189 L

Look at the history of every vigorous movement born spontaneously of the Holy Ghost; there comes a time when its true spiritual power dies, and it dies in correspondence to the success of the organisation. Every denomination or missionary enterprise departs from its true spiritual power when it becomes a successful organisation, because the advocates of the denomination or of the missionary enterprise after a while have to see first of all to the establishment and success of their organisation, while the thing which made them what they are has gone like a corn of wheat into the ground and died.

He Shall Glorify Me, 493 R

In chapter 23 Jeremiah points out very clearly how degeneration starts and continues. When an organisation is maintained by pagan methods it becomes aggressive, intolerant, and quite unlike anything that takes its standard from Jesus Christ. There may be no trace of this in the individual lives of those belonging to the organisation; they may be truly humble saints. We are apt to say we are battling for God's glory when we are battling for our own organisation; union with Jesus Christ is the one essential.

Notes on Jeremiah, 1426 L

Whenever an organisation begins to be conscious of itself, its spiritual power goes because it is living for its own propaganda. Movements which were started by the Spirit of God have crystallised into something God has had to blight because the golden rule for spiritual work has been departed from. (See John 12:24.)

Disciples Indeed, 406 R

Within recent years missionary organisation from the human standpoint has almost reached the limit of perfection. But if all this perfection of organisation does is to make men discover a new sense of responsibility without an emphatic basing of everything on Redemption, it will end in a gigantic failure. To-day many are interested in the foreign field because of a passionate interest in something other than the Lord Jesus and His command—"Go ye therefore, and make disciples." All this organisation ought to mean that we can go ahead as never before; but if once the dethronement of Jesus creeps in, the finest organisation will but perfect the lock which cannot open of itself.

So Send I You, 1331 L

Jesus Christ owns the harvest which is produced in men by the distress of conviction of sin; and it is this harvest we have to pray that labourers may be thrust out to reap. We may be taken up with the activities of a denomination, or be giving ourselves up to this committee and that, whilst all about us people are ripe unto harvest and we do not reap one of them, but waste our Lord's time in over-energised activities for furthering some cause or denomination.

So Send I You, 1324 R

PASSION

Nowadays the great passion is the passion for souls, but you never find that passion mentioned in the New Testament; it is the passion for Christ that the New Testament mentions. It is not a passion for men that saves men; a passion for men breaks human hearts. . . . Whenever the passion for souls obscures the passion for Christ, Satan has come in as an angel of light.

Approved Unto God, 18 R

God never makes us bloodless stoics; He makes us passionate saints. The word used of Jesus Christ has in it the very essence of Christianity—our Lord's "passion"; you could never speak of His passionlessness; the one characteristic of our Lord's life was its condensed intensity.

Biblical Ethics, 113 L

People have the idea that Christianity and Stoicism are alike; the writings of the stoics sound so like the teaching of Jesus Christ, but just at the point where they seem most alike, they are most divergent. A stoic overcomes the world by making himself indifferent, by passionlessness; the saint overcomes the world by passionateness, by the passion of his love for Jesus Christ.

The Highest Good—The Pilgrim's Song Book, 535 L

We think that sobriety and capability go together, but it is not always so. A man may be sober and incapable as well as drunk and incapable. Paul warns against the enthusiasm according to wine, but he says we have no business to be nondescript, negative people, drunk neither one way nor the other; we must be enthusiastic. *"Be being filled."* The teaching of the New Testament presents the passion of life.

The Place of Help, 1045 L

Beware of passion that makes you reach for position, because it will end in spiritual infamy. Passion is the combination of desire and pride with a wild reach of possibility. The desire may be for a big or a little thing, but the instant result of anything done at the spur of passion lands you in a wilderness of disgust, nursing wounded pride.

Not Knowing Whither, 878 R

Christianity overcomes the world by passion, not by passionlessness. Passion is usually taken to mean something from which human nature suffers; in reality it stands for endurance and high enthusiasm, a radiant intensity of life, life at the highest pitch all the time without any reaction. That is what Paul means by "Be being filled."

The Place of Help, 1045 L

PAST AND PRESENT

Things are bad and difficult now, but not a tithe as difficult as they used to be. It is of no use to pray for the old days; stand square where you are and make the present better than any past has been. Base all on your relationship to God and go forward, and presently you will find that what is emerging is infinitely better than the past ever was. The present excels the past because we have the wealth of the past to go on.

Shade of His Hand, 1224 L

(Continued)

PAST AND PRESENT
(Continued)

Never limit God by remembering what you have done in the past. When you come into relation with the Reality of Redemption God creates something in you that was never there before; it is the active working of the life of God in you; consequently you can do now what you could not do before.

God's Workmanship, 415 R

There is a tendency in us all to mourn over something—to say that the past was a great deal better than the present, or that the future will be better; the worst time we ever lived in is the present—forgetting that we never lived in any other time!

Shade of His Hand, 1222 L

Here is the day, O Lord, Thy day, cause it to shine for ever in our individual lives like a jewel.

Knocking at God's Door, February 16, 639 L

There is no more glorious opportunity than the day in which we live for proving in personal life and in every way that we are confident in God.

The Place of Help, 997 L

The Gospel of the grace of God takes the stain of memory from a worker, not by making him ignore the past, but by enabling him to see that God can make it of service in his work for God.

The Place of Help, 1005 R

You may know that God has wonderfully used a man in the past, but never make that your ground for heeding what he says now, for at any minute a man may be out of touch with God (cf. 1 Corinthians 9:27). Never pin your faith to a man's reputation as a servant of God; always watch for the Holy Spirit.

Conformed to His Image, 356 R

There is no obstacle, nothing in the past or the present or in his heredity, that can stand in a man's way if he will only make room for Jesus Christ.

He Shall Glorify Me, 508 R

The unfathomable sadness of the "might have been"! God never opens doors that have been closed. He opens other doors, but He reminds us that there are doors which we have shut, doors which need never have been shut, imaginations which need never have been sullied. Never be afraid when God brings back the past. Let memory have its way. It is a minister of God with its rebuke and chastisement and sorrow. God will turn the "might have been" into a wonderful culture for the future.

My Utmost for His Highest, April 3, 766 L

Our yesterdays present irreparable things to us; it is true that we have lost opportunities which will never return but God can transform this destructive anxiety into a constructive thoughtfulness for the future. Let the past sleep, but let it sleep on the bosom of Christ.

My Utmost for His Highest, December 31, 861 R

We limit the Holy One of Israel by remembering what we have allowed Him to do for us in the past, and by saying—"Of course I cannot expect God to do this thing." The thing that taxes almightiness is the very thing which as disciples of Jesus we ought to believe He will do.

My Utmost for His Highest, February 27, 754 L

Beware of harking back to what you once were when God wants you to be something you have never been.

Our Brilliant Heritage, 952 R

We sit down under the tyranny of a devil's lie and say, "I can't undo the past": you cannot, but God can. God can make the past, as far as our spiritual life is concerned, as if it had never been and even in its worst features He can make it bring out the "treasures of darkness."

Notes on Isaiah, 1383 R

Watch how we limit the Lord by remembering what we have allowed Him to do for us in the past: "I always failed there, and I always shall"; consequently we do not ask for what we want, "It is ridiculous to ask God to do this." If it is an impossibility, it is the thing we have to ask. If it is not an impossible thing, it is not a real disturbance. God will do the absolutely impossible.

My Utmost for His Highest, February 29, 754 R

PATIENCE

To "wait on the Lord," and to "rest in the Lord," is an indication of a healthy, holy faith, while impatience is an indication of an un-healthy, un-holy unbelief.

Christian Disciplines, Volume 2,
The Discipline of Patience, 334 L

People who are right with God are often guilty of the most ugly characteristics and you are astounded that they do not see it: but wait; if they go on with God, slowly and surely God's Spirit will educate them from the general principles to the particular items, until after a while they are as careful as can be down to the "jots" and "tittles" of their life, thereby proving their sanctification in the growing manifestation of the new disposition God has given them. No wonder the Book of God counsels us to be patient with ourselves and with one another!

Biblical Psychology, 198 R

It takes a long time to realise what Jesus is after, and the person you need most patience with is yourself. God takes deliberate time with us; He does not hurry, because we can only appreciate His point of view by a long discipline.

The Place of Help, 1016 R

If your hopes are being disappointed just now it means that they are being purified. There is nothing noble the human mind has ever hoped for or dreamed of that will not be fulfilled. Don't jump to conclusions too quickly; many things lie unsolved, and the biggest test of all is that God looks as if He were totally indifferent. Remain spiritually tenacious.

God's Workmanship, 463 R

Patience is the result of well-centred strength; it takes the strength of Almighty God to keep a man patient. No one can remain under and endure what God puts a servant of His through unless he has the power of God. We read that our Lord was "crucified through weakness," yet it took omnipotent might to make Him weak like that.

The Love of God—The Message of Invincible Consolation, 674 L

Patience is not the same as endurance because the heart of endurance is frequently stoical, whereas the heart of patience is a blazing love that sees intuitively and waits God's time in perfect confidence.

Our Portrait in Genesis, 966 L

(Continued)

PATIENCE *(Continued)*

It is impossible to be patient and proud because pride weakens into lust, and lust is essentially impatient. Noah stands for all time as the embodiment of the patience of hope.

Our Portrait in Genesis, 966 L

All through the Bible, emphasis is laid steadily on patience. A man's patience is tested by three things—God, himself, and other people. An apt illustration is that of a bow and arrow in the hand of an archer. God is not aiming at what we are, nor is He asking our permission. He has us in His hands for His own purpose, and He strains to the last limit; then when He lets fly, the arrow goes straight to His goal. Acquire your soul with patience. Don't get impatient with yourself.

Shade of His Hand, 1223 L

Think of the invincible, unconquerable, unwearying patience of Jesus—"Come unto Me."

My Utmost for His Highest, October 8, 831 R

PATRIOTISM / NATIONALISM

The missionary of the Cross is not first a British or an American subject, but a Christian. The missionary is not a sanctified patriot, but one whose sympathies have broken all parochial bounds and whose aims beat in unison with God's own heart.

Christian Disciplines, Volume 2,
The Discipline of Loneliness, 323 R

Once the crisis of identification with Jesus is passed, the characteristic of the life is that we keep open house for the universe. The saint is at home anywhere on Mother Earth; he dare be no longer parochial or denominational; he belongs to no particular crowd, he belongs to Jesus Christ. A saint is a sacramental personality, one through whom the presence of God comes to others (see John 7:37–39).

The Love of God—The Making of a Christian,
681 R

As saints, we are cursed, not blessed, by patriotism. The idea of nations is man's, not God's. When Our Lord establishes His Kingdom there will be no nations, only the great Kingdom of God. That is why His Kingdom is not built up on civilised life.

Not Knowing Whither, 908 L

"And He is the propitiation for our sins: and not for ours only, but also for the sins of the whole world" (1 John 2:2).

The key to the missionary message is the remissionary aspect of Christ's life, not His kindness and His goodness, and His revealing of the Fatherhood of God; the great limitless significance is that He is the propitiation for our sins. The missionary message is not patriotic: it is irrespective of nations and of individuals; it is for the whole world.

My Utmost for His Highest, October 15, 834 L

The Holy Ghost sheds abroad the love of God in our hearts, and the love of God is world-wide; there is no patriotism in the missionary message. This does not mean that patriots do not become missionaries, but it does mean that the missionary message is not patriotic. The missionary message is irrespective of all race conditions, it is for the whole world. "God so loved the world . . ."

So Send I You, 1329 L

PEACE

The peace of this world can never be the peace of God. The peace of physical health, of mental healthy-mindedness, of prosperous circumstances, of civilisation—not one of these is the peace of God, but the outcome of the souls of men being garrisoned by the prince of this world (see Luke 11:21).

The Highest Good—The Pilgrim's Song Book,
526 R

The path of peace for us is to hand ourselves over to God and ask Him to search us, not what we think we are, or what other people think we are, or what we persuade ourselves we are or would like to be, but, "Search me out, O God, explore me as I really am in Thy sight."

Biblical Psychology, 184 R

The peace of sins forgiven, the peace of a conscience at rest with God, is not the peace that Jesus imparts. Those are the immediate results of believing and obeying Him, but it is His own peace He gives, and He never had any sins to be forgiven or an outraged conscience to appease. Have you ever received His peace? When you are right with God, receive your peace by studying in consecrated concentration our Lord Himself; it is the peace that comes from looking at His face and remembering the undisturbed condition of our Lord in every set of circumstances.

Christian Disciplines, Volume 1,
The Discipline of Peril, 300 R

Let your requests be made known unto God. And the peace of God, which passeth all understanding, shall guard your hearts and your thoughts in Christ Jesus" (RV); the poising power of the peace of God will enable you to steer your course in the mix-up of ordinary life.

The Moral Foundations of Life, 721 R

In all the rush of life, in working for our living, in all conditions of bodily life, wherever God engineers our circumstances—"My peace"; the imperturbable, inviolable peace of Jesus imparted to us in every detail of our lives.

Our Brilliant Heritage, 924 R

The coming of Jesus Christ is not a peaceful thing; it is a disturbing thing, because it means the destruction of every peace that is not based on a personal relationship to Himself.

The Place of Help, 1003 L

It is an easy business to preach peace when you are in health and have everything you want, but the Bible preaches peace when things are in a howling tumult of passion and sin and iniquity; it is in the midst of anguish and terror that we realise who God is and the marvel of what He can do.

Notes on Isaiah, 1380 L

What kind of peace had Jesus Christ? A peace that kept Him for thirty years at home with brothers and sisters who did not believe in Him; a peace that kept Him through three years of popularity, hatred, and scandal; and He says, "My peace I give unto you"; "let not your heart be troubled," i.e., see that your heart does not get disturbed out of its relationship to Me.

The Shadow of an Agony, 1183 R

There is one unmistakable witness that Jesus promised us, and that is the gift of His peace. "My peace I give unto you." No matter how complicated the circumstances may be, one moment of contact with Jesus and the fuss is gone, the panic is gone, all the shallow emptiness is gone, and His peace is put in, absolute tranquillity, because of what He says—"All power is given unto Me."

So Send I You, 1326 R

(Continued)

PEACE (Continued)

If I was peaceful and happy, living a clean upright life, why should Jesus Christ come with a standard of holiness I never dreamt of? Simply because that peace was the peace of death, a peace altogether apart from God. The coming of Jesus Christ to the natural man means the destruction of all peace that is not based on a personal relationship to Himself.

Biblical Ethics, 115 L

PEOPLE (See HUMANITY)

PERCEPTION

The characteristic of a man without the Spirit of God is that he has no power of perception; he cannot perceive God at work in the ordinary occurrences. The marvellous, uncrushable characteristic of a saint is that he does discern God.

Biblical Psychology, 170 R

We all see the common occurrences of daily life, but who amongst us can perceive the arm of the Lord behind them? who can perceive behind the thunder the voice of God? The characteristic of the man without the Spirit of God is that he has no power of perception; he cannot perceive God's working behind ordinary occurrences.

If Thou Wilt Be Perfect, 571 R

If my ruling disposition is self-interest, I perceive that everything that happens to me is always for or against my self-interest; if, on the other hand, my ruling disposition is obedience to God, I perceive Him to be at work for my perfecting in everything that happens to me.

The Moral Foundations of Life, 707 L

PERSECUTION

In Matthew 10:34 Jesus told the disciples that they would be opposed not only in private life, but that the powers of state would oppose them and they would have to suffer persecution, and some even crucifixion. Don't say, "But that was simply meant for those days." If you stand true to Jesus Christ you will find that the world will react against you with a butt, not with a caress, annoyed and antagonistic (see John 15:18–20).

Approved Unto God, 16 R

The tendency to-day is to say, "Live a holy life, but don't talk about it; don't give your testimony; don't confess your allegiance to Jesus, and you will be left alone." . . . People are not persecuted for living a holy life; it is the confession of Jesus that brings the persecution.

Approved Unto God, 16 R

There is a saying of Bacon's to the effect that if prosperity is the blessing of the Old Testament, adversity is the blessing of the New; and the apostle Paul says that "all that will live godly in Christ Jesus shall suffer persecution" (2 Timothy 3:12).

Baffled to Fight Better, 52 L

I have no business to stir up the hatred of the world through a domineering religious opinionativeness—that has nothing whatever to do with the spirit of Jesus; I am never told to rejoice when men separate me from their company on that account; but when in all modesty I am standing for the honour of Jesus Christ and a crisis arises when the Spirit of God requires that I declare my otherworldliness, then I learn what Jesus meant when He said, men will hate you. It is the hatred of the world expressed to the otherworldly standpoint once it is made clear.

Biblical Ethics, 100 L

"I have given them Thy word; and the world hated them, because they are not of the world, even as I am not of the world" (John 17:14 RV). The hatred of the world is its intense objection to the principles exhibited by the saint, and frequently it is the best specimens of the worldly spirit who positively hate and detest the otherworldly spirit of the saint. It is not that they hate you personally; they may be very kind to you, but they hate what you represent of Jesus Christ.

Biblical Ethics, 100 L

Most of us live our life in the world without ever discovering its hatred, but it is there, and a crisis may suddenly arise and bring it to a head; then we are appalled to find the meaning of Our Lord's words, "And ye shall be hated of all men for My name's sake."

Biblical Ethics, 100 L

Jesus said, "Leap for joy" when they shall "separate you from their company and cast out your name as evil, for the Son of man's sake," not for some crotchety notion or faddy idea of your own, or for some principle you have wedded yourself to, but *for My sake.*

Biblical Psychology, 189 R

At heart men are antagonistic to the lordship of Jesus Christ. It is not antagonism to creeds or points of view, but antagonism encountered for My sake. Many of us awaken antagonism by our way of stating things; we have to distinguish between being persecuted for some notion of our own and being persecuted "for My sake."

The Highest Good—The Pilgrim's Song Book, 532 L

Try and work your home life or your business life according to the rule of Jesus Christ and you will find that what He said is true: you will be put out of court as a fool, and we don't like to be thought fools. That

is the persecution that many a man and woman has to go through if they are true to Jesus Christ, a continual semi-cultured sneering ridicule; nothing can stand that but absolute devotion to Jesus Christ; a creed will never stand it. Christianity is other-worldliness in the midst of this-worldliness.

The Highest Good, 542 R

I may be such a pig-headed cross-patch, and have such determined notions of my own, that no one can live with me. That is not suffering for the Son of Man's sake; it is suffering for my own sake.

The Moral Foundations of Life, 731 R

If any man will live godly, he shall suffer persecution. If a man wants success and a good time in the actual condition of things as they are, let him keep away from Jesus Christ, let him ignore His claims and the heroism of His holiness; there is no commercial value in it.

Shade of His Hand, 1233 R

PERSONALITY

We are so mysterious in personality, there are so many forces at work in and about us which we cannot calculate or cope with, that if we refuse to take the guidance of Jesus Christ, we may, and probably shall be, deluded by supernatural forces far greater than ourselves.

Biblical Psychology, 190 R

As long as we are flippant and stupid and shallow and think that we know ourselves, we shall never give ourselves over to Jesus Christ; but when once we become conscious that we are infinitely more than we can fathom, and infinitely greater in possibility either for good or bad than we can know, we shall be only too glad to hand ourselves over to Him.

Biblical Psychology, 214 L

(Continued)

PERSONALITY *(Continued)*

Psalm 139 is the classic in all literature concerning a man's personality. In this Psalm the tendency in man which makes him want to examine himself takes the form of prayer, "O Lord, explore me." The Psalmist implies: "Thou art the God of the early mornings and late at nights, the God of the mountains and the fathomless deep; but, my God, my soul has farther horizons than the early mornings, deeper darkness than the nights of earth; higher heights than any mountain peaks, greater depths than any sea in nature; search *me* out, and see if there be any way of grief in me."

The Moral Foundations of Life, 705 L

PERSPECTIVE

"Thine eyes shall see the king in his beauty: they shall behold a far stretching land ['a land of far distances,' mg]" (Isaiah 33:17 RV). The forward look is the look that sees everything in God's perspective whereby His wonderful distance is put on the things that are near. Caleb had the perspective of God; the men who went up with him saw only the inhabitants of the land as giants and themselves as grasshoppers. Learn to take the long view and you will breathe the benediction of God among the squalid things that surround you. Some people never get ordinary or commonplace, they transfigure everything they touch because they have got the forward look which brings their confidence in God out into the actual details of life.

Conformed to His Image, 368 R

"*But I would ye should understand, brethren, that the things which happened unto me have fallen out rather unto the furtherance of the gospel*" (*Philippians 1:12*).

The fortune of misfortune! That is Paul's way of looking at his captivity. He does not want them to be depressed on his account, or to imagine that God's purpose has been hindered; he says it has not been hindered, but furthered. The very things that looked so disastrous have turned out to be the most opportune, so that on this account his heart bounds with joy, and the note of rejoicing comes out through the whole Letter.

Conformed to His Image, 373 R

We only see another in the light of what we think he is; it takes an amount of surgery on the inside to make us see other people as they really are, and it is the same with what we think about God; we take the facts revealed in the Bible and try to fit them into our own ideas of what God is like.

Disciples Indeed, 388 R

Remember that a disciple is committed to much more than belief in Jesus; he is committed to his Lord's view of the world, of men, of God and of sin. Take stock of your views and compare them with the New Testament, and never get tricked into thinking that the Bible does not mean what it says when it disagrees with you. Disagree with what our Lord says by all means if you like, but never say that the Bible does not mean what it says.

The Highest Good, 545 R

Take the Bible attitude to men on the whole; civilisations are despatched at a minute's notice, armies come together and annihilate one another and God seems to pay no attention. His attitude is one which makes us blaspheme and say that He does not care an atom for human beings. Jesus Christ says He does; He says He is a Father, and that He, Jesus, is exactly like His Father. The point is that Jesus saw life from God's standpoint; we don't.

The Highest Good, 549 L

God has so constituted things that prayer on the basis of Redemption alters the way a man looks at things. Prayer is not a question of altering things externally, but of working wonders in a man's disposition. When you pray, *things* remain the same, but *you* begin to be different.

If Ye Shall Ask, 609 R

How complete must be my hold on Thee else through sheer futility I wilt and wander and am only weak. In my present mood I am inclined to give way to the feeling of having missed the mark. Lord, deal with my mind and outlook.

Knocking at God's Door, September 13, 647 R

"For our light affliction, which is but for a moment, worketh for us a far more exceeding and eternal weight of glory"; the apostle seems to be putting things the wrong way round. Surely the affliction is the heavy thing and the glory the light thing! No, Paul is putting it in the right way; he puts the emphasis on the weight of glory resulting from the light affliction. Again, everything is determined by the standpoint you take.

The Love of God—The Message of Invincible Consolation, 671 L

If you are being trained as an art student you will first of all be taught to see things as a whole, in mass outline, and then in detail. The meaning of perspective is that we keep the view of the whole whilst paying attention to the detail.

Our Brilliant Heritage, 938 L

If I have the disposition of a fault-finder, I am a most uncomfortable person to live with, but if the love of God has been shed abroad in my heart, I begin to see extraordinary self-sacrifice under the roughest of exteriors. I begin to see nobility where before I only saw meanness, because I see only what I bring with me the power of seeing—a most humiliating thing to realise!

The Place of Help, 1004 R

We only see along the line of our prejudices until the surgery of events alters our outlook.

He Shall Glorify Me, 489 L

When you are identified with Jesus Christ you become a new creation in the same surroundings. You see life differently because of the moral transfiguration of the regeneration of the Son of God.

The Shadow of an Agony, 1163 R

It is a great thing to have our spiritual sight tested by the Celestial Optician, to watch the way in which He rectifies and readjusts our sight.

So Send I You, 1326 R

PESSIMISM

There is a passion of pessimism at the heart of human life and there is no "plaster" for it; you cannot say, "Cheer up, look on the bright side"; there is no bright side to look on. There is only one cure and that is God Himself, and God comes to a man in the form of Jesus Christ.

Baffled to Fight Better, 51 L

If a man faces actual things as they are and thinks them right out, he must be a pessimist. Most of us are either too thick-headed, or too prejudiced, or too religious, to think right out to the bottom board of things, until the tension comes and obliges us to face them; then we find out who are the men who point the finest way of thinking.

Shade of His Hand, 1197 R

(Continued)

PESSIMISM *(Continued)*

In the Bible you never find the note of the pessimist. In the midst of the most crushing conditions there is always an extraordinary hopefulness and profound joy, because God is at the heart.

The Highest Good—Thy Great Redemption,
566 L

PHARISEE / PHARISAISM

The nature of Pharisaism is that it must stand on tiptoe and be superior. The man who does not want to face the foundation of things becomes tremendously stern and keen on principles and on moral reforms. A man who is hyper-conscientious is nearly always one who has done something irregular or who is morbid; either he is close on the verge of lunacy, or he is covering up something wrong by tremendous moral earnestness along certain lines of reform.

Baffled to Fight Better, 71 L

A Pharisee shuts you up, not by loud shouting, but by the unanswerable logic he presents; he is bound to principles, not to a relationship. There is a great amount of Pharisaism abroad to-day, and it is based on "devotee-ness" to principles. Devotion to a cause is the great mark of our day, and in religion it means being devoted to the application of religious principles. A disciple of Jesus Christ is devoted to a Person, not to principles.

Baffled to Fight Better, 71 L

The modern Pharisee is the one who pretends to be the publican—"Oh, I would never call myself a saint!" Exaggerated self-depreciation and exaggerated conceit are both diseased.

Disciples Indeed, 393 R

All the ordinances to which the Pharisees held had been given by God, but the Pharisees had become second editions of the Almighty; they had usurped the place of God. There is always a danger of Pharisee-ism cropping up. In our own day its form is evangelical; man becomes a little god over his own crowd doctrinally.

Our Brilliant Heritage, 945 R

PIETY / PIOUS TALK

There is no room in the New Testament for sickly piety, but room only for the robust, vigorous, open-air life that Jesus lived—*in* the world but not *of* it, the whole life guided and transfigured by God. Beware of the piety that is not stamped by the life of God, but by the type of a religious experience. Be absolutely and fiercely godly in your life, but never be pious.

Approved Unto God, 5 L

The greatest insult you can offer God is pious talk unless it is backed up by holy actions.

Biblical Ethics, 99 R

Pious talk paralyses the power to live piously, the energy of the life goes into the talk—sanctimonious instead of sanctified. Unless your mind is free from jealousy, envy, spite, your pious words only increase your hypocrisy.

Disciples Indeed, 402 R

Piety always pretends to be going through what it is not.

Not Knowing Whither, 903 L

PILGRIMS ON EARTH

The Songs of Ascents* are the autobiography of the children of God; they reveal their inner secrets. These psalms express not the outward, but the inward condition of the children of God, when they realise that they are pilgrims. We do not immediately realise that we are pilgrims; when a child is born into the world it is welcomed and for a time it feels perfectly happy and at home. Neither when we are born again do we realise at once that we are pilgrims; rather, we feel more at home on the earth than ever; we have come into contact with the Creator of it all, and

Heaven above is brighter blue,
Earth around a sweeter green.

But as we go on, this sense of at-home-ness disappears and ultimately we realise a deep alienation to all that the world represents, and we recognise that we are "strangers and pilgrims on the earth," that "here we have no continuing city." That mood is represented in these Psalms. God seems to delight to stir up our nests; it is not the devil who does it, but God; this is curiously unrecognised on our part.

The Highest Good—The Pilgrim's Song Book,
526 L
*Psalms 120–128: songs originally sung by
those making their annual religious pilgrimages
to Jerusalem, ascending Mount Zion

As Christians it is more important to know how to live than what to live on. The attitude of the Christian is not, "I'm but a stranger here; heaven is my home," but rather "I'm not a stranger here." A stranger is exonerated from many things for which God holds us responsible. Jesus asked His Father to treat His disciples not as strangers but as inmates of the world and to keep them from the evil (John 17:15). We have to live in the heavenly places while here on earth.

The Highest Good, 540 R

PLANS / PROGRAMMES

God begins a work by the inspiration of the Holy Spirit for His own ends entirely and we get caught up into His purpose for that thing; then we begin to introduce our own plans—"I want *this* to produce *that*," and we storm the throne of God along that line; and the first thing God does is *not* to do it, and we say, "That must be the devil." Beware of making God an item, even the principal item, in your programme. God's ways are curiously abrupt with programmes; He seems to delight in breaking them up.

Our Portrait in Genesis, 976 R

POSSESSIONS

The thing that leads me wrong always and every time is what I am persuaded I possess. The thing that is mine is the thing I have with the power to give it. All that I want to possess without the power to give, is of the nature of sin. God has no possessions; consequently I cannot rob God of anything, but I rob myself of God every time I stick to what I possess. Immediately I abandon to God I get that which possesses me but has no possessions with it; there is nothing to keep. Being possessed by God means an untrammelled human life.

God's Workmanship, 422 L

(Continued)

POSSESSIONS (Continued)

Our Lord Jesus Christ became poor for our sakes not as an example, but to give us the unerring secret of His religion. Professional Christianity is a religion of possessions that are devoted to God; the religion of Jesus Christ is a religion of personal relationship to God, and has nothing whatever to do with possessions. The disciple is rich not in possessions, but in personal identity.

Approved Unto God, 8 L

The disciple realises that his life does not consist in the abundance of things he possesses, because what we possess often possesses us—we are possessed by possessions. "This is mine, you must not touch it!" When we become rich towards God it will show in the details of our actual life.

Bringing Sons Unto Glory, 233 R

"For a man's life consisteth not in the abundance of the things which he possesseth" (Luke 12:15).
    This statement of Our Lord's needs careful consideration because we dislike it strongly. The whole teaching of Jesus is opposed to the idea of civilisation, viz., possessing things for myself—"This is mine." The sense of property is connected, not with the lasting element of our personality, but with that which has to do with sin; it is the sense of property that makes me want to gratify myself. Jesus Christ had no sense of property; there was never any attempt to gratify Himself by possessing things for Himself—"the Son of man hath not where to lay His head." What was His, He gave—"I lay down My life. . . . I lay it down of Myself."

God's Workmanship, 422 L

Abraham came back exceedingly wealthy, but he kept tryst with God over his possessions. Beware of not keeping tryst with God over your possessions, whether they be material or not. It is perilously possible not

to, but to make your spiritual life depend on the abundance of things you possess.

Not Knowing Whither, 871 L

"Blessed are the meek: for they shall inherit the earth." The gift here is the heritage of the earth by being fool enough to let other people have it at present. Jesus Christ taught that any one who possesses property of any nature has got to go through a baptism of bereavement in connection with it before he can be His disciple. The rich young ruler is a good specimen of possession (see Luke 18:22–23). The craze nowadays for those of us who have no property is to take the liberty of hauling to pieces those who have; but Jesus Christ turns it round the other way—"Do you possess *anything*, any property of pride, any sense of goodness, any virtue, any gift? Then you will have to go through intolerable bereavement before you can ever be My disciple." Intellectually that is inconceivable; spiritually it is clear to everyone who is rightly related to the Lord.

The Highest Good, 541 R

How many people do you know who have their godliness incarnated in economy? Are you one of them? If we can save and do justly with money, we are absolutely certain we are right in the sight of God. The thing about our Lord and His teaching which puts Him immeasurably away from us nowadays is that He is opposed to all possessions, not only of money and property, but any kind of possession. That is the thing that makes Him such a deep-rooted enemy to the modern attitude to things.

The Highest Good, 547 L

Anything we possess as our own, as a possession of our own personality, is the very essence and principle of sin at work. "If any man will come after Me," said Jesus, "let him deny himself"; literally, let him give up his right to himself to Me, "and take up his cross daily, and follow Me." Our Lord said this over and over again, but we have come to the conclusion that He did not mean what He said and we piously and reverently pass it over.

If Thou Wilt Be Perfect, 574 R

One of the most subtle errors is that God wants our possessions; they are not any use to Him. God does not want our possessions; He wants us.

If Thou Wilt Be Perfect, 603 L

Every possession is tainted with a want. . . . Every possession produces an appetite that clings.

Not Knowing Whither, 871 R

There comes a time when the only way to save what is of enormous value to a life is to cast away all its possessions. "Thy life will I give unto thee for a prey"—you will have nothing else, but you will escape with your life. There is a time when a man may have to lose everything he has got in order to save himself (see Mark 8:35).

Shade of His Hand, 1202 R

The sense of possession is a snare to true spiritual life. . . . No sense of property or possession can go along with an abiding detachment. In civilised life it is the building up of possessions that is the snare—This is *my* house, *my* land; these are *my* books, and *my* things—imagine when they are touched! I am consumed with distress. Over and over again Jesus Christ drives this point home—Remember, don't have your heart in your possessions; let them come and go.

Shade of His Hand, 1214 R

We estimate by what a man possesses; God's only concern is what a man *is*. There is only one thing that will endure and that is personality: no possessions, no pretence, nothing in the way of what men call greatness will last. All the rest is trappings; in their right place, great and good trappings, but Satan wants to keep our minds on them.

Notes on Isaiah, 1377 L

POVERTY

Voluntary poverty was the marked condition of Jesus (see Luke 9:58), and the poverty of God's children in all ages is a significant thing. To-day we are ashamed and afraid to be poor. The reason we hear so little about the inner spiritual side of external poverty is that few of us are in the place of Jesus, or of Paul. The scare of poverty will knock the spiritual backbone out of us unless we have the relationship that holds. The attitude of Our Lord's life was that He was disconnected with everything to do with things that chain people down to this world; consequently He could go wherever His Father wanted Him to.

Approved Unto God, 8 R

Jesus Christ nowhere stands with the anti-property league. It is an easy business for me to mentally satirise the man who owns land and money when I don't. It is easy for me to talk about what I could do with a thousand pounds if I had it; the test is what I do with the 2½d* I have got. It may be hard for a rich man to enter into the kingdom of heaven, but it is just as hard for a poor man to seek first the kingdom of God. It is not eternal perdition, it is the perdition of losing the soul for this life. Jesus thought as much of the possibility of losing the highest good through poverty as through riches.

The Highest Good, 547 L
Two pence and a half penny, i.e., next to nothing

(Continued)

POVERTY (Continued)

The blood of the majority of Christians flows in hard cash. If ever we are to be loosened from the thing which keeps us poor in relation to God, we must shed our blood right out. "As having nothing, and yet possessing all things." The poverty of God's children in all ages is a significant thing, and the poverty has to come through calamity.

Bringing Sons Unto Glory, 233 R

We have grown literally afraid of being poor. We despise anyone who elects to be poor in order to simplify and save his inner life. If he does not join the general scramble, and pant with the moneymaking street, we deem him spiritless and lacking in ambition. We have lost the power of imagining what the ancient idealisation of poverty could have meant—the liberation from material attachments, the unbribed soul, the manlier indifference, the paying our way by what we are or do, and not by what we have; the right to fling away our life at any moment irresponsibly, the more athletic trim, in short, the moral fighting shape.

Christian Disciplines, Volume 2,
The Discipline of Loneliness, 321 L

To-day we are so afraid of poverty that we never dream of doing anything that might involve us in being poor. We are out of the running of the mediaeval monks who took on the vow of poverty. Many of us are poor, but none of us chooses to be. These men chose to be poor, they believed it was the only way they could perfect their own inner life.

Shade of His Hand, 1242 L

POWER

It is not the length of time we give to a thing that matters, but whether the time we give opens the door to the greatest power in our life. The greatest factor in life is that which exerts most power, not the element which takes most time. The five minutes we give to the words of Jesus the first thing in the morning are worth more than all the rest of the day.

Our Brilliant Heritage, 952 R

"And he said, Thy name shall be called no more Jacob, but Israel: for thou hast striven with God and with men, and hast prevailed." The warrior of God is not the man of muscle and a strong jaw, but the man of un-utterable weakness, the man who knows he has not any power; Jacob is no longer strong in himself, he is strong only in God; his life is no longer marked by striving, but by reliance on God. You cannot imitate reliance on God.

Our Portrait in Genesis, 978 L

PRAISE

Everything that God has created is like an orchestra praising Him. "All Thy works shall praise Thee." In the ear of God everything He created makes exquisite music, and man joined in the paean of praise until he fell; then there came in the frantic discord of sin. The realisation of Redemption brings man by way of the minor note of repentance back into tune with praise again. The angels are only too glad to hear that note, because it blends man into harmony again (see Luke 15:10).

Praising God is the ultimate end and aim of all we go through. "Whoso offereth praise glorifieth Me." What does it matter whether you are well or ill! whether you have money or none! It is all a matter of indifference; but one thing is not a matter of indifference, and that is that we are pleasing to the ears of God.

Approved Unto God, 4 L

It is a good thing to begin prayer with praising God for His attributes, and for the way those attributes have been brought to bear on our personal salvation. Let your mind soak in the deliverance of God, and then praise Him for them.

The Highest Good—The Pilgrim's Song Book, 533 L

PRAYER

We do not pray at all until we are at our wits' end. " . . . their soul fainted in them. *Then* they cried unto the Lord in their trouble" (Psalm 107:5–6). During this war many a man has prayed for the first time in his life. When a man is at his wits' end it is not a cowardly thing to pray, it is the only way he can get in touch with Reality.

Baffled to Fight Better, 72 R

Much of our praying has nothing in it; it is not the talk of a child to his Father when he has come up against things or is hurt. "Ask, and it shall be given you," Jesus says. We do not ask, we worry; whereas one minute in prayer will put God's decree at work, viz., that He answers prayer on the ground of Redemption.

Baffled to Fight Better, 73 R

The time a Christian gives to prayer and communion with God is not meant for his natural life, but meant to nourish the life of the Son of God in him. God engineers the circumstances of His saints in order that the Spirit may use them as the praying-house of the Son of God. If you are spiritual the Holy Spirit is offering up prayers in your bodily temple that you know nothing about; it is the Spirit making intercession in you (see Romans 8:26–27).

Biblical Ethics, 103 R

We hear it said that "Prayer alters things"; prayer not so much alters things as alters

the man who prays, and he alters things. When I am born from above the life of the Son of God is born in me, and I have to take time to nourish that life. The essential meaning of prayer is that it nourishes the life of the Son of God in me and enables Him to manifest Himself in my mortal flesh.

Biblical Ethics, 103 R

We cannot talk to God unless we walk with Him when we are not talking.

He Shall Glorify Me, 495 R

Prayer is not to be used as the petted privilege of a spoiled child seeking for ideal conditions in which to indulge his spiritual propensities *ad lib**; the purpose of prayer is the maintenance of fitness in an ideal relationship with God amid conditions which ought not to be merely ideal but really actual. . . . The purpose of prayer is to reveal the presence of God equally present all the time in every condition.

Christian Disciplines, Volume 2,
The Discipline of Prayer, 308 L
**Without restraint or limit*

We can always do what we want to do if we want to do it sufficiently keenly. Do it now, "enter into thy closet"; and remember: it is a place selected to pray in, not to make little addresses in, or for any other purpose than to pray in, never forget that. . . . It is to be a selected place, a secret shut-in place, where no one ever guesses what you are doing.

Christian Disciplines, Volume 2,
The Discipline of Prayer, 311 R

Prayer is not logical; it is a mysterious moral working of the Holy Spirit.

Christian Disciplines, Volume 2,
The Discipline of Prayer, 315 R

(Continued)

PRAYER *(Continued)*

Matthew 5:23–24: "Therefore if thou bring thy gift to the altar, and there rememberest that thy brother hath ought against thee; leave there thy gift before the altar, and go thy way; first be reconciled to thy brother, and then come and offer thy gift."

If you have incurred a debt and not paid it, or cared about paying it, or have spoken in the wrong mood to another, or been vindictive—these and similar things produce a wrong temper of soul and you cannot pray in secret; it is no use trying to pray until you do what the Lord says. The one thing that keeps us from doing it is pride, and pride has never yet prayed in the history of mankind.

Christian Disciplines, Volume 2,
The Discipline of Prayer, 312 L

"Again I say unto you, That if two of you shall agree on earth . . . ."

We need to know this simple, direct truth about praying in public. . . . Agreement in purpose on earth must not be taken to mean a predetermination to agree together to storm God's fort doggedly till He yields. It is far from right to agree beforehand over what we want, and then go to God and wait, not until He gives us His mind about the matter, but until we extort from Him permission to do what we had made up our minds to do before we prayed; we should rather agree to ask God to convey His mind and meaning to us in regard to the matter.

Christian Disciplines, Volume 2,
The Discipline of Prayer, 313 R

The prayer of the feeblest saint on earth who lives in the Spirit and keeps right with God is a terror to Satan.

Christian Disciplines, Volume 2,
The Discipline of Prayer, 317 R

Agreement in purpose on earth is not a public presentation of persistent begging which knows no limit, but a prayer which is conscious that it is limited through the moral nature of the Holy Ghost. It is really "symphonising" on earth with our Father Who is in heaven.

Christian Disciplines, Volume 2,
The Discipline of Prayer, 313 R

Learn to be vicarious in public prayer. Allow two rivers to come through you: the river of God, and the river of human interests. Beware of the danger of preaching in prayer, of being doctrinal.

Disciples Indeed, 399 L

We are not beggars on the one hand or spiritual customers on the other; we are God's children, and we just stay before Him with our broken treasures or our pain and watch Him mend or heal in such a way that we understand Him better.

Christian Disciplines, Volume 2,
The Discipline of Prayer, 313 L

The very powers of darkness are paralysed by prayer. No wonder Satan tries to keep our minds fussy in active work till we cannot think to pray.

Disciples Indeed, 397 L

God is not meant to answer *our* prayers; He is answering the prayer of Jesus Christ in our lives; by our prayers we come to discern what God's mind is, and that is declared in John 17.

Disciples Indeed, 397 L

God never answers prayer to prove His own might.

Disciples Indeed, 396 R

If we realise the intense sacredness of a human soul in God's sight we will no longer romp in where angels fear to tread; we will pray and wait.

Disciples Indeed, 411 L

The knowledge of where people are wrong is a hindrance to prayer, not an assistance. 'I want to tell you of the difficulties so that you may pray intelligently." The more you know the less intelligently you pray because you forget to believe that God can alter the difficulties.

God's Workmanship, 419 R

Watch how God will upset our programmes if we are in danger of making our little Christian habits our god. Whenever we begin to worship our habit of prayer or of Bible reading, God will break up that time. We say—"I cannot do this, I am praying; it is my hour with God." No, it is our hour with our habit; we pray to a habit of prayer.

Our Brilliant Heritage, 933 L

Prayer is other than meditation; it is that which develops the life of God in us. When a man is born from above, the life of the Son of God begins in him, and he can either starve that life or nourish it. Prayer is the way the life of God is nourished. Our Lord nourished the life of God in Him by prayer; He was continually in contact with His Father.

If Ye Shall Ask, 608 L

We heard it said that we shall suffer if we do not pray; I question it. What will suffer if we do not pray is the life of God in us; but when we do pray and devote the dawns to God His nature in us develops; there is less self-realisation and more Christ-realisation.

He Shall Glorify Me, 501 L

We generally look upon prayer as a means of getting things for ourselves; whereas the Bible idea of prayer is that God's holiness and God's purpose and God's wise order may be brought about, irrespective of who comes or who goes. Our ordinary views of prayer are not found in the New Testament.

If Ye Shall Ask, 608 L

Remember, what makes prayer easy is not our wits or our understanding, but the tremendous agony of God in Redemption. A thing is worth just what it costs. Prayer is not what it costs us, but what it cost God to enable us to pray. It cost God so much that a little child can pray. It cost God Almighty so much that anyone can pray.

If Ye Shall Ask, 611 R

We have to get down to the level where the reality works out, and the whole counsel comes back to this, "Watch and pray"—the secret of the sacred simplicity of prayer. Prayer imparts the power to walk and not faint, and the lasting remembrance of our lives is of the Lord, not of us.

If Ye Shall Ask, 613 R

We think of prayer as a preparation for work, or a calm after having done work, whereas prayer is the essential work. It is the supreme activity of everything that is noblest in our personality.

If Ye Shall Ask, 628 L

To ask how we are to get our prayers answered is a different point of view from the New Testament. According to the New Testament, prayer is God's answer to our poverty, not a power we exercise to obtain an answer.

If Ye Shall Ask, 632 L

"Unite my heart to fear Thy Name." My soul is all abroad because of the meanness, the self-consciousness, the less-than-the-best, which hover around and prevent me as I pray. Lord, be almighty for me!

Knocking at God's Door, July 17, 645 L

(Continued)

PRAYER (Continued)

O Lord, explore down to the deepest springs of my spirit where the Spirit maketh intercession for us, and read the prayers I cannot utter.

Knocking at God's Door, December 6, 651 L

Prayer that is not an effort of the will is unrecognised by God. "If ye abide in Me, and My words abide in you, ye shall ask what ye will, and it shall be done unto you," said Jesus. That does not mean ask anything you like, but ask what you *will*. What are you actively willing? ask for that. We shall find that we *ask* very few things.

The Moral Foundations of Life, 709 R

We have to pray with our eyes on God, not on the difficulties.

God's Workmanship, 450 R

Never *say* you will pray about a thing; *pray about it.* Our Lord's teaching about prayer is so amazingly simple but at the same time so amazingly profound that we are apt to miss His meaning. The danger is to water down what Jesus says about prayer and make it mean something more common sense; if it were only common sense, it was not worth His while to say it. The things Jesus says about prayer are supernatural revelations.

Our Brilliant Heritage, 951 L

There is no snare or danger of infatuation or pride or the "show business" in prayer. Prayer is a hidden, obscure ministry which brings forth fruit that glorifies the Father.

Our Brilliant Heritage, 953 R

Prayer means that we get into union with God's view of other people. Our devotion as saints is to identify ourselves with God's interests in other lives. God pays no attention to our personal affinities; He expects us to identify ourselves with *His* interests in others.

The Psychology of Redemption, 1090 R

Every time we pray our horizon is altered, our attitude to things is altered, not sometimes but every time, and the amazing thing is that we don't pray more.

The Place of Help, 1050 R

We are challenged straight away by the difference between our view of prayer and Our Lord's view. Prayer to us is not practical it is stupid, and until we do see that prayer is stupid, that is, stupid from the ordinary natural common-sense point of view, we will never pray. "It is absurd to think that God is going to alter things in answer to prayer!" But that is what Jesus says He will do. It sounds stupid, but it is a stupidity based on His Redemption.

So Send I You, 1323 L

Prayer the Battle (Ephesians 6:11–20)
The armour is for the battle of prayer. "Take up the whole armour of God. . . . Stand therefore, . . ." and then pray. The armour is not to fight in, but to shield us while we pray. Prayer is the battle.

So Send I You, 1324 L

Mark the significance of the term "labour." We refuse to pray unless we get thrills. May God save us from that counterfeit of true prayer; it is the intensest form of spiritual selfishness. We have to labour, and to labour along the line of His direction. Jesus Christ says—*Pray.* It looks stupid; but when we labour at prayer results happen all the time from His standpoint, because God creates something in answer to, and by means of prayer, that was not in existence before. *"Labour."* It is the one thing we will not do. We will take open-air meetings, we will preach—but labour at prayer! There is nothing thrilling about a labouring man's work, but it is the labouring man who makes the conceptions of the genius possible; and it is the labouring saint who makes the conceptions of his Master possible.

So Send I You, 1325 L

Prayer is the answer to every problem there is. How else could Our Lord's command in John 14:1 be fulfilled in our experience? How could we have an untroubled heart if we believed that the heathen who had not heard the Gospel were damned? What would the Redemption of Jesus Christ be worth, of what use would the revelation given in John 3:16 be, if it depended on the laggard laziness of Christians as to whether men are to be saved or not?

So Send I You, 1325 R

We have continually to pull ourselves up short and recognise the amazing simplicity of Jesus Christ's counsel. The reason we get perplexed is that we do not believe He is Sovereign Lord; we do not believe that He will never forget anything we remember; we conjure up a hundred and one things that we imagine He has forgotten. Instead of praying to the Lord of the harvest to thrust out labourers, we pray—"O Lord, keep my body right; see after this matter and that for me." Our prayers are taken up with our concerns, our own needs, and only once in a while do we pray for what He tells us to.

So Send I You, 1327 L

'But thou, when thou prayest, enter into thy closet, and when thou hast shut thy door, pray to thy Father which is in secret," i.e., get a place for prayer where no one imagines that that is what you are doing, shut the door and talk to God in secret. It is impossible to live the life of a disciple without definite times of secret prayer.

Studies in the Sermon on the Mount, 1455 R

Whenever the insistence is on the point that God answers prayer, we are off the track. The meaning of prayer is that we get hold of God, not of the answer.

My Utmost for His Highest, February 7, 747 L

"When thou prayest, enter into thy closet, and when thou hast shut thy door, pray to thy Father which is in secret" (Matthew 6:6).

Get into the habit of dealing with God about everything. Unless in the first waking moment of the day you learn to fling the door wide back and let God in, you will work on a wrong level all day; but swing the door wide open and pray to your Father in secret, and every public thing will be stamped with the presence of God.

My Utmost for His Highest, August 23, 815 R

In his prayer (Isaiah 37:16–20) Hezekiah tells God what he knows God knows already. That is the meaning of prayer—I tell God what I know He knows in order that I may get to know it as He does (cf. Matthew 6:8). It is not true to say that a man learns to pray in calamities, he never does; he calls on God to deliver him, but he does not pray (see Psalm 107:6, 13, 19). A man only learns to pray when there is no calamity.

Notes on Isaiah, 1382 L

PRAYER, INTERCESSION

The subject of intercessory prayer is weakened by the neglect of the idea with which we ought to start. We take for granted that prayer is preparation for work, whereas prayer is *the* work, and we scarcely believe what the Bible reveals, viz., that through intercessory prayer God creates on the ground of the Redemption; it is His chosen way of working.

Christian Disciplines, Volume 2, The Discipline of Prayer, 317 L

(Continued)

PRAYER, INTERCESSION
(Continued)

We lean to our own understanding, or we bank on service and do away with prayer, and consequently by succeeding in the external we fail in the eternal, because in the eternal we succeed only by prevailing prayer.

Christian Disciplines, Volume 2,
The Discipline of Prayer, 317 L

Intercession does not develop the one who intercedes; it blesses the lives of those for whom he intercedes. The reason so few of us intercede is because we don't understand this.

Disciples Indeed, 387 L

By intercessory prayer we can hold off Satan from other lives and give the Holy Ghost a chance with them. No wonder Jesus put such tremendous emphasis on prayer!

Disciples Indeed, 397 L

There is only one field of service that has no snares, and that is the field of intercession. All other fields have the glorious but risky snare of publicity; prayer has not. The key to all our work for God is in that one word we are apt to despise—"Pray." And prayer is "labourer" work.

If Ye Shall Ask, 631 R

If I am a Christian, I am not set on saving my own skin, but on seeing that the salvation of God comes through me to others, and the great way is by intercession.

Disciples Indeed, 396 L

When we pray we give God a chance to work in the unconscious realm of the lives of those for whom we pray; when we come into the secret place it is the Holy Ghost's passion for souls that is at work, not our passion, and He can work through us as He likes.

Studies in the Sermon on the Mount, 1455 L

The Bible knows nothing about a gift of prayer; the only prayer the Bible talks about is the prayer that is able to bring down something from God to men.

Disciples Indeed, 396 R

The illustrations of prayer our Lord uses are on the line of importunity, a steady, persistent, uninterrupted habit of prayer.

Disciples Indeed, 396 R

The reason for intercession is not that God *answers* prayer, but that God tells us to pray.

Disciples Indeed, 396 R

The meaning of prayer is that I bring power to bear upon another soul that is weak enough to yield and strong enough to resist; hence the need for strenuous intercessory prayer.

Disciples Indeed, 397 R

When God puts a weight on you for intercession for souls don't shirk it by talking to them. It is much easier to talk to them than to talk to God about them—much easier to talk to them than to take it before God and let the weight crush the life out of you until gradually and patiently God lifts the life out of the mire. That is where very few of us go.

God's Workmanship, 419 R

Whenever Our Lord spoke of importunity in intercession it was never for ourselves but for others. When by imperceptible degrees we stop praying for ourselves, we are "getting there."

Not Knowing Whither, 888 R

If I allow the saintly conscience to have way in me it will mean that I keep my own life steadfastly open towards God and keep steadfastly related to Him on the line of intercessory prayer for others. The clearing house for a guilty conscience is that by our intercession Jesus repairs the damage done to other lives, and the consolation to our conscience is amazing. The saintly conscience means that I maintain an open scrutiny before God, and that I carry out the sensitiveness gained there all through my life.

Our Brilliant Heritage, 936 R

The incalculable power of intercession comes in here. A Christian father or mother or teacher or friend can anticipate that moment in the life of their child or teacher or friend, so that when the awakening comes, the Spirit of God in answer to believing prayer holds off the world, the flesh and the devil and introduces the Friend of friends, the Lord Jesus Christ. I wish I could convey to you the imperative importance of intercessory prayer.

The Philosophy of Sin, 1117 L

I do believe that by intercessory prayer, as Jesus Himself has told us, the great power of God works in ways we cannot conceive.

The Philosophy of Sin, 1117 L

Our part in intercessory prayer is not to enter into the agony of intercession, but to utilise the common-sense circumstances God has placed us in, and the common-sense people He has put us amongst by His providence, to bring them before God's throne and give the Holy Spirit a chance to intercede for them. That is how God is going to sweep the whole world with His saints.

So Send I You, 1293 R

The Holy Spirit does reveal what is wrong in others, but His discernment is never for purposes of criticism, but for purposes of intercession. When the Holy Spirit reveals something of the nature of sin and unbelief in another, His purpose is not to make us feel the smug satisfaction of a critical spectator, "Well, thank God, I am not like that"; but to make us so lay hold of God for that one that God enables him to turn away from the wrong thing.

Studies in the Sermon on the Mount, 1461 L

Intercession means that we rouse ourselves up to get the mind of Christ about the one for whom we pray.

My Utmost for His Highest, March 30, 764 R

When we lose sight of God we become hard and dogmatic. We hurl our own petitions at God's throne and dictate to Him as to what we wish Him to do. We do not worship God, nor do we seek to form the mind of Christ. If we are hard towards God, we will become hard towards other people.

My Utmost for His Highest, March 30, 764 R

Get into the real work of intercession, and remember it is a work, a work that taxes every power; but a work which has no snare.

My Utmost for His Highest, March 30, 765 L

Beware of imagining that intercession means bringing our personal sympathies into the presence of God and demanding that He does what we ask.

My Utmost for His Highest, May 4, 776 R

Vicarious intercession means that we deliberately substitute God's interests in others for our natural sympathy with them.

My Utmost for His Highest, May 4, 776 R

Discernment is God's call to intercession, never to fault finding.

My Utmost for His Highest, May 3, 776 R

(Continued)

PRAYER, INTERCESSION
(*Continued*)

Preaching the gospel has a snare; intercessory prayer has none.

My Utmost for His Highest, March 30, 765 L

The real business of your life as a saved soul is intercessory prayer. Wherever God puts you in circumstances, pray immediately, pray that His Atonement may be realised in other lives as it has been in yours. Pray for your friends *now*; pray for those with whom you come in contact *now*.

My Utmost for His Highest, June 20, 793 L

PREACHERS / PREACHING

Paul gives Timothy indications of the right lines of work: he is to concentrate on the deposit of truth conveyed by the words of Scripture. As a preacher never have as your ideal the desire to be an orator or a beautiful speaker; if you do, you will not be of the slightest use. Read Matthew 23, and Mark 7, and see the rugged, taste-shattering language of Our Lord. An orator moves men to do what they are indifferent about; a preacher of the Gospel has to move men to do what they are dead-set against doing, viz., giving up the right to themselves.

Approved Unto God, 6 R

The one calling of a New Testament preacher is to uncover sin and reveal Jesus Christ as Saviour; consequently he cannot be poetical, he has to be surgical. We are not sent to give beautiful discourses which make people say, "What a lovely conception that is," but to unearth the devil and his works in human souls. We have to probe straight down where God has probed us, and the measure of the probing is the way God has probed us.

Approved Unto God, 7 L

Be keen in sensing those Scriptures that contain the truth which comes straight home, and apply them fearlessly. The tendency nowadays is to get a truth of God and gloss it over. Always keep the sense of the passage you expound. For example, in Malachi 2:13 the prophet tells the people that God will not regard their offerings, though they cover "the altar of the Lord with tears, with weeping, and with crying out." The context gives the reason: there is a wrong temper of mind and secret immorality.

Approved Unto God, 7 L

Let your text get such hold of you that you never depart from its application. Never use your text as a title for a speculation of your own, that is being an impertinent exploiter of the word of God.

Approved Unto God, 7 R

Whenever Paul talks about his call to preach the gospel, it is a "woe is unto me, if I preach not the gospel!" (1 Corinthians 9:16). It is not a calm, quiet choice, but a necessity laid upon him, an overmastering sense of call. The great note of Paul's life is that he is mastered by his mission; he cannot get away from it.

Approved Unto God, 9 L

The great passion in much of the preaching of to-day is to secure an audience. As workers for God our object is never to secure our audience, but to secure that the Gospel is presented to men. Never presume to preach unless you are mastered by the motive born of the Holy Ghost: "For I determined not to know any thing among you, save Jesus Christ, and Him crucified."

Approved Unto God, 10 R

Avoid the temptation to be slovenly in your mind and be deluded into calling it "depending on the Spirit." Don't misapply Matthew 10:19-20. Carelessness in spiritual matters is a crime.

Approved Unto God, 11 L

Keep yourself full to the brim in reading; but remember that the first great Resource is the Holy Ghost Who lays at your disposal the Word of God. The thing to prepare is not the sermon, but the preacher.

Approved Unto God, 11 R

A preacher must remember that his calling is different from every other calling in life; his personality has to be submerged in his message (cf. John 3:30). An orator has to work *with* men and enthuse them; a New Testament preacher has to come *upon* men with a message they resent and will not listen to at first.

Approved Unto God, 12 L

It is easy to tell men they must be saved and filled with the Holy Ghost; but we have to live amongst men and show them what a life filled with the Holy Ghost ought to be. A preacher has to come upon men with a message and a testimony that go together. The great pattern for every witness is the abiding Witness, the Lord Jesus Christ. He came down on men from above; He stood on our level, with what men never had, in order to save men.

Approved Unto God, 12 L

As preachers we are privileged by God to stand steadfast against any element that lowers His standard. We are called upon to confront the world with the Gospel of Christ, not to start off on side tracks of our own.

Approved Unto God, 12 R

Never choose a text, let the text choose you. . . . When a text has chosen you, the Holy Spirit will impress you with its inner meaning and cause you to labour to lead out that meaning for your congregation.

Approved Unto God, 13 L

Do we come to the Bible to be spoken to by God, to be made "wise unto salvation," or simply to hunt for texts on which to build addresses? There are people who vagabond through the Bible, taking sufficient only out of it for the making of sermons; they never let the word of God walk out of the Bible and talk to them. Beware of living from hand to mouth in spiritual matters; do not be a spiritual mendicant.

Our Brilliant Heritage, 954 R

The danger is to preach a subjective theology, i.e., that something wells up on the inside. The Gospel of the New Testament is based on the absoluteness of revelation; we cannot get at it by our common sense. If a man is to be saved it must be from outside; God never pumps up anything from within. As a preacher, base on nothing less than revelation, and the authenticity of the revelation depends on the character of the one who brings it. Our Lord Jesus Christ put His impress on every revelation from Genesis to Revelation.

Approved Unto God, 14 L

The only safety for the preacher is to face his soul not with his people, or even with his message, but to face his soul with his Saviour all the time.

Approved Unto God, 14 R

In preaching the Gospel remember that salvation is the great thought of God, not an experience. Experience is the gateway through which salvation comes into our conscious life, the evidence of a right relationship to Jesus Christ. Never preach experience; preach the great thought of God that lies behind.

Approved Unto God, 15 L

(Continued)

PREACHERS / PREACHING *(Continued)*

"He must increase, but I must decrease." That is the only standard for the preacher of the Gospel. John the Baptist is stating the truth that we have no right as preachers on the ground of our personality, but only because of the message we proclaim.

Approved Unto God, 15 R

So many preach the human aspect of Christ, His sympathy for the bereaved and the suffering and sin-stained, and men listen whilst Christ is brought down to their conditions; but a preacher has to bring the Gospel of God to men's needs, and to do this he has to uncover their need and men resent this—"I don't want to accept the verdict on myself that Jesus Christ brings; I don't believe I am so sinful as He reveals." A man never believes what Jesus Christ says about the human heart until the Holy Ghost gives him the startling revelation of the truth of His diagnosis (see Mark 7:20–23).

Approved Unto God, 15 R

Do we bear the marks of the Lord Jesus in our preaching, or do we leave our congregations with the impression of how sweet and winsome we are? Whether Paul's words were stinging or comforting, for praise or for condemnation, the one impression left was Jesus Christ and Him crucified, not Jesus Christ risen and exalted, but *crucified*.

Approved Unto God, 18 L

"*In pureness, in knowledge, in long-suffering, in kindness, in the Holy Ghost, in love unfeigned*" (*2 Corinthians 6:6 RV*).

"In kindness"—be perfectly clear and emphatic with regard to your preaching of God's truth, but amazingly kind in your treatment of people. Some of us have a hard, metallic way of dealing with people which never has the stamp of the Holy Ghost on it.

Facing Reality, 41 R

The reason some of us have no power in our preaching, no sense of awe, is that we have no passion for God, but only a passion for Humanity. The one thing we have to do is to exhibit Jesus Christ crucified, to lift Him up all the time. "*I, if I be lifted up from the earth, will draw all men unto Me.*"

Approved Unto God, 18 L

The call to preach is not because I have a special gift, or because Jesus has sanctified me, but that I have had a glimpse of God's meaning in the Cross, and life can never be the same again. The passion of Paul's preaching is the suffering of God Almighty exhibited in the Cross of Christ. Many who are working for God ought to be learning in the School of Calvary.

Approved Unto God, 18 R

Eliphaz makes out that Job's problems are not what he thinks they are; he tries to wear down Job's opposition by sheer ponderosity, i.e., saying nothing with terrific emphasis.

Baffled to Fight Better, 64 L

It is difficult to evade pose* in religious life because it is of the nature of unconscious priggishness. If you have the idea that your duty is to catch other people, it puts you on a superior platform at once and your whole attitude takes on the guise of a prig. This too often is the pose of the earnest religious person of to-day. Of all the different kind of men one meets the preacher takes the longest to get at, for this very reason; you can get at a doctor or any professional man much more quickly than you can a professionally religious man.

Baffled to Fight Better, 66 L
Implies an attitude deliberately assumed in order to impress others.

The preacher is there not by right of his personality or oratorical powers, but by right of the message he proclaims.

Biblical Ethics, 105 R

"Ye shall know them by their fruits"
(Matthew 7:16; see Matthew 7:15–20).

Jesus told His disciples to test preachers and teachers not by the fact that they prophesied in His name, but by their fruits. How many of us do?

Biblical Ethics, 122 L

Beware lest activity in proclaiming the Truth should mean a cunning avoidance of spiritual concentration in intercession.

Disciples Indeed, 397 R

If you stand true as a disciple of Jesus He will make your preaching the kind of message that is incarnate as well as oral.

Disciples Indeed, 397 L

Beware of stealing the hearts of the people of God in your mind. If once you get the thought, "It is my winsome way of putting it, my presentation of the truth that attracts"— the only name for that is the ugly name of thief, stealing the hearts of the sheep of God who do not know why they stop at you. Keep the mind stayed on God, and I defy anyone's heart to stop at you; it will always go on to God.

If Thou Wilt Be Perfect, 600 R

". . . *that they may see your good works*"
(Matthew 5:16).

Our Lord did not say "that you may preach the right thing." It is an easy business to preach, an appallingly easy thing to tell other people what to do; it is another thing to have God's message turned into a boomerang—"You have been teaching these people that they should be full of peace and of joy, but what about yourself? Are *you* full of peace and joy?" The truthful witness is the one who lets his light shine in works which exhibit the disposition of Jesus; one who *lives* the truth as well as preaches it.

The Love of God—The Ministry of the Unnoticed, 663 R

We may see no result in our congregation, but if we have presented the truth and anyone has seen it for one second, he can never be the same again; a new element has come into his life. It is essential to remember this and not to estimate the success of preaching by immediate results.

The Moral Foundations of Life, 697 L

We all know the boomerang effect of messages; after we have preached the Spirit of God comes and says, "What about you?"

Biblical Ethics, 122 R

God's denunciation will fall on us if in our preaching we tell people they must be holy and we ourselves are not holy. If we are not working out in our private life the messages we are handing out, we will deepen the condemnation of our own souls as messengers of God.

Disciples Indeed, 398 L

A twofold line runs all through God's Book, and especially in the Epistles of St. Paul, with regard to public preaching and teaching and dealing with people in private: Be as stern and unflinching as God Almighty in your preaching, but as tender and gentle as a sinner saved by grace should be when you deal with a human soul. To-day the order is being reversed and modern teaching is amazingly "easy-osy."

The Philosophy of Sin, 1135 L

It is one thing to thrill an audience with fine rhetoric, or by a magnetic personality, but the New Testament order of preaching is that of John the Baptist—"He must increase, but I must decrease."

The Place of Help, 1027 L

Preaching is worthy in God's sight when it costs something, when we are really living out what we preach.

The Servant as His Lord, 1284 L

(Continued)

PREACHERS / PREACHING *(Continued)*

You have preached to others? Yes, and God blessed your preaching, but from the second you begin to neglect the side issues of your life, that moment God begins to leave you alone as a worker for Him. God grant you may get back again, all the avenues clearly open to Him, avenues of heart and head and body and soul.

Workmen of God, 1362 L

If the preaching of a servant of God does not make me brace myself up and watch my feet and my ways, one of two things is the reason—either the preacher is unreal, or I hate being better. At some time or other all of us have had a detestation of being better.

Notes on Jeremiah, 1428 R

The test that prophets preach from the presence of God is that fruit appears, not in the shape of converts, but in the shape of godly living. "Ye shall know them by their fruits." The test is—How many people stop being mean,* being impure, stop committing sin? how many people learn to live rightly? The sign that God is in the word and making it living is the fruit of godliness in the lives of those who speak it and in the lives of their hearers.

Notes on Jeremiah, 1429 R
*Refers to something or someone ordinary, common, low, or ignoble rather than cruel or spiteful.

The insistent need in practical Christianity is to rely on the Spirit of God; it is the only way to kill the arrogant impudence of preachers. I look upon a congregation as those whom I have to induce to come to God—and I am made of the same stuff as they are!

Notes on Isaiah, 1383 L

Never water down God's word to suit men's experience. We palliate the truth of God because it offends, while in personal dealing our tendency is to be vindictive and hard. Be possessed with unflinching courage in preaching the truth of God, but when you deal with sinners, remember who you are. God tells Ezekiel to be concentrated on the message He gives him, no matter what result.

Notes on Ezekiel, 1476 R

"Because, even because, they have seduced My people, saying, 'Peace; and there is no peace'" (Ezekiel 13:10 RV).
Prophetic opportunism means preaching the truth of God, but without regard to being consistent with His holiness.

Notes on Ezekiel, 1481 L

The only reason for my being in the preacher's place is that I have heard God's voice and He has done something in me which He can for them; and I deliver God's message, knowing that the Spirit will apply it as I rely upon Him. Beware of ignoring the ministry of the Spirit by relying on your sensible knowledge of the people you talk to. The great snare in modern Christian enterprise is this very thing—"Do remember the people you are talking to." We have to stay true to God and His message, not to our knowledge of the people. We must not consider what the people want but what God wants us to present to them, and as we rely on His Spirit we find God works His marvels in His own way.

Notes on Isaiah, 1383 L

PREDESTINATION
(See also ELECTION)

We must be careful not to confuse the predestination of God by making His election include every individual; or to have the idea that because God elected a certain nation through whom His salvation was to come, therefore every individual of that nation is elected to salvation. The history of the elect nation disproves this, but it does not alter God's purpose for the nation. Individuals of the elect nation have to be saved in the same way as individuals of nations that have not been elected.

So Send I You, 1317 R

Election refers to the unchangeable purpose of God, not to the salvation of individuals. Each individual has to choose which line of predestination he will take—God's line or the devil's line. Individual position is determined by individual choice, but that is neither here nor there in connection with God's purpose for the human race.

So Send I You, 1317 R

Individuals enter into the realisation of the creative purpose of God for the human race by being born again of the Spirit; but we must not make the predestination of God for the race to include every individual, any more than God's predestination for the elect nation included every individual. Salvation is of universal application, but human responsibility is not done away with.

So Send I You, 1318 L

The election of God by creation is an illustration of, though not the same as, "the election of grace." Election by creation means that God created the people known as Israel for one purpose—to be His servants until through them every nation should come to know Him. The "election of grace" is that anyone, Jew or Gentile, can, by God's free grace, enter into relationship with Him in and through our Lord Jesus Christ. The realisation of the election of grace by regeneration, and of being thereby perfectly fitted for glorifying God, is the most joyful realisation.

Notes on Ezekiel, 1482 R

PREJUDICE

"Being the son (as was supposed) of Joseph" *(Luke 3:23 RV).*

There were many pre-conceptions about our Lord in His day, and this was a prevalent one. We do not bring with us those pre-conceptions, but we bring others; we have made up our mind that God will only come along certain lines, and like the religious people of His day, when He comes on another line, we do not recognise Him. It is difficult for anyone brought up with religious conceptions to get rid of them in the right way.

Bringing Sons Unto Glory, 238 L

In national life and in personal life delusion always arises when a word has been spoken by God and been perverted by prejudice. Beware what you are for and what you are against.

Notes on Ezekiel, 1484 L

Preaching from prejudice is dangerous; it makes a man dogmatic and certain that he is right. The question for each of us to ask ourselves is this: Would I recognise God if He came in a way I was not prepared for—if He came in the bustle of a marriage feast, or as a Carpenter? That is how Jesus Christ appeared to the prejudices of the Pharisees, and they said He was mad.

Baffled to Fight Better, 52 L

A prejudice is a foreclosed judgement without having sufficiently weighed the evidence. Not one of us is free from prejudices, and the way we reveal them most is by being full of objection to the prejudices of other people. If we stick obstinately to any line of prejudice, there will come the surgery of events that will shift us out of it. Watch that you do not make an issue with God; it is a dangerous thing to do.

Baffled to Fight Better, 84 R

(Continued)

PREJUDICE (Continued)

"How can ye believe, which receive glory one of another, and the glory that cometh from the only God ye seek not?" (John 5:44 RV).

These words of Jesus bring out the very essence of prejudice, viz., to foreclose judgement without sufficiently weighing the evidence. "It is a moral impossibility for you to believe in Me," Jesus says, "not because you are bad, but because you have another standard in view; you seek honour one of another." Remember, we only see along the line of our prejudice, and prejudice means ignorance; we are always prejudiced over what we know least about and we foreclose our judgement about it—"I have sealed the question, docketed it and put it into a pigeon-hole and I refuse to say anything more about it" (cf. John 9:22). Then it is impossible for you to see along any other line until you are willing to take the packet out of the pigeon-hole, unseal it and open the question again. Every point of view which I hold strongly makes me prejudiced and I can see nothing else but that point of view; there is a ban of finality about it which makes me intolerant of any other point of view.

Bringing Sons Unto Glory, 238 R

We only see along the line of our prejudices—our evangelical or un-evangelical prejudices, the prejudices of our belief or of our agnosticism; we cannot see otherwise until events operate on us. The surgery of events is a most painful thing. It has taken a devilish thing like this war to root up the prejudices of men who were misrepresenting God to themselves.

Baffled to Fight Better, 84 R

PRESENCE OF GOD

God cannot come to me in any way but His own way, and His way is often insignificant and unobtrusive.

Disciples Indeed, 389 R

"In every thing give thanks," says Paul, not—Give thanks *for* everything, but give thanks that in everything that transpires there abides the real Presence of God. God is more real than the actual things— "therefore will not we fear, though the earth be removed."

The Place of Help, 1026 R

The purpose of prayer is to reveal the presence of God equally present all the time in every condition.

Christian Disciplines, Volume 2,
The Discipline of Prayer, 308 L

PRETENCE / PRETENDING

It is appallingly easy to pretend. If once our eyes are off Jesus Christ, pious pretence is sure to follow . . . . not hypocrisy (a hypocrite is one who tries to live a two-fold life for his own ends and succeeds), but a desperately sincere effort to be right when we know we are not.

Studies in the Sermon on the Mount, 1468 L

We have to beware of pretence in ourselves. It is an easy business to appear to be what we are not. It is easy to talk and to preach, and to preach our actual life to damnation. It was realising this that made Paul say— "I keep under my body, . . . lest that by any means, when I have preached to others, I myself should be a castaway." The more facile the expression in words, the less likely is the truth to be carried out in life. There is a peril for the preacher that the listener has not, the peril of expressing a thing and letting the expression react in the exhaustion of never doing it.

Studies in the Sermon on the Mount, 1468 R

PRIDE

God alters our estimates, and we shall find that God gives us a deeper horror of carnality than ever we had of immorality; a deeper horror of the pride which lives clean amongst men but lifts itself against God, than of any other thing. Pride is the central citadel of independence of God.

Biblical Psychology, 171 R

How does Jesus Christ treat me? Let me receive the Holy Spirit and I will very soon know. He will treat me as He treats every man—mercilessly with regard to sin.

We say, "O Lord, leave a little bit of pride, a little bit of self-realisation." God can never save human pride. Jesus Christ has no mercy whatever when it comes to conviction of sin. He has an amazing concern for the sinner, but no pity for sin.

Conformed to His Image, 372 R

It is easy to be shocked at immorality, but how much education in the school of Christ, how much reliance on the Holy Spirit, does it take to bring us to the place where we are shocked at pride against God? That sensitiveness is lacking to-day.

Conformed to His Image, 373 R

Certain forms of sin shock us far more than they shock God. The sin that shocks God, the sin that broke His heart on Calvary, is not the sin that shocks us. The sin that shocks God is the thing which is highly esteemed among men—self-realisation, pride, my right to myself. . . . We have to remember that in the sight of God there are no social conventions, and that external sins are no whit worse in His sight than the pride which hates the rule of the Holy

Ghost while the life is morally clean. May God have mercy on any one of us who forgets this, and allows spiritual pride or superiority and a sense of his own unsulliedness, to put a barrier between him and those whom God has lifted from depths of sin he cannot understand.

Conformed to His Image, 380 R

Self-complacency and spiritual pride are always the beginning of degeneration. When I begin to be satisfied with where I am spiritually, instantly I begin to degenerate.

Disciples Indeed, 394 L

There is no pride equal to spiritual pride, and no obstinacy equal to spiritual obstinacy, because they are nearest to the throne of God, and are most like the devil.

Disciples Indeed, 394 L

The only reason I can't get to God is pride, no matter how humble I seem.

Disciples Indeed, 394 L

The only sacrifice acceptable to God is "a broken and a contrite heart," not a moral upright life built on pride. When I stand on the basis of penitence, God's salvation is manifested immediately.

Disciples Indeed, 394 L

We are apt to tone down the things Our Lord tiraded against—pride, self-realisation, etc. When a man is guilty of wrong things, he recognises instantly that there is a chance of being delivered; but the righteous man sits self-governed in his own right; he is his own god.

Shade of His Hand, 1218 L

(Continued)

PRIDE *(Continued)*

The thing that makes me feel I am different from "the common herd" never came from God: I am not different. Remember, the same stuff that makes the criminal makes the saint.

Disciples Indeed, 403 L

In the majority of cases we don't care a bit about a soul rebelling against Jesus Christ, but we do care about his humiliating us.

Disciples Indeed, 411 R

The real attitude of sin in the heart towards God is that of being without God; it is pride, the worship of myself, that is the great atheistic fact in human life.

God's Workmanship, 446 R

There is more pride in human grief and misery than in joy and health; certain elements in human sorrow are as proud as the devil himself. There are people who indulge in the luxury of misery; they are always talking of the agonising and distressing things—"No one ever suffered as I do; there is a special element in my suffering, it is isolated." At the back of it is terrific pride; it is weeping that will not stoop.

He Shall Glorify Me, 489 L

We are to be of the stamp of Our Lord and Master, and the prigs of His day called Him a glutton and a winebibber; they said He was not dealing with the profound things. Beware of the production of contempt for others by thinking that they are shallow. To be shallow is not a sign of being wicked; the ocean has a shore. The shallow amenities of life are appointed of God and are the things in which Our Lord lived, and He lived in them as the Son of God. It is easier for personal pride not to live in them. Beware of posing as a profound person; God became a Baby.

Not Knowing Whither, 884 L

There is a subtle thing that goes by the name of unworthiness which is petulant pride with God. When we are shy with other people it is because we believe we are superior to the average person and we won't talk until they realise our importance. Prayerlessness with God is the same thing; we are shy with God not because we are unworthy, but because we think God has not given enough consideration to our case; we have some peculiar elements He must be pleased to consider. We have to go to school in order to learn not to take ourselves seriously and to get the genuine unworthiness which no longer is shy before God.

If Ye Shall Ask, 629 L

When a man really sees himself as the Lord sees him, it is not the abominable sins of the flesh that shock him, but the awful nature of the pride of his own heart against Jesus Christ.

My Utmost for His Highest, March 8, 757 R

Pride submerges itself and becomes piety, but it is just as devilish.

Notes on Jeremiah, 1429 R

Pride in its most estimable as well as its most debased form is self-deification; it is not a yielding to temptation from without, but a distinct alteration of relationships within. Watch where you are not willing to give up your self-confident obstinacy in little things, and you will know how much pride there is in your heart.

Notes on Ezekiel, 1484 R

PRINCIPLES

Nothing must switch the disciple's loyalty to his Lord by loyalty to principles deduced from His teaching. There are no infallible principles, only an infallible Person.

Disciples Indeed, 406 L

The one mark of a disciple is moral originality. The Spirit of God is a well of water in the disciple, perennially fresh. When once the saint begins to realise that God engineers circumstances, there will be no more whine, but only a reckless abandon to Jesus. Never make a principle out of your own experience; let God be as original with other people as He is with you.

Our Brilliant Heritage, 947 R

In the Christian domain we make the blunder of trying to guide our life by the principles of Jesus Christ's teaching. The basis of Christianity is not primarily virtue and honesty and goodness, not even holiness, but a personal relationship to God in Jesus Christ which works out all the time by "spontaneous moral originality." Principles are of a lesser order, and if they are applied apart from the life of Jesus Christ they may become anti-Christian.

Shade of His Hand, 1235 R

PRIORITIES

We reverse the teaching of Jesus: we don't seek first the Kingdom of God we seek every other thing first, and the result accords with what Jesus said: the word He puts in is choked and becomes unfruitful.

Conformed to His Image, 376 L

PROMISES OF GOD

Think of the ridiculously legal way we treat the promises; we say to God, "You made this promise now fulfil it." The promise itself is the fulfillment; God's presence is *in* the promise. No one can fulfil a promise but the one who made it. "For all the promises of God in Him are yea, and in Him Amen, unto the glory of God by us" (2 Corinthians 1:20), not "yea and Amen" to faith, but *in* Christ Jesus.

Notes on Isaiah, 1381 R

Whenever you debate with a promise of God, watch how you begin to manœuvre by your own prudence—but you can't sleep at night.

Our Portrait in Genesis, 976 L

The God who guides the stars, unhasting and unresting, will as assuredly fulfil what He has promised.

Notes on Isaiah, 1384 R

PROPHET(S) / PROPHECY, OLD TESTAMENT

A prophet is not a sanctified gypsy telling fortunes, but one who speaks as he is moved by the Holy Spirit within.

Christian Disciplines, Volume 2,
The Discipline of Loneliness, 330 R

The great inspiring Mind behind the prophets and the apostles is not an ingenious human mind, but the Mind of Almighty God. "For the prophecy came not in old time by the will of man: but holy men of God spake *as they were moved by the Holy Ghost*" (2 Peter 1:21).

Notes on Isaiah, 1369 R

(Continued)

PROPHET(S) / PROPHECY, OLD TESTAMENT (Continued)

The prophets speak with all the blood and passion of their natures; they do not stand off like a superior authority, they are wrapped up in their prophecy. Notice the identification of the prophet with the life of his time; we gather our spiritual skirts from touching the life of the time we are in. These men did not; they stood for God in every condition of things.

Notes on Isaiah, 1369 R

The 53rd chapter of Isaiah stands alone as a great burst of amazing prophecy. The greatest spiritual exposition of the Lord Jesus Christ is not in the New Testament; it is in this chapter, given by a man who lived hundreds of years before Christ was born. If you want to know the characterisation of the Person of Christ you will find it here, sketched by His Father, through the mouth of Isaiah.

Notes on Isaiah, 1387 L

PROSPERITY

In times of prosperity we are apt to forget God; we imagine it does not matter whether we recognise Him or not. As long as we are comfortably clothed and fed and looked after, our civilisation becomes an elaborate means of ignoring God.

The Highest Good—The Pilgrim's Song Book, 529 R

We blunder when we try to make out that the prosperity referred to in the Old Testament is intended for us in this dispensation. Plainly that prosperity has never yet been fulfilled in the history of the world; it is going to be fulfilled, but it does not refer to this dispensation, which is the dispensation of the humiliation of the saints, not of their glorification. One of Satan's greatest

delusions is to decoy folks off on to blessings that are merely secondary.

The Highest Good—The Pilgrim's Song Book, 526 R

A man's idea of prosperity is according to where his hopes are founded—on God or on a hearsay God; on the living God, or on ideas of God.

Christian Disciplines, Volume 2, The Discipline of Loneliness, 332 L

PSYCHOLOGY, CHRISTIAN

Christian Psychology is based on the knowledge of the Lord Jesus Christ, not on the knowledge of ourselves.

The Psychology of Redemption, 1061 L

In Christian Psychology we have not to introspect as we do in natural psychology; we have to accept the revelations given to us in and through our Lord Jesus Christ; that is, we must take all our bearings from the Son of God, not from our natural wits. We have not to study and understand ourselves; but to understand the manifestation in us of the life of the Son of God Who became Son of Man, the Lord Jesus Christ.

The Psychology of Redemption, 1061 L

PUNISHMENT

Cain takes God's punishment, which is His mercy, and perverts it into a penal decree making it impossible for him to come back. He entrenches himself in despair as a garment and spits back accusations against God—"See what You have done; I can't get back." When we are punished by God for wrong-doing our attitude is apt to be—"Oh well, it's no use trying to do any better; God has sent me from His presence, and I can't get back; I can do as I like now." Beware of making the despairing-sulk complaint, which is found in all of us, a threatening accusation against God. God can never forgive despair. The door is always open to God until I shut it. God never shuts it; I shut it, then I lose the key and say, "It's all up; whatever I do now God is entirely to blame."

Our Portrait in Genesis, 962 R

A man may sin magnificently, but he is punished drearily. The whole of our prison system is a day after day nemesis which makes men wish they had died rather than that the gates of paradise had clanged behind them.

God's Workmanship, 463 R

"And it came to pass, when they were in the field, that Cain rose up against Abel his brother, and slew him" (Genesis 4:8).

No man can murder his brother who has not first murdered God in himself. Cain's crime is more than murdering his brother; it is a deeper crime within that crime, viz., the putting up of his whole nature against God, and, finally, accusing God for his punishment—"Of course, my sin is unpardonable if You are a holy God, but You are to blame for being a holy God."

Our Portrait in Genesis, 962 L

PURITY

If you want to know what a pure heart is, read the life of the Lord Jesus Christ as recorded in the New Testament. His is a pure heart; anything less is not.

The Highest Good, 541 R

The seal of doom in a man is that he cannot believe in purity, and this can only be accounted for by an internal twist; no man gets there easily.

Not Knowing Whither, 888 R

"Mortify therefore your members which are upon the earth; fornication, uncleanness, passion, evil desire, and covetousness, the which is idolatry" (Colossians 3:5 RV).

In this passage Paul mentions things that are of the nature of rubbish, and he mentions them in their complete ugliness . . . and he says, "Mortify them, destroy them by neglect." Certain things can only be dealt with by ignoring them; if you face them you increase their power. It is absurd to say, Pray about them; when once a thing is seen to be wrong, don't pray about it, it fixes the mind on it; never for a second brood on it; destroy it by neglect.

Biblical Ethics, 104 L

No man or woman on earth is immune; each one of us knows the things we should not think about, or pray about, but resolutely neglect. It is a great thing for our moral character to have something to ignore. It is because these things are not understood that there is so much inefficiency in spiritual life. What Christianity supplies is "the expulsive power of a new affection."

Biblical Ethics, 104 L

The touchstone of truth is not a big intellect but a pure heart—a holy man.

Biblical Ethics, 122 L

There is a difference between innocence and purity. Innocence is the true condition of a child; purity is the characteristic of men and women. Innocence has always to be shielded; purity is something that has been tested and tried and has triumphed; something that has character at the back of it, that can overcome, and has overcome.

Biblical Psychology, 175 R

(Continued)

PURITY (Continued)

Innocence in a child's life is a beautiful thing, but men and women ought not to be innocent; they ought to be tested and tried and pure. No man is born pure: purity is the outcome of conflict. The pure man is not the man who has never been tried, but the man who knows what evil is and has overcome it.

Studies in the Sermon on the Mount, 1444 R

"How then can I do this great wickedness, and sin against God?" (Genesis 39:9).

The phrase "complete steel" is Milton's definition of chastity, and is peculiarly appropriate to Joseph. Personal chastity is an impregnable barrier against evil. Like virtue, chastity is not a gift, but an attainment of determined integrity. Unsoiledness may be nothing more than necessity, the result of a shielded life, and is no more chastity than innocence is purity. Virtue and chastity are forged by me, not by God. You can't drown a cork, and you can't defile Joseph.

Our Portrait in Genesis, 980 R

The man who discovers that he can find no way out may go into the pigsty and let every passion have its way; but when a man has been gripped by purity and has seen God if only for one minute, he may try and live in a pigsty but he will find he cannot; there is something that produces misery and longing even while he lets loose his passions.

Shade of His Hand, 1198 L

Disinclination to sin is not virtue, any more than innocence is purity. Innocence has always to be shielded; purity is something that has been tested and tried and has triumphed, something that has character at the back of it, that can overcome, and has overcome. Virtue is acquired, and so is purity.

The Shadow of an Agony, 1182 L

. . . with the purity Jesus Christ puts in He can take us where He went Himself, and make us capable of facing the vilest moral corruption unspotted; He will keep us as pure as He is Himself.

Studies in the Sermon on the Mount, 1447 L

Virtue is the overcoming by moral strength an inclination to go the other way.

Notes on Isaiah, 1379 L

PURPOSE

Our lives mean much more than we can tell; they fulfil some purpose of God about which we know nothing; our part is to trust in the Lord with all our heart and not lean to our own understanding. Earthly wisdom can never come near the threshold of the Divine; if we stop short of the Divine we stop short of God's purpose for our lives.

Bringing Sons Unto Glory, 236 L

The destiny of mankind in the purpose of God is not to do something, but to *be* something—"that they may be one, even as We are one."

Bringing Sons Unto Glory, 236 R

After sanctification it is difficult to state what your aim in life is, because God has taken you up into His purposes. The design for God's service is that He can use the saint as His hands or His feet. Jesus taught that spiritually we should "grow as the lilies," bringing out the life that God blesses.

Conformed to His Image, 371 R

Nothing can hinder God's purpose in a personal life but the person himself.

Disciples Indeed, 394 R

To-day we hold conferences and conventions and give reports and make our programmes. None of these things were in the life of Jesus, and yet every minute of

His life He realised that He was fulfilling the purpose of His Father (e.g. John 9:4). How did He do it? By maintaining the one relationship, and it is that one relationship He insists on in His disciples, and it is the one we have lost in the rubbish of modern civilisation.

The Highest Good, 548 R

To say that if a man is committing sin he will hinder the purpose of God, is not true; if a *leader* is trying to serve his own ends, he will hinder the purpose of God. For instance, if I were to try and utilise this house of God* for my own ends, the atmosphere of the house would be damaged instantly. Personal sin does not present a barrier in God's house, although it does put a barrier between the one who is sinning and God; but immediately anyone tries to utilise God's house, or God's people, or God's things for his own purposes and ends, then the atmosphere is altered at once.

Not Knowing Whither, 870 L
*The Bible Training College, London

Individually we may thwart God's purpose in our lives for a time, but God's purpose will be fulfilled, wherever we end. Human free will is God's sovereign work, and God not only respects it in man but He delights to posit it in him. I have perfect power not to do God's will, and I have that power by the sovereign will of God; but I can never thwart God's will ultimately.

Not Knowing Whither, 879 R

We have to be for God's purpose, and God cannot explain His purpose until it happens.

Not Knowing Whither, 907 L

God brings His purposes to pass in spite of all men may do, and often through what they do, and He will utilise the very things which look as if they were going dead against their fulfilment; God goes steadily on and involves us in the fulfilment.

Our Portrait in Genesis, 981 R

We have no conception of what God is aiming at, and it gets more and more vague as we go on. At the beginning of our Christian life we have our own particular notions as to what God's purpose is—we are meant to go here, or there; or, God has called us to do this or that piece of work. We go and do the thing and still we find the big compelling of God remains. The majority of the work we do is so much scaffolding to further the purpose of the big compelling of God. "He took unto Him the twelve." He takes us all the time; there is more than we have got at, something we have not seen.

The Place of Help, 1039 L

There is a purpose in every life that is in God's keeping of which we know little, but which He will fulfil if we let Him rightly relate us to Himself.

The Servant as His Lord, 1262 R

"And straightway He constrained His disciples to get into the ship, and to go to the other side. . . ." (Mark 6:45; see verses 45–52).

What is my dream of God's purpose? His purpose is that I depend on Him and on His power now. If I can stay in the middle of the turmoil calm and unperplexed, that is the end of the purpose of God. God is not working towards a particular finish; His end is the process—that I see Him walking on the waves, no shore in sight, no success, no goal, just the absolute certainty that it is all right because I see Him walking on the sea. It is the process, not the end, which is glorifying to God.

My Utmost for His Highest, July 28, 806 L

(Continued)

PURPOSE *(Continued)*

The first thing that happens after we have realised our election to God in Christ Jesus is the destruction of our prejudices and our parochial notions and our patriotisms; we are turned into servants of God's own purpose. . . . And when we are born again we are brought into the realisation of God's great purpose for the human race, viz., I am created for God, He made me. Beware lest you forget God's purpose for your life.

My Utmost for His Highest, September 21, 825 L

We have to see that we keep the windows of our soul open to God's creative purpose for us, and not confuse that purpose with our own intentions. Every time we do so, God has to crush our intentions and push them on one side, however it may hurt, because they are on the wrong line. We must beware lest we forget God's purpose for our life.

So Send I You, 1317 R

READINESS

Readiness means a right relationship to God and a knowledge of where we are at present. We are so busy telling God where we would like to go. . . . We wait with the idea of some great opportunity, something sensational, and when it comes we are quick to cry—"Here am I." Whenever Jesus Christ is in the ascendant, we are there; but we are not ready for an obscure duty.

My Utmost for His Highest, April 18, 771 L

Readiness for God means that we are ready to do the tiniest little thing or the great big thing, it makes no difference. We have no choice in what we want to do; whatever God's programme may be we are there, ready.

My Utmost for His Highest, April 18, 771 L

Keep your soul fit to manifest the life of the Son of God. Never live on memories; let the word of God be always living and active in you.

My Utmost for His Highest, May 14, 780 R

READING *(See BOOKS)*

REALITY *(See also FACTS)*

In the invincible blackness caused by Job's condition death seems the only way out. In every age which has seen a great upheaval the initial stage has always been marked by the advocacy of suicide, which is an indication of the agony produced by facing things as they are. The basis of things is wild. The only way you can live your life pleasantly is by being either a pagan or a saint; only by refusing to think about things as they are can we remain indifferent.

Baffled to Fight Better, 50 R

Our Lord always dealt with the "basement" of life, i.e., with the real problem; if we only deal with "the upper storey" we do not realise the need of the Redemption; but once we are hit on the elemental line, as this war has hit men, everything becomes different. There are many men to-day who for the first time in their lives find themselves in the midst of the elemental with no civilised protection, and they go through appalling agony.

Baffled to Fight Better, 50 L

It is quite possible to be a sincere person, to be in earnest in proclaiming the truth of God, and yet not have one iota of reality along with it. This does not mean that the sincere person is a hypocrite or a sham, but it does mean that he has never understood that God wants him to be *real*.

He Shall Glorify Me, 513 L

Let us face life as it is, not as we feel it ought to be, for it never will be what it ought to be until the kingdom of this world is become the kingdom of our Lord, and of His Christ.

Christian Disciplines, Volume 1,
The Discipline of Peril, 294 L

The lives that are getting stronger are lives in the desert, deep-rooted in God; they always remind you of God whenever you come in contact with them.

Disciples Indeed, 411 L

"And they come unto thee as the people cometh, and they sit before thee as My people, and they hear thy words, but do them not" (Ezekiel 33:31 RV).

God not only requires us to have a right attitude to Him, He requires us to allow His truth to so react in us that we are actively related to Him. These people flocked to Ezekiel like disciples to a teacher; they looked exactly like God's children; the difference was not on the outside but on the inside, and it would take the penetration of God to see it; but it was all pose, they were not real.

God's Workmanship, 446 R

The strength of a *real* man or *real* woman cannot be estimated.

He Shall Glorify Me, 513 R

If we are in Christ the whole basis of our goings is God, not conceptions of God, not ideas of God, but God Himself. We do not need any more ideas about God; the world is full of ideas about God; they are all worthless, because the ideas of God in anyone's head are of no more use than our own ideas. What we need is a real God, not more ideas about Him.

If Thou Wilt Be Perfect, 587 R

How many of us spend our time expecting that we will be something we are not. "Oh the time is coming when I am going to be so and so." It never will come; the time is always *now*. The amazing thing about the salvation of our Lord is that He brings us into contact with the reality that is, until we are just like children, continually seeing the wonder and beauty of things around us.

The Moral Foundations of Life, 710 L

We long for some thing that is not and shut our eyes to the thing that is. When the Lord Jesus awakens us to reality by new birth and brings us in contact with Himself, He does not give us new fathers and mothers and new friends; He gives us new sight, that is, we focus our eyes on the things that are near and they become wonderfully distant. "Put thy distance on the near." This craving to go somewhere else, to see the things that are distant, arises from a refusal to attend to what is near.

The Moral Foundations of Life, 710 R

One soul attending to reality is an emancipation to hundreds more.

The Moral Foundations of Life, 711 R

The discipline of disillusionment brings us to the place where we see men and women as they are, and yet there is no cynicism, we have no stinging, bitter things to say. Many of the cruel things in life spring from the fact that we will suffer from illusions; we are not true to one another as facts, we are only true to our ideas of one another. Everything is either delightful and fine, or else mean and dastardly, according to our own ideas. Jesus Christ is the Master of the human soul, He knows what is in the human heart (see Mark 7:21–22), and He has no illusions about any man.

The Place of Help, 1000 L

(Continued)

REALITY (*Continued*)

We can be spiritual in prayer meetings, in congenial spiritual society, in what is known as Christian work, but we cannot be spiritual in drudgery. . . . We are trying to develop a life that is sanctified and holy but it is spiritually inefficient—it cannot wash feet, it cannot do secular things without being tainted. Spiritual means *real*, and the only type of spiritual life is the life of our Lord Himself; there was no sacred and secular in His life, it was all real.

The Place of Help, 1037 L

Everything man has ever done is constantly being obliterated; everything a man fights for and lives for passes; he has so many years to live and then it is finished. This is neither fiction nor dumps*. In true thinking of things as they are, there is always a bedrock of unmitigated sadness. Optimism is either religious or temperamental. No man who thinks and faces life as it actually is, can be other than pessimistic. There is no way out unless he finds it by his religious faith or is blinded by his temperament.

Shade of His Hand, 1195 R
*Despondency

The Bible always emphasises the facts of life as they are. Whenever Jesus Christ applied His teaching to actual life He focused it round two points—marriage and money. If the religion of Jesus Christ and the indwelling of the Spirit of God cannot deal with these things and keep a man and woman as God wants them to be, His religion is useless.

Shade of His Hand, 1210 L

The peril of the inevitable barriers is that if I have not faced the facts sufficiently, I am apt to blame God for them. There is one fact more that I do not know, and that fact lies entirely with God, not with me. It is no use to spend my time saying, I wish I was not like this; I am just like it. The practical point in Christianity is—Can Jesus Christ and His religion be of any use to me as I am, not as I am not? Can He deal with me where I am, in the condition I am in?

Shade of His Hand, 1217 R

If I want to get at reality my conscience must witness as well as my emotions. I may talk like an archangel and live like a pig; I may write magnificent stuff and have fine conceptions, and people may be thrilled, but that does not prove that I have touched reality.

The Shadow of an Agony, 1162 L

"Not every one that saith unto Me, Lord, Lord, shall enter into the kingdom of heaven; but he that doeth the will of my Father which is in heaven" (Matthew 7:21).

Our Lord is warning that it is possible to wear the label without having the goods; possible for a man to wear the badge of being His disciple when he is not. Labels are all right, but if we mistake the label for the goods we get confused.

Studies in the Sermon on the Mount, 1470 L

"And then will I profess unto them, I never knew you: depart from Me, ye that work iniquity" (Matthew 7:23).

In these solemn words Jesus says He will have to say to some Bible expositors, some prophetic students, some workers of miracles—"Depart from Me, ye that work iniquity." To work iniquity is to twist out of the straight; these men have twisted the ways of God and made them unequal. "I never knew you"—you never had My Spirit, you spoke the truth and God honoured it, but you were never *of* the truth. "Depart from Me," the most appallingly isolating and condemning words that could be said to a human soul.

Studies in the Sermon on the Mount, 1470 R

Come unto Me" (Matthew 11:28).

Nothing is so important as to keep right spiritually. The great solution is the simple one—"Come unto Me." The depth of our reality, intellectually, morally and spiritually, is tested by these words. In every degree in which we are not real, we will dispute rather than come.

My Utmost for His Highest, August 19, 814 L

REASON / RATIONALISM

Reason is our guide among the facts of life, but it does not give us the explanation of them. Sin, suffering, and the Book of God all bring a man to the realisation that there is something wrong at the basis of life, and it cannot be put right by his reason.

Baffled to Fight Better, 50 L

The basis of things fundamentally is not reasonable; if it were, God would be cruel to allow what He does. Our reason is simply an instrument, the way we explain things; it is not the basis of things. The problems of life are only explainable by means of a right relationship to God.

Conformed to His Image, 377 R

Thank God for logic and for reason; they are instruments for expressing our life, but life itself is not reasonable.

The Psychology of Redemption, 1102 R

The basis of things is not rational, but tragic. Reason is our guide among facts as they are, but reason cannot account for things being

as they are. This does not mean that a man is not to use his reason; reason is the biggest gift he has.

Shade of His Hand, 1194 R

The rationalist says that everything in between birth and death is discernible by human reason; but the actual experience of life is that things do not run in a reasonable way; there are irrational elements to be reckoned with.

Shade of His Hand, 1194 R

Logic and reason are always on the hunt for definition, and anything that cannot be defined is apt to be defied. Rationalism usually defies God and defies life; it will not have anything that cannot be defined on a rational basis, forgetting that the things that make up elemental human life cannot be defined.

Baffled to Fight Better, 56 R

Things cannot be worked out on a logical line; there is always something incalculable. You may think to reach your goal through obedience to a set of principles, but you will find it won't work that road. Solomon says that neither the good man nor the bad man ends where you expect him to. All you can say is that every man has his own setting from a starting-point he knows nothing about.

Shade of His Hand, 1235 R

Nothing bold has ever been done in the name of rationalism. In all the big crises of life the rationalist is at a discount. He is great at writing books, at pointing out the futilities of religion, etc., but no rationalist has ever produced the heroism, the adventure, or the nobility that the people and the things he criticised have produced.

Shade of His Hand, 1241 L

(Continued)

REASON / RATIONALISM (Continued)

If you go on the economical basis you get into confusion. Rationalism makes us timid, shrewd in criticising, but nothing else. We never do the things that foolish people do.

Shade of His Hand, 1241 L

Sum up your life as it actually is, and, unless you look at actual things from a religious or a temperamental or an intellectual standpoint, everything is to be said for this philosophy: Eat, drink and be merry, for tomorrow we die. If Rationalism is the basis of things, that is undoubtedly the most reasonable thing to do. But if the basis of things is tragic, then the Bible standpoint comes nearer the solution, and Nietzsche is nearer the truth than any rationalist. Nietzsche declares that the basis of things is tragic, and that the way out is by the merciless Superman; the Bible reveals that the basis of things is tragic, and that the way out is by Redemption.

Shade of His Hand, 1195 R

RECOGNITION

"This wisdom have I seen also under the sun, and it seemed great unto me: There was a little city, and few men within it; and there came a great king against it, and besieged it, and built great bulwarks against it: now there was found in it a poor wise man, and he by his wisdom delivered the city; yet no man remembered that same poor man. Then said I, Wisdom is better than strength: nevertheless the poor man's wisdom is despised, and his words are not heard" (Ecclesiastes 9:13–16).

We do not put any price at all on wisdom when we have got what wisdom brings. When we attain success we do not remember the one who gave us the right counsel; the wise man who guided things aright is not taken into account. When a thing is

done successfully in the Army or the Navy, it is very rarely the men of the regiment or the crew that are mentioned but only the figure head at the top. Any man with wisdom knows that that kind of preference is conceded, and there is no use losing heart over it. The discerning man understands that it is what lies behind the scenes that accounts for success. In the same way there has often been a remarkably good but obscure woman behind a prominent man who has done great things. Solomon's counsel is to take into account the fact that you cannot expect to be recognised. Remember that your lasting relationship is with God; otherwise you will find heartbreak and disappointment and become cynical.

Shade of His Hand, 1237 R

Paul is like a musician who does not heed the approval of the audience if he can catch the look of approval from his Master.

My Utmost for His Highest, March 17, 760 L

Never court anything other than the approval of God.

My Utmost for His Highest, April 24, 773 L

REDEMPTION

"Oh, but I don't feel worthy." Of course you are not worthy! Not all your praying or obedience can ever make you worthy. Leave yourself absolutely in His hands, and see that you plunge yourself deep down in faith on the revelation that you are made one with God through the Redemption of Jesus Christ.

Approved Unto God, 23 R

The New Testament never says that Jesus Christ came primarily to teach men: it says that He came to reveal that He has put the basis of human life on Redemption; that is, He has made it possible for any and every man to be born into the Kingdom where He lives (see John 3:3). Then when we are born again His teaching becomes a description of what God has undertaken to make a man if he will let His power work through him. So long as a man has his morality well within his own grasp he does not need Jesus Christ—"For I came not to call the righteous, but sinners," said Jesus. When a man has been hard hit and realises his own helplessness he finds that it is not a cowardly thing to turn to Jesus Christ, but the way out which God has made for him.

Baffled to Fight Better, 50 R

The religion of Jesus Christ is not a religion of ethical truth, but of Redemption. The teachings of Jesus have not made so much difference to the world as the teachings of Socrates and Plato, but to those who are born from above they make all the difference.

The Highest Good—Thy Great Redemption, 558 L

Jesus Christ undertakes to enable a man to withstand every one of the charges made by Satan. Satan's aim is to make a man believe that God is cruel and that things are all wrong; but when a man strikes deepest in agony and turns deliberately to the God manifested in Jesus Christ, he will find Him to be the answer to all his problems.

Baffled to Fight Better, 51 R

God's conscience means He has to forgive completely and finally redeem the human race. The point about Christian forgiveness is not that God puts snow over a dungheap, but that He turns a man into the standard of the Forgiver.

The Shadow of an Agony, 1163 L

The cry on the cross, "My God, My God, why hast Thou forsaken Me?" is not the desolation of an isolated individual: it is the revelation of the heart of God face to face with the sin of man, and going deeper down than man's sin can ever go in inconceivable heartbreak in order that every sin-stained, hell-deserving sinner might be absolutely redeemed. If the Redemption of Christ cannot go deeper down than hell, it is not redemption at all.

The Highest Good—Thy Great Redemption, 558 L

"And apart from shedding of blood there is no remission." God redeemed the world by shedding His blood, by putting the whole passion of the Godhead into it. He did not become interested and put one arm in to help the human race up; He went into the Redemption absolutely, there was nothing of Himself left out. Am I willing to put my whole self into becoming His? or am I one of those who accept His salvation, but thoroughly object to giving up my right to myself to Him? Unless I am willing to shed my blood for Him my Christianity is not worth anything.

Biblical Ethics, 110 L

The great marvellous revelation of Redemption is that it atones for everyone; men are "condemned to salvation" through the Cross of Christ. (See also UNIVERSALISM)

Conformed to His Image, 344 R

The Redemption of the human race does not necessarily mean the salvation of every individual. Redemption is of universal application, but human responsibility is not done away with. Jesus Christ states emphatically that there are possibilities of eternal damnation for the man who positively* neglects or positively rejects His Redemption.

The Psychology of Redemption, 1084 R
*Independent; unrelated to anything else

(Continued)

REDEMPTION *(Continued)*

The Redemption covers more than men and women, it covers the whole earth; everything that has been marred by sin and the devil has been completely redeemed by Jesus Christ. " . . . new heavens and a new earth, wherein dwelleth righteousness"—nothing that defiles can be on it at all; at present that is absolutely inconceivable to us.

Biblical Ethics, 100 R

God has paid the price of redeeming a race that had become degenerate; He is not *going to* redeem it, He *has* redeemed it. The Gospel is just that—good news about God, that He has redeemed the human race. "God was in Christ, reconciling the world unto Himself. . . ." Is the Gospel, as it is popularly presented, good news about God, or is it a misrepresentation of God? It is not good news about God unless it presents the revelation that God has put the basis of human life on Redemption.

Biblical Ethics, 110 L

The Redemption means a great deal more than my personal salvation and yours; that is a mere outcome; pseudo-evangelism is apt to make it the great thing. The great thing according to the New Testament is not that the Redemption touches *me*, but that it avails for the whole human race.

Biblical Ethics, 110 R

Redemption means a great deal more than a man is conscious of. The Redemption is not only for mankind, it is for the universe, for the material earth; everything that sin and the devil have touched and marred has been completely redeemed by Jesus Christ. There is a day coming when the Redemption will be actually manifested, when there will be "a new heaven and a new earth," with a new humanity upon it.

Conformed to His Image, 343 R

What has God redeemed? Everything that sin and Satan have touched and blighted, God has redeemed; Redemption is complete. We are not working *for* the redemption of the world, we are working *on* the Redemption, which is a very different thing.

Our Brilliant Heritage, 932 R

The first result of the Redemption of Jesus Christ in human life is havoc. If any human life can stand before God on its own basis, Calvary is much ado about nothing. If it can be proved that rationalism is the basis of human life, then the New Testament is nonsense; instead of its being a revelation, it is a cunningly devised fable. There is no need for redemption, Jesus Christ is nothing but a martyr, one of whom it was true that He was stricken, smitten of God and afflicted.

The Psychology of Redemption, 1090 L

The statement that a man who gives his life for his king and country thereby redeems his soul, is a misapprehension of New Testament revelation. Redemption is not a man's bit. "Greater love hath no man than this, that a man lay down his life for his friends," has nothing to do with Christianity; an atheist will do this, or a blackguard, or a Christian; there is nothing divine about it, it is the great stuff that human nature is made of. The love of God is manifested in that He laid down His life for His enemies, something no man can do. Paul says the fundamental revelation of the New Testament is that God redeemed the whole human race when they were spitting in His face, as it were.

The Shadow of an Agony, 1159 R

If we estimate things from the standpoint of a man's life, Redemption will seem "much ado about nothing." But when we come to a big Judgement Day like a European war, when individual lives apparently amount to nothing, and human lives are being swept away by the thousand, the "bottom board" is knocked out of our ignorance, and we begin to see that the basis of things is not rational, but wild and tragic. It is through these glimpses that we understand why the New Testament was written, and why there needed to be a Redemption made by Jesus Christ, and how it is that the basis of life is redemptive.

The Shadow of an Agony, 1158 L

When you come to your wits' end, remember there is a way out, viz., personal relationship to God through the Redemption of Jesus Christ.

The Shadow of an Agony, 1190 R

REGRET

The sense of the irreparable is one of the greatest agonies in human life. Adam and Eve entered into the sense of the irreparable when the gates of Paradise clanged behind them. Cain cried out—"My punishment is greater than I can bear." Esau "found no place of repentance, though he sought it diligently with tears." There are things in life which are irreparable; there is no road back to yesterday.

Job's sense of the irreparable brought him face to face with the thing God was face to face with, and when a man gets there he begins to see the meaning of the Redemption. . . . Through Jesus Christ's Redemption the way is opened back to yesterday, out of the blunders and blackness and baffling into a perfect simplicity of relationship to God.

Baffled to Fight Better, 49 R, 51 L

RELATIONSHIP WITH GOD

Maintain your personal relationship with God at all costs. Never allow anything to come between your soul and God, and welcome anyone or anything that leads you to know Him better.

Approved Unto God, 13 R

When a worker jealously guards his secret life with God the public life will take care of itself.

Disciples Indeed, 411 L

"Therefore I say unto you, Take no thought for your life, what ye shall eat, or what ye shall drink; nor yet for your body, what ye shall put on. Is not the life more than meat, and the body than raiment?" (Matthew 6:25).

Jesus does not say, "Blessed is the man who does not think about anything"; that man is a fool; He says, "Be carefully careless about everything saving one thing, viz., your relationship to God." . . . Jesus is saying that the great care of the life is to put the relationship to God first and everything else second. Our Lord teaches a complete reversal of all our practical sensible reasonings.

Studies in the Sermon on the Mount, 1458 L

Paul was not given a message or a doctrine to proclaim; he was brought into a vivid, personal, overmastering relationship to Jesus Christ. Verse 16 is immensely commanding—"to make thee a minister and a witness." There is nothing there apart from the personal relationship. Paul was devoted to a Person not to a cause. He was absolutely Jesus Christ's; he saw nothing else; he lived for nothing else. "For I determined not to know any thing among you, save Jesus Christ, and Him crucified."

My Utmost for His Highest, January 24, 742 R

(Continued)

RELATIONSHIP WITH GOD *(Continued)*

It is because people live in the things they possess instead of in their relationship to God, that God at times seems to be cruel. There are a thousand and one interests that God's providential hand has to brush aside as hopelessly irrelevant to His purpose, and if we have been living in those interests, we go with them (cf. Luke 12:15).

So Send I You, 1317 L

RELATIONSHIPS, HUMAN

How impatient we are in dealing with others! Our attitude implies that we think God is asleep. When we begin to reason and work in God's way, He reminds us first of all how long it took Him to get us where we are, and we realise His amazing patience and we learn to come on other lives from above. As we learn to rely on the Spirit of God He gives us the resourcefulness of Jesus.

The Moral Foundations of Life, 732 L

We all have natural affinities—some people we like and others we do not; some people we get on well with and others we do not. Never let those likes and dislikes be the rule of your Christian life. "If we walk in the light, as He is in the light, we have fellowship one with another," i.e., God gives us fellowship with people for whom we have no natural affinity.

Studies in the Sermon on the Mount, 1452 R

It takes a long time to get the full force of our Lord's statements. "I say unto you, Love your enemies"—an easy thing to do when you have no enemies; an impossible thing when you have. "Bless them that curse you"—easy when no one is cursing you, but impossible when someone is.

Studies in the Sermon on the Mount, 1453 R

When a man does love his enemies, he knows that God has done a tremendous work in him, and every one else knows it too.

Studies in the Sermon on the Mount, 1453 L

"Or what man is there of you, whom if his son ask bread, will he give him a stone?" (Matthew 7:9).

The illustration of prayer that Our Lord uses here is that of a good child asking for a good thing. We talk about prayer as if God heard us irrespective of the fact of our relationship to Him (cf. Matthew 5:45). Never say it is not God's will to give you what you ask; don't sit down and faint, but find out the reason, turn up the index. Are you rightly related to your wife, to your husband, to your children, to your fellow-students— are you a "good child" there? "Oh, Lord, I have been irritable and cross, but I do want spiritual blessing." You cannot have it; you will have to do without until you come into the attitude of a good child.

My Utmost for His Highest, August 24, 815 R

The bitterest hurt in life is to be wounded in the house of your friends; to be wounded by an enemy is bad enough, but it does not take you unawares; you expect it in a measure.

Baffled to Fight Better, 68 L

A retreat from comradeship is nearly always covered by a terrific amount of utterance either in writing or speech.

Baffled to Fight Better, 70 L

The expectation of the heart must be based on this certainty: "in all the world there is none but Thee, my God, there is none but Thee." Until the human heart rests there, every other relationship in life is precarious and will end in heart-break. There is only one Being Who can satisfy the last aching abyss of the human heart, and that is the Lord Jesus Christ.

The Moral Foundations of Life, 706 L

The whole history of envy and cruelty in human relationships is summed up in the demand for infinite satisfaction from human hearts; we will never get it, and we are apt to become cruel, vindictive, bitter, and often criminal. When once the heart is right with God and the real centre of the life satisfied, we never expect or demand infinite satisfaction from a finite heart; we become absolutely kind to all other hearts and never become a snare.

The Moral Foundations of Life, 706 L

God introduces us to people who conduct themselves to us as we have conducted ourselves to Him, and if we do not recognise what He is doing we will ride a moral hobby-horse—"I will not be treated like that." There is no further inspiration possible from the Spirit of God until that temper of mind is gone. "Take heed to your spirit, that ye deal not treacherously." Our Lord always puts His finger unerringly on the thing that is wrong. *"First be reconciled . . ."* (Matthew 5:24).

The Moral Foundations of Life, 717 R

Every man in the sight of God has an equal right to life, and if a man takes away the life of another, his own life shall be taken away. The right of life is insisted on all through the Bible. As long as I do not murder anyone outright the law cannot touch me, but is there someone dependent on me to whom in the tiniest way I am not giving the right to live? someone for whom I am cherishing an unforgiving dislike? "Whosoever hateth his brother is a murderer," says John (1 John 3:15). One of the terrors of the Day of Judgement will be our indifference to the rights of life.

Biblical Ethics, 95 R

The greatest problems of conscience are not the wrong things we have done, but wrong relationships. We may have become born again, but what about those we have wronged? It is of no use to sit down and

say, "It is irreparable now; I cannot alter it." Thank God He can alter it!

The Philosophy of Sin, 1111 R

The shores of life are strewn with ruined friendships, irreparable severances through our own blame or others', and when the Holy Spirit begins to reveal the tremendous twist, then comes the strange distress, "How can we repair it?" Many a sensitive soul has been driven into insanity through anguish of mind because he has never realised what Jesus Christ came to do, and all the asylums in the world will never touch them in the way of healing; the only thing that will is the realisation of what the death of Jesus means, viz., that the damage we have done may be repaired through the efficacy of His Cross.

The Philosophy of Sin, 1111 R

REMEMBRANCE (*See* MEMORY)

REPENTANCE

Because a man has altered his life it does not necessarily mean that he has repented. A man may have lived a bad life and suddenly stop being bad, not because he has repented, but because he is like an exhausted volcano. The fact that he has become good is no sign of his having become a Christian. The bedrock of Christianity is repentance.

Baffled to Fight Better, 83 L

Repentance means that I estimate exactly what I am in God's sight and I am sorry for it, and on the basis of the Redemption I become the opposite. The only repentant man is the holy man, i.e., the one who becomes the opposite of what he was because something has entered into him.

Baffled to Fight Better, 83 R

(Continued)

REPENTANCE (Continued)

Strictly speaking, repentance is a gift of
God. No man can repent when he chooses.
A man can be remorseful when he chooses,
but remorse is a lesser thing than repentance. Repentance means that I show my
sorrow for the wrong thing by becoming
the opposite.

Baffled to Fight Better, 85 L

The old Puritans used to pray for "the gift
of tears." A man has the power to harden
himself against one of God's greatest gifts. If
in order to dissolve a piece of ice, you take a
hammer and smash it up, you simply break
it into so many pieces of ice; but put the ice
out in the sunshine and it quickly disappears. That is just the difference between
man's handling of wrong and God's. Man's
handling may cause it to crumble, but it is
only so much crumbled-up wrong; when
God handles it, it becomes repentance, and
the man turns to God and his life becomes a
sacrament of experimental repentance.

Baffled to Fight Better, 85 L

Repentance to be true must issue in holiness, or it is not New Testament repentance.
Repentance means not only sorrow and distress for the wrong done, but the acceptance
of the Atonement of Jesus which will make
me what I have never been—holy.

Bringing Sons Unto Glory, 225 R

Never mistake remorse for repentance;
remorse simply puts a man in hell while he
is on earth; it carries no remedial quality
with it at all, nothing that betters a man.

Conformed to His Image, 348 R

Repentance is the experimental side of
Redemption and is altogether different from
remorse or reformation. "Repentance" is a ·
New Testament word and cannot be applied
outside the New Testament. We all experience remorse, disgust with ourselves over

the wrong we have done when we are found
out by it, but the rarest miracle of God's
grace is the sorrow that puts an end for ever
to the thing for which I am sorry. Repentance involves the receiving of a totally new
disposition so that I never do the wrong
thing again.

Conformed to His Image, 349 R

Experimentally the meaning of life is to
attain the excellency of a broken heart,
for that alone entails repentance and
acceptance, the two great poles of Bible
revelation. "The sacrifices of God are a
broken spirit"—why, we do not know, but
God has made it so. The one thing we are
after is to avoid getting broken-hearted.

The Highest Good, 550 L

"And the Lord said unto Cain, Why art
thou wroth? and why is thy countenance
fallen? If thou doest well, shalt thou not be
accepted?" (Genesis 4:6–7). These verses
present God doing for Cain what He did
for Adam and Eve—giving him a Divine
opportunity for repentance. Remorse is
never repentance; remorse is the rebellion
of man's own pride which will not agree
with God's judgement on sin but accuses
God because He has made His laws too
stern and holy.

Our Portrait in Genesis, 962 L

"And He said unto him, what is thy name? And
he said, Jacob" (Genesis 32:27).
    The confession has to be made: That is
my name—supplanter; sneak; there is no
palliation. Jacob had to get to the place
where he willingly confesses before God
the whole guilt of usurping the birthright.
This is full and profound and agonising
repentance.

Our Portrait in Genesis, 978 L

When you have been through a bereavement, or have thought you would be found
out in a wrong and were not, there is the

danger of reacting into a rash spell of devotion. You read your Bible and say things to God, but there is no reality in it. It is like the reaction of a man after a drinking bout; he mistakes his remorse for repentance. Repentance is not a reaction, remorse is. Remorse is—I will never do the thing again. Repentance is that I deliberately become the opposite to what I have been.

Shade of His Hand, 1211 L

The prevailing attitude to-day is the healthy-minded attitude that treats remorse as a disease of the nerves and sin as a mere intellectual nuisance—"Do things; don't give way to absurd self-examination." Jesus Christ stands for the unhindered facing of the world, the flesh and the devil, and an equally unhindered facing of God, and such a facing will always bring a man to the evangelical attitude—"Just as I am." Beware of bracing yourself up to be cheerful when you should be broken up into repentance.

Notes on Jeremiah, 1393 R

RESPONSIBILITY

The characteristic of a man who is not based on the issue of his life is an incessant cunning, crafty, commercial worry. Our Lord was absolutely devoid of that. What we call responsibility our Lord never had, and what He called responsibility men are without. Men do not care a bit for Jesus Christ's notion of their lives, and Jesus does not care for our notions. There is the antagonism. If we were to estimate ourselves from our Lord's standpoint, very few of us would be considered disciples.

The Highest Good, 548 R

We won't accept the responsibility of life as God gives it to us; we only accept responsibility as we wish to take it, and the responsibility we wish to take is to save our own skins, make comfortable positions for ourselves and those we are related to, exert ourselves a little to keep ourselves clean and vigorous and upright; but when it comes to following out what Jesus says, His sayings are nothing but jargon. We name the Name of Christ but we are not based on His one issue of life, and Jesus says, "What shall it profit a man, if he shall gain the whole world"—and he can easily do it—"and lose his own soul?"

The Highest Good, 549 L

God will do everything I cannot do, but He will do nothing He has constructed me to do.

The Moral Foundations of Life, 702 L

"O Jerusalem, Jerusalem, thou that killest the prophets, and stonest them which are sent unto thee, how often would I have gathered thy children together, even as a hen gathereth her chickens under her wings, and ye would not! Behold, your house is left unto you desolate" (Matthew 23:37–38).

Is yours a desolated life, deserted in soul? Then in plain honesty don't blame your father or mother or anyone in your family; don't blame the fact that you had no education, or that someone thwarted you when you were sixteen, or that you were heartbroken when you were twenty-four, or had a business disaster when you were thirty. These things may be facts, but they are not to the point. Nothing that transpires outside me can make the tiniest difference to me morally unless I choose to let it. The desolation described by Jesus was brought on by the people of God themselves and by them alone.

The Servant as His Lord, 1269 R

(Continued)

RESPONSIBILITY *(Continued)*

In individual experience no one person is ever entirely to blame—"my father is to blame, my mother, my heredity"—everybody and everything but myself. It is impossible for human wisdom to apportion the blame. Remember the one fact more which God alone knows.

Our Portrait in Genesis, 969 R

Beware of obeying anyone else's obedience to God because it means you are shirking responsibility yourself.

Our Portrait in Genesis, 970 L

To enter into peace for ourselves without becoming either tolerantly un-watchful of other lives or an amateur providence over them, is supremely difficult. God holds us responsible for two things in connection with the lives He brings around us in the apparent haphazard of His providence, viz., insistent waiting on God for them, and inspired instruction and warning from God to them. The thing that astonishes us when we get through to God is the way God holds us responsible for other lives.

Our Portrait in Genesis, 978 R

REST

"And I will give you rest." Rest means the perfection of motion. "I will give you rest," that is, "I will stay you." Not—"I will put you to bed and hold your hand and sing you to sleep"; but—"I will get you out of bed, out of the languor and exhaustion, out of being half dead while you are alive; I will so imbue you with the spirit of life that you will be stayed by the perfection of vital activity." It is not a picture of an invalid in a bathchair, but of life at such a pitch of health that everything is at rest, there is no exhaustion without recuperation.

Our Brilliant Heritage, 946 L

"And I will give you rest" (Matthew 11:28).

Jesus says "Come unto Me . . . and I will give you rest," i.e., Christ-consciousness will take the place of self-consciousness. Wherever Jesus comes He establishes rest, the rest of the perfection of activity that is never conscious of itself.

My Utmost for His Highest, August 20, 814 R

RESURRECTION

There had been resurrections before the resurrection of Jesus Christ, but they were all resuscitations to the same kind of life as heretofore. Jesus Christ rose to a totally new life, and to a totally different relationship to men and women.

The Psychology of Redemption, 1096 L

RETRIBUTION

There is a difference between retaliation and retribution. The basis of life is retribution—"For with what judgement ye judge, ye shall be judged: and with what measure ye mete, it shall be measured to you again." This statement of our Lord's is not a haphazard guess; it is an eternal law and it works from God's throne right down. Life serves back in the coin you pay. You are paid back what you give not necessarily by the same person; and this holds with regard to good as well as evil. If you have been generous, you will meet generosity again through someone else; if you have been shrewd in finding out the defects of others, that is the way people will judge you. Jesus Christ never allows retaliation, but He says that the basis of life is retribution. If my enemy turns and gives proof of his sorrow, I am not to meet him with retaliation.

He Shall Glorify Me, 507 L

REVELATION, BOOK OF

If we are ever going to understand the Book of the Revelation we have to remember that it gives the programme of God, not the guess of a man. "Write the things which thou hast seen, and the things which are, and the things which shall be hereafter." The Apostle is writing what the Spirit revealed to him—that is the origin of the Book.

He Shall Glorify Me, 497 L

Apocalyptic literature is never easy to understand; its language is either a revelation or fantastic nonsense. We study it and worry over it and never begin to make head or tail of it, while obedience will put us on the line of understanding. Spiritual truth is never discerned by intellect, only by moral obedience. God brings His marvels to pass in lives by means of prayer, and the prayers of the saints are part of God's programme.

He Shall Glorify Me, 497 L

REVELATION OF GOD

There are three ways in which we can responsibly receive communications from God: by giving deliberate thoughtful attention to the Incarnation, by identifying ourselves with the Church, and by means of Bible revelation. God gave Himself in the Incarnation; He gives Himself to the Church; and He gives Himself in His Word; and these are the ways He has ordained for conveying His life to us.

Approved Unto God, 4 R

In the New Testament we deal not with the shrewd guesses of able men, but with a supernatural revelation, and only as we transact business on that revelation do the moral consequences result in us.

Approved Unto God, 14 L

It is of importance to note that the Bible reveals that our Redeemer entered into the world through the woman. Man, as man, had no part whatever in the Redemption of the world; it was "the seed of the woman." In Protestant theology and in the Protestant outlook we have suffered much from our opposition to the Roman Catholic Church on this one point, viz., intense antipathy to Mariolatry, and we have lost the meaning of the woman side of the revelation of God. All that we understand by womanhood and by manhood, all that we understand by fatherhood and motherhood, is embraced in the term "El Shaddai" (Genesis 17:1 RV).

Biblical Psychology, 143 L

Be sceptical of any revelation that has not got as its source the simplicity by means of which a "babe" can enter in, and which a "fool" can express.

Conformed to His Image, 358 R

That God is love is a revelation. Unless I am born from above, what is the use of telling me God is love? To me He is not love. Where is the love of God in war? in suffering? in all the inevitable inequalities of life? No one who faces facts as they are could ever prove that God is love unless he accepts the revelation of His love made by Jesus Christ.

The Place of Help, 1004 L

REVERENCE

If we have never had the experience of taking our commonplace religious shoes off our commonplace religious feet, and getting rid of all the undue familiarity with which we approach God, it is questionable whether we have ever stood in His presence. The people who are flippant and familiar are those who have never yet been introduced to Jesus Christ. After the amazing delight and liberty of realising what Jesus Christ *does*, comes the impenetrable darkness of realising Who He *is*.

My Utmost for His Highest, January 3, 735 R

REWARD

We have the delight of giving our lives as a lovegift to Jesus Christ. "He that loseth his life for My sake shall find it." Reward is the ultimate delight of knowing that God has fulfilled His purpose in my life; it is not a question of resting in satisfaction, but the delight of being in perfect conscious agreement with God.

He Shall Glorify Me, 522 L

"It is required in stewards, that a man be found faithful"—not successful. The anticlimax comes when we look for rewards—"If I am good, I shall be blessed." The logic of mathematics does not amount to anything in the spiritual realm.

Shade of His Hand, 1226 L

RICH YOUNG RULER

To the rich young ruler Jesus said, "Loosen yourself from your property because that is the thing that is holding you." The principle is one of fundamental death to possessions while being obliged to use them. "Sell that thou hast . . ."—reduce yourself till nothing remains but your consciousness of yourself, and then cast that consciousness at the feet of Christ. That is the bedrock of intense spiritual Christianity. The moral integrity of this man made him see clearly what Jesus meant.

If Thou Wilt Be Perfect, 602 L

RIGHT TO MYSELF

"If any man will come after Me," said Jesus, "the condition is that he must leave something behind," viz., his right to himself. Is Jesus Christ worth it, or am I one of those who accept His salvation but thoroughly object to giving up my right to myself to Him?

Facing Reality, 31 R

What then is our cross? Our cross is something that comes only with the peculiar relationship of a disciple to Jesus. It is the sign that we have denied our right to ourselves and are determined to manifest that we are no longer our own; we have given away for ever our right to ourselves to Jesus Christ.

Facing Reality, 31 R

We need to remember that we cannot train ourselves to be Christians; we cannot discipline ourselves to be saints; we cannot bend ourselves to the will of God: we have to be broken to the will of God. There must be a break with the dominant ruler. We may be clean and upright and religious, we may be Christian workers and have been mightily used of God; but if the bedrock of self-realisation has not been blasted out by our own free choice at the Cross of Christ, shipwreck is the only thing in the end.

Facing Reality, 32 L

Naturally, a man regards his right to himself as the finest thing he has, yet it is the last bridge that prevents Jesus Christ having His way in a life.

Disciples Indeed, 395 L

'If you are going to be My disciple," Jesus says, "you must give up your right to yourself." Jesus Christ came to do what I could not do, viz., alter my heredity, and the point for me is, am I going to let Him do it?

Biblical Ethics, 110 L

We say we can do what we like with our bodies; we cannot. If I try to satisfy any appetite on the basis of my right to myself, it means there is a spirit of antagonism to Jesus Christ at work in me; if I recognise that my body is the temple of the Holy Ghost, it is a sign that my life is based on the Cross.

Biblical Ethics, 112 L

It is not true that everything in life apart from Christ is bad; there are many virtues that are good and moral; pride and self-interest are remarkably fine things in some aspects, "highly esteemed among men," but when I see Jesus Christ I have to go to their moral death. Any fool will give up wrongdoing and the devil, if he knows how to do it; but it takes a man in love with Jesus Christ to give up the best he has for Him. Jesus Christ does not demand that I give up the wrong, but the right, the best I have for Him, viz., my right to myself. Will I agree to go through my "white funeral" and say I deliberately cut out my claim to my right to myself, deliberately go to the death of my self-will? If I will, instantly the Spirit of God begins to work, and slowly the new mind is formed.

The Shadow of an Agony, 1187 L

"If any man would come after Me, let him deny himself," i.e., "deny his right to himself." Jesus never swept men off their feet in ecstasy; He always talked on the line that left a man's will in the ascendant until he saw where he was going. It is impossible for a man to give up his right to himself without knowing he is doing it.

Disciples Indeed, 395 L

My right to myself is not merely something I claim, but something that continually makes me insist on my own way.

Disciples Indeed, 403 L

The only thing I can give to God is "my right to myself" (Romans 12:1). If I will give God that, He will make a holy experiment out of me, and God's experiments always succeed.

Our Brilliant Heritage, 947 R

The right to ourselves is the only thing we have to give to God.

The Psychology of Redemption, 1092 L

RIGHTEOUS INDIGNATION

We need to be reminded of the presentation of Jesus in the New Testament for the Being pictured to us nowadays would not perturb anybody; but He aroused His whole nation to rage. Read the records of His ministry and see how much blazing indignation there is in it. For thirty years Jesus did nothing, then for three years He stormed every time He went down to Jerusalem. Josephus says He tore through the Temple courts like a madman. We hear nothing about that Jesus Christ to-day. The meek and mild Being pictured to-day makes us lose altogether the meaning of the Cross.

The Highest Good, 551 L

The thing that awakens indignation in us is the thing that upsets our present state of comfort and society. The thing that made Jesus Christ blaze was pride that defied God and prevented Him from having His right with human hearts.

The Highest Good, 551 R

RIGHTEOUSNESS

Righteousness—Conformity to a Right Standard — where no one but God sees us. That is where very few of us are Christians.

Biblical Ethics, 94 L

The righteous man is the one whose inner intention is clearly revealed in his outer intention; there is no duplicity, no internal hypocrisy.

Biblical Ethics, 94 R

Imputed righteousness must never be made to mean that God puts the robe of His righteousness over our moral wrong, like a snow-drift over a rubbish heap; that He pretends we are all right when we are not. The revelation is that "Christ Jesus . . . is made unto us . . . righteousness"; it is the distinct impartation of the very life of Jesus on the ground of the Atonement, enabling me to walk in the light as God is in the light, and as long as I remain in the light God sees only the perfections of His Son. We are "accepted in the Beloved."

Conformed to His Image, 367 L

RIGHTS

The teaching of the Sermon on the Mount is the exact opposite of the modern jargon about "equal rights"; "Why shouldn't I do this? I'm within my rights." Of course you are, but never call yourself a Christian if you reason like that because a Christian is one who sacrifices his liberty for the sake of others, for Jesus Christ's sake.

Biblical Ethics, 96 L

Any fool can insist on his rights, and any devil will see that he gets them; but the Sermon on the Mount means that the only right the saint will insist on is the right to give up his rights.

He Shall Glorify Me, 516 R

We begin to debate and say, "Why shouldn't I do this? I'm within my rights." That idea is so foreign to Our Lord's conception that He has made no provision for it. The passion of Christianity is that I deliberately sign away my own rights and become a bondslave of Jesus Christ.

He Shall Glorify Me, 516 R

Equal duties, not equal rights, is the keynote of the spiritual world; equal rights is the clamour of the natural world. The protest of power through grace, if we are following Jesus, is that we no longer insist on our rights, we see that we fulfil our duty.

If Thou Wilt Be Perfect, 600 L

The characteristic of a Christian is that he has the right not to insist on his rights. That will mean that I refuse to do certain things because they would cause my brother to stumble. To me the restrictions may be absurd and narrow-minded; I can do the things without any harm; but Paul's argument is that he reserves the right to suffer the loss of all things rather than put an occasion to fall in his brother's way. The Holy Ghost gives us the power to forgo our rights.

The Moral Foundations of Life, 702 R

It would seem the wisest thing in the world for Abraham to choose; it was his right, and the people round him would consider him a fool for not choosing (see Genesis 13:5–13). Many of us do not go on in our spiritual life because we prefer to choose what is our right instead of relying upon God to choose for us. We have to learn to walk according to the standard that has its eye on God.

Not Knowing Whither, 871 R

In the life of faith God allows us to get into a place of testing where the consideration of our own welfare would be the right and proper thing if we were not living the life of faith; but if we are living the life of faith, we will heartily waive our own rights in favour of those whose right it is not, and leave God to choose for us. Whenever we make "right" our guidance, we blunt our spiritual insight. The greatest enemy of the life with God is not sin, but the good that is not good enough.

Not Knowing Whither, 871 R

We have the perfect right not to insist on our rights; it is the privilege of a Christian to waive his rights; but we do not always recognise that we must insist on those associated with us getting their rights. If they prefer to take the line of faith that we take, that is their responsibility, but we are not exonerated from seeing that they get their rights.

Not Knowing Whither, 874 R

"Agree with thine adversary quickly" (Matthew 5:25).

To see that my adversary gives me my rights is natural; but Jesus says that it is a matter of eternal and imperative importance to me that I pay my adversary what I owe him. From our Lord's standpoint it does not matter whether I am defrauded or not; what does matter is that I do not defraud. Am I insisting on my rights, or am I paying what I owe from Jesus Christ's standpoint?

My Utmost for His Highest, June 30, 796 R

RISK

Our attitude is that if we are extravagant a rainy day will come for which we have not laid up. You cannot lay up for a rainy day and justify it in the light of Jesus Christ's teaching. We are not Christians at heart; we don't believe in the wisdom of God, but only in our own. We go in for insurance and economy and speculation, everything that makes us secure in our own wisdom.

Shade of His Hand, 1242 L

In the natural world it is a real delight to be faced with risk and danger, and in the spiritual world God gives us the "sporting chance." He will plant us down amongst all kinds of people and give us the amazing joy of proving ourselves "a living sacrifice" in those circumstances.

Facing Reality, 35 R

Beware lest your attitude to God's truth reminds Him that He is very unwise. Everything worth while in life is dangerous, and yet we would have God such a tepid Being that He runs no risks!

Disciples Indeed, 388 R

If you believe in Jesus, you will not spend all your time in the smooth waters just inside the harbour, full of exhilaration and delight, but always moored; you will have to go out through the harbour bar into the great deeps of God and begin to know for yourself, begin to get spiritual discernment. If you do not cut the moorings, God will have to break them with a storm and send you out. Why not unloosen and launch all on God and go out on the great swelling tide of His purpose?

Our Brilliant Heritage, 952 L

Jesus Christ demands of the man who trusts in Him the same reckless sporting spirit that the natural man exhibits in his life. If a man is going to do anything worth while, there are times when he has to risk everything on a leap, and in the spiritual world Jesus Christ demands that we risk everything we hold by our common-sense and leap into what He says. Immediately we do, we find that what He says fits on as solidly as our common-sense.

Studies in the Sermon on the Mount, 1459 L

ROUTINE *(See ORDINARY)*

RUSH (See HURRY)

SABBATH

Being not under the law but under grace means that we fulfil all the old law easily and a good deal more. With regard to the Sabbath, Jesus said "the Son of man is Lord also of the sabbath." That means we have to remember that Jesus Christ is the Lord of the one day that is His, though we can rob Him of it. When we recognise that the Sabbath day belongs to God, every other day that we give over to Him is our gift. The same with regard to money and possessions. The giving of the tenth is not a sign that it all belongs to God, but a sign that the tenth belongs to God and the rest is ours, and we are held responsible for what we do with it.

Notes on Jeremiah, 1421 L

SACRED AND SECULAR

Our whole being, not one aspect of it, has to be brought to comprehend the love of God. We are apt to co-ordinate our spiritual faculties only; our lack of co-ordination is detected if we cannot pass easily from what we call the secular to the sacred. Our Lord passed from the one to the other without any break; the reason we cannot is that we are not pressed on to the life of God. We have made "a world within the world" of our own which we have to guard jealousy: "I must not do this and that"; "I must keep myself entirely here." That is not the life of God at all, it is not genuine enough; it is artificial and cannot stand the strain of actual life.

Approved Unto God, 5 L

The difficulty in Christian work to-day is that we put it into a sphere that upsets the reasoning of things—this sphere for sacred and that for secular; this time for activity and that for study. God will never allow us to divide our lives into sacred and secular, into study and activity. We generally think of a student as one who shuts himself up and studies in a reflective way, but that is never revealed in God's book. A Christian's thinking ought to be done in activities, not in reflection, because we only come to right discernment in activities. Some incline to study naturally in the reflective sense, others incline more to steady active work; the Bible combines both in one life.

Approved Unto God, 7 L

Sometimes we are fresh for a prayer meeting but not fresh for cleaning boots!

My Utmost for His Highest, January 20, 741 L

Don't shut up any avenue of your nature; let God come into every avenue, every relationship, and you will find the nightmare curse of "secular and sacred" will go.

Disciples Indeed, 409 L

The idea of the "missionary" class, the "ministerial" class, the "Christian worker" class has arisen out of our ideas of civilised life, not out of the New Testament faith and order. The New Testament faith and order is that as Christians we do not cease to do our duty as ordinary human beings, but in addition we have been given the key to the missionary message, viz., the proclaiming of the remissionary purpose of the Life and Death of Our Lord.

So Send I You, 1328 L

In Jesus Christ there was nothing secular and sacred; it was all real, and He makes His disciples like Himself.

Studies in the Sermon on the Mount, 1452 L

SACRIFICE

Some people spend their lives sacrificing themselves for other people, with the only result that the people for whom the sacrifice is made become more and more selfish. Whenever the Holy Ghost inspires the sacrifice, it is the sacrifice of ourselves for Jesus' sake, and that never blights, but always blesses. Half the heart-breaks and difficulties which some of us have hurried ourselves into would have been prevented if we had only dared to obey God in the power of the Spirit.

Biblical Ethics, 124 L

The only way we can offer a spiritual sacrifice to God is to do what He tells us to do, discipline what He tells us to discipline.

Not Knowing Whither, 897 R

Sacrifice for love is never conscious; sacrifice for duty always has margins of distress. The nature of love is to give, not to receive. Talk to a lover about giving up anything, and he doesn't begin to understand you!

Our Portrait in Genesis, 972 R

If you have got bitter and sour, you will probably find it is because God brought you a blessing and you clutched it for yourself; whereas if you had poured it out unto the Lord, you would have been the sweetest person out of heaven. If we are craving spiritual sponges, always taking these things to ourselves, we shall become a plague; other people will not get their horizon enlarged through us because we have never learned to pour out anything unto the Lord.

The Place of Help, 1024 R

The Apostle Paul literally fulfilled what we mean by this phrase, the altar of fellowship; he offered himself liberally and freely to God, and then offered himself at the hands of God, freely and fully, for the service of God among men, whether or not men understood him. "And I will very gladly spend and be spent for you; though the more abundantly I love you, the less I be loved." Do we know anything about this altar of fellowship whereby we offer back to God the best He has given us, and then let Him re-offer it as broken bread and poured-out wine to His other children?

The Place of Help, 997 L

SADDUCEE

The Sadducee is the type of person who in all ages destroys the treasure of the spirit; he is a common-sense individual.

The Highest Good, 552 L

If I work for God because I know it brings me the good opinion of those whose good opinion I wish to have, I am a Sadducee. The one great thing is to maintain a spiritual life which is absolutely true to Jesus Christ and to the faith of Jesus Christ.

The Highest Good, 553 R

SAFETY / SECURITY

"He only is my rock . . ." (Psalm 62:6).
    A rock conveys the idea of an encircling guard, as that of a mother watching her child who is learning to walk; should the child fall, he falls into the encircling love and watchfulness of the mother's care. "The Lord is my rock," my encircling guard. Where did the Psalmist learn this truth? In the school of silent waiting upon God. The Rock of Ages is the great sheltering encirclement; we are watched over by the Mother-guardianship of God. "I am El-Shaddai," the Father-Mother God. He is my high tower and my defence. The Lord Himself is our inviolable place of safety.

The Place of Help, 1013 R

(Continued)

SAFETY / SECURITY
(Continued)

Jesus says, Your Father, who looks after the sparrows, will care for you; fear not therefore. It is not to be a life of self-interest at all. When God calls us He never gives security; He gives us a knowledge of Himself. We reveal how much we believe in the things Jesus said when we reason like this—"Is this God's will for me? No, it can't be because there is no security." "It is enough for the disciple that he be as his Master." Jesus never had any home of His own, never a pillow on which to lay His head. His poverty was a deliberate choice. We may have to face destitution in order to maintain our spiritual connection with Jesus, and we can only do that if we love Him supremely.

> *The Servant as His Lord, 1280 L*

Just as nations place their confidence for security in armaments or arbitration (as the whim takes them) and neglect the worship of God as the only security, so individuals may easily place confidence in the amenities of society, in civilised entrenchments, in a good home and a good situation, and belittle the one abiding security—IN GOD!

> *Christian Disciplines, Volume 1,*
> *The Discipline of Peril, 295 R*

It is impossible to guard our spirit; the only One Who can guard all its entrances is God.

> *If Thou Wilt Be Perfect, 577 R*

SAINT

A saint is not an ethereal creature too refined for life on this earth; a saint is a mixture of the Divine and the human that can stand anything.

> *Biblical Ethics, 105 R*

A saint is not a human being who is trying to be good, trying by effort and prayer and longing and obedience to attain as many saintly characteristics as possible; a saint is a being who has been re-created. "If any man is in Christ, he is a new creation."

> *Biblical Psychology, 202 R*

The dominant thing about a saint is not self-realisation, but the Lord Himself; consequently a saint can always be ignored because to the majority of eyes our Lord is no more noticeable in the life of a saint than He was to men in the days of His flesh. But when a crisis comes the saint is the one to whom men turn; and the life which seemed colourless is seen to be the white light of God.

> *Our Brilliant Heritage, 934 L*

Why should we play at being Christians? We are told that to be an experimental Christian means we understand the plan of salvation; the devil understands that, but he is not a saint. A saint is one who, on the basis of the Redemption of Jesus Christ, has had the centre of his life radically altered, and has deliberately given up his right to himself. This is the point where the moral issue comes, the frontier whereby we get in contact with God. Intellect will not bring us there, but moral obedience only, and an agony opens the door to it.

> *The Shadow of an Agony, 1166 R*

The popular view of a saint is an anaemic young man with one foot in the grave, or an old woman, or an innocent, sweet young lady—anyone who has not enough original sin to be bad. The New Testament view of a saint is a more rugged type. You and I are a mixture of dust and Deity, and God takes that sordid human stuff and turns it into a saint by Regeneration. A saint does not mean a man who has not enough sin to be bad, but a man who has received from Jesus Christ a new heredity that turns him into another man.

The Shadow of an Agony, 1169 R

Notice God's unutterable waste of saints. According to the judgement of the world, God plants His saints in the most useless places. We say—"God intends me to be here because I am so useful." God puts His saints where they will glorify Him, and we are no judges at all of where that is.

My Utmost for His Highest, August 10, 810 R

The New Testament idea of a saint is not a cloistered sentiment gathering around the head of an individual like a halo of glory, but a holy character reacting on life in deeds of holiness.

*Christian Disciplines, Volume 1,
The Discipline of Suffering, 286 L*

SALVATION

Most of us take our salvation much too cheaply.

Baffled to Fight Better, 53 R

The measure of the salvation of Jesus is not that it does for the best man we know, but that it does for the worst and most sin-stained. There is no son of man that need despair, Jesus Christ can reproduce His saving work in any and every man, blessed be the Name of God!

Bringing Sons Unto Glory, 221 L

The Cross of Christ means that the salvation of God goes deeper down than the deepest depths of iniquity man can commit. No man can get beyond the reach of Jesus: He made a way back to the throne of God from the very heart of hell by His tremendous Atonement.

Bringing Sons Unto Glory, 234 R

Jesus Christ does not add one burden to the lives of men; He imparts the power to live up to what we know we ought; that is the meaning of His salvation.

The Highest Good, 543 L

No man is so laboured or crushed as the man who, with the religion of ideals, finds he cannot carry them out. There are many more men in that attitude than is supposed. Men are kept away from Jesus Christ by a sense of honesty as much as by dishonesty. "I don't deny that Jesus Christ saves—but if you only knew me!—the mistakes I have made, the wrong things I have done, the blundering things—I should be a perfect disgrace to Him." Our Lord says to such a one, "Come unto Me . . . , and I will give you rest."

The Shadow of an Agony, 1179 L

Everything that Satan and sin have marred, God holds in an unimpaired state for every son of man who will come to Him by the way back which Jesus Christ has made.

Our Portrait in Genesis, 961 R

Salvation is God's grace to sinful men, and it takes a lifetime to say the word properly.

The Philosophy of Sin, 1112 L

The next thing we have to learn by contact with Jesus Christ is this, that if the whole human race—everybody, good, bad and indifferent—is lost, we must have the boundless confidence of Jesus Christ Himself about us; that is, we must know that He can save anybody and everybody.

Workmen of God, 1343 R

SANCTIFICATION

Sanctification begins at regeneration, and goes on to a second great crisis, when God, upon an uttermost abandonment in consecration, bestows His gracious work of entire sanctification. The point of entire sanctification is reached not by the passing of the years but by obedience to the heavenly vision and through spiritual discipline.

> *Christian Disciplines, Volume 2,*
> *The Discipline of Loneliness, 323 L*

The only way we are going to overcome the world as Jesus overcame it is by experimental sanctification. We are to live in heavenly places in Christ Jesus while on this earth and among worldly people. That is the glorious discipline of the sanctified life.

> *Biblical Ethics, 99 R*

If I do not put to death the things in me which are not of God, they will put to death the things that are of God.

> *Biblical Ethics, 116 R*

"Knowing this, that our old man is crucified with Him. . ." (Romans 6:6).

What is our "old man"? The disposition of sin in us discovered by the incoming Spirit of God when we are born from above. A Christian experiencing the first work of God's regenerating grace begins to discern this disposition, and the issue is clear that that old disposition must be crucified or the Spirit of Christ must be crucified; the two cannot remain long together. Paul states triumphantly, "knowing this, that our old man was crucified with Him. . . ." It was not a divine anticipation on the part of the Apostle Paul; it was a very radical, definite experience.

> *Facing Reality, 33 L*

There are things in a man's natural life that are fine and beautiful, but when a man comes to Jesus Christ, he has to forgo them, and go to their "white funeral." This is a phrase Tennyson uses in speaking of the "white funeral"* of the single life; and that aspect is the only one that suits the spiritual life. . . . There is any amount in paganism that is good and virtuous, but if I am going on with Jesus Christ, I have to give those things a "white funeral," make a termination of them, and we very often get there through disenchantment.

> *The Shadow of an Agony, 1187 L*
> **Phrase from Tennyson's poem "To H.R.H.*
> *Princess Beatrice"; to Chambers, a white*
> *funeral meant a passage from one stage of life*
> *to another; leaving the past behind and moving*
> *into the future; he often used it to mean death*
> *to self and a complete surrender to God.*

When we are rightly related to God as Jesus was, the spiritual life becomes as natural as the life of a child. The one dominant note of the life after sanctification is the simplicity of a child, full of the radiant peace and joy of God. "Except ye . . . become as little children . . ."

> *Bringing Sons Unto Glory, 221 R*

We are apt to mistake the sovereign works of Grace in salvation and sanctification as being final—they are only beginnings.

> *Bringing Sons Unto Glory, 221 L*

One of the worst sins amongst us is that we are more interested in the most recent views on sanctification than we are in the testimonies in God's Book. Any excitable, hysterical testimony from a tide of revival is apt to be more welcome to the majority of sanctified people than the bedrock teaching of the New Testament. With what result? ". . . because they had no root, they withered away." Picture those silent years in the life of Our Lord, shielded by His Father, until all the tremendous forces of His life were developed and grasped.

> *Bringing Sons Unto Glory, 222 L*

We are saved and sanctified for God, not to be specimens in His showroom, but for God to do with us even as He did with Jesus, make us broken bread and poured-out wine as He chooses. That is the test—not spiritual fireworks or hysterics, not fanaticism, but a blazingly holy life that "confronts the horror of the world with a fierce purity," chaste physically, morally and spiritually, and this can only come about in the way it came about in the life of Our Lord.

Bringing Sons Unto Glory, 226 L

We are apt to make sanctification the end; it is only the beginning. Our holiness as saints consists in the exclusive dedication to God of all our powers.

Bringing Sons Unto Glory, 229 L

Sanctification means a radical and absolute identification with Jesus until the springs of His life are the springs of my life. "Faithful is He that calleth you, who also will do it."

Conformed to His Image, 358 R

". . . *work out your own salvation*" (*Philippians 2:12*).

"*The normal course of all religious experience is expansion followed by concentration.*" — *Forsyth*

When God gives a vision of what sanctification means or what the life of faith means, we have instantly to pay for the vision, and we pay for it by the inevitable law that "expansion must be followed by concentration." . . . Every expansion of brain and heart that God gives in meetings or in private reading of the Bible must be paid for inevitably and inexorably by concentration on our part, not by consecration. God will continually bring us into circumstances to make us prove whether we will work out with determined concentration what He has worked in.

Conformed to His Image, 358 R

The great fever in people's blood to-day is, "Do something"; "Be practical." The great need is for the one who is un-practical enough to get down to the heart of the matter, viz., personal sanctification. Practical work not based on an understanding of what sanctification means is simply beating the air.

Disciples Indeed, 402 R

The test of sanctification is not our talk about holiness and singing pious hymns; but, what are we like where no one sees us? with those who know us best?

Disciples Indeed, 402 R

You can always test the worth of your sanctification. If there is the slightest trace of self-conscious superiority about it, it has never touched the fringe of the garment of Christ.

Disciples Indeed, 403 L

Some people pray and long and yearn for the experience of sanctification, but never get anywhere near it; others enter in with a sudden marvellous realisation. Sanctification is an instantaneous, continuous work of grace; how long the approach to it takes depends upon ourselves, and that leads some to say sanctification is not instantaneous. The reason why some do not enter in is because they have never allowed their minds to realise what sanctification means.

If Ye Shall Ask, 623 R

Beware of the idea of sanctification that makes a man say—"Now I am sanctified I can do what I like." If he does, he is immoral. Even Christ pleased not Himself. If our experience of sanctification ends in pious sentiment, the reason is that it has never dawned on us that we must deliberately set our sanctified selves apart for God's use as Jesus did.

So Send I You, 1314 R

(Continued)

SANCTIFICATION (*Continued*)

In sanctification the regenerated soul deliberately gives up his right to himself to Jesus Christ, and identifies himself entirely with God's interest in other men.

My Utmost for His Highest, January 10, 738 L

No one enters into the experience of entire sanctification without going through a "white funeral"—the burial of the old life. If there has never been this crisis of death, sanctification is nothing more than a vision. There must be a "white funeral," a death that has only one resurrection—a resurrection into the life of Jesus Christ. Nothing can upset such a life; it is one with God for one purpose, to be a witness to Him.

My Utmost for His Highest, January 15, 739 R

SARCASM

There is a difference between sarcasm and irony (cf. Job 12:1–3). Sarcasm is the weapon of the weak man; the word literally means to tear flesh from the bone. Both Isaiah and the apostle Paul make free use of irony, but they never use sarcasm. If a weak man is presented with facts he cannot understand, he invariably turns to sarcasm.

Baffled to Fight Better, 64 L

SATAN / SATANIC

Sin never frightened Jesus; the devil never frightened Him. Face Jesus Christ with all the power of the devil: He was manifested, that He might destroy the works of the devil. Are you being tripped up by the subtle power of the devil? Remember, Jesus Christ has power not only to release you, but to make you more than conqueror over all the devil's onslaughts.

Conformed to His Image, 372 R

Jesus Christ claims that He can do in human nature what human nature cannot do for itself, viz., "destroy the works of the devil," remove the wrong heredity and put in the right one. He can satisfy the last aching abyss of the human heart; He can put the key into our hands which will give the solution to every problem that ever stretched before our minds. He can soothe by His pierced hands the wildest sorrow with which Satan or sin or death ever racked humanity.

Biblical Ethics, 128 L

Satan, however, is as subtle as God is good, and he tries to counterfeit everything God does, and if he cannot counterfeit it, he will limit it. Do not be ignorant of his devices!

Biblical Psychology, 167 R

The most outrageous moment for the devil will be when he finds that in spite of himself he has done God's will; and the same with the man who has been serving his own ends.

Disciples Indeed, 389 L

When we say a thing is "Satanic" we mean something abominable according to our standards: the Bible means something remarkably subtle and wise. Satanic temptations are not bestial, those temptations have to do with a man's own stupidity and wrongdoing.

Disciples Indeed, 407 L

Satan does not tempt to gross sins; the one thing he tempts to is putting myself as master instead of God.

Disciples Indeed, 407 R

Don't run away with the idea that everything that runs contrary to your complacent scheme of things is of the devil.

Disciples Indeed, 409 R

Nothing blinds the mind to the claims of Jesus Christ more effectually than a good, clean-living, upright life based on self-realisation. For a thing to be Satanic does not mean that it is abominable and immoral. The satanically managed man is moral, upright, proud, and individual; he is absolutely self-governed and has no need of God.

The Psychology of Redemption, 1093 L

When men go into external sins Satan is probably as much upset as the Holy Ghost, but for a different reason. Satan knows perfectly well that when men go into external sin and upset their lives, they will want another Ruler, a Saviour, a Deliverer; but as long as he can keep them in peace and unity and harmony apart from God he will do so.

The Servant as His Lord, 1260 L

SCANDAL

Scandal should be treated as you treat mud on your clothes. If you try and deal with it while it is wet, you rub the mud into the texture, but if you leave it till it is dry you can flick it off with a touch; it is gone without a trace. Leave scandal alone; never touch it.

Studies in the Sermon on the Mount, 1449 R

SCEPTIC / SCEPTICISM

Our Lord was always stern with disbelief, i.e., scepticism, because there is always a moral twist about scepticism. Never place an agnostic in the same category as a sceptic. An agnostic is one who says, "There is more than I know, but I have not found anyone who can tell me about it." Jesus is never stern with that attitude; but He is stern with the man who objects to a certain way of getting at the truth because he does not like that way.

The Moral Foundations of Life, 697 L

SCIENCE

If the Bible agreed with modern science, in about fifty years both would be out of date. All scientific findings have at one time been modern.

Biblical Psychology, 204 R

Our Lord did not say He was "all truth" so that we could go to His statements as to a text-book and verify things; there are domains, such as science and art and history, which are distinctly man's domains and the boundaries of our knowledge must continually alter and be enlarged; God never encourages laziness. The question to be asked is not, "Does the Bible agree with the findings of modern science?" but, "Do the findings of modern science help us to a better understanding of the things revealed in the Bible?"

God's Workmanship, 424 L

SECOND COMING OF CHRIST

The only way to wait for the Second Coming is to watch that you do what you should do so that *when* He comes is a matter of indifference. It is the attitude of a child, certain that God knows what He is about. When the Lord does come it will be as natural as breathing. God never does anything hysterical, and He never produces hysterics.

Our Portrait in Genesis, 966 L

(Continued)

SECOND COMING OF CHRIST *(Continued)*

We are to "meet the Lord in the air." Is that conceivable to you? If it is, it certainly is not conceivable to me. I do not know how I am going to stay up "in the air" with the Lord; but that is no business of mine; all I know is that God's Book reveals that we shall do so.

Biblical Psychology, 213 R

"This same Jesus," who trod this earth with naked feet, "and wrought with human hands the creeds of creeds," is coming again, visibly and blessedly coming to earth again, when the petition will be fulfilled, "Thy kingdom come." All that men have ever dreamed of Utopias and of Golden Ages will fade into foolish fancies beside the wonder of that blessed Age, that blessed period of Christ's reign among men. We have to remain stedfastly certain in Him, not go out of Him to see when He is coming; it is to be prophetic *living* as well as prophetic study. To the saint everything is instinct with the purpose of God. History is fulfilling prophecy all the time.

God's Workmanship, 446 R

We are apt to make the mistake of looking for God to put things ostensibly right immediately. If we dwell much on the Second Coming without having a right spiritual relationship to God, it will make us ignore the need for spiritual tenacity.

God's Workmanship, 463 R

Jesus said, "The kingdom of God cometh not with observation." I believe in the Second Coming, but not always in its advocates. They are apt to ignore altogether what Jesus said.

The Servant as His Lord, 1276 R

SELF-DENIAL

Self-denial and self-sacrifice are continually spoken of as being good in themselves; Our Lord never used any such affectation. He aimed a blow at the mistake that self-denial is an end in itself. He spoke of self-denial and self-sacrifice as painful things that cost and hurt (see Matthew 10:38–39). The term self-denial has come to mean giving up things; the denial Jesus speaks of is a denial right out to my right to myself, a clean sweep of all the decks to the mastership of Jesus.

Approved Unto God, 17 R

Self-denial must have its spring in personal outflowing love to Our Lord; we are no longer our own; we are spoilt for every other interest in life saving as we can win men to Jesus Christ. The one great spring of sacrifice is devotion to Jesus, "For My sake."

Approved Unto God, 17 R

Paul argues in this way: If anything in me, right or wrong, is hindering God's work and causing another to stumble, I will give it up, even if it is the most legitimate thing on earth (see 1 Corinthians 8:13). People say, "Why cannot I do this?" For pity's sake do it! There is no reason why you shouldn't; there is neither right nor wrong about it; but if your love for Jesus Christ is not sufficient to disentangle you from a thousand and one things that would develop you, you know nothing about being His servant.

Approved Unto God, 21 L

"If any man will come after Me, let him deny himself." What is the meaning of these words from the lips of Jesus? He is not teaching us to deny one part of ourselves in order to benefit another part of ourselves, which is what self-denial has come to mean. The full force of our Lord's words is—"let him deny his right to himself; let him give up his right to himself to Me."

Facing Reality, 31 L

SELF-INDULGENCE

Jesus Christ is merciless to self-realisation, to self-indulgence, pride, unchastity, to everything that has to do with the disposition you did not know you had till you met Him. The Redemption does not tinker with the externals of a man's life; it deals with the disposition. "And they that are of Christ Jesus have crucified the flesh with the passions and the lusts thereof" (Galatians 5:24). No one is really Christ's till that is done.

Biblical Ethics, 116 R

Self-indulgence is a refusal to struggle, a refusal to make ourselves fit. We must be right ourselves before we can help others to be right.

The Place of Help, 1008 R

"I said in mine heart, Go to now, I will prove thee with mirth, therefore enjoy pleasure: and, behold, this also is vanity. I said of laughter, It is mad: and of mirth, What doeth it?" (Ecclesiastes 2:1–2).

Solomon was sick of trying to find any rationality at the back of things; he revolted from it, and indulged every passion and appetite without restraint. Always distinguish between the man who is naturally given to passion and appetite and the man who goes into these things from revolt. There is an irony and a bitterness and a criminality about the man who does it in revolt. In the same way there is a difference between laughter that is natural and laughter that is a revolt. There is nothing more awful than to hear laughter that is a revolt.

Shade of His Hand, 1197 R

Beware of any belief that makes you self-indulgent; it came from the pit, no matter how beautiful it sounds.

My Utmost for His Highest, August 27, 816 R

SELFISHNESS / SELF-INTEREST

When God's providence involves us unexpectedly in all sorts of complications, the test comes on two lines—Will I have faith in God; and will I ally myself with those who rescue the down-trodden irrespective of their beliefs? It is instructive to note in the Bible that faint-heartedness arises whenever self-interest begins to get luxurious. The sign of faint-heartedness in individuals is in the languid talk of "someone else" when there is anything to be done.

Not Knowing Whither, 872 R

"Thou art Simon. . . . thou shalt be called Cephas." Jesus writes the new name in those places in our lives where He has erased our pride and self-sufficiency and self-interest. Some of us have the new name in spots only—like sanctified measles.

Our Brilliant Heritage, 946 R

One of the reasons we lose fellowship with God is that we will explain and vindicate ourselves; we will not let God hunt through us and chase out the interests of self-will and self-assertion.

The Place of Help, 1036 R

If we are yearning to recover God, what we need is to get to the point of deciding against the self-assertiveness of our own hearts, and letting God teach us how to pay the price of our dreams.

The Place of Help, 1037 L

Paul was absolutely Christ-centred; he had lost all interest in himself in an absorbing passionate interest in Christ. Very few saints get where he got, and we are to blame for not getting there.

Conformed to His Image, 375 R

(Continued)

SELFISHNESS / SELF-INTEREST (Continued)

One of the most deeply ingrained forms of selfishness in human nature is that of misery. The isolation of misery is far more proud than any other form of conceit.

Shade of His Hand, 1236 L

If we only give up something to God because we want more back, there is nothing of the Holy Spirit in our abandonment; it is miserable commercial self-interest.

My Utmost for His Highest, March 12, 758 R

SELF-PITY

You cannot be too severe with self-pity in yourself or in others. Be more merciless with yourself than you are with others.

Disciples Indeed, 411 L

You could never awaken self-pity in the Apostle Paul; you might starve him or imprison him, but you could never knock out of him that uncrushable gaiety and certainty of God.

He Shall Glorify Me, 510 R

Why our Lord said that self-pity was of the devil is that self-pity will prevent us appreciating God's deliverance. When we begin to say "Why has this happened to me?" "Why does poverty begin to come to me?" "Why should this difficulty come, this upset?" it means that we are more concerned about getting our own way than in esteeming the marvellous deliverance God has wrought. We read of God's people of old that "They soon forgot His works," and we are in danger of doing the same unless we continually lift up our eyes to God and bless Him for His deliverances.

The Highest Good—The Pilgrim's Song Book, 533 R

Self-pity is taking the wrong standpoint, and if self-pity is indulged in, before long we will take part in the decaying thing instead of in that which grows more and more into the glory of God's presence.

The Love of God—The Message of Invincible Consolation, 671 R

What does it matter if external circumstances are hard? Why should they not be! If we give way to self-pity and indulge in the luxury of misery, we banish God's riches from our own lives and hinder others from entering into His provision. No sin is worse than the sin of self-pity, because it obliterates God and puts self-interest upon the throne.

My Utmost for His Highest, May 16, 781 L

SELF-REALISATION

Self-realisation is a modern phrase—"Be moral, be religious, be upright, in order that you may realise yourself." Nothing blinds the mind to the claims of Jesus more effectually than a good moral life based on the disposition of self-realisation.

Biblical Ethics, 116 L

From man's standpoint, self-realisation is full of light and wisdom; from God's standpoint, it is the dark night of the soul. Romans 7 describes the giving way of the foundations of self-realisation.

Biblical Ethics, 116 R

The modern jargon is all for self-realisation; we educate ourselves for the purpose of self-realisation; we select our friendships for self-realisation purposes. Jesus says, "Whosoever shall lose his life for My sake"— deliberately fling it away—"shall find it." The one great dominant recognition is that my personal self belongs to Jesus Christ.

The Servant as His Lord, 1270 R

It is a slander to the Cross of Christ to say we believe in Jesus and please ourselves all the time, choosing our own way.

The Highest Good—Thy Great Redemption,
559 R

SELF-RELIANCE

Never allow in yourself or in others the phrase "I can't"; it is unconscious blasphemy. If I put my inability as a barrier, I am telling God there is something He has not taken into account. Every element of self-reliance must be slain by the power of God.

Approved Unto God, 19 L

The people who say "I can't" are those who have a remnant of self-reliance left; a true saint never says "I can't," because it never occurs to him that he can! Complete weakness is always the occasion of the Spirit of God manifesting His power. Never allow anything to be in you that the Cross of Christ condemns.

Approved Unto God, 19 L

SENSUAL / SENSUALITY

Once allow suspicion of God and of His goodness and justice to enter into a man's mind and the floodgates of sensuality are opened. We mean by "sensuality," the life that draws its sustenance from natural surroundings, guided by a selfishly appointed purpose.

The Philosophy of Sin, 1109 L

Paul says, "Mortify the deeds of the body"; mortify means to destroy by neglect. . . . If I take any part of my natural life and use it to satisfy myself, that is sensuality. A Christian has to learn that his body is not his own.

The Shadow of an Agony, 1175 R

Every religious sentiment that is not worked out in obedience, carries with it a secret immorality; it is the way human nature is constituted. Whenever I utilise myself for my own ends, I am giving way to sensuality, and it is done not only physically, but mentally also; and one of the most humiliating things for a Christian is to realise how he does it. The impertinence of mental sensuality lies in the refusal to deny the right of an undisciplined intelligence that is contrary to Jesus Christ.

The Shadow of an Agony, 1175 R

SENT BY GOD

"And how shall they preach unless they be sent?"
(Romans 10:15).

The Christian worker must be sent; he must not elect to go. Nowadays that is the last thing thought of; it is a determination on the part of the individual—"This is something I can do, and I am going to do it." Beware of demanding that people go into work; it is a craze; the majority of saved souls are not fit to feed themselves yet.

How am I to know I have been sent of God? Firstly, by the realisation that I am utterly weak and powerless and if I am to be of any use to God, God must do it all the time. Is this the humiliating certainty of my soul, or merely a sentimental phrase? Secondly, because I know I have to point men to Jesus Christ, not to get them to think what a holy man I am. The only way to be sent is to let God lift us right out of any sense of fitness in ourselves and place us where He will.

Approved Unto God, 8 L

(Continued)

SENT BY GOD (Continued)

Before ever God can use us as workers He has to bring us to a place of entire poverty, where we shall have no doubt as to where we are, "Here I am, absolutely no good!" Then God can send us, but not until then. We put hindrances in the way of God's working by trying to do things for Him. The impatience of modern life has so crept into Christian work that we will not settle down before God and find out what He wants us to do.

Approved Unto God, 9 L

SERIOUS / SOLEMN

The one thing about Our Lord that the Pharisees found it hard to understand was His gaiety in connection with the things over which they were appallingly solemn. And what puzzled the religious people of Paul's day was his uncrushable gaiety; he treated buoyantly everything that they treated most seriously. Paul was in earnest over one thing only, and that was his relationship to Jesus Christ. There he was in earnest, and there they were totally indifferent.

Our Brilliant Heritage, 944 L

Reverence and solemnity are not the same. Solemnity is often nothing more than a religious dress on a worldly spirit.

Our Brilliant Heritage, 944 R

I have determinedly to take no one seriously but God, and the first person I have to leave severely alone as being the greatest fraud I have ever known is myself.

Not Knowing Whither, 881 R

SERMON ON THE MOUNT

What is the good of telling me to love my enemies—and that "Blessed are the pure in heart"? You may talk like that to further orders, but it does not amount to anything. Jesus Christ did not come to teach men to be or do any of these things: He did not come primarily to teach; He came to make a man the possessor of His own disposition, the disposition portrayed in the Sermon on the Mount.

Biblical Ethics, 111 L

In the training of art students, the master does not merely tell them what is wrong in a design; he puts the right design beside the wrong and lets them judge for themselves, and that is exactly what Jesus Christ did all through the Sermon on the Mount.

The Highest Good, 546 R

So many of us think only of the visible things, whereas the real concentration, the whole dead-set of the life, should be where our Lord put it in the huge "nugget" of truth which we call the Sermon on the Mount. There our Lord says, in effect, "Take no thought for your life; be carefully careless about everything saving one thing, your relationship to God." Naturally, we are apt to be carefully careless about everything saving that one thing.

The Love of God—The Message of Invincible Consolation, 672 L

Once a week at least read the Sermon on the Mount and see how much you have hearkened to it—"Love your enemies, bless them that curse you"; we do not listen to it because we do not want to. We have to learn to hearken to Jesus in everything, to get into the habit of finding out what He says.

Our Brilliant Heritage, 930 R

It is ingrained in our thinking that competition and rivalry are essential to the carrying on of civilised life; that is why Jesus Christ's statements seem wild and ridiculous. They are the statements either of a madman or of God Incarnate. To carry out the Sermon on the Mount is frankly impossible to anyone but a fool, and who is the fool? The man who has been born again and who dares to carry out in his individual life the teaching of Jesus. And what will happen? The inevitable result, not the success he would otherwise have. A hard saying, but true.

Our Portrait in Genesis, 963 R

The Sermon on the Mount is not a set of principles to be obeyed apart from identification with Jesus Christ. The Sermon on the Mount is a statement of the life we will live when the Holy Spirit is getting His way with us.

The Psychology of Redemption, 1069 R

Our Lord began His discourse by saying, "Blessed are. . . . " and His hearers must have been staggered by what followed. According to Jesus Christ they were to be blessed in every condition which from earliest childhood they had been taught to regard as a curse.

Studies in the Sermon on the Mount, 1441 L

The Beatitudes seem merely mild and beautiful precepts for unworldly people and of very little use for the stern world in which we live. We soon find, however, that they contain the dynamite of the Holy Ghost; they explode like a spiritual "mine" when the circumstances of our lives require them to do so, and rip and tear and revolutionise all our conceptions.

Studies in the Sermon on the Mount, 1441 L

If the old commandments were difficult, our Lord's principles are unfathomably more difficult. Our Lord goes behind the old law to the disposition. Everything He teaches

is impossible unless He can put into us His Spirit and remake us from within. The Sermon on the Mount is quite unlike the Ten Commandments in the sense of its being absolutely unworkable unless Jesus Christ can remake us.

Studies in the Sermon on the Mount, 1443 L

SERVANT OF GOD

If we trace the lineaments of the servants of God in the Bible, we find a servant of God to be altogether different from an instrument of God. An instrument of God is one whom God takes up and uses and puts down again. A servant of God is one who has given up for ever his right to himself, and is bound to his Lord as His slave.

Christian Disciplines, Volume 1,
The Discipline of Divine Guidance, 274 R

A man may be used as an instrument of God without being a servant of God.

Christian Disciplines, Volume 2,
The Discipline of Loneliness, 329 R

The whole idea of the prayers of the saints is that God's holiness, God's purpose and God's wise ways may be brought about irrespective of who comes or goes. The notion has grown almost imperceptibly that God is simply a blessing machine for men—"If I link myself on to God He will see me through"; instead, the human race is meant to be the servant of God, a different thing altogether.

He Shall Glorify Me, 497 R

(Continued)

SERVANT OF GOD (Continued)

"What then? notwithstanding, every way, whether in pretence, or in truth, Christ is preached; and I therein do rejoice, yea, and will rejoice" (Philippians 1:18).

This brings us up against a big problem, a problem our Lord refers to in Matthew 7:21–23. Because God honours His word no matter how preached or by whom, we naturally infer that if His word is blessed, souls saved, demons cast out, mighty works done, surely the preacher must be a servant of God. It does not follow by any means. An instrument of God and a servant of God ought to be identical, but our Lord's words and Paul's are instances where they are not. It does not impair the inspiration of the Gospel to have it preached by a bad man, but the influence of the preacher, worthy or unworthy, apart altogether from his preaching, has a tremendous effect.

Conformed to His Image, 374 L

"I have had visions on the mount," "wonderful times of communion with God"—but is it turning you into an individual infinitely superior to your Lord and Master? one who won't wash feet, but will only give himself up to certain types of meeting?

Disciples Indeed, 396 L

"If I then, the Lord and the Master, have washed your feet, ye also ought to wash one another's feet": the highest motive is the only motive for the lowliest service. Where do we stand in God's sight under that scrutiny?

Disciples Indeed, 396 L

As you go on with God He will give you thoughts that are a bit too big for you. God will never leave a servant of His with ideas he can easily express; He will always express through him more than he can grasp.

Disciples Indeed, 409 R

Our Lord makes the test of goodness not only goodness in intention, but the active carrying out of God's will. Beware of confounding appearance and reality, of judging only by external evidence. God honours His word no matter who preaches it. The men Jesus Christ refers to in [Matthew 7] verse 21 were instruments, but an instrument is not a servant. A servant is one who has given up his right to himself to the God Whom he proclaims, a witness to Jesus, i.e., a satisfaction to Jesus Christ wherever he goes.

Studies in the Sermon on the Mount, 1469 R

Paul's idea of service is the same as our Lord's: "I am among you as He that serveth"; "ourselves your servants for Jesus' sake." We have the idea that a man called to the ministry is called to be a different kind of being from other men. According to Jesus Christ, he is called to be the "door-mat" of other men; their spiritual leader, but never their superior.

My Utmost for His Highest, February 23, 752 R

The ecclesiastical idea of a servant of God is not Jesus Christ's idea. His idea is that we serve Him by being the servants of other men. Jesus Christ out-socialists the socialists. He says that in His Kingdom he that is greatest shall be the servant of all. The real test of the saint is not preaching the gospel, but washing disciples' feet, that is, doing the things that do not count in the actual estimate of men, but count everything in the estimate of God.

My Utmost for His Highest, February 25, 753 L

Paul delighted to spend himself out for God's interests in other people, and he did not care what it cost. We come in with our economical notions—"Suppose God wants me to go there—what about the salary? What about the climate? How shall I be looked after? A man must consider these things." All that is an indication that we are serving God with a reserve.

My Utmost for His Highest, February 25, 753 L

If you want to know what a servant of God is to be like, read what Isaiah says in this chapter* and the following ones about the great Servant, Jesus Christ. The characteristics of the great Servant must be the characteristics of every servant; it is the identification of the servant of God with the immortal characteristics of God Himself.

Notes on Isaiah, 1384 L
**Isaiah 42*

The whole conception of the work of a servant of God is to lift up the despairing and the hopeless. Immediately you start work on God's line He will bring the weak and infirm round you; the surest sign that God is at work is that that is the class who come—the very class we don't want, with the pain and the distress and limitation. We want the strong and robust, and God gathers round us the feeble-minded, the afflicted and weak.

Notes on Isaiah, 1385 L

SERVICE

Are we willing to be broken bread and poured-out wine in Jesus Christ's hands for others? to be spoilt for this age, for this life, this time, spoilt from every standpoint saving as we can disciple men and women to Him? My life as a worker is the way I say "Thank you" to God for His unspeakable salvation.

Approved Unto God, 6 R

Remember you are accountable to no one but God; keep yourself for His service along the line of His providential leading for you, not on the line of your temperament.

Approved Unto God, 8 R

If you want to remain a full-orbed grape you must keep out of God's hands for He will crush you; wine cannot be had in any other way.

Approved Unto God, 21 R

We must not dictate to Jesus as to where we are going to serve Him.

Facing Reality, 32 R

"He that believeth on Me, as the scripture hath said, out of his belly shall flow rivers of living water" (John 7:38).

How anxious we are to serve God and our fellow men to-day! Jesus Our Lord says we must pay attention to the Source—belief in Him, and He will look after the outflow. He has promised that there shall be "rivers of living water," but we must not look at the outflow, nor rejoice in successful service. "Notwithstanding in this rejoice not, that the spirits are subject unto you; but rather rejoice, because your names are written in heaven" (Luke 10:20).

Facing Reality, 34 R

If you are going to live for the service of your fellow-men, you will certainly be pierced through with many sorrows, for you will meet with more base ingratitude from your fellow-men than you would from a dog. You will meet with unkindness and "two-facedness," and if your motive is love for your fellow-men, you will be exhausted in the battle of life. But if the mainspring of your service is love for God, no ingratitude, no sin, no devil, no angel, can hinder you from serving your fellow-men, no matter how they treat you. You can love your neighbour as yourself, not from pity, but from the true centring of yourself in God.

Biblical Psychology, 191 R

(Continued)

SERVICE (Continued)

Nothing is cleaner or grander or sweeter than light. Light cannot be soiled; a sunbeam may shine into the dirtiest puddle, but it is never soiled. A sheet of white paper can be soiled, so can almost any white substance, but you cannot soil light. Men and women who are rightly related to God can go and work in the most degraded slums of the cities, or in the vilest parts of heathendom where all kinds of immorality are practised, without being defiled because God keeps them like the light, unsullied.

Biblical Psychology, 189 L

Whenever success is made the motive of service, infidelity to our Lord is the inevitable result. (Cf. Luke 10:20.)

Disciples Indeed, 410 L

We make the mistake of imagining that service for others springs from love of others; the fundamental fact is that supreme love for our Lord alone gives us the motive power of service to any extent for others—"ourselves your servants for Jesus' sake." That means I have to identify myself with God's interests in other people, and God is interested in some extraordinary people, viz., in you and in me, and He is just as interested in the person you dislike as He is in you.

Conformed to His Image, 370 R

To be everlastingly on the look-out to do some work for God means I want to evade sacramental service—"I want to do what I want to do." Maintain the attitude of a child towards God and He will do what He likes with you. If God puts you on the shelf it is in order to season you. If He is pleased to put you in limited circumstances so that you cannot go out into the highways of service, then enter into sacramental service. Once you enter that service, you can enter no other.

Conformed to His Image, 371 L

May God save us from Christian service which is nothing more than the reaction of a disappointed, crushed heart, seeking surcease from sorrow in social service. Christian service is the vital, unconscious result of the life of a believer in Jesus.

Facing Reality, 34 R

Christian service is not our work; loyalty to Jesus is our work.

Disciples Indeed, 410 L

Nothing hoodwinks us more quickly than the idea that we are serving God.

Disciples Indeed, 411 R

"Let not your heart be troubled." When we dream of ourselves in God's service our hearts do get troubled—"I think this is what God is preparing me for." God is not preparing you for anything; obedience is its own end in the purpose of God; be faithful to Him. Never say, "I wonder what God is doing with me just now." That is no business of yours, and the Spirit of God will never give you an answer. If you are spiritual I defy you to tell anyone what God is preparing you for; the preparation is His end.

God's Workmanship, 426 R

Being seated together in heavenly places in Christ Jesus does not mean lolling about on the mount of transfiguration, singing ecstatic hymns, and letting demon-possessed boys go to the devil in the valley; it means being in the accursed places of this earth as far as the walk of the feet is concerned, but in undisturbed communion with God.

If Thou Wilt Be Perfect, 588 R

Notice the words that Our Lord glorified. A word that was scorned when He came was the word "servant," yet Jesus said: "I am among you as He that serveth," and, whosoever of you will be the chiefest, shall be servant of all." Our Lord took words that were despised and transfigured their meaning; He did things that were commonplace and sordid and ordinary and transfigured them. Our Lord was the unconscious light in the midst of the most ordinary circumstances conceivable.

The Love of God—The Ministry of the Unnoticed, 662 R

Jesus Christ counts as service not what we do for Him, but what we are to Him, and the inner secret of that is identity with Him in person. "That I may know Him."

The Moral Foundations of Life, 725 R

"And Abraham rose up early in the morning . . . and went unto the place of which God had told him" (Genesis 22:3).

Always guard against self-chosen service for God; self sacrifice may be a disease. God chose the crucible for Abraham, and Abraham made no demur, he went steadily through. If God has made your cup sweet, drink it with grace; if He has made it bitter, drink it in communion with Him. If it is a hard time of difficulty in the providential order of God, go through with it, but never choose your own service. If God has given the command, He will look after everything; your business is to get up and go, and smilingly wash your hands of the consequences.

Not Knowing Whither, 900 R

Fuss is always a sign of fever. A great many people mistake perspiration in service for inspiration in devotion. The characteristic of a man who has come to God is that you cannot get him to take anyone seriously but God.

The Place of Help, 1042 L

With us, Christian service is something we do; with Jesus Christ it is not what we *do for* Him, but what we *are to* Him that He calls service.

The Place of Help, 1029 L

After the Resurrection, Jesus Christ did not invite the disciples to a time of communion on the Mount of Transfiguration; He said—"Feed My sheep."

The Psychology of Redemption, 1093 R

There is so much self-chosen service; we say—"I think I will do this, and that for God." Unless we work for God in accordance with His supernatural call, we shall meet havoc and disaster and upset. The moment that the consciousness of the call of God dawns on us, we know that it is not a choice of our own at all; the consciousness is that of being held by a power we do not fully know.

So Send I You, 1290 L

We make a blunder when we fix on the particular location for our service and say— "God called me *there*." When God shifts the location, the battle comes—will I remain consistent to what I have said I am going to do, or be true to the insurgent call of God, and let Him locate me where He likes?

So Send I You, 1290 R

We are so busy telling God where we should like to go. Most of us are waiting for some great opportunity, something that is sensational, then we cry—"Here am I; send me." Whenever Jesus is in the ascendant, in revival times, when the exciting moment comes, we are there; but readiness for God and for His work means that we are ready to do the tiniest thing or the great big thing, it makes no difference.

So Send I You, 1296 R

(Continued)

SERVICE *(Continued)*

Be ready for the sudden surprise visits of Our Lord, and remember there is no such thing as prominent service and obscure service; it is all the same with God, and God knows better than ourselves what we are ready to do.

So Send I You, 1297 R

Pain in God's service always leads to glory. We want success; God wants glory. Some of us have the notion, till God shakes it out of us, that we are saved and sanctified to have a holy hilarious time before God and among men. Never! We are saved and sanctified to be the servants of men—"ourselves your servants for Jesus' sake."

Notes on Isaiah, 1385 R

SEX

If your religion does not make you a better man, it is a rotten religion. The test of true religion is when it touches these four things—food, money, sex and mother earth. These things are the test of a right sane life with God, and the religion that ignores them or abuses them is not right.

Shade of His Hand, 1227 L

Remember we are to be not numskulls, but holy men, full-blooded and holy to the last degree, not anaemic creatures without enough strength to be bad. The relation to life ordained by Jesus Christ does not unsex men and women, but enables them to be holy men and women.

Shade of His Hand, 1227 L

Four things—sex, money, food, and mother earth—make a man a king and a woman a queen, or they make a man a beast and a woman a she devil.

Shade of His Hand, 1230 L

The three main sensibilities in a man's life are sex, money and food. What has he to do with them? They are not sinful; they are plain facts which can be either devilish or sublime. Whenever Jesus Christ brought His teaching to a focus it was on two points, viz., Marriage and Money. In ordaining sex God took the bigger risk and made either the most gigantic blunder or the most sublime thing. Sex has to be controlled, so have money and food. By what? By the highest.

The Shadow of an Agony, 1176 L

We hear the talk nowadays of an "impossible chastity." Chastity is undesirable if I want to be a beast; but no holiness or rectitude of character is impossible; it is simply undesirable if I prefer the other way.

Shade of His Hand, 1229 L

SHAKESPEARE, WILLIAM

In Shakespeare's writings there is an undercurrent of faith which makes him the peculiarly valuable writer he is, and makes him more at home to those who understand the Bible point of view than to those who do not.

Shade of His Hand, 1195 R

SHALLOW AND PROFOUND

Our lives are lived in two compartments, the shallow and the profound, and both domains are to be God's. There is always the temptation to live only in the profound, and to despise others for not understanding our profundity. We are apt to forget that God is in the shallow as well as in the profound. We have to see that we live our shallow life in as godly a manner as we live the profound.

The Place of Help, 1021 R

One of the greatest defects in Christianity is that it is not shallow enough. . . . It is religious enough, supernormally moral, but not able to eat, drink and be merry. Jesus Christ made the shallow and the profound, the give and the take, one. The art of shallow conversation is one that is rarely learned. It is a great gift as well as a real ministration to be able to say nothing cleverly. It is an insult to be everlastingly introducing subjects that make people think on the deepest lines. It takes all the essence of Christianity to be shallow properly.

Shade of His Hand, 1221 L

To be shallow is not a sign of being wicked, nor is shallowness a sign that there are no deeps; the ocean has a shore. The shallow amenities of life, eating and drinking, walking and talking, are all ordained by God. These are the things in which Our Lord lived. He lived in them as the Son of God, and He said that "the disciple is not above his Master." . . . We are so abominably serious, so desperately interested in our own characters, that we refuse to behave like Christians in the shallow concerns of life.

My Utmost for His Highest, November 22, 847 R

SILENCE

God will give us the blessings we want if we won't go any further, but His silence is the sign that He is bringing us into this marvellous understanding of Himself.

If Ye Shall Ask, 619 R

As long as we have the idea only that God will bless us in answer to prayer, He will do it, but He will never give us the grace of a silence. If He is taking us into the understanding that prayer is for the glorifying of His Father, He will give us the first sign of His intimacy—silence. The devil calls it unanswered prayer; in the case of Martha

and Mary the Spirit of God called it a sign that He loved them, and because He loved them and knew they were fit to receive a bigger revelation than ever they dreamed of, He stayed where He was.

If Ye Shall Ask, 619 R

SIMPLICITY

Do not mistake simplicity for stupidity. By "simplicity" is meant the simplicity that was in Jesus Christ. Paul says, "I fear, lest by any means . . . your minds should be corrupted from the simplicity that is in Christ" (2 Corinthians 11:3).

Biblical Psychology, 199 L

Beware of the people who tell you life is simple. Life is such a mass of complications that no man is safe apart from God. Coming to Jesus does not simplify life; it simplifies my relationship to God.

Disciples Indeed, 395 R

As we go on in the Christian life it gets simpler, for the very reason that we get less inclined to say, "Now, why did God allow this and that?"

The Place of Help, 1039 R

Beware of believing that the human soul is simple; look at yourself, or read the 139th Psalm, and you will soon find the human soul is much too complex to touch. When an intellectualist says that life is simple, you may be sure he is sufficiently removed from facts to have no attention paid to him. Things look simple as he writes about them, but let him get "into the soup," and he will find they are complicated. The only simple thing in human life is our relationship to God in Christ.

The Shadow of an Agony, 1174 R

(Continued)

SIMPLICITY *(Continued)*

The essence of the Gospel of God working through conscience and conduct is that it shows itself at once in action. God can make simple, guileless people out of cunning, crafty people; that is the marvel of the grace of God. It can take the strands of evil and twistedness out of a man's mind and imagination and make him simple towards God, so that his life becomes radiantly beautiful by the miracle of God's grace.

Biblical Psychology, 199 L

SIN

No man is held responsible by God for having an heredity of sin: what God holds a man responsible for is refusing to let Jesus Christ deliver him from it when he sees that that is what He came to do (see John 3:19).

Baffled to Fight Better, 63 L

Sin is not man's problem, but God's. God has taken the problem of sin into His own hands and solved it, and the proof that He has is the Cross of Calvary. The Cross is the Cross of God.

Baffled to Fight Better, 83 L

Remember what sin is: fundamental independence of God; the thing in me that says, I can do without God, I don't need Him. The hatred of the world has its source there.

Biblical Ethics, 100 L

It was the tragedy caused by sin that made new birth necessary. It sounds much more sensible to say that if a man goes on evolving and developing he will become a spiritual being; but once get a dose of "the plague of your own heart" and you will find that things are as the Bible says they are, tragically wrong.

Biblical Ethics, 102 R

If you are not delivered from any particular element of sin, the reason is either you don't believe God can deliver you or you don't want Him to

Biblical Ethics, 112 R

According to the Bible, sin is doing without God. Sin is not wrong doing; it is wrong *being*, deliberate and emphatic independence of God. That may sound remote and far away from us, but in individual experience it is best put in the terms of "my claim to my right to myself."

Biblical Ethics, 129 R

The essential nature of sin is my claim to my right to myself.

Bringing Sons Unto Glory, 220 L

Every other view of sin, saving the Bible view, looks on sin as a disease, a weakness, a blunder, an infirmity; the Bible revelation shows sin to be an anarchy, not a missing of the mark merely, but a refusal to aim at the mark.

Christian Disciplines, Volume 2,
The Discipline of Patience, 335 R

Read John 3:19 and you will see how our Lord uses the word "darkness." "This is the judgement," He says, i.e., the critical moment, "that the light is come into the world, and men loved the darkness rather than the light; for their works were evil" (RV). On another occasion Jesus said, "If therefore the light that is in thee be darkness, how great is that darkness!" Darkness is my own point of view; when once I allow the prejudice of my head to shut down the witness of my heart, I make my heart dark.

Biblical Psychology, 178 R

A darkened heart is a terrible thing, because a darkened heart may make a man peaceful. A man says—"My heart is not bad, I am not convicted of sin; all this talk about being born again and filled with the Holy Spirit is so much absurdity." The natural heart needs the Gospel of Jesus, but it does not want it; it will fight against it, and it takes the convicting Spirit of God to make men and women know they need to experience a radical work of grace in their hearts.

Biblical Psychology, 179 L

And this is the condemnation," said Jesus, "that light is come into the world, and men loved darkness rather than light, because their deeds were evil" (John 3:19). "Darkness" is my own point of view, my prejudices and preconceived determinations; if the Spirit of God agrees with these, well and good; if not, I shall go my own way.

Biblical Psychology, 203 R

Many of us do believe in Jesus; we have received the Holy Spirit and know we are children of God, and yet we won't make the moral decision about sin, viz., that it must be killed right out in us. It is the great moment of our lives when we decide that sin must die right out, not be curbed or suppressed or counteracted, but crucified. It is not done easily; it is only done by a moral wrench. We never understand the relation between a human life and the Cross of Christ until we perform a moral act and have the light of God thrown upon reality.

Conformed to His Image, 361 L

To say that what God condemned in the Cross was social sins is not true; what God condemns in the Cross is *sin* which is away further down than any moral quirks.

Conformed to His Image, 375 R

The essence of sin is the refusal to recognise that we are accountable to God at all.

The Moral Foundations of Life, 710 L

Beware of attempting to diagnose sin unless you have the inner pang that you are one of the worst sinners.

Disciples Indeed, 403 L

Whenever you talk about sin, it must be "my" sin. So long as you speak of "sins" you evade Jesus Christ for yourself.

Disciples Indeed, 403 L

Our Lord never sympathised with sin; He came to "proclaim liberty to the captives," a very different thing. We have to see that we don't preach a theology of sympathy, but the theology of a Saviour from sin.

Disciples Indeed, 403 R

When you come in contact with the great destructive sins in men's lives, be reverent with what you don't understand. God says, "Leave that one to Me."

Disciples Indeed, 411 R

I will do anything rather than take the responsibility on myself for having done wrong: or if I do accept the responsibility, I defy God to readjust me; the one is as bad as the other. I either refuse to say I have sinned, or I admit I have sinned and refuse to let God save me; I won't allow God to have the last word; I have the last word and intend to stick to it.

Our Portrait in Genesis, 961 R

The Bible always speaks of sin as it appears in its final analysis. Jesus does not say, "You must not covet because it will lead to stealing"; He says, "You must not covet because it *is* stealing." He does not say, "You must not be angry with your brother because it will lead to murder"; He says, "You must not be angry with your brother because it *is* murder." "Whosoever hateth his brother is a murderer" (1 John 3:15). When the climax of these things is reached we begin to see the meaning of Calvary.

Our Portrait in Genesis, 980 L

(Continued)

SIN (Continued)

To sin alone is never possible.

The Philosophy of Sin, 1108 L

It is only the right view of sin and right thinking about sin that ever will explain Jesus Christ's Life and Death and Resurrection. It is sin that He came to cope with; He did not come to cope with the poor little mistakes of men; they cope with their own mistakes; He came to give them a totally new stock of heredity; that is, He came to implant into them His own nature, so that Satan's power in the soul is absolutely destroyed, not counteracted.

The Philosophy of Sin, 1109 R

No wonder God's Book says, "the way of transgressors is hard." Could God have made it more terrible than He has for man to go astray? Could He have put the danger signals more clearly than He has? The way is absolutely strewn with alarm signals; it is impossible to go wrong easily.

The Philosophy of Sin, 1124 R

A man may look all right in his ostensible religious life, he may have had a vivid religious history, but his private life may be rotten. It is a terrible thing to become blunt and insensitive. Sin destroys the power of knowing that we sin.

The Place of Help, 1054 R

The knowledge of evil that came through the Fall gives a man a broad mind, but instead of instigating him to action it paralyses his action. Men and women whose minds are poisoned by gross experience of evil are marvellously generous with regard to other people's sins; they argue in this way—"To know all is to pardon all." Every bit of their broadmindedness paralyses their power to *do* anything.

The Servant as His Lord, 1266 R

Always beware of an estimate of life which does not recognise the fact that there is sin.

My Utmost for His Highest, June 24, 794 L

One of the first things we discover in dealing with the big universal problem is that it is mirrored in each individual life.

The Shadow of an Agony, 1174 R

When a man sins magnificently he is always punished monotonously; that is the ingenuity of punishment.

The Place of Help, 1057 L

Sin is a disposition of self-love that obeys every temptation to its own lordship. Sin is literally self-centred rule, a disposition that rules the life apart from God.

The Philosophy of Sin, 1125 R

SINLESS PERFECTION

The sinless perfection heresy arises out of this confusion—it says that because the disposition of sin is removed, it is impossible to sin. The inclination to sin, thank God, is removed, but never the possibility. If the power to disobey were removed, our obedience would be of no value, for we should cease to be morally responsible. It is gloriously possible not to sin, but never impossible to sin, because we are moral agents.

The Philosophy of Sin, 1125 R

The one thing that will enable us to stop sinning is the experience of new birth, i.e., entire sanctification. When we are born into the new realm the life of God is born in us, and the life of God in us cannot sin (1 John 3:9). That does not mean that we cannot sin; it means that if we obey the life of God in us, we *need not* sin. God never takes away our power to disobey; if He did, our obedience would be of no value, for we should cease to be morally responsible. By regeneration God puts in us the power not to sin.

The Psychology of Redemption, 1070 R

No good man is impeccable; that is, he never arrives at the place where it is impossible to sin. A man is able not to sin, but it never becomes impossible for him to sin.

Shade of His Hand, 1227 R

Sin was in existence in Jeremiah's day, and in John Wesley's day, and it is in our existence in our day, but in very different guises. To-day we have to fight the Higher Thought teaching, the Mind Cure teaching, Christian Science; the one great objection of all these is to sin. Sin to them is a mere nuisance.

Notes on Jeremiah, 1394 L

" . . . saying Peace, peace; when there is no peace" (Jeremiah 6:14).
    "They treat the healing of the hurt of My people as a trifling, temperamental matter; there is no such thing as the grace of shame amongst them." The majority of people do not see what is wrong, and the talk of a prophet like Jeremiah is nonsense. We never can face the things that are wrong, apart from God, without getting insane. If sin is a trifling thing and we can preach to the healing of people and bring peace on any other line, then the tragedy of the Cross is a huge blunder.

Notes on Jeremiah, 1400 R

SLEEP

I wonder if we have ever considered the Bible implications about sleep? It is not true to say that sleep is simply meant for physical recuperation; surely much less time than God has ordered would have served that purpose. The Revised Version suggests a deeper, profounder ministry for sleep than mere physical recuperation. "For so He giveth unto His beloved *in* sleep." The deepest concerns of our souls, whether they be good or bad, are furthered during sleep. It is not merely a physical fact that you go to bed perplexed and wake clear-minded; God has been ministering to you during sleep. Sometimes God cannot get at us until we are asleep.

The Highest Good—The Pilgrim's Song Book, 536 R

Sleep is God's celestial nurse who croons away our consciousness, and God deals with the unconscious life of the soul in places where only He and His angels have charge. As you retire to rest, give your soul and God a time together, and commit your life to God with a conscious peace for the hours of sleep, and deep and profound developments will go on in spirit, soul and body by the kind creating hand of our God.

The Highest Good—The Pilgrim's Song Book, 537 L

We do not sufficiently realise the need to pray when we lie down at night, "Deliver us from the evil one." It puts us in the attitude of asking the Lord to watch our minds and our dreams, and He will do it.

The Philosophy of Sin, 1115 R

"The sleep of a labouring man is sweet, whether he eat little or much: but the abundance of the rich will not suffer him to sleep" (Ecclesiastes 5:12).
    The sleep of a labouring man is sweet; it recreates him. The Bible indicates that sleep is not meant only for the recuperation of a man's body, but that there is a tremendous furtherance of spiritual and moral life during sleep.

Shade of His Hand, 1215 L

(Continued)

SLEEP (Continued)

In the Bible there are times when in the deep slumber of the body God has taken the souls of His servants into deeper communion with Himself (e.g. Genesis 2:21, 15:12). Often when a problem or perplexity harasses the mind and there seems no solution, after a night's rest you find the solution easy, and the problem has no further perplexity. Think of the security of the saint in sleeping or in waking, "Thou shalt not be afraid for the terror by night, nor for the arrow that flieth by day."

The Highest Good—The Pilgrim's Song Book, 537 L

SLOTHFULNESS (See LAZINESS)

SOCIAL WORK

Social reform is part of the work of ordinary honourable humanity and a Christian does it because his worship is for the Son of God, not because he sees it is the most sensible thing to do. The first great duty of the Christian is not to the needs of his fellow-men, but to the will of his Saviour.

The Psychology of Redemption, 1080 L

It is an interesting study in psychology to watch people who are engaged in drastic social and rescue work and find out whether they are doing it for a surcease from their own troubles, to get relief from a broken heart. In a great many cases the worker wants a plaster for his own life. He takes up slum work, not because it is the great passion of his life, but because he must get something to deliver him from the gnawing pain of his own heart. The people he works amongst are often right when they say he is doing it to save his own soul.

Shade of His Hand, 1209 R

SOCIETY (See CIVILISATION)

SOLITARINESS

There is such a thing as an obsession of solitariness. Hermits, ascetics and celibates cut themselves off in revolt—"Because I cannot find peace or joy or happiness in the tyranny of civilised life or in commerce, and I cannot be an idle tramp, I become a solitary and live a sequestered life." Solomon points out what history has proved that this is an experiment that ends disastrously, because a man cannot shut out what is inside by cutting himself off from the outside.

Shade of His Hand, 1209 R

[A] man may say: "I believe in quiet mysticism, cutting myself off from everything around and getting at things by a spiritual life of my own." The monks in the Middle Ages refused to take the responsibilities of life by shutting themselves away from the world, and people to-day seek to do the same by cutting themselves off from this and that relationship. Paul says: "Beware of those who ignore the basis of human life." If I refuse to accept nations or churches or human beings as facts, I shall find I have nothing to help solve the problems that arise.

The Shadow of an Agony, 1173 R

"Oh that I had wings like a dove! Then would I fly away, and be at rest." The desire is to be solitary—"If only I could get away and be quiet; if only I could live in a sunrise or a sunset!" We have to find our true life in things as they are with that on the inside which keeps us right. The true energy of life lies in being rightly related to God, and only there is true joy found.

Shade of His Hand, 1209 R

Jesus Christ was rarely alone; the times when He was alone are distinctly stated. Solitariness to be beneficial must never be sought and must never be on account of sin. If I choose solitariness, I go back into active life with annoyance and a contempt for other people, proving that my seeking solitariness was selfish.

Conformed to His Image, 362 L

A man who lives a mystical life or an intellectual life frequently has an attitude of lofty contempt towards others. No man has any right to maintain such an attitude towards another human being, watching him as a spectator for purposes of his own, as journalistic copy, or as a religious specimen; if he does he ceases to be a human being by pretending to be more.

Shade of His Hand, 1226 R

No room is allowed either in the Old or New Testament for mysticism pure and simple, because that will mean sooner or later an aloofness from actual life, a kind of contempt expressed or implied by a superior attitude, by occult relationships and finer sensibilities. That attitude is never countenanced in the Bible.

Shade of His Hand, 1195 L

SOLITUDE

Solitude with God repairs the damage done by the fret and noise and clamour of the world. To have been on the mount with God means that we carry with us an exhilaration, an incommunicable awe.

Christian Disciplines, Volume 2,
The Discipline of Loneliness, 318 L

The enemy goes all he can against our communion with God, against our solitude with God; he tries to prevent us from drawing our breath in the fear of the Lord.

Disciples Indeed, 397 R

The nutriment of a man's life comes when he is alone with God; he gets his direction in the desert experiences.

He Shall Glorify Me, 491 R

Any soul who has not that solitary place alone with God is in supreme peril spiritually. Let us ask ourselves if we have allowed the solitary places to be broken down or built over with altars that look beautiful, and people passing by say "How religious that man or woman must be." Such an altar, if there is no other in the solitary place, is an insult to the deep work of God in our souls.

He Shall Glorify Me, 511 R

Profoundly speaking, we are not here to work for God. Absorption in practical work is one of the greatest hindrances in preventing a soul discerning the call of God. Unless active work is balanced by a deep isolated solitude with God, knowledge of God does not grow and the worker becomes exhausted and spent out.

Not Knowing Whither, 901 R

When God gets us alone by affliction, heartbreak, or temptation, by disappointment, sickness, or by thwarted affection, by a broken friendship, or by a new friendship—when He gets us absolutely alone, and we are dumbfounded and cannot ask one question, then He begins to expound. . . . There are whole tracts of stubbornness and ignorance to be revealed by the Holy Spirit in each one of us, and it can only be done when Jesus gets us alone. Are we alone with Him now, or are we taken up with little fussy notions, fussy comradeships in God's service, fussy ideas about our bodies? Jesus can expound nothing until we get through all the noisy questions of the head and are alone with Him.

My Utmost for His Highest, January 13, 739 L

SONG OF SOLOMON

The daring sufficiency of the Song of Songs is an example of how easy it is to make that sublime Song grovel in Eastern voluptuousness and sensual wallowing; but for the soul walking alone with God its language is the choicest in the whole Bible to adequately express the eternal pleasure of this blessed loneliness.

Christian Disciplines, Volume 2,
The Discipline of Loneliness, 331 R

SORROW

Job's actual life looked exactly the same after his suffering as before to anyone who does not know the inner history. That is the disguise of the actual. There is always this difference in the man who has been through real trouble—his society is enlarged in every direction, he is much bigger minded, more generous and liberal, more capable of entertaining strangers. One of the greatest emancipators of personal life is sorrow.

Baffled to Fight Better, 85 R

We can fathom our own natures by the things we sorrow over. . . . Jeremiah has been called "the weeping prophet," and in his Lamentations we find that the secret of his sorrow is Jerusalem, the city of his love . . . and we remember with adoring wonder that Our Lord is known throughout all generations as "a Man of sorrows."

He Shall Glorify Me, 511 L

Every forgiven soul will love the world so much that he hates to death the sin that is damning men; to love the world in any other sense is to be an enemy of God: to love the world as God loves it is to spend and be spent that men might be saved from their sins.

He Shall Glorify Me, 512 L

To-day there are in our midst many so-called Christian movements, but they bear the characteristic of being without sorrow for sin and without sympathy for suffering.

He Shall Glorify Me, 512 R

In our mental outlook we have to reconcile ourselves to the fact that sin is the only explanation as to why Jesus Christ came, the only explanation of the grief and the sorrow that there is in life.

The Place of Help, 1043 L

"Now is my soul troubled; and what shall I say? Father, save me from this hour. But for this cause came I unto this hour" (John 12:27).
     Jesus Christ is asking God to save Him *out of* the hour, not *from* it. All through, that is the inner attitude of Jesus Christ; He received Himself in the fires of sorrow; it was never "Do not let the sorrow come." That is the opposite of what we do; we pray, "Oh, Lord, don't let this or that happen to me"; consequently all kinds of damaging and blasphemous things are said about answers to prayer. You hear of one man who has gone safely through battles, and friends tell him it is in answer to prayer; does that mean that the prayers for the men who have gone under have not been answered? We have to remember that the hour of darkness will come in every life. It is not that we are saved from the hour of sorrow, but that we are delivered in it.

The Place of Help, 1043 R

People say there ought to be no sorrow; but the fact remains that there *is* sorrow; there is not one family just now without its sorrow, and we have to learn to receive ourselves in its fires. If we try to evade sorrow and refuse to lay our account with it, we are foolish, for sorrow is one of the biggest facts in life, and there is no use saying it ought not to be; it is. It is ridiculous to say things ought not to be when they are.

The Place of Help, 1043 R

A man who wants to find an explanation of why things are as they are is an intellectual lunatic. There is nothing gained by saying, "Why should there be sin and sorrow and suffering?" They *are*; it is not for me to find out why God made what I am pleased to consider a mistake; I have to find out what to do in regard to it all.

The Place of Help, 1043 R

Jesus Christ's attitude is that I have to receive myself in the fires of sorrow. . . . sorrow does not necessarily make a man better; sorrow burns up a great amount of unnecessary shallowness; it gives me my self, or it destroys me. If a man becomes acquainted with sorrow, the gift it presents him with is his self.

The Place of Help, 1043 R

You always know the person who has been through the fires of sorrow and has received himself; you never smell the fire on him, and you are certain you can go to him when you are in trouble. It is not the man with the signs of sorrow on him who is helpful, but the one who has gone through the fires and received himself; he is delivered from the small side of himself, and has ample leisure for others. The one who has not been through the fires of sorrow has no time for you and is inclined to be contemptuous and impatient. If I have received myself in the fires of sorrow, then I am good stuff for other people in the same condition.

The Place of Help, 1044 R

"*A Man of sorrows, and acquainted with grief*" (*Isaiah 53:3*).

We are not acquainted with grief in the way in which Our Lord was acquainted with it; we endure it, we get through it, but we do not become intimate with it.

My Utmost for His Highest, June 23, 794 L

"*It is better to go to the house of mourning, than to go to the house of feasting: for that is the end of all men; and the living will lay it to his heart*" (*Ecclesiastes 7:2*).

Solomon does not mean us to live as some folks who seem never to be happy unless they are at a funeral. He means us to keep at the basis of things, to scrape through the veneer and face things, and we learn to do this better in mourning than in feasting.

Shade of His Hand, 1220 R

Many a man has found God in the belly of hell during the war. He has come face to face with God through having had things stripped off and having to face the fact that the basis of life is tragedy. . . . No man who faces the ultimate tragedy in another's life can be the cheap and easy cynic we are all apt to be without thinking. . . . Go to the house of mourning and see your friend dead, and it will alter your attitude to things.

Shade of His Hand, 1221 L

SOVEREIGNTY OF GOD

Everything the devil does, God over-reaches to serve His own purpose.

Disciples Indeed, 389 L

Some people believe in an omnipotence with no character; they are shut up in a destiny of hopelessness; Jesus Christ can open the door of release and let them right out. There is no door that man or devil has closed but Jesus Christ can open it; but remember, there is the other side, the door He closes no man can open.

If Thou Wilt Be Perfect, 605 R

SOVEREIGNTY OF GOD
(Continued)

Every now and again when you look at life from a certain angle it seems as if evil and wrong and legalised iniquity are having it all their own way and you feel that everything must go to pieces; but it doesn't; around it is the sovereignty of God.

God's Workmanship, 451 L

You cannot prove that God is love if you have not been born from above, because everything around you disproves it. Take the war and the ruination going on just now: it is absurd to say that it is just and reasonable; it is tragic and wrong; and yet when you are born from above you are able to discern the "arm of the Lord" behind it all, but it takes the nature of Jesus Christ to see it; human nature apart from Him is unable to do so.

He Shall Glorify Me, 504 L

". . . He that openeth, and no man shutteth; and shutteth, and no man openeth" (Revelation 3:7).

The word "door" is used elsewhere in the New Testament for privileges and opportunities ("For a great door and effectual is opened unto me," 1 Corinthians 16:9); but here it means that Jesus Christ's sovereignty is effective everywhere; it is He Who opens the door and He Who shuts. "Behold, I have set before thee an open door, and no man can shut it." Behind the devil is God. God is never in a panic; nothing can be done that He is not absolute Master of, and no one in earth or heaven can shut a door He has opened, nor open a door He has shut. God alters the inevitable when we get in touch with Him.

If Thou Wilt Be Perfect, 604 R

Another evidence of new birth is that we see the rule of God. We no longer see the haphazard of chance or fate, but by the experience of new birth we are enabled to see the rule of God everywhere.

The Psychology of Redemption, 1069 R

Isaiah's message needs to come home to us to-day, viz., that God is behind the devil, not the devil behind God; all the great world forces are in front of God, and they cannot do a thing without His permission. To-day we are so emphasising the freedom of the human will that we are forgetting the sovereignty of God; consequently when we come up against the forces at work in the world we are paralysed by fear and get into despair, which we need never have done if we had been built up in faith in God.

Notes on Isaiah, 1376 L

All through Isaiah there is the confidence that God is reigning and ruling; the devil likes to make us believe that we are in a losing battle. Nothing of the sort! we have to overcome all the things that try to obscure God. The rugged truths of Isaiah point out not only the appalling state of the world as it is, but that we have to live a holy life in it by the power of God, not a sequestered life in particular temples or rituals, but real genuine magnificent men and women of God, no matter what the devil or the world or the flesh may do.

Notes on Isaiah, 1379 R

SPECULATION

There is no book which lends itself more readily to speculation than the Bible, and yet all through the Bible warns against it. By speculation we mean taking a series of facts and weaving all kinds of fancies round them. In Deuteronomy 29:29 ("The secret things belong unto the Lord our God: but those things which are revealed belong unto us and to our children for ever. . ."), and Revelation 5:3 ("And no man in heaven, nor in earth, neither under the earth, was able to open the book, neither to look thereon"), the bounds of human knowledge with regard to Bible revelation are fairly well marked. What is revealed in God's Book is for us; what is not revealed is not for us. Speculation is searching into what is not revealed.

Biblical Psychology, 162 L

The day we live in is a day of wild imaginations everywhere, unchecked imaginations in music, in literature, and, worst of all, in the interpretation of Scripture. People are going off on wild speculations; they get hold of one line and run clean off at a tangent and try to explain everything on that line, then they go off on another line: none of it is in accordance with the Spirit of God. There is no royal road for bringing our brains into harmony with the Spirit God has put in our hearts; we do not get there all at once, but only by steady discipline.

Biblical Psychology, 208 R

SPEECH (See also TONGUE)

When Paul mentions the matter of conversation, he says, "See that your speech is edifying"— good building-up stuff, not sanctimonious talk, but real solid stuff that makes people stronger in the Word of God, stronger in character, stronger in practical life.

Workmen of God, 1363 R

Our Lord said "Out of the abundance of the heart the mouth speaketh." But remember when it is that our speech reveals what is in our heart, viz., when we are brought to a sudden crisis and the whole nature expresses itself. The majority of us are much too cunning to express what is in our heart until we are brought to a crisis; then the true state of our heart is out instantly.

Notes on Isaiah, 1372 R

If I want to know what my heart is like, let me listen to my mouth, in an unguarded frame, for five minutes!

Biblical Psychology, 168 R

SPIRITUAL CARE / CURE OF SOULS

When someone comes to you with a question which makes you feel at your wits' end, never say, "I can't make head or tail of it." Of course you cannot. Always take the case that is too hard for you to God, and to no one else, and He will give you the right thing to say.

Approved Unto God, 22 L

Never believe what people tell you about themselves. There is only one person in a thousand who can actually tell you his or her symptoms; and beware of the people who can tell you where they are spiritually. I mean by that, never be guided by what people tell you; rely on the Spirit of God all the time you are probing them.

Workmen of God, 1341 R

When we come across a foul-mouthed, blasphemous man any number of us are ready to reprove him for the one who will try to discover why he speaks thus. Job is looking for someone who will understand what lies behind his talk, but he finds only those who are far removed from his problem.

Baffled to Fight Better, 55 L

Unless you are out amongst the tremendous facts of God's revelation in the Bible, unless you know how to take breezy walks through that Book, unless you know how to walk up and down that country and take in the air of God's hills and get thoroughly robust and continually change your walk amongst those facts, you are sure to catch the diseases of the souls you are dealing with.

Workmen of God, 1342 R

(Continued)

SPIRITUAL CARE / CURE OF SOULS *(Continued)*

Dealing with souls is tenfold more dangerous than dealing with bodies. Unless you are in a healthy, vigorous condition with God, you will catch the disease of the soul you are dealing with instead of helping to cure it.

Workmen of God, 1342 R

Do not get confused because when you have to face backsliders you find you cannot deal with them as you deal with any ordinary sinner. Their hearts are frozen, they are not convicted of sin, they are absolutely dull and dead towards all God wants. They will tell you quite mechanically, "Oh yes, I once knew God, I did experience this and that, but I deliberately stepped aside." The process may be gradual, but the backsliding condition is reached by forsaking God and taking up with something else.

Workmen of God, 1349 L

When you come to deal with backsliders, one of the greatest dangers is that they spread their disease more quickly than any other. The presence of one backslider is a peril to a whole community.

Workmen of God, 1349 L

Never sympathise with a soul whose case makes you come to the conclusion that God is hard. God is tenderer than anyone we can conceive of, and if a man cannot get through to Him it is because there is a secret thing he does not intend to give up. It is impossible to deal poetically with a case like that; you have to go right down to the root of the trouble until there is antagonism and pain and resentment against the message.

Approved Unto God, 7 L

If God is going to give you power, Christian worker, to work for the cure of souls in their worst form, among the "two-faced" and the hypocritical, remember, first He will give

you such an insight into the possibilities of your own sinfulness, and then such a comprehension of the marvels of His grace and wonderful salvation that you will have all the subtlety Nathan had. You will not be silent; you will speak out.

Workmen of God, 1352 R

If you are going to work for the cure of souls, you cannot choose the kind of souls you are going to work with.

Workmen of God, 1352 R

The wonder of our Lord Jesus Christ is just this, that you can face Him with any kind of men or women you like, and He can cure them and put them into a right relationship with God.

Workmen of God, 1353 R

Jesus Christ faces fearlessly the question of sin and wrong, and He teaches us to face it fearlessly also. There is no circumstance so dark and complicated, no life so twisted, that He cannot put right.

Studies in the Sermon on the Mount, 1448 R

You cannot be sure that the man you are dealing with will always be the same; at any second he may alter. You see someone set on a line you know to be wrong, but remember, at any second the universe of his desire may change. To remember this will bring a tremendous hopefulness and cure us of our unbelief about any life.

Biblical Ethics, 93 R

If you get your little compartment of texts, and search them out and say, "I know how to deal with this soul," you will never be able to deal with it; but if you realise your absolute helplessness and say, "My God, I cannot touch this life; I do not know where to begin, but I believe that Thou canst do it," then you can do something.

Workmen of God, 1355 R

SPIRITUAL DANGER

The great peril is the peril within, which men never think of as a peril. My right to myself, self-pity, self-conceit, consideration for my progress, my ways of looking at things, those things are the Satanic perils which will keep us in perfect sympathy with Satan.

Biblical Psychology, 144 L

The majority of us are shockingly ignorant about ourselves simply because we will not allow the Spirit of God to reveal the enormous dangers that lie hidden in the centre of our spirit. Jesus Christ taught that dangers never come from outside, but from within.

Biblical Psychology, 179 R

"The kings of the earth believed not, neither all the inhabitants of the world, that the adversary and the enemy should enter into the gates of Jerusalem" (Lamentations 4:12 RV).

That ancient peril is apt to repeat itself to-day, viz., a proud arrogancy arising from intellectual confidence in God's prophetic word, irrespective of the heart's condition. God has not any favourites outside faithfulness. . . . It is possible to build up a false security, as Israel and Judah did of old, based on God's own prophetic word, but which ignores heart purity and humility before Him.

Christian Disciplines, Volume 1,
The Discipline of Peril, 294 R

In estimating the dangers which beset us we have to remember that they are not haphazard, but things that will happen. Our Lord told His disciples to lay their account with peril, with hatred, in fact He tells them to leap for joy "when men shall hate you, and when they shall separate you from their company, and shall reproach you and cast out your name as evil, for the Son of man's sake" (Luke 6:22–23). We are apt to look at this alternative as a supposition, but Jesus says it will happen and must be estimated. It is never wise to under-estimate an enemy. We look upon the enemy of our souls as a conquered foe; so he is, but only to God, not to us.

The Highest Good—The Pilgrim's Song Book, 531 L

Always remain alert to the fact that where anyone has gone back is exactly where we all may go back ("Wherefore let him that thinketh he standeth take heed lest he fall"). You have borne the burden and heat of the day, been through the big test, now beware of the undertime, the after-part of the day spiritually.

The Place of Help, 998 R

It is the least likely thing that is the peril. The Bible characters never fell on their weak points but on their strong ones; unguarded strength is double weakness. It is in the after-part of the day spiritually that we have to be alert.

The Place of Help, 998 R

After a big transaction with God the current of your life heads you straight out to sea, right over the harbour bar, every sail set; now be alert for the spiritual undertow that would suck you back. The undercurrent is always most dangerous just where the river merges with the sea. The undercurrent is of the same nature as the river and will take you back into its swirling current; not out into the main stream, but back to the shipwrecks on the bank. The most pitiable of all wrecks are those inside the harbour.

The Place of Help, 999 L

It is quite possible to be enchanted with Jesus Christ and with His truth and yet never to be changed by it. . . . There is a real peril in being enchanted but unchanged.

The Place of Help, 1038 R

(Continued)

SPIRITUAL DANGER
(Continued)

Life is a far greater danger than death. . . .
The possibilities of life are awful. Think—
are you absolutely certain that you are
not going to topple headlong over a moral
precipice before you are three years older?
. . . it does us good, although it frightens us,
to look at the possibilities of life. May God
help us to face the issues.

The Servant as His Lord, 1254 L

There is no snare, or any danger of infatuation or pride in intercession; it is a hidden
ministry that brings forth fruit whereby the
Father is glorified.

My Utmost for His Highest, June 7, 788 L

SPIRITUAL GIFTS

Spiritual gifts must be dealt with in the
same way as natural gifts. Spiritual gifts are
not glorified gifts; they are the gift of the
Spirit. "Now there are diversities of gifts,
but the same Spirit." None of the gifts Paul
mentions in 1 Corinthians 12:8–11 are
natural gifts.

If Thou Wilt Be Perfect, 580 R

The danger is to say, "How highly favoured
I must be if God gives me this great gift";
"what a wonderful person I must be." We
never talk like that, but the slightest
thought that looks upon the gifts of the
Spirit as a favour to us is the first thing that
will take us out of the central point of Jesus
Christ's teaching. Never look at the work of
God in and through you; never look at the
way God uses you in His service; immediately you do, you put your mind away from
where Jesus Christ wants to get it. Gifts are
gifts, not graces.

If Thou Wilt Be Perfect, 580 R

SPIRITUAL GROWTH

We have to recognise that we are one half
mechanical and one half mysterious; to live
in either domain and ignore the other is to
be a fool or a fanatic. The great supernatural
work of God's grace is in the incalculable
part of our nature; we have to work out in
the mechanical realm what God works in in
the mysterious realm.

Biblical Ethics, 107 L

Spiritual maturity is not reached by the
passing of the years, but by obedience
to the will of God. Some people mature
into an understanding of God's will more
quickly than others because they obey
more readily; they more readily sacrifice
the life of nature to the will of God; they
more easily swing clear of little determined
opinions. It is these little determined
opinions, convictions of our own that
won't budge, that hinder growth in grace
and makes us bitter and dogmatic, intolerant, and utterly un-Christlike.

Bringing Sons Unto Glory, 221 R

There are stages in spiritual development
when God allows us to be dull, times when
we cannot realise or feel anything. It is one
of the greatest mercies that we have those
blank spaces, for this reason, that if we go
on with spiritual perception too quickly we
have no time to work it out; and if we have
no time to work it out it will react in stagnation and degeneration. Work out what
God works in—work it out through your
fingertips, through your tongue, through
your eyes; then when that is worked out,
God will flood your soul with more light.

Bringing Sons Unto Glory, 222 R

The whole art of spirituality is that my
human nature should retire and let the new
disposition have its way.

Conformed to His Image, 348 L

As you go on towards maturity watch the by-path meadows—"I have been so blessed of God here; this is where I ought to stay." Read the life of Jesus; He kept His eye fixed on the one purpose His Father had for His life, which He calls going "up to Jerusalem," and we have to go with Him there.

Bringing Sons Unto Glory, 222 R

There is nothing simpler under heaven than to become a Christian, but after that it is not easy; we have to leave "the word of the beginning of Christ," and "press on unto full growth" (Hebrews 6:1 RV).

Conformed to His Image, 347 L

Romans 12:2 is the apostle Paul's passionate entreaty that we should rouse ourselves out of that stagnation which must end in degeneration, in which we are ensnared by thinking because it is "all of grace" there is no need for "gumption." Grace, Grit, Glory is the graduation course.

Conformed to His Image, 368 L

We must take the pains to make ourselves visibly all that God has made us invisibly.

Conformed to His Image, 360 L

The first essential in spiritual construction is to clear away the rubbish. Nehemiah could not begin to build until the rubbish had been dealt with (see Nehemiah 4:2). Rubbish is waste matter, and there is the moral equivalent of rubbish which must be dealt with before we can begin to build a spiritual character. We do not start with a clean sheet; we start with a sheet that is like a palimpsest, a manuscript that has been written on twice, and if the right chemical is used, the first writing is seen. We all have hereditary writing in us which is so much rubbish to be removed.

Biblical Ethics, 104 L

The full growth in the Great Life is to "Believe also in Me" about everything. "Make room for Me, especially in matters where you cannot go; bring the child's mind to what I have said about them." We want to be our own Lord and master, to get everything solved for ourselves; Jesus says, "Look unto Me, and be ye saved." To commit his life and reasoning to Jesus Christ's attitude takes a man right out of himself and into Jesus Christ. This is not rational; it is redemptive.

Facing Reality, 38 R

Measure your growth in grace by your sensitiveness to sin.

Disciples Indeed, 404 L

We are apt to be busy about everything but that which concerns our spiritual progress, and at the end of a profitless day we snatch up a Bible or *Daily Light* and read a few verses, and it does us good for precisely three-quarters of a second. We have to take time to be diligent.

The Moral Foundations of Life, 711 R

"Consider the lilies of the field, how they grow"—in the dark! We are apt to consider a lily when it is in the sunshine only, but for the greater part of the year it is buried in the ground; and we imagine that we are to be always above ground, shedding perfume and looking beautiful; or continually being cut and put into God's show-room to be admired, forgetting altogether that we cannot be as lilies unless we have spent time in the dark, totally ignored. As a disciple, Jesus says, consider your hidden life with God.

The Moral Foundations of Life, 712 L

(Continued)

SPIRITUAL GROWTH
(Continued)

Every domain of our life which comes under the apprehension of the Spirit of God is a call to cultivate that particular domain for Him. The trouble is that we won't break up the new soil of our lives for God.

Disciples Indeed, 400 R

Prayer is not meant to develop us, but to develop the life of God in us after new birth.

The Psychology of Redemption, 1083 L

SPIRITUAL WARFARE

When you meet the hatred of the whole world-system unspiritual people around you will laugh to scorn the idea that you have a struggle on hand, but you realise that you are wrestling not against flesh and blood, but against the spiritual hosts of wickedness in the heavenly places.

Biblical Ethics, 100 L

"Who shall separate us from the love of Christ? Shall . . . nakedness, or peril, or sword?" (Romans 8:35).

The Apostle Paul seems to be never tired of comparing the Christian life to a fight, and a fight against tremendous odds, but always a winning fight. In these verses Paul brings before our contemplation every conceivable battlefield; every manoeuvre and strategy of the enemy is embraced, no phase of his tactics is left out, and in it all he says we are "more than conquerors through Him that loved us."

The Servant as His Lord, 1251 R

There is such a thing as being haunted on the inside of the life. It begins when a man tampers with the borders of spiritualism and communicates with supernatural powers; he opens the unconscious part of his personality to all kinds of powers he cannot control.

Shade of His Hand, 1212 R

There are supernatural powers and agencies that can play with us like toys whenever they choose unless we are garrisoned by God. The New Testament continually impresses this upon us: "For we wrestle not against flesh and blood, but against principalities, against powers, against the rulers of the darkness of this world, against spiritual wickedness in the high places." According to the Bible, spiritualism is not a trick; it is a fact.

The Servant as His Lord, 1263 R

We are not meant to be "carried to heaven on flow'ry beds of ease"; we are given the fighting chance, and it is a glorious fight. Jesus Christ came to fit men to fight; He came to make the lame, the halt, the paralysed, the all but sin-damned, into terrors to the prince of this world. . . . No man is a match for that warfare unless he is saved by God's grace.

The Servant as His Lord, 1248 L

STRENGTH

The phrase, "the weakness of God," is astonishing, but scriptural. "The weakness of God is stronger than men" (1 Corinthians 1:25). Our astonishment arises from the fact that what we call strength from the natural standpoint may be weakness; and that what God calls strength is too often esteemed by men as weakness. It was so in the life of Jesus Christ judged from the standpoint of the natural man.

Christian Disciplines, Volume 2,
The Discipline of Patience, 337 L

Many workers have gone out with high courage and fine impulses, but with no intimate fellowship with Jesus Christ, and before long they are crushed. They do not know what to do with the burden; it produces weariness, and people say—"What an embittered end to such a beginning!" "Roll thy burden upon the Lord" (see Psalm 37:5 RV)—you have been bearing it all; deliberately put one end on the shoulders of God.

My Utmost for His Highest, April 13, 769 R

The test of the worker is that he knows he has been enabled by the Lord Jesus; therefore he works and learns to do it better all the time. The realisation that my Lord has enabled me to be a worker keeps me strong enough never to be weak.

Conscious obtrusive weakness is natural unthankful strength; it means I refuse to be made strong by Him. When I say I am too weak it means I am too strong; and whenever I say "I can't" it means "I won't." When Jesus Christ enables me, I am omnipotently strong all the time. Paul talks in paradoxes, "for when I am weak, then am I strong."

Approved Unto God, 4 L

To think along Pentecostal lines means that we have received the Holy Spirit, and this should be sufficient for us to see that we have the ability to do the things that are demanded by God. It is a crime for a saint to be weak in God's strength.

Biblical Ethics, 122 R

The child of God who walks alone with Him is not dependent on places and moods but carries to the world the perpetual mystery of a dignity, unruffled, and unstung by insult, untouched by shame and martyrdom.

Christian Disciplines, Volume 2,
The Discipline of Loneliness, 318 R

The realisation that my strength is always a hindrance to God's supply of life is a great eye-opener. A man who has genius is apt

to rely on his genius rather than on God. A man who has money is apt to rely on money instead of God. So many of us trust in what we have got in the way of possessions instead of entirely in God. All these sources of strength are sources of double weakness.

God's Workmanship, 438 R

The life of a saint reveals a quietness at the heart of things; there is something firm and dependable, because the Lord is the strength of the life.

The Moral Foundations of Life, 701 R

The Bible indicates that a man always falls on his strongest point. Abraham, the man of faith, fell through unbelief; Moses, the meek man, fell through losing his temper; Elijah, the courageous man, fell through losing heart; and Solomon, the most colossally wise, wealthy, luxurious, superb king, fell through grovelling, sensual idolatry.

Shade of His Hand, 1196 R

"To them that have no might He increaseth strength." God comes and takes us out of our sentimentality, and our complaining turns into a psalm of praise. The only way to know the strength of God is to take the yoke of Jesus upon us and learn of Him.

"The joy of the Lord is your strength." Where do the saints get their joy from? If we did not know some saints, we would say—"Oh, he, or she, has nothing to bear." Lift the veil. The fact that the peace and the light and the joy of God are there is proof that the burden is there too. The burden God places squeezes the grapes and out comes the wine; most of us see the wine only. No power on earth or in hell can conquer the Spirit of God; in a human spirit, it is an inner unconquerableness.

If you have the whine in you, kick it out ruthlessly. It is a positive crime to be weak in God's strength.

My Utmost for His Highest, April 14, 770 L

(Continued)

STRENGTH (Continued)

We think it a sign of real modesty to say at the end of a day—"Oh, well, I have just got through, but it has been a severe tussle." And all the Almighty God is ours in the Lord Jesus! And He will tax the last grain of sand and the remotest star to bless us if we will obey Him.

My Utmost for His Highest, May 16, 781 L

"They that wait upon the Lord . . . shall walk, and not faint" (Isaiah 40:31).
There is no thrill in walking; it is the test of all the stable qualities. To "walk and not faint" is the highest reach possible for strength.

My Utmost for His Highest, July 20, 803 L

STUDY / PREPARATION

If you lack education, first realise it; then cure it.

Approved Unto God, 11 L

If we wish to excel in secular things, we concentrate; why should we be less careful in work for God? Don't get dissipated; determine to develop your intellect for one purpose only—to make yourself of more use to God. Have a perfect machine ready for God to use.

Approved Unto God, 11 L

Take time before God and find out the highest ideal for an address. Never mind if you do not reach the ideal, but work at it, and never say fail. By work and steady application you will acquire the power to do with ease what at first seemed so difficult.

Approved Unto God, 11 L

The work we do in preparation is meant to get our minds into such order that they are at the service of God for His inspiration.

Disciples Indeed, 400 L

Nothing that has been discovered by anyone else is of any use to you until you re-discover it. Be careful to use your own mental eyes, and the eyes of those who can help you to see what you are looking at. Drummond said that Ruskin taught him to *see*. Be careful to develop the power of perceiving what you look at, and never take an explanation from another mind unless you see it for yourself.

Approved Unto God, 13 L

When you try and re-state to yourself what you implicitly feel to be God's truth, you give God a chance to pass that truth on to someone else through you.

Approved Unto God, 13 R

To talk about "getting a message," is a mistake. It is preparation of myself that is required more than of my message.

Disciples Indeed, 400 L

In immediate preparation don't call in the aid of other minds; rely on the Holy Spirit and on your own resources, and He will select for you. Discipline your mind by reading and by building in stuff in private; then all that you have assimilated will come back.

Approved Unto God, 11 R

The great thing is not to hunt for texts, but to live in the big comprehensive truths of the Bible and texts will hunt you.

Disciples Indeed, 399 R

Inspiration won't come irrespective of study, but only because of it. Don't trust to inspiration; use your own "axe" (Psalm 74:5). Work! Think! Don't luxuriate on the mount!

Disciples Indeed, 404 L

It is by thinking with your pen in hand that you will get to the heart of your subject.

Disciples Indeed, 399 L

Don't go to your Bible in a yawning mood.

Disciples Indeed, 400 L

Don't insult God by telling Him He forgot to give you any brains when you were born. We all have brains; what we need is *work*.

Disciples Indeed, 404 R

A subject has never truly gripped you until you are mentally out of breath with it.

Disciples Indeed, 405 L

If I make my study a place of stern industry, it will act as an inspiration every time I go into it; but if I am lazy there, the place will revenge itself on me.

Disciples Indeed, 405 L

Look at the laborious way of a scientist in finding out the secrets of Nature, and then look at our own slipshod ignorance with regard to God's Book. If the worker will obey God's way he will find he has to be everlastingly delving into the Bible and working it out in circumstances; the two always run together.

The Love of God—The Message of Invincible Consolation, 673 L

Watch the care students take in other domains of life, and then think of our own laziness and the way we continually fall back and say, "It can't be done." All we need is grit and gumption and reliance on the Holy Spirit. We must bring the same determined energy to the revelations in God's Book as we bring to earthly professions. Most of us leave the sweat of brain outside when we come to deal with the Bible.

The Moral Foundations of Life, 715 R

When once the mind begins to think, the horizon is continually broadening and widening, there is a general unsettlement, and

the danger is to go back to the old confined way and become fanatical and obstinate. This explains why some people who really are God's children have such an inveterate dislike of study.

The Moral Foundations of Life, 718 L

We hear it asked, "What is the good of all this study and reading of the Bible? We get no 'change' out of it." Most of us want something to show for what we do. We are not interested in God's life in us, but only in our life in God. We are not after the development of the unconscious life of the Son of God in us, but after the "small change" which enables us to say, "I did this and that." The life of the Son of God grows feebler in a life of that order.

The Psychology of Redemption, 1072 L

One way in which Satan comes as an angel of light to Christians to-day is by telling them there is no need to use their minds. We *must* use our minds; we must keep the full power of our intellect ablaze for God on any subject that awakens us in our study of His word, always keeping the secret of the life hid with Christ in God. Think of the sweat and labour and agony of nerve that a scientific student will go through in order to attain his end; then think of the slipshod, lazy way we go into work for God.

So Send I You, 1330 R

If there ever was a need, it is for people to search and ransack this Book and get at what God says. How much time have you given to finding out what the Bible has to say? An hour a day? "Oh, I cannot give an hour." Half an hour? "Oh no, I cannot give that." Five minutes? "Yes, I could do that." Well, have you done it? Five minutes a day out of twenty-four hours to find out what the word of God says! No wonder God says, "My people doth not consider."

Workmen of God, 1358 R

(Continued)

STUDY / PREPARATION
(Continued)

Preparation is not something suddenly accomplished, but a process steadily maintained. It is easy to imagine that we get to a settled state of experience where we are complete and ready; but in work for God it is always preparation and preparation.

So Send I You, 1297 L

SUBMISSION

When we are young in grace there is a note of independence about our spiritual life—"I don't intend anyone to tell me what to do; I intend to serve God as I choose." It is an independence based on inexperience, an immature fellowship; it lacks the essential of devotion. Some of us remain true to the independent following and never get beyond it; but we are built for God, Himself, not for service for God, and that explains the submissions of life. We can easily escape the submissions if we like to rebel against them, but the Spirit of God will produce the most ghastly humiliation if we do not submit. Since we became disciples of Jesus we cannot be as independent as we used to be.

Facing Reality, 35 R

"And He went down with them, . . . and was subject unto them" (Luke 2:51).

An extraordinary exhibition of submissiveness! and "the disciple is not above his master." Think of it: thirty years at home with brothers and sisters who did not believe in Him! We fix on the three years which were extraordinary in Our Lord's life and forget altogether the earlier years at home, thirty years of absolute submission. Perhaps something of the same kind is happening to you, and you say—"I don't know why I should have to submit to this." Are you any better than Jesus Christ? "As He is, so are we in this world." The explanation of

it all is Our Lord's prayer—"that they may be one, even as We are one." If God is putting you through a spell of submission, and you seem to be losing your individuality and everything else, it is because Jesus is making you one with Him.

The Love of God—The Ministry of the Unnoticed, 664 L

"The Father abiding in Me doeth His works" (John 14:10 RV). Our Lord habitually submitted His will to His Father; that is, He engineered nothing but left room for God. The modern trend is dead against this submission; we do engineer, and engineer with all the sanctified ingenuity we have, and when God suddenly bursts in in an expected way, we are taken unawares. It is easier to engineer things than determinedly to submit all our powers to God. We say we must do all we can: Jesus says we must let God do all He can.

The Moral Foundations of Life, 726 L

SUCCESS

Success means to end with advantage. What is the Christian standard of success? Jesus Christ distinctly recognises that we have to succeed, and He indicates the kind of success we must have. The advantage with which we are to end is that we become preserving salt and shining lights; not losing our savour but preserving health, and not covering our light with a bushel but letting it shine.

Biblical Psychology, 189 L

"And straightway He constrained His disciples to get into the ship, and to go to the other side . . ." (Mark 6:45).

We are apt to imagine that if Jesus Christ constrains us and we obey Him, He will lead us to great success; but He does not. We would have thought these men would have had a most successful time, but their obedience led them into a great disaster. If our Lord has ever constrained you, and you obeyed Him, what was your dream of His purpose? Never put your dream of success as God's purpose for you; His purpose may be exactly the opposite.

God's Workmanship, 425 L

We have an idea that God is leading us to a certain goal; He is not. The question of getting to a particular end is a mere incident. "For I know the plans that I am planning for you, saith the Lord, plans of welfare, and not of calamity, to give you an expected end" (see Jeremiah 29:11). What men call the process, God calls the end. If you can stay in the midst of the turmoil unperplexed and calm because you see Jesus, that is God's purpose in your life; not that you may be able to say, "I have done this and that and now it's all right." God's purpose for you is that you depend upon Him and His power *now*; that you see Him walking on the waves—no shore in sight, no success, just the absolute certainty that it is all right because you see Him.

God's Workmanship, 426 L

We are not called to be successful in accordance with ordinary standards, but in accordance with a corn of wheat falling into the ground and dying, becoming in that way what it never could be if it were to abide alone.

He Shall Glorify Me, 493 R

"And in the morning, rising up a great while before day, He went out, and departed into a solitary place, and there prayed" (Mark 1:35).

This incident in the life of Our Lord occurred after what one would call a most successful day. . . . Our Lord had called the men who were to be His disciples, and they had promptly left all and followed Him; He had had a triumphant time in Capernaum, casting out demons and setting men and women free. The fame and success of this mysterious Being grew, and we read that "all the city was gathered together at the door." It was after this time of eminent success in relieving men and blessing them that Jesus departed into a solitary place and spent the night in prayer. . . .

Where do we place the night of prayer and the dawn of intercession in our soul's calendar? do we place it after a day of marvellous success in work for God? If we do not, our souls are in peril.

He Shall Glorify Me, 510 L, 511 L

We are not here to win souls, to do good to others; that is the natural outcome, but it is not our aim, and this is where so many of us cease to be followers. We will follow God as long as He makes us a blessing to others, but when He does not we will not follow. Suppose Our Lord had measured His life by whether or not He was a blessing to others! Why, He was a "stone of stumbling" to thousands, actually to His own neighbours, to His own nation, because through Him they blasphemed the Holy Ghost, and in His own country "He did not many mighty works there because of their unbelief" (Matthew 13:58). If Our Lord had measured His life by its actual results, He would have been full of misery.

The Love of God—The Ministry of the Unnoticed, 667 L

Watch where Jesus went. The one dominant note in His life was to do His Father's will. His is not the way of wisdom or of success, but the way of faithfulness.

The Love of God—Now Is It Possible, 686 R

The great cry of modern enterprise is success; Jesus says we cannot be successful in this age. This is the age of the humiliation of the saints; that means we have to stand true to Jesus Christ while the odds are crushingly against Him all the time.

The Servant as His Lord, 1283 L

(Continued)

SUCCESS (Continued)

The afterwards of success for God produces the feeling—Was it worthwhile? The coward fears before danger; the heroic spirit fears afterwards. It was after the victory, when Abraham went into the valley of the afterwards, that God said to him—"Fear not, Abram: I am thy shield, and thy exceeding great reward."

Not Knowing Whither, 875 L

The test of the life of a saint is not success, but faithfulness as a steward of the mysteries of God in human life as it actually is (cf. Luke 6:40). We will put up success as the aim in Christian work; the one thing glorifying to God is the glory of God manifested in human lives unobtrusively. The "show business" belongs to the pagan order of things; devotion to God in actual human conditions belongs to the Redemptive order. A Christian is one who has learned to live the life hid with Christ in God in human conditions.

Not Knowing Whither, 906 R

It is your relationship to God which fits you to live on the earth in the right way, not necessarily the successful way. Sometimes you will have the worst of it for doing right.

Shade of His Hand, 1234 L

Popular Christianity says, "We must succeed." The Book of Revelation says success cannot be marked; it is impossible. The New Testament conception of spirituality in the world is a forlorn hope always, by God's design. Take the parable of the Sower, which is the key to all the parables: only one-fourth of the seed sown brings forth fruit in this dispensation. We are determined to be successful; the Apostle Paul says we are called upon to be faithful (1 Corinthians 4:1–2).

The Servant as His Lord, 1275 L

Look at Jesus as He was when He was here; it was anything but glory. He was easily ignorable, saving to those who knew Him intimately; to the majority of men He was "as a root out of a dry ground." For thirty years He was obscure, then for three years He went through popularity, scandal, and hatred; He succeeded in gathering a handful of fishermen as disciples, one of whom betrayed Him, one denied Him, and all forsook Him; and He says, "It is enough for you to be like that." The idea of evangelical success, Church prosperity, civilised manifestation, does not come into it at all. When we fulfil the conditions of spiritual life we become unobtrusively real.

The Servant as His Lord, 1279 L

It is not what a man achieves, but what he believes and strives for that makes him noble and great.

Not Knowing Whither, 912 L

SUFFERING

Peter is talking about suffering, and he says "the time is come that judgement must begin at the house of God."* Where is the house of God? My body. As a child of God I have no right to go through a dispensation of suffering without asking my Father the reason for it. It may be suffering because of a purpose of God which He cannot explain to you, but He makes you know in your inmost heart that all is well (see verse 19). Or it may be suffering for chastisement and discipline. An undisciplined saint is inclined either to despise the chastening and say it is of the devil, or else to faint when he is rebuked, and cave in. The writer to the Hebrews says: "If you are a saint you will be chastened, be careful, see that you don't despise it."

Approved Unto God, 9 R
*1 Peter 4:17

We begin our religious life by believing our beliefs, we accept what we are taught without questioning; but when we come up against things we begin to be critical, and find out that the beliefs, however right, are not right for us because we have not bought them by suffering. What we take for granted is never ours until we have bought it by pain. A thing is worth just what it costs. When we go through the suffering of experience we seem to lose everything, but bit by bit we get it back.

Facing Reality, 25 L

When I suffer and feel I am to blame for it, I can explain it to myself; when I suffer and know I am not to blame, it is a harder matter; but when I suffer and realise that my most intimate relations think I am to blame, that is the limit of suffering. That is where the scourge of suffering lashed Job; the power of the sneer of Satan has come now into his most intimate relationships.

Baffled to Fight Better, 49 L

It is always well to note the things in life that your explanations do not cover. Job is facing a thing too difficult for him to solve or master; he realises that there is no way out.

Baffled to Fight Better, 50 L

We must beware in our attitude toward people who are suffering that we do not blunder by imagining our point of view to be the only one.

Baffled to Fight Better, 55 L

When anyone is in pain the thing that hurts more than anything else is pose, and that is what Job is fighting against here. No one revolts against a thing without a reason for doing so, not necessarily a wrong reason, because revolt is of a moral order. If we come across a counterfeit, reality is sure to be found somewhere. Job is up against the religious pose of men who do not begin to understand where his sorrow lies. . . .

What looks like revolt against God may really be not against God at all, but against the presentation being given of Him.

Baffled to Fight Better, 66 L

We have to be careful lest we take on the religious pose, or the evangelical pose, or the denominational pose, or any pose that is not real, when we come across suffering in which there is no deliverance and no illumination. The only thing to do is to be reverent with what we do not understand. The basis of things is tragic; therefore God must find the way out, or there is no way out. Human reasoning and a human diagnosis of things will do exactly what Job's friends did, viz.: belittle the grief.

Baffled to Fight Better, 67 L

There was a larger, grander society in Job's actual life after his suffering. In his Epistle Peter refers to the people who have plenty of time for you; they are those who have been through suffering, but now seem full of joy (see 1 Peter 4:12–19). If a man has not been through suffering he will snub you unless you share his interests; he is no more concerned about you than the desert sand; but those who have been through things are not now taken up with their own sorrows; they are being made broken bread and poured-out wine for others. You can always be sure of the man who has been through suffering, but never of the man who has not.

Baffled to Fight Better, 85 R

You cannot think of a home to-day that is without suffering. The war has knocked on the head the stupid temperamental idea that "every cloud has a silver lining"; there are clouds in countless lives with an inkier lining inside than outside. It is an insult to tell such people to "Cheer up and look on the bright side"; their lives are blasted for all time from every standpoint saving Jesus Christ's.

Biblical Ethics, 121 L

(Continued)

SUFFERING (Continued)

The remarkable thing is that it is rarely the one who suffers who turns against God; it is the lookers-on who turn against God because they do not see the one fact more in the life which gives God room to work. Those who look on are apt to come to the conclusion either that the one who suffers is a sinner, or that God is cruel; they take the line of Job's comforters. Why there should be suffering we do not know; but we have to remain loyal to the character of God as revealed by Jesus Christ in the face of it.

Biblical Ethics, 121 L

"For hereunto were ye called: because Christ also suffered for you, leaving you an example, that ye should follow His steps: Who did no sin, neither was guile found in His mouth: Who, when He was reviled, reviled not again; when He suffered, threatened not . . ." (1 Peter 2:21–23 RV).

Peter makes it perfectly clear and unambiguous how we are to "follow His steps," viz., in the way we suffer as Christians. "Who did no sin, neither was guile found in His mouth: . . . when He suffered, threatened not." "Follow His example there," says Peter; just as Christ exhibited an unthreatening spirit when He suffered, we are to do the same. No human being can suffer wrongfully without finding the spirit of threatening awakened in him, a spirit which if put into words would be—"I'll make that person smart! The idea of saying that about me!" If we are born again of the Holy Ghost the disposition of Jesus in us will enable us to "follow His steps" so that when we suffer wrongfully, we do not threaten.

Bringing Sons Unto Glory, 232 L

The Lamentations are not the expression of the grief of a disappointed man; the peculiar element in Jeremiah's sorrow is that he is identifying himself with an unrepentant people. (Cf. Daniel 9:4-20.) We suffer on account of our own wrong or the wrong of others, but that is not vicarious suffering. Jeremiah's grief personifies vicariously the grief of the whole nation. Am I prepared to be a scapegoat for the sins of others for which they are still unrepentant?

Conformed to His Image, 362 L

The saint who is being made into bread knows that his Father knows best, and that He would never allow the suffering if He had not some purpose. Ill-tempered people, hard circumstances, poverty, wilful misunderstandings and estrangements, are all millstones. Had Jesus any of these things in His own life? He had a devil in His company for three years; He lived at home with brothers and sisters who did not believe in Him; He was continually thwarted and misunderstood by the Pharisees, and He says, "the disciple is not above his Master." If we have the tiniest element of self-pity in us God dare not put us anywhere near the millstones. When these experiences come, remember God has His eyes on every detail.

The Servant as His Lord, 1283 R

Suffering is the touchstone of saintliness, just as temptation is, and suffering wrongfully will always reveal the ruling disposition because it takes us unawares.

Bringing Sons Unto Glory, 232 L

The awful problem of suffering continually crops up in the Scriptures, and in life and remains a mystery. . . . Perhaps to be able to explain suffering is the clearest indication of never having suffered.

Christian Disciplines, Volume 1,
The Discipline of Suffering, 281 L

The unexplained things in life are more than the explained. God seems careless as to whether men understand Him or not; He scarcely vindicates His saints to men.

Christian Disciplines, Volume 1,
The Discipline of Suffering, 281 R

It is an insult to take the temperamental line in dealing with a human being— "Cheer up, look on the bright side"; there are some types of suffering before which the only thing you can do is to keep your mouth shut. There are times when a man needs to be handled by God, not by his fellow men, and part of the gift of man's wisdom is to know how to be reverent with what he does not understand.

Conformed to His Image, 355 R

When things go well a man does not want God, but when things get difficult and suffering begins to touch him, he finds the problem of the world inside his own skin.

Conformed to His Image, 376 L

The citadel of true religion is personal relationship to God, let come what will.

Where does our mind rest regarding suffering? The Bible makes little of physical suffering. The modern mind looks on suffering and pain as an unmitigated curse; the Bible puts something akin to purifying in connection with suffering, e.g., "for he that hath suffered in the flesh hath ceased from sin" (1 Peter 4:1). The thing that moves us is the pathos arising from physical suffering; the anguish of a soul trying to find God we put down to lunacy.

Conformed to His Image, 376 R

The war has produced anticlimaxes in hundreds of lives, men are maimed and useless for fulfilling their ambitions. You rarely hear a man who has been through the real agony of suffering say that he disbelieves in God; it is the one who watches others going through suffering who says he disbelieves in God. In the suffering there is a compensation which cannot be got at in any other way. It is not seen from the outside because the compensation cannot be articulately stated.

Shade of His Hand, 1226 L

"Blessed are ye, when men shall revile you, and persecute you, and shall say all manner of evil against you falsely, for My sake. Rejoice, and be exceeding glad." That is the mark of a Christian from our Lord's standpoint. Many of us are persecuted because we have crotchety notions of our own, but the mark of a disciple is suffering "for My sake." Have you ever suffered anything for His sake?

The Highest Good, 542 R

In Romans 8:18 ("For I reckon that the sufferings of this present time are not worthy to be compared with the glory which shall be revealed in us") Paul is stating that it is the standpoint of the worker which determines everything. If you think of suffering affliction you will begin to write your own epitaph, begin to dream of the kind of tombstone you would like. That is the wrong standpoint. Have your standpoint in the heavenlies, and you will not think of the afflictions but only of the marvellous way God is working out the inner weight of glory all the time, and you will hail with delight the afflictions which our Lord tells us to expect (John 16:33), the afflictions of which James writes (James 1:2), and of which Peter writes (1 Peter 4:12).

The Love of God—The Message of Invincible Consolation, 671 L

A man may be perfected through suffering or be made worse through suffering; it depends on his disposition.

The Place of Help, 1000 R

(Continued)

SUFFERING (Continued)

The picture of God in the Bible is of One who suffers, and when the mask is torn off life and we see all its profound and vast misery, the suffering, sorrowing God is the only One who does not mock us. "He was despised, and rejected of men; a man of sorrows, and acquainted with grief" (Isaiah 53:3 RV).

God's Workmanship, 461 L

The counterfeit of true spirituality is that produced by creeds. When one has been bereaved the most trying person is the one with a creed who can come with didactic counsel with regard to suffering; but turn to a book like the Book of Job where nothing is taught at all, but wonderful expression is given to the real suffering of life, and the mere reading of it brings consolation to a breaking heart.

The Place of Help, 1032 R

"Anguish" comes from a word meaning to press tightly, to strangle, and the idea is not a bit too strong for the things people are going through. They are not sentimental things, but real things, where every bit of a man's life is twisted and wrung out to the last ebb. Can the love of God in Christ hold there, when everything says that God is cruel to allow it, and that there is no such thing as justice and goodness? Shall anguish separate us from the love of God? No, we are more than conquerors in it, not by our own effort but by the fact that the love of God in Christ holds.

The Servant as His Lord, 1277 R

The way of approach to the holy ground of God is nearly always through suffering; we are not always in the natural mood for it, but when we have been ploughed into by suffering or sorrow, we are able to approach the moral frontiers where God works.

The Shadow of an Agony, 1159 L

SUPERSTITION

A mascot is a talisman of some sort the presence of which is supposed to bring good luck. The persistence of the superstitious element is one of the most indelible stains on the character of otherwise good people, and it abounds in our own day. A re-awakening of superstition always follows on the heels of gross materialism in personal and in national life.

Our Portrait in Genesis, 974 R

SURPRISE (See also EXPECTANCY)

Never be surprised at what God does, but be so taken up with Him that He may continue to do surprising things through you.

Our Brilliant Heritage, 942 R

Do you believe in a miracle-working God, and will you go out in surrender to Him? Have you faith in your holiness or in God? faith in your obedience or in God? Have you gone out in surrender to God until you would not be an atom surprised at anything He did? No one is surprised over what God does when once he has faith in Him. Have you a supernatural God, or do you tie Him up by the laws of your own mind?

The Love of God—Now Is It Possible, 685 L

We have not to depend on the prayers of other people, not to look for the sympathy of God's children, but to be ready for the Lord. It is this intense reality of expecting Him at every turn that gives life the attitude of child wonder that Jesus wants it to have. When we are rightly related to God, life is full of spontaneous joyful uncertainty and expectancy—we do not know what God is going to do next; and He packs our life with surprises all the time.

So Send I You, 1296 L

The element of surprise is always the note of the life of the Holy Ghost in us. We are born again by the great surprise—"The wind bloweth where it listeth, and thou hearest the voice thereof, but knowest not whence it cometh, and whither it goeth: so is every one that is born of the Spirit" (John 3:8 RV). Men cannot tie up the wind, it blows where it lists; neither can the work of the Holy Spirit be tied up in logical methods.

So Send I You, 1295 R

Jesus rarely comes where we expect Him; He appears where we least expect Him, and always in the most illogical connections. The only way a worker can keep true to God is by being ready for the Lord's surprise visits. It is not service that matters, but intense spiritual reality, expecting Jesus Christ at every turn. This will give our life the attitude of child-wonder which He wants it to have. If we are going to be ready for Jesus Christ, we have to stop being religious (that is, using religion as a higher kind of culture) and be spiritually real.

My Utmost for His Highest, March 29, 764 L

SURRENDER

There is no bigger word and no word made more shallow than "surrender." To say "I surrender all" may be blethering sentiment, or it may be the deep passionate utterance of the life.

The Highest Good—Thy Great Redemption, 560 R

When I stop telling God what I want, He can catch me up for what He wants without let or hindrance. He can crumple me up or exalt me; He can do anything He chooses. He simply asks me to have implicit faith in Himself and in His goodness.

My Utmost for His Highest, November 10, 843 L

It means more to surrender to God for Him to do a big thing than to surrender a big thing to God. We have to surrender our mean little notions for a tremendous revelation that takes our breath away.

The Love of God—Now Is It Possible, 684 R

God has no respect for anything we bring Him; He is after one thing only, and that is our unconditional surrender to Him.

Our Brilliant Heritage, 945 L

To go out in surrender to God means the surrendering of the miserable sense of my own un-importance. Am I willing to surrender that mean little sense for the great big idea God has for me? Am I willing to surrender the fact that I am an ignorant, useless, worthless, too-old person? There is more hindrance to God's work because people cling to a sense of unworthiness than because of conceit.

The Love of God—Now Is It Possible, 684 R

Faith means implicit confidence in Jesus, and that requires not intellect only but a moral giving over of myself to Him. . . . It is this point of moral surrender that nearly every man "shies off." We sentimentally believe, and believe, and believe, and nothing happens. We pray "Lord, increase our faith," and we try to pump up the faith, but it does not come. What is wrong? The moral surrender has not taken place. Will I surrender from the real centre of my life, and deliberately and wilfully stake my confidence on what Jesus Christ tells me?

Facing Reality, 36 L

(Continued)

SURRENDER (Continued)

Over and over again the Holy Spirit brings us to the place which in evangelical language is called "full surrender." Remember what full surrender is. It is not giving up this thing and that, but the deliberate giving up of my right to my individual self. As long as we are slaves to our ideas of individuality we distort the presentation of our Lord's teaching about discipleship.

The Servant as His Lord, 1273 L

You are getting tired of life as it is, tired of yourself as you are, getting sour with regard to the setting of your life; lift your eyes for one moment to Jesus Christ. Do you want, more than you want your food, more than you want your sleep, more than you want anything under heaven, or in heaven, that Jesus Christ might so identify you with Himself that you are His first and last and for ever? God grant that the great longing desire of your heart may begin to awaken as it has never done, not only the desire for the forgiveness of sins, but for identification with Jesus Himself until you say, "I live; yet not I, but Christ liveth in me."

God's Workmanship, 420 R

Sacrifice in the Bible means that we give to God the best we have; it is the finest form of worship. Sacrifice is not giving up things, but giving to God with joy the best we have. We have dragged down the idea of surrender and of sacrifice; we have taken the life out of the words and made them mean something sad and weary and despicable; in the Bible they mean the very opposite.

The Love of God—Now Is It Possible, 684 R

SYMPATHY

There is a difference between the human sympathy we give to a discouraged or broken-hearted man and what the Holy Spirit will do for him. We may sit down beside a broken-hearted man and pour out a flow of sympathy, and say how sorry we are for him, and tell him of other people with broken hearts; but all that only makes him more submissive to being broken-hearted. When our Lord sympathises with the heart broken by sin or sorrow, He binds it up and makes it a new heart, and the expectation of that heart ever after is from God.

The Moral Foundations of Life, 706 L

If you accept sympathy from those who have not heard the call of God, it will so blunt your own sense of His call that you become useless to Him. Every saint must stand out absolutely alone. Beware lest the sympathy of others competes with God for the throne of your life. Don't look for a comrade other than God when God speaks to you; through *you* will come His purpose.

Not Knowing Whither, 865 R

We need to be warned against the books that pander to our weak side, and the folks who say—"Poor fellow, he couldn't help it." It may be a kindly thing to say, but some things should not be treated with kindness. There is a tyrannical order which runs all through life, and if we get slopped over with sentiment we are not only unfit for life, but are of no use whatever to lay hold of God's order in the midst of things as they are.

Shade of His Hand, 1214 L

Whenever we step back from identification with God's interest in others into sympathy with them, the vital connection with God has gone; we have put our sympathy, our consideration for them, in the way, and this is a deliberate rebuke to God.

My Utmost for His Highest, May 3, 776 R

Identification is the key to intercession, and whenever we stop being identified with God, it is by sympathy, not by sin.

My Utmost for His Highest, May 3, 776 R

TEACHERS / TEACHING

The test of an instructor in the Christian Church is that he is able to build me up in my intimacy with Jesus Christ; not that he gives me new ideas, but I come away feeling I know a bit more about Jesus Christ. To-day the preacher is tested, not by the building up of saints but on the ground of his personality.

Facing Reality, 27 L

God uses children, and books, and flowers in the spiritual instruction of a man, but He seldom uses the self-conscious prig who consciously instructs. . . . There are no experts in spiritual matters as there are in scientific matters . . . because the very nature of spiritual instruction is that it is unconscious of itself; it is the life of a child, manifesting obedience, not ostentation. Our Lord describes the spiritual expert in Matthew 18:4—"Whosoever therefore shall humble himself as this little child, the same is greatest in the kingdom of heaven."

Baffled to Fight Better, 61 L

Beware of the trick of exposition which externalises Scripture so that we teach but never learn its lessons.

Christian Disciplines, Volume 2,
The Discipline of Prayer, 308 R

There is a snare in being able to talk about God's truth easily because frequently that is where it ends. If we can express the truth well, the danger is that we do not go on to know more. Most of us can talk piously; we have the practice but not the power.

Studies in the Sermon on the Mount, 1449 L

Testify to what the Lord has done for you; but at the peril of being cast away as reprobate silver, presume to preach or teach what you have not bought by suffering.

Christian Disciplines, Volume 2,
The Discipline of Loneliness, 319 R

If you teach anything out of an idle intellect, you will have to answer to God for it.

Disciples Indeed, 409 R

The one test of a teacher sent from God is that those who listen see and know Jesus Christ better than ever they did. If you are a teacher sent from God your worth in God's sight is estimated by the way you enable people to see Jesus.

If Thou Wilt Be Perfect, 600 R

The teacher sent from God is the one who clears the way to Jesus and keeps it clear; souls forget altogether about him because the vision of Jesus is the only abiding result. When people are attracted to Jesus Christ through you, see always that you stay on God all the time, and their hearts and affections will never stop at you.

If Thou Wilt Be Perfect, 600 R

The enervation that has crippled many a church, many a Sunday School class and Bible class, is that the pastor or teacher has won people to himself, and the result when they leave is enervating sentimentality. The true man or woman of God never leaves that behind; every remembrance of them makes you want to serve God all the more.

If Thou Wilt Be Perfect, 600 R

If we as preachers or teachers are rightly related to God in obedience, God is continually pouring through us. When we stop obeying Him, everything becomes as hard and dry as a ditch in mid summer. When we are placed in a position by God and we keep rightly related to Him, He will see to the supply.

The Moral Foundations of Life, 732 R

(Continued)

TEACHERS / TEACHING
(*Continued*)

The teacher who succeeds best with children is the one who does things before them; it is no use teaching children abstract stuff. That is why it is necessary in teaching a young life, whether young in years of the flesh or the spirit, for a teacher to attend more to what he does than to what he says. The crystallising point of our Lord's teaching lies here, and the reason our Lord condemned the Pharisees was that "they say, and do not." Everyone has a perfect right to come and ask those of us who teach whether we practise what we teach. The influence of our teaching is in exact proportion to our practical doing.

The Moral Foundations of Life, 722 R

If you are called to preach, preach; if you are called to teach, teach. Keep obedient to God on that line. The proof that you are on God's line is that other people never credit you with what comes through you. Jesus said, "Let your light so shine before men, that they may see your good works, and glorify your Father which is in heaven." Go on doing God's will, and you will be recreated while you do it.

The Moral Foundations of Life, 732 R

There is a danger with the children of God of getting too familiar with sublime things. We talk so much about these wonderful realities, and forget that we have to exhibit them in our lives. It is perilously possible to mistake the exposition of the truth for the truth; to run away with the idea that because we are able to expound these things we are living them too. Paul's warning comes home to us—". . . lest that by any means, when I have preached to others, I myself should be a castaway."

Our Brilliant Heritage, 925 L

God brings His own particular teachers into our lives, and we have to watch that we do not slack off in our loyalty to them. Loyalty to teachers is a very rare thing. The man or woman used by God to teach me is not necessarily the one used to teach you. We must not foist our teachers on everyone else. Are we loyal to our teachers, or are we spiritual butterflies? Does every new-comer on the highway of spiritual life switch us off on to a new line?

Our Brilliant Heritage, 954 L

The great snare is to seek acceptance with the people we talk to, to give people only what they want; we have no business to wish to be acceptable to the people we teach. "Study to show thyself approved"—unto the saints? No, "unto God." I have never known a man or woman who taught God's word to be always acceptable to other people.

The Philosophy of Sin, 1113 R

Man cannot order the seasons or make the seed to grow (cf. Jeremiah 33:20); and as preachers and teachers we are powerless to make saints. Our duty is to put the seed into the right place and leave the rest to God. It would be foolish for a farmer to sow his seed and tell his servants to watch it; he must sow his seed in the right place and then trust in God and Nature, and by and by he will reap his harvest. So all we can do is to sow the seed of the Word of God in the hearts of the hearers.

The Servant as His Lord, 1281 R

The lost sight of God inevitably follows spiritual teaching that has not a corresponding balance of private prayer.

Disciples Indeed, 397 R

To develop your expression in public you must do a vast amount of writing in private. Write out your problems before God. Go direct to Him about everything.

Disciples Indeed, 400 L

TEACHINGS OF JESUS

A good way to find out how much stodge there is in our spiritual life is to read the Sermon on the Mount and see how obtuse we are to the greater part of what Jesus Christ taught.

Disciples Indeed, 405 L

If you have never been brought close enough to Jesus to realise that He teaches things that grossly offend you as a natural man, I question whether you have ever seen Him.

Disciples Indeed, 406 R

Immediately you get out of touch with God, you are in a hell of chaos. That is always in the background of the teaching of Jesus. (Cf. Matthew 5:21–26.) That is why the teaching of Jesus produces such consternation in the natural man.

Disciples Indeed, 406 R

If we would have the blunt courage of ordinary human beings and face the teachings of Jesus, we would have to come to one of two conclusions—either the conclusion His contemporaries came to, that He was devil-possessed, or else to the conclusion the disciples came to, that He is God Incarnate.

The Highest Good, 550 R

The teaching of Jesus Christ comes with astonishing discomfort to begin with, because it is out of all proportion to our natural way of looking at things; but Jesus puts in a new sense of proportion, and slowly we form our way of walking and our conversation on the line of His precepts: Remember that our Lord's teaching applies only to those who are His disciples.

Studies in the Sermon on the Mount, 1441 L

Notice the apparent unsatisfactoriness of the answers of Jesus Christ. He never once answered a question that sprang from a man's head, because those questions

are never original; they always have the captious note about them. The man with that type of question wants to get the best of it logically. In Luke 13:23–24, a certain devout man asked Jesus a question, "Lord, are there few that be saved?" and Jesus replied, "Strive to enter in at the strait gate," i.e., "See that your own feet are on the right path." Our Lord's answers seem at first to evade the issue, but He goes underneath the question and solves the real problem. He never answers our shallow questions; He deals with the great unconscious need that makes them arise. When a man asks an original question out of his own personal life, Jesus answers him every time.

Studies in the Sermon on the Mount, 1466 R

We can always find a hundred and one reasons for not obeying our Lord's commands, because we will trust our reasoning rather than His reason, and our reason does not take God into calculation.

Studies in the Sermon on the Mount, 1451 R

TEMPTATION

If Our Lord was led into temptation, it behoves us not to rush into it. "Resist the devil," not attack him. Our Lord taught us to pray—"Lead us not into temptation." When once we know that we are stronger through testing, the danger is real to seek it.

Bringing Sons Unto Glory, 226 L

Every temptation of Satan is perfectly wise. The wisest, shrewdest, subtlest things are said by Satan, and they are accepted by everybody as the acme of human philosophy; but when the Spirit of God is at work in a man, instantly the hollow mockery at the heart of what Satan is trying to do is seen. When we understand the inwardness of the temptation we see how Satan's strategy is turned into confusion by the Spirit of God.

Bringing Sons Unto Glory, 227 L

(Continued)

TEMPTATION *(Continued)*

If you remain true to your relationship
to Jesus Christ the things that are either
right or wrong are never the problem; it is
the things that are right but which would
impair what He wants you to be that are
the problem.

Disciples Indeed, 395 R

The old Puritan idea that the devil tempts
men had this remarkable effect: it produced the man of iron who fought; the
modern idea of blaming his heredity or his
circumstances produces the man who succumbs at once.

Disciples Indeed, 407 L

The popular idea of temptation is that it is
towards evil, meaning that we can see it to
be evil by our common sense; but temptation is always a short cut to good; the mind
is perplexed—"I wonder if this is the way
of God?" If I yield to the temptation the
devil gets his way, as he did with Judas in
the last extreme.

He Shall Glorify Me, 501 R

Temptation is not sin; temptation must
always be possible for our sonship to be of
worth to God. It would be no credit for God
to bring mechanical slaves to glory—"for
it became Him . . . in bringing many sons
unto glory"—not slaves, not useless chan-
nels, but vigorous, alert, wide-awake men
and women, with all their powers and faculties devoted absolutely to God.

The Philosophy of Sin, 1123 R

Temptation trains innocence into character or else into corruption.

The Philosophy of Sin, 1125 L

The moments of severest temptation are the
moments of His divinest succour.

Disciples Indeed, 407 R

Temptation is not towards what we
understand as evil, but towards what
we understand as good (cf. Luke 16:15).
Temptation is something that for a while
completely baffles us; we do not know
whether it is towards a right thing or
not. Spiritual life is attained, not by a
necromantic magic pill, but by moral
choices, whereby we test the thing that
presents itself to us as being good.

The Philosophy of Sin, 1126 R

Temptation is a short cut to what is good,
not to what is bad. Satan came to our Lord
as an angel of light, and all his temptations
centre around this point—"You are the Son
of God, then do God's work in Your own
way; put men's needs first, feed them, heal
their sicknesses, and they will crown You
King." Our Lord would not become King
on that line; He deliberately rejected the
suggested short cut, and chose the long trail,
evading none of the suffering involved
(cf. John 6:15).

The Place of Help, 995 L

We are apt to imagine that when we are
saved and sanctified we are delivered from
temptation; we are not; we are loosened
into it. Before we are born again, we are not
free enough to be tempted, neither morally
nor spiritually. Immediately we are born
into the Kingdom of God, we get our first
introduction into what God calls temptation, viz., the temptations of His Son.

The Psychology of Redemption, 1078 R

In the temptation of our Lord the compromise for good ends is pictured: "Don't be so
stern against sin; compromise judiciously
with evil and You will easily win Your
Kingship of men." When we become rightly
related to God our intellect is apt to say

TEMPTATION OF JESUS

exactly the same thing: "Don't be narrow; don't be so pronounced against worldliness, you will upset your friends." Well, upset them, but never upset the main thing that God is after. There is always the tendency to compromise and we have to be roused up to recognise it. We have to walk in very narrow paths before God can trust us to walk in the wide ones. We have to be limited before we can be un-limited.

The Moral Foundations of Life, 731 L

When we are born from above, the central citadel of the devil's attack is the same in us as it was in our Lord—viz., to do God's will in our own way.

The Psychology of Redemption, 1079 R

Always remain alert to the fact that where one man has gone back is exactly where any one may go back (see 1 Corinthians 10:13). You have gone through the big crisis; now be alert over the least things; take into calculation the "retired sphere of the leasts."

My Utmost for His Highest, April 19, 771 R

Do not forecast where the temptation will come; it is the least likely thing that is the peril. In the aftermath of a great spiritual transaction the "retired sphere of the leasts" begins to tell; it is not dominant, but remember it is there, and if you are not warned, it will trip you up. You have remained true to God under great and intense trials; now beware of the undercurrent.

My Utmost for His Highest, April 19, 771 R

Unguarded strength is double weakness, because that is where the "retired sphere of the leasts" saps. The Bible characters fell on their strong points, never on their weak ones.

My Utmost for His Highest, April 19, 771 R

In each of the three never-to-be-forgotten pictures which our Lord has given us,* the temptation of Satan centres round this point—"You are the Son of God, then do God's work in Your own way; assert Your prerogative of Sonship." . . . He [Jesus] deliberately rejected the suggested "short cut" and chose the "long, long trail," evading none of the suffering involved.

The Psychology of Redemption, 1079 R
*Matthew 4:1–11

Temptation yielded to is lust deified. In the Bible, the term "lust" is used of other things than merely of immorality. It is the spirit of, "*I must have it at once*; I will have my desire gratified, and I will brook no restraint." Each temptation of our Lord contains the deification of lust—"You will get the Kingship of the world at once by putting men's needs first; use signs and wonders, and You will get the Kingship of men at once; compromise with evil, judiciously harmonise with natural forces, and You will get the Kingship of men at once." At the heart of every one of our Lord's answers are these words: "For I came down from heaven not to do Mine own will, but the will of Him that sent Me" (John 6:38); that is, "I came to do God's work in His way, not in My own way, although I am the Son of God."

The Psychology of Redemption, 1081 L

The idea that because Jesus Christ was without sin, therefore He could not be tempted, has become woven into religious belief. If that were so, the record of His temptation is a mere farce. Could Jesus Christ be tempted? Undoubtedly He could, because temptation and sin are not the same thing. "In all points tempted, . . . yet without sin."

Shade of His Hand, 1227 R

(Continued)

TEMPTATION OF JESUS

(Continued)

We can never fathom the agony in Gethsemane, but at least we need not misunderstand it. . . . We must read the record of the
agony in the light of the temptation three
years previously. There are three recorded
temptations, and three recorded spells of
agony in Gethsemane, "And when the devil
had ended all the temptation, he departed
from Him for a season." In Gethsemane he
came back, and was again overthrown.

The Psychology of Redemption, 1086 L

TESTIMONY

It is easier to stand true to a testimony
mildewed with age, because it has a
dogmatic ring about it that people agree
with, than to talk from your last moment
of contact with God.

Disciples Indeed, 407 R

If my testimony makes anyone wish to
emulate me, it is a mistaken testimony; it
is not a witness to Jesus.

Disciples Indeed, 408 R

Beware of your testimony when you can give it without thinking.

God's Workmanship, 464 L

To say a thing is the sure way to thinking
it. That is why it is so necessary to testify to
what Jesus Christ has done for us. A testimony gets hold of the mind as it has hold
of the heart; but the same thing is true of
the opposite: if we say a wrong thing often
enough we begin to think it.

If Thou Wilt Be Perfect, 576 R

TESTING

Stedfastly endure the trial and you will
get direction from it. "What I tell you in
the darkness, that speak ye in the light"
(Matthew 10:27 RV). Darkness is the time
to listen, not to speak; if you do speak, you
will speak in the wrong mood; you will
be inclined to criticise God's providential
arrangements for other lives and to tell Him
He has no business to allow these things.
As long as you are in the dark you do not
know what God is doing; immediately you
get into the light, you discover it. "Because
thou hast kept the word of My patience. . ."
(Revelation 3:10). The test always comes
along the line of patience.

He Shall Glorify Me, 488 R

Darkness is not synonymous with sin; if
there is darkness spiritually it is much
more likely to be the shade of God's hand
than darkness on account of sin; it may be
the threshold of a new revelation coming
through a big break in personal experience. Before the dawn there is desolation;
but wait, the dawn will merge into glorious
day—". . . the light of dawn, that shineth
more and more unto the perfect day." If you
are experiencing the darkness of desolation
on individual lines, go through with it, and
you will find yourself face to face with Jesus
Christ as never before. "I am come that
they might have life"—life in which there
is no death—"and that they might have it
more abundantly."

He Shall Glorify Me, 489 R

"What I tell you in darkness"—watch where
God puts you into darkness, and when you
are there, keep your mouth shut. Are you in
the dark just now in your circumstances, or
in your life with God? Then remain quiet.
If you open your mouth in the dark, you
will talk in the wrong mood: darkness is the
time to listen. Don't talk to other people
about it; don't read books to find out the

reason of the darkness, but listen and heed. If you talk to other people, you cannot hear what God is saying. When you are in the dark, listen, and God will give you a very precious message for someone else when you get into the light.

My Utmost for His Highest, February 14, 749 R

"And He said unto them, Let us go over unto the other side of the lake. And they launched forth" (Luke 8:22).

"If you obey Jesus you will have a life of joy and delight." Well, it is not true. Jesus said to the disciples—"Let us go to the other side of the lake," and they were plunged into the biggest storm they had ever known. You say, "If I had not obeyed Jesus I should not have got into this complication." Exactly. The problems in our walk with God are to be accounted for along this line, and the temptation is to say, "God could never have told me to go there; if He had done so this would not have happened." We discover then whether we are going to trust God's integrity or listen to our own expressed scepticism. Scepticism of the tongue is only transitional; real scepticism is wrung out from the man who knows he did not get where he is on his own account—"I was not seeking my own; I came deliberately because I believe Jesus told me to, and now there is the darkness and the deep and the desolation."

He Shall Glorify Me, 502 L

Patience has the meaning of testing—a thing drawn out and tested, drawn out to the last strand in a strain without breaking, and ending in sheer joy. The strain on a violin string when stretched to the uttermost gives it its strength; and the stronger the strain, the finer is the sound of our life for God, and He never strains more than we are able to bear.

The Love of God—The Ministry of the Unnoticed, 669 L

It is the trial of our faith that makes us wealthy towards God.

Not Knowing Whither, 865 R

Just where Jesus does not seem to be, when it looks as if the waves would overwhelm them, the Son of God comes walking on the top of those very billows. As we go on in our spiritual life we get into similar conditions; they are not symbolic, but the actual conditions of our lives. God engineers us out of our sequestered places and brings us into elemental conditions, and we get a taste of what the world is like because of the disobedience of man. We realise then that our hold on God has been a civilised hold; we have not really believed in Him at all. When we get out on to the deep and the darkness we realise what a wonderful thing the Psalmist says—"Therefore will not we fear, though the earth be removed. . . ." But it takes some confidence in God to say that when everything you trust in has gone.

He Shall Glorify Me, 502 R

It is those you have been the means of blessing who keep you from the onslaughts of the enemy. We shall be amazed to find how much we are indebted to people we never think about, simply because they were introduced to God through us, and in our difficulties they come to our aid.

The Highest Good—The Pilgrim's Song Book, 537 R

If you are outside the crucible you will say that Jesus Christ is cruel, but when you are in the crucible you see that it is a personal relationship with Himself that He is after all the time. He is after the true gold, and the devil is after it too.

Not Knowing Whither, 900 R

(Continued)

TESTING *(Continued)*

Look back over your life in grace, whether long or short, and ask yourself which are the days that have furthered you most in the knowledge of God—the days of sunshine and peace and prosperity? Never! The days of adversity, the days of strain, the days of sudden surprises, the days when the earthly house of this tabernacle was strained to its last limit, those are the days when you learned the meaning of this passion of "Go."

The Philosophy of Sin, 1114 R

Any great calamity in the natural world—death, disease, bereavement—will awaken a man when nothing else would, and he is never the same again. We would never know the "treasures of darkness" if we were always in the place of placid security.

The Philosophy of Sin, 1115 L

Never misunderstand the shadow of God's hand. When He puts us there it is assuredly to lead us into the inner meaning of Philippians 3:10—"that I may know Him." The stern discipline that looks like distress and chastisement turns out to be the biggest benediction; it is the shadow of God's hand that keeps us perfectly fitted in Him.

So Send I You, 1318 R

We say many things which we believe, but they have never been tested. Discipline has to come through all the things we believe in order to turn them into real spiritual possessions. It is the trial of our faith that is precious. "Hang in" to Jesus Christ against all odds until He turns your spiritual beliefs into real possessions.

The Place of Help, 998 L

God has hidden the glory of His teaching in the experience of temptation. "Count it all joy, my brethren, when ye fall into manifold temptations," says the Apostle James. "To him that overcometh, to him will I give of the hidden manna." The feast is just beyond the fight; when you have been through the fight, there is the wondrous joy and triumph of the feast. We learn to thank God for the trial of our faith because it works patience.

The Place of Help, 1010 L

The thing that is precious in the sight of God is faith that has been tried. Tried faith is spendable; it is so much wealth stored up in heaven, and the more we go through the trial of our faith, the wealthier we become in the heavenly regions.

The Place of Help, 1010 L

We have to beware lest we think we are tempted as no one else is tempted. What we go through is the common inheritance of the race, not something no one ever went through before. It is most humiliating to be taken off our pedestal of suffering and made to realise that thousands of others are going through the same thing as we are going through.

The Psychology of Redemption, 1082 R

It is a disastrous thing for a man never to be ragged, an appalling thing to be a privileged young man! A lad who has been his mother's pet and has been brought up like a hothouse plant is totally unprepared for the scathing of life as it is, and when he is flung out into the rugged realities of life, he suffers intolerably. Conceive the suffering of a lad who has been sheltered, never had anything go against him, never been thwarted, when the tension does come.

Shade of His Hand, 1210 L

God is not concerned about our plans; He does not say—"Do you want to go through this bereavement, this upset?" He allows these things for His own purpose. The things we are going through are either making us sweeter, better, nobler men and women, or they are making us more captious and fault-finding, more insistent upon our own way. The things that happen either make us fiends or they make us saints; it depends entirely upon the relationship we are in to God.

My Utmost for His Highest, May 22, 783 L

It is the trial of our faith that makes us wealthy in heaven. We want the treasure on earth all the time. We interpret answers to prayer on the material plane only, and if God does not answer there, we say He does not answer at all. "Treasure in heaven" is faith that has been tried, otherwise it is only possible gold.

So Send I You, 1304 R

Faith is the trend of the life all through, and everything that is not "hid with Christ in God" is against it. The trial of faith always comes in such a way that it is a perplexity to know what to do. You get advice that sounds wise, it has your welfare in view; everything seems right, and yet there is the feeling that there is an error at the heart of it.

Notes on Isaiah, 1382 L

We say, "sorrow, disaster, calamity"; God says, "chastening," and it sounds sweet to Him though it is a discord in our ears. Don't faint when you are rebuked, and don't despise the chastenings of the Lord. "In your patience possess ye your souls." If God has given you a time of rest, then lie curled up in His leaves of healing.

The Love of God—The Ministry of the Unnoticed, 669 L

THEOLOGY

Do I believe in God apart from my reasoning about Him? Theology is a great thing; so is a man's creed; but God is greater than either, and the next greatest thing is my relationship to Him.

Baffled to Fight Better, 53 R

Theology is second, not first; in its place it is a handmaid of religion, but it becomes a tyrant if put in the first place. The great doctrines of predestination and election are secondary matters; they are attempts at definition; but if we take sides with the theological method we will damn men who differ from us without a minute's hesitation.

Baffled to Fight Better, 65 L

If we insist that a man must believe the doctrine of the Trinity and the inspiration of the Scriptures before he can be saved, we are putting the cart before the horse. All that is the effect of being a Christian, not the cause of it; and if we put the effect first we produce difficulties because we are putting thinking before life. Jesus says, "Come unto Me, and if you want to know whether My teaching is of God, do His will." A scientist can explain the universe in which common-sense men live, but the scientific explanation is not first; life is first. The same with theology; theology is the systematising of the intellectual expression of life from God; it is a mighty thing, but it is second, not first.

Baffled to Fight Better, 78 R

We usually mean by theology something remote that has to do with controversy, something whereby our mind is tied up in knots and our practical life left alone. In the Bible theology is immensely practical.

Bringing Sons Unto Glory, 233 L

It is vastly important to remember that our duty is to fit our doctrines to our Lord Jesus Christ and not to fit our Lord into our doctrines.

Christian Disciplines, Volume 2, The Discipline of Patience, 338 L

The first thing that goes when you begin to think is your theology. If you stick too long to a theological point of view you become stagnant, without vitality.

Disciples Indeed, 409 L

(Continued)

THEOLOGY (Continued)

Substratum—an under stratum or layer, a fundamental element that does not appear, but on which all that does appear rests.

There is a difference between the Christian foundation and my experience of it. I can no more experience the foundation of my faith than a building can experience its foundation; but the two must be associated. Dissatisfaction in the Christian life is sure to arise if the foundations are ignored. Because men cannot experience the foundations of the Christian faith they are apt to discard them as unnecessary: they are more necessary than all the experiences which spring from them. To say "You don't need theology to save a soul" is like saying "What is the good of a foundation? What we want is a house." The good of the foundation is that when the storms come, nothing can wreck the "house" that is built on the foundation (see Matthew 7:24–27).

He Shall Glorify Me, 522 L

Theology is the science of Christianity; much that is wrongly called theology is mere psychological guess-work, verifiable only from experience. Christian theology is the ordered exposition of revelation certainties.

He Shall Glorify Me, 523 L

Whenever we put theology or a plan of salvation or any line of explanation before a man's personal relationship to God, we depart from the Bible line, because religion in the Bible is not faith in the rule of God, but faith in the God Who rules.

Shade of His Hand, 1201 L

THINKING

Watch what you say you don't understand—you understand only too clearly.

Disciples Indeed, 408 R

You can never become a Christian by thinking; you can only become a Christian by receiving something from God; but you must think after you are a Christian. Some folks have a cowardly fear of intellect in spiritual matters. After the war the most energetic thinking will have to be done by Christians; we must think as we have never thought before, otherwise we will be outstripped by those who think on lines which ignore Jesus Christ and endeavour to prove that the Redemption is not necessary.

Biblical Ethics, 105 R

Thinking is not of first importance, but it is of mighty importance secondarily. The man who prefers to be lazy in his spiritual life may do well enough, but it is the man who has thought on the basis of things who is able to give intelligent help to those who are up against it. Men have been hit during the war and few of us have been able to help them; we are inarticulate; we don't know how to put things because we have not thought about them. "My people doth not consider," says God; they do not think.

Biblical Ethics, 106 R

The reason why average Christian workers remain average Christian workers is that they are grossly ignorant about things for which they see no immediate use. The majority of us are brought up on spooned meat*—"for when by reason of the time ye ought to be teachers, ye have need again that some one teach you the rudiments of the first principles of the oracles of God; and are become such as have need of milk, and not of solid food" (Hebrews 5:12 RV).

Bringing Sons Unto Glory, 240 L
*Liquefied food that requires no chewing or effort—baby food

Until a man is born again his thinking goes round and round in a circle and he becomes intoxicated with his own importance. When he is born again there is a violent readjustment in his actual life, and when he begins to think along Jesus Christ's line there is just as tremendous a revolution in his thinking processes.

Bringing Sons Unto Glory, 240 R

We are called upon not only to be right in heart, but to be right in thinking. When we have become personally related to Jesus Christ we have to do the thing that is in our power to do, viz., think aright. In Philippians 4:8–9 Paul gives the rule for the thinking life of the Christian. Have we ever given our brains the task of concentrated thinking along that line? "Finally, brethren, whatsoever things are true, whatsoever things are honest, whatsoever things are just, whatsoever things are pure, whatsoever things are lovely, whatsoever things are of good report; if there be any virtue, and if there be any praise, *think on these things*."

Bringing Sons Unto Glory, 241 L

One is made to turn with weary exhaustion from the unthinking, hand to mouth experience of much of the religious literature of the day. To *think* as a Christian is a rare accomplishment, especially as the curious leaven which puts a premium on ignorance works its sluggish way.

Christian Disciplines, Volume 1,
The Discipline of Divine Guidance, 273 L

To speak of Plato to the majority of Christian preachers, particularly holiness preachers, would be to meet not a consciousness of ignorance, but a blatant pride which boasts of knowing nothing outside the Bible, which, in all probability, means knowing nothing inside it either. Christian thinking is a rare and difficult thing; so many seem unaware that the first great commandment according to our Lord is, "Thou shalt love the Lord thy God . . . from all thy mind. . . ."

Christian Disciplines, Volume 1,
The Discipline of Divine Guidance, 273 L

If thinking gives you a headache, it is a sign that you have brains.

The Moral Foundations of Life, 696 R

Our thinking is based not on Hebrew Wisdom and confidence in God, but on the Wisdom of the Greeks, which is removed from practical life, and on that basis we persuade ourselves that if a man knows a thing is wrong he will not do it. That is not true. The plague with me, apart from the grace of God, is that I know what is right, but I'm hanged if I'll do it! What I want to know is, can anyone tell me of a power that will alter my "want to"? Education will never alter the "want to," neither will high ideals nor vowing; that is where the great fundamental mistake in dealing with human problems has been made. It is only when a man is born from above of the Spirit of God that he finds the "want to" is altered.

Shade of His Hand, 1229 R

There is no jump into thinking; it is only done by a steady determined facing of the facts brought by the engineering of circumstances. God always insists that I think *where I am.*

Disciples Indeed, 409 L

Never cease to think until you think things home and they become character.

Disciples Indeed, 409 L

Before the mind has begun to grapple with problems it is easy to talk; when the mind has begun to grapple with problems it is a humiliating thing to talk.

Disciples Indeed, 409 R

Unless you think, you will be untouched, unbroken, by the truths you utter.

Disciples Indeed, 409 R

(Continued)

THINKING (*Continued*)

Never stop learning. People stagnate, not through backsliding, but because they stop learning and harden into a wrong mental poise.

He Shall Glorify Me, 522 R

Run your idea for all it is worth. When we are young we think things are simpler than they are; we have an idea for every domain. A man says he is a materialist, or an agnostic, or a Christian, meaning he has only one main idea, but very few will run that idea for all it is worth, yet this is the only way to discover whether it will work, and the same thing is true in the idea of the Christian religion that God is Love.

The Love of God, 658 L

It is the extraordinary thinker, the man with the extreme experience, rather than the average man, who gets at the truth at the basis of things. When we deal with great thinkers like Solomon or Shakespeare we get to the truth of things; we do not get the truth through experience.

Shade of His Hand, 1222 R

The great need for the saint is to get his brains at work on the Word of God; otherwise he will stagnate, no matter how much he may name the Name of God.

Notes on Isaiah, 1377 R

Most of us do not think; we live healthy ordinary lives and don't bother about thinking at all; but when an upheaval comes from underneath proving that the basis of things is not rational, we find the value of the Bible attitude, which is that the basis of things is tragic and not rational, and the war has proved that the Bible is right. We have to live based on our relationship to God in the actual condition of things as they are.

Shade of His Hand, 1222 R

We do not think on the basis of Christianity at all. We are taught to think like pagans for six days a week and to reverse the order for one day; consequently in critical moments we think as pagans and our religion is left in the limbo of the inarticulate.

Shade of His Hand, 1229 L

THOUGHTS / THOUGHT LIFE

We are responsible for our habits of thinking, and Paul in these passages* is dealing with the phase of mental life in which a man can choose his thinking and is able to express it in words. The old idea that we cannot help evil thoughts has become so ingrained in our minds that most of us accept it as a fact. But if it is true, then Paul is talking nonsense when he tells us to choose our thinking, to think only on those things that are true, and honourable, and just, and pure.

The Moral Foundations of Life, 702 L
*See Philippians 4:8–9; 2 Corinthians 10:5

Never pray about evil thoughts; it will fix them in the mind. "Quit"—that is the only thing to do with anything that is wrong; to ruthlessly grip it on the threshold of your mind and allow it no more way. If you have received the Holy Spirit, you will find that you have the power to bring "every thought into captivity to the obedience of Christ."

The Moral Foundations of Life, 706 R

Our minds are apt to be all abroad, like an octopus with its tentacles out to catch everything that comes along—newspaper garbage, spiritualistic garbage, advertisement garbage, we let them all come and make a dumping ground of our heads, and then sigh and mourn and say we cannot think right thoughts. Beware of saying you cannot help your thoughts; you can; you have all the almighty power of God to help you. We have to learn to bring every thought into captivity to the obedience of Christ, and it takes time. We want to reach it in a moment like a rocket, but it can only be done by a gradual moral discipline, and we do not like discipline; we want to do it all at once.

The Moral Foundations of Life, 719 L

A wrong temper of mind is the most blame-worthy thing there is. It is not only what we say but what we think that tells.

So Send I You, 1299 R

Things of Good Report . . . literally, the things that have a fine face, a winning and attractive tone about them. What should we be like after a year of thinking on these things? We might not be fatter, but I am certain we should look pleasanter! When we do think about the things of good report we shall be astonished to realise where they are to be found; they are found where we only expected to find the opposite. When our eyes are fixed on Jesus Christ we begin to see qualities blossoming in the lives of others that we never saw there before. We see people whom we have tabooed and put on the other side exhibiting qualities we have never exhibited, although we call ourselves saved and sanctified.

The Moral Foundations of Life, 720 L

Beware what you brood on in secret, for the fateful opportunity will come when God and the devil will meet in your soul, and you will do according to your brood-ing, swept beyond all your control. This is a law as sure as God is God. . . . Beware of saying, "Oh well, it doesn't matter much what I think about in secret"; it does, for the opportunity will come when what you think about in secret will find expression and spurt out in an act.

Our Portrait in Genesis, 980 L

We cannot think anything without the thought having its consequence.

Shade of His Hand, 1240 R

TIME

Take time. Remember we have all the time there is. The majority of us waste time and want to encroach on eternity. "Oh well, I will think about these things when I have time." The only time you will have is the day after you are dead, and that will be eternity. An hour, or half an hour, of daily attention to and meditation on our own spiritual life is the secret of progress.

The Moral Foundations of Life, 712 L

Remember, no man has time to pray; he has to take time from other things that are valu-able in order to understand how necessary time for prayer is.

The Psychology of Redemption, 1090 R

Jesus said that the cares of this world and the lust of other things would choke His word. We can choke God's word with a yawn; we can hinder the time that should be spent with God by remembering we have other things to do. "I haven't time!" Of course you have not time! *Take* time; strangle some other interests and make time to realise that the centre of power in your life is the Lord Jesus Christ and His Atonement. Paul limited his knowledge to that one thing—"I determined not to know any thing among you, save Jesus Christ, and Him crucified." We have to learn to concentrate our affinities, to determine to be limited.

Our Brilliant Heritage, 953 R

(Continued)

TIME (Continued)

God grant we may be roused up in the spiritual domain to put energy and vim into our work and never say, "I can't; I have no time." Of course you have not; no man worthy of the name ought to have time to give to God; he has to take it from other things until he knows how God values time.

Workmen of God, 1364 R

God's dates are not man's. God seems to pay no attention to our calendars; He has a calendar of His own in which He suddenly surprises a man in the midst of his days. Leave room for God. We expect God only on special days, in particular meetings; that is not God's way. He comes suddenly, at midnight or at noonday.

Notes on Isaiah, 1372 L

Time is nothing to God.

Conformed to His Image, 377 R

TONGUE (See also SPEECH)

The Bible reveals the tongue to be the worst enemy a man has (see James 3:6–8). . . . if we are not born again our words rankle and sting and annoy and spread destruction.

The Highest Good—The Pilgrim's Song Book, 527 R

TRIAL (See TESTING)

TRUST

Trustfulness is based on confidence in God whose ways I do not understand; if I did, there would be no need for trust.

He Shall Glorify Me, 487 R

Naturally, we do not love God, we mistrust Him; consequently in thinking we are apt to apply to God what should be applied to Satan. Satan uses the problems of this life to slander God's character; he tries to make us think that all the calamities and miseries and wrongs spring from God.

Biblical Psychology, 177 R

Whenever I say "I want to reason this thing out before I can trust," I will never trust. The reasoning out and the perfection of knowledge come after the response to God has been made.

God's Workmanship, 414 L

When we have the simple, childlike trust in God that Jesus exhibited, the overflowing grace of God will have no limits, and we must set no limits to it.

The Highest Good—Thy Great Redemption, 564 R

It is very necessary to be brought to the stage of trust in our experience of suffering; perhaps we are brought to it most acutely when in the case of someone we love we have to look up mutely to God and say, "I don't understand it at all, but go on with what You are doing." That marks a real stage of learning to trust in God, and it is a step towards something still further on.

Christian Disciplines, Volume 1, The Discipline of Suffering, 284 R

It is not our trust that keeps us, but the God in whom we trust who keeps us. We are always in danger of trusting in our trust, believing our belief, having faith in our faith. All these things can be shaken; we have to base our faith on those things which cannot be shaken (see Hebrews 12:27).

The Highest Good—The Pilgrim's Song Book, 533 L

Beware of the thing that makes you go down before God and sway from side to side spiritually—"I don't know what to do"; then don't do anything. "I don't see anything"; well, don't look for anything. "I thought by this time I should see something"; if you don't, be foolish enough to trust in God. It is the height of madness from common-sense standpoints to have faith in God.

Not Knowing Whither, 881 R

"If God would only come down and explain everything to me, I would have faith in Him," we say; and yet how little trust we are inclined to have in God, even when we have had an experience of His grace and a revelation of Himself. We sink back to the experience instead of being confident in the God Who gave us the experience. Experience is never the ground of our trust; it is the gateway to the One Whom we trust.

Not Knowing Whither, 866 R

It is a very great lesson, which few of us learn, that when God gives us nothing it is because we are inside Him, and by determining to do something we put ourselves outside Him. Abraham would not stay in the land when the famine came because there was nothing; he would not trust God for a child because there was not one. God kept giving Abraham "nothing," i.e., Himself, and by determining to do something Abraham jumped outside God, and came to find that he was putting himself in the relationship of the Everlasting No. There are things God tells us to do without any light or illumination other than just the word of His command, and if we do not obey it is because we are independently strong enough to wriggle out of obeying. All God's commands are enablings, therefore it is a crime to be weak in His strength.

Not Knowing Whither, 880 L

Personal contact with Jesus alters everything. Be stupid enough to come and commit yourself to what He says. The attitude of coming is that the will resolutely lets go

of everything and deliberately commits all to Him.

My Utmost for His Highest, June 11, 790 L

Never trust any man or woman, and never trust yourself; trust only the grace of God. As sure as we put our trust in man, no matter how good, we learn that the human heart is a cunning house of deceit.

Notes on Jeremiah, 1408 R

Don't glory in man, for the best of men are but the best of men; bank on God alone.

Notes on Jeremiah, 1397 R

TRUTH

Truth is not a system, not a constitution, nor even a creed; the Truth is the Lord Jesus Christ Himself, and He is the Truth about the Father just as He is the Way of the Father. Our tendency is to make truth a logical statement, to make it a principle instead of a Person.

Christian Disciplines, Volume 1,
The Discipline of Peril, 298 L

A truth may be of no use to us just now, but when the circumstances arise in which that truth is needed, the Holy Spirit will bring it back to our remembrance. This accounts for the curious way in which the statements of Jesus emerge; we say: "I wonder where that word came from?" It came from the unconscious mind; the point is, are we going to obey it?

The Moral Foundations of Life, 707 R

(Continued)

TRUTH (Continued)

There is no such thing as a *wrong* wrong, only a *right* that has gone wrong. Every error had its start in a truth, else it would have no power.

Disciples Indeed, 393 R

Most of us prefer to live in a particular phase of the Truth, and that is where we get intolerant and pigheaded, religiously determined that everyone who does not agree with us must be wrong. We preach in the Name of God what He won't own.

Disciples Indeed, 398 L

Watch the tendency which is in us all to try and safeguard God's truth. The remarkable thing is that God never safeguards His own truth; He leaves statements in this Book we can easily misrepresent; the only test is the Holy Spirit who leads us into all truth.

Conformed to His Image, 357 L

Many of the theological terms used nowadays have no grip; we talk glibly about sin, and about salvation, but let the truth be presented along the line of a man's deep personal need, and at once it is arresting.

Disciples Indeed, 398 R

The first moment of thinking alters our life. If for one moment we have discerned the truth, we can never be the same again; we may ignore it, or forget it, but it will not forget us. Truth once discerned goes down into the subconscious mind, but it will jump up in a most awkward way when we least expect it.

The Moral Foundations of Life, 696 R

Our tendency is to put truth into a dogma: Truth is a Person. "I am . . . the Truth," said Jesus.

Our Portrait in Genesis, 959 L

With God a thing is never too good to be true; it is too good not to be true.

The Highest Good—The Pilgrim's Song Book, 535 R

It is never right to do wrong in order that right may come, although it may seem justifiable from every standard saving one. In the long run you can never produce right by doing wrong, yet we will always try to do it unless we believe what the Bible says. If I tell a lie in order to bring about the right, I prove to my own conviction that I do not believe the One at the back of the universe is truthful. Judge everything in the light of Jesus Christ, who is The Truth, and you will never do the wrong thing, however right it looks.

Our Portrait in Genesis, 967 R

No man is ever the same after listening to the truth; he may say he pays no attention to it, he may appear to forget all about it, but at any moment the truth may spring up into his consciousness and destroy all his peace of mind.

Disciples Indeed, 397 R

UNBELIEF

Un-belief is a fretful, worrying, questioning, annoying, self-centred spirit. To believe is to stop all this and let God work.

If Thou Wilt Be Perfect, 586 L

We reveal the impoverished meanness of our conceptions by the words we use in the actual business of life—"economy," "insurance," "diplomacy." These words cover by euphemism our ghastly disbelief in our Heavenly Father.

The Place of Help, 992 R

Whenever our spiritual life is unsatisfactory it is because we have said to God—"I won't"; "You can't expect me to trust You." Then we must take the consequences. "And He did not many mighty works there because of their unbelief." If Jesus Christ has done no mighty works for me it is either because I don't believe He can, or I don't want Him to.

Shade of His Hand, 1224 R

The great paralysis of our heart is unbelief. Immediately I view anything as inevitable about any human being, I am an unbeliever.

Disciples Indeed, 386 R

We say—"If I really could believe!" The point is—If I really *will* believe. No wonder Jesus Christ lays such emphasis on the sin of unbelief. "And He did not many mighty works there because of their unbelief." If we really believed that God meant what He said—what should we be like!

My Utmost for His Highest, July 9, 799 R

To some people every day brings fresh causes to disbelieve God, and to others new opportunities of praising and knowing God. This is not because the one is in physical health and the other not, but because one has a moral twist and the other has not. Disbelief in God is never only intellectual; it is moral.

Notes on Jeremiah, 1415 L

Anything Jesus Christ revealed may be missed. The disbelief of the human mind always wastes itself in the sentimental idea that God would never let us miss the greatest good. Jesus says He will; that is why we don't like Him, and that is why the teaching of to-day is not the teaching of the Jesus Christ of the New Testament.

The Highest Good, 545 L

UNCONSCIOUS (SUBCONSCIOUS) MIND

Most of what we hear passes out of our conscious mind into our unconscious mind and we think we have forgotten it, but we have not; we never forget anything; we cannot always recall it when we want to, but that is a different matter. We forget nothing; it is there, although not in the conscious mind, and when certain circumstances arise, suddenly the thing we thought we had forgotten is there to our amazement right enough. This is exactly what Jesus said the Holy Ghost would do, "He shall . . . bring all things to your remembrance whatsoever I have said unto you." The Holy Spirit is forming the unconscious mind all the time, and as we "mop up" His teaching—simply take it in, not try to estimate it as we would a mathematical study—we shall find God is putting in the right soil for His life to grow in. Our one concern is to keep in the right atmosphere.

The Psychology of Redemption, 1072 L

When a man is related to God through Jesus Christ, God protects not only the conscious life but the unconscious life as well.

Shade of His Hand, 1212 R

An island of the sea is easily explored, yet it may prove to be but the top of a mountain, the greater part of which is hidden under the sea, going down to deeper depths than we can fathom. So our personality is infinitely more than we can be conscious of; consequently we must never estimate ourselves by the part we are conscious of, or be so stupid as to say we are only what we are conscious of. We are all in danger of doing this until we come across things in ourselves that surprise us.

The Servant as His Lord, 1263 L

UNIVERSALISM

(See also COMPROMISE)

The revelation given through Jesus Christ is that the human race has been redeemed. "It is finished," and in the Cross of Jesus Christ all men are condemned to salvation. That is very different from what is called Universalism. The redemption is of universal application, but human responsibility is not done away with. Universalism looks like a Christian flower, but it has not its roots in the Christian faith. Jesus Christ is most emphatic on the fact that there are possibilities of eternal damnation for the man who positively neglects or positively rejects His redemption.

The Place of Help, 1046 R

USEFULNESS

Has God put you on the shelf deliberately? Why cannot He be glorified by a man in the dust as well as in the sunshine? We are not here to tell God what to do with us, but to let Him use us as He chooses. Remember, God's main concern is that we are more interested in Him than in work for Him. Once you are rooted and grounded in Christ the greatest thing you can do is to *be*. Don't try and be useful; be yourself and God will use you to further His ends.

Facing Reality, 28 L

We constantly ask, "Am I of any use?" If you think you are, it is questionable whether you are being used by the Holy Spirit at all. It is the things you pay no attention to that the Holy Spirit uses.

Disciples Indeed, 410 R

There is a great danger in asking, "What is the use of it?" There is no *use* in it at all. If you want a life of usefulness, don't be a Christian after Our Lord's stamp; you will be much more useful if you are not. The cry for

the standard of usefulness knocks the spiritual Christian right out; he dare not touch it if he is going to remain true to his Master. Take the life of Our Lord: for three years all He did was to walk about saying things and healing sick people—a useless life, judged from every standard of success and of enterprise. If Our Lord and His disciples had lived in our day, they would have been put down as a most unuseful crowd. In spiritual matters we can never calculate on the line of—"What is the use of it?"

The Love of God—The Ministry of the Unnoticed, 664 R

Your dead-set determination to be of use never means half so much as the times you have not been thinking of being used—a casual conversation, an ordinary word, while your life was "hid with Christ in God."

Disciples Indeed, 410 R

The true character of the loveliness that tells for God is always unconscious. Conscious influence is priggish and un-Christian. When we begin to wonder whether we are of any use, we instantly lose the bloom of the touch of the Lord. Jesus says—"He that believeth on Me," out of him "shall flow rivers of living water." If we begin to examine outflow, we lose touch with the Source. We have to pay attention to the Source and God will look after the outflow.

The Love of God—The Ministry of the Unnoticed, 661 R

The one great need is not to face our beliefs and our creeds, or the question whether we are of any use or not, but to face our Lord. This attitude of being ready to face Him means more and more disentanglement from so-called religious work, and more and more intense spiritual reality in so-called secular work. The whole meaning of the Christian life from Our Lord's standpoint is to be ready for Him.

So Send I You, 1295 L

We have nothing to do with our "usability," but only with our relationship to Jesus Christ; nothing must be allowed to come in between.

If Thou Wilt Be Perfect, 581 L

We can all do the heroic thing, but can we live in the drab humiliating valley where there is nothing amazing, but mostly disaster, certainly humiliation, and emphatically everything drab and dull and mean?* That is where Jesus Christ lived most of His life. The reason we have to live in the valley is that the majority of people live there, and if we are to be of use to God in the world we must be useful from God's standpoint, not from our own standpoint or the standpoint of other people.

The Love of God—The Ministry of the Unnoticed, 665 L
Ordinary, common, low, or ignoble.

It is a misconception to imagine that God is bound up in His instruments; He uses forces and powers for His own ends, but they must never be mistaken for Himself. An instrument conveys God's message, and a man used by God ought to be a holy man: but it does not always follow that he is (cf. Matthew 7:21–22).

The Place of Help, 1017 L

We are apt to have the idea that we can only estimate what God is in us by what He does through us. What about our Lord and Master; what did He do? The marvellous thing about Him is what He did not do. Think what an ignominious failure His life was, judged from every standpoint but

God's. Our Lord did not say that signs and wonders would not follow, but that the one set purpose for us is that we do God's will in His way, not in our way.

The Psychology of Redemption, 1080 R

[Our Lord] went through villages and cities where He was marvellously used, but the great characteristic of His earthly life was that He stedfastly set His face to go to Jerusalem; He never stayed in a place because He had been of use there (Mark 1:37–38). Beware of the sweet sisters and beloved brothers who say to you, "Now do consider whether you will not be of more use here than anywhere else." . . . The measure of our service for God is not our usefulness to others. We have nothing to do with the estimate of others, nor with success in service; we have to see that we fulfil our ministry.

The Psychology of Redemption, 1094 R

God sows His saints in the most useless places, according to the judgment of the world. Where they will glorify Him is where God puts His saints, and we are no judge at all of where that is. . . . People say, "Don't be so absurd as to go and bury yourself there." We have to let God sacrifice us as He likes, and go where He sends us. Never be deluded into making this statement: "I am here because I am so useful"; say rather, "I am here because God wants me here." The one lodestar of the saint is God Himself, not estimated usefulness.

The Servant as His Lord, 1284 L

We have to get rid of this notion—"Am I of any use?" and make up our minds that we are not, and we may be near the truth. It is never a question of being of use, but of being of value to God Himself. When we are abandoned to God, He works through us all the time.

My Utmost for His Highest, February 21, 752 L

VALUE OF PERSONS
(See also AGING)

There is engrained in the depths of human nature a dislike of the general ruck of mankind, in spite of all our modern jargon about "loving Humanity." We have a disparaging way of talking about the common crowd: the common crowd is made up of innumerable editions of you and me.

Conformed to His Image, 366 R

Ask the Holy Spirit to enable your mind to brood for one moment on the value of the "nobody" to Jesus. The people who make up the common crowd are nobodies to me, but it is astonishing to find that it is the nobodies that Jesus Christ came to save. The terms we use for men in the sense of their social position are nothing to Him.

Conformed to His Image, 366 R

VENGEANCE

Vengeance is probably the most tyrannical passion of the carnal mind. The first wonderful thing done by the new life given to us by the Holy Spirit is to loosen the heart, and as we obey the Spirit the manifestation in the life becomes easier.

Biblical Psychology, 167 R

The deepest-rooted passion in the human soul is vengeance. Drunkenness, sensuality, and covetousness go deep, but not so deep as vengeance. . . . Vengeance is the most deeply rooted passion in the human soul, and the impersonation of it is the devil. The devil has an absolute detestation of God, an immortal hatred of God.

Biblical Psychology, 172 R

VINDICATION
(See ARGUE / ARGUMENT)

VISION

We can all see visions and dream dreams, but they are not woven into the texture of our life, and unless we are willing to pay the price of expansion we will drift from our ideals.

God's Workmanship, 465 R

The most unwholesome people spiritually are those who like to have their emotions stirred by prayer meetings and devotional readings, but they never act them out.
. . . When the Spirit of God stirs you, make as many things inevitable as possible, let the consequences be what they will. It is in such crises in spiritual life as these that Jesus says, "Come unto Me . . . and I will give you rest." He will make a man able to work out in actual life what he sees by the power of vision.

God's Workmanship, 465 R

God has to season us; there has to be a time of humiliation before the vision is turned into verity. We have to learn not only how useless we are, but how marvellously mighty God is. "Many are called, but few prove the choice ones."

So Send I You, 1294 R

God gives us the vision; then He takes us down to the valley to batter us into the shape of the vision, and it is in the valley that so many of us faint and give way. Every vision will be made real if we will have patience. Think of the enormous leisure of God! He is never in a hurry. We are always in such a frantic hurry.

My Utmost for His Highest, July 6, 798 R

The vision is not a castle in the air, but a vision of what God wants you to be. . . . If you have ever had the vision of God, you may try as you like to be satisfied on a lower level, but God will never let you.

My Utmost for His Highest, July 6, 798 R

"And let us not be weary in well-doing: for in due season we shall reap, if we faint not" (Galatians 6:9 RV).

We all experience the weariness that comes from wrongdoing, but I want to mention the weariness which annoys us because we don't know how it came; why our life suddenly lost all its interest. The point to note is that weariness does come in well-doing, when everything becomes listless. It has no business to be though— it is a sickness of the soul. What is the cure? The cure is that of a right vision. Every man has the power to slay his own weariness, not by "bucking up" as you do physically, but by suddenly looking at things from a different standpoint.

The Place of Help, 1057 L

God gives us the vision; then He takes us down to the valley to batter us into its shape, and it is in the valley that we faint and give way, while all the time God is wanting to get us through to the veritable reality.

So Send I You, 1293 R

The proof that we have the vision is that we are reaching out for more than we have grasped. It is a bad thing to be satisfied spiritually.

My Utmost for His Highest, May 2, 776 L

Each one of us has a counterpart somewhere in the experiences of these three men of God. In the case of Abraham, the valley of humiliation lasted thirteen years; Moses, forty years; Isaiah, a few minutes. No two of us are alike; each one stands alone before God. Your valley may be a darkness where you have nothing but your duty to guide you; no voice, no thrill, but just steady, plodding duty; or it may be a deep agonising dejection at the realisation of your unfitness and uncleanness and insufficiency. Let God put you on His wheel and whirl you as He likes, and as sure as God is God and you are you, you will turn out exactly in accordance

with the vision He gave you. Don't lose heart in the process.

So Send I You, 1295 R

If we have only what we have experienced, we have nothing; if we have the inspiration of the vision of God, we have more than we can experience. Beware of the danger of relaxation spiritually.

My Utmost for His Highest, May 2, 776 L

A man with the vision of God is not devoted to a cause or to any particular issue; he is devoted to God Himself. You always know when the vision is of God because of the inspiration that comes with it; things come with largeness and tonic to the life because everything is energised by God.

My Utmost for His Highest, May 2, 776 L

VOCATION

Our Lord's vocation, which He accepted at His baptism, was His identification with sin. Our vocation is to fulfil the anticipations of God and to become His sons and daughters. The majority of us so harp on the ordinary evangelical line that we thank God for saving us and then leave the thing alone. We cannot grow *into* holiness, but we must grow *in* it. Are we accepting our vocation and determining to let the Son of God manifest Himself in our mortal flesh?

The Psychology of Redemption, 1075 R

Watch the barriers God puts into your life. The natural life says, "I ought to be this and that." But God has told you you cannot. Woe be to you if you hanker for a second after the thing about which God has said "No" to you. If you do, you will put to death the life of God in you. Are you willing to accept the barrier from Him? It may be a barrier with regard to personal ambition for His service.

The Psychology of Redemption, 1076 R

(Continued)

VOCATION (Continued)

Have we received this ministry from Jesus, "As Thou hast sent Me into the world, even so have I also sent them into the world"? How did the Father send Him? "For I came down from heaven, not to do Mine own will, but the will of Him that sent Me." The first obedience of Jesus was to the will of His Father, not to the needs of men. Then our first accepted vocation is not to help men, but to obey God, and when we accept that vocation we enter into relationship with the despised and the neglected. It is always easy to neglect a man or woman who deliberately accepts the aim of his life from the Lord Jesus.

The Psychology of Redemption, 1077 L

VOWING / VOWS

The Old Testament Scriptures always regard the oath as a peculiar sacrament. If you read what the Bible says about vowing you will see how culpably negligent we are in the way we promise. If we do not fulfil a promise, we damage our moral and spiritual life. It is infinitely better to refuse to promise anything, even in the most superficial relationships, than to promise and not perform. Spiritual leakages are accounted for in this way.

Not Knowing Whither, 899 L

Solomon's advice is—Don't vow, for if you make a vow even in ordinary matters and do not keep it, you are the worse for it. . . . We reap terrific damage to our own characters when we vow and do not perform. . . . Don't pile up vows before men, and certainly not before God.

Shade of His Hand, 1212 L

WAITING

The waiting time is always the testing time. How we hurry people into work for God! A thrilling experience, an ecstasy of spiritual emotion, a heavenly vision, and, "I am called of God to preach"! Are you? Get back to God's Book. If you are called to preach, God will put you through mills you never dreamed of.

Bringing Sons Unto Glory, 222 L

The majority of us know nothing about waiting; we don't wait, we endure. Waiting means that we go on in the perfect certainty of God's goodness—no dumps or fear. The attitude of the human heart towards God Who promises should be to give Him credit for being as honest as He ought to be, and then to go on in the actual life as if no promise had been made. That is faithful waiting.

Not Knowing Whither, 894 R

To wait upon God is not to sit with folded hands and do nothing, but to wait as men who wait for the harvest. The farmer does not wait idly but with intense activity; he keeps industriously "at it" until the harvest. To wait upon God is the perfection of activity. We are told to "rest in the Lord," not to rust.

The Place of Help, 1013 L

WAR*

*Chambers' references to war usually refer to World War I (1914–1918).

One thing the war has done is to knock on the head all such shallow optimism as telling people to "look on the bright side of things"; or that "every cloud has a silver lining": there are some clouds that are black all through.

Baffled to Fight Better, 48 L

This question is on the lips of people to-day: Is war of the devil or of God? It is of neither. It is of man, though God and the devil are both behind it. War is a conflict of wills, either in individuals or in nations, and just now there is a terrific conflict of wills in nations. If I cannot make my will by diplomacy bear on other people, then the last resort is war, and always will be until Jesus Christ brings in His kingdom.

Christian Disciplines, Volume 1,
The Discipline of Peril, 292 L

We must take heed that in the present calamities, when war and devastation and heart-break are abroad in the world, we do not shut ourselves up in a world of our own and ignore the demand made on us by our Lord and our fellow-men for the service of intercessory prayer and hospitality and care.

Christian Disciplines, Volume 1,
The Discipline of Peril, 293 L

The war has put an end to a great deal of belief in our beliefs. Coleridge's criticism of many so-called Christians was that they did not believe in God, but only believed their beliefs about Him. A man up against things as they are feels that he has lost God, while in reality he has come face to face with Him. It is not platitudes that tell here, but great books, like the Book of Job, which work away down on the implicit line. There are many things in life that look like irresponsible blunders, but the Bible reveals that God has taken the responsibility for these things, and that Jesus Christ has bridged the gap which sin made between God and man; the proof that He has done so is the Cross. God accepts the responsibility for sin, and on the basis of the Redemption men find their personal way out and an explanation.

Baffled to Fight Better, 50 L

Our Lord insists on the inevitableness of peril. Right through His talks with His disciples, without panic and without passion

and without fear, He says: "You must lay your account with this sort of thing, with war, with spite, with hatred, with jealousy, with despisings, with banishment, and with death. I have told you these things, that when they happen, you may remember that I told you of them, and not be scared."

Christian Disciplines, Volume 1,
The Discipline of Peril, 292 L

There is one thing worse than war, and that is sin. The thing that startles us is not the thing that startles God. We get tremendously scared when our social order is broken up, and well we may. We get terrorised by hundreds of men being killed, but we forget that there is something worse—sinful, dastardly lives being lived day by day, year in and year out, in our villages and towns—men without one trace of cleanness in their moral lives. That is worse.

Christian Disciplines, Volume 1,
The Discipline of Peril, 292 R

How many of us in times of peace and civilisation bother one iota about the state of men's hearts towards God? Yet these are the things that produce pain in the heart of God, not the wars and the devastation that so upset us. The human soul is so mysterious that in the moment of a great tragedy men get face to face with things they never gave heed to before, and in the moment of death it is extraordinary what takes place in the human heart towards God.

Christian Disciplines, Volume 1,
The Discipline of Peril, 292 R

There is something worse than war, and that is the average run of commercial business life in piping times of peace; it does not destroy a man's body, but it almost damns his soul; it makes a cultured detester of the one who competes against him.

He Shall Glorify Me, 483 R

(Continued)

WAR *(Continued)*

At present in the history of the world it is the hour and the power of darkness. During the war some of the biggest intellectual juggling tricks have been performed trying to make out that war is a good thing; war is the most damnably bad thing. Because God overrules a thing and brings good out of it does not mean that in itself that thing is a good thing. We have not been getting "acquainted with grief"; we have tried to juggle with the cause of it. If the war has made me reconcile myself with the fact that there is sin in human beings, I shall no longer go with my head in the clouds, or hidden in the sand like an ostrich, but I shall be wishing to face facts as they are.

The Place of Help, 1043 L

The intense awful crisis of the war will be followed by years of drudgery for the lives that are left—shattered nerves, maimed men, and marred lives. We get our moments of light and insight when we see what God is after, and then we come to where there is no crisis, but just the ordinary life to be lived. By and by God will give an unveiled year and reveal the wonder of what He has been doing in us all the time.

The Psychology of Redemption, 1072 R

To call war either diabolical or Divine is nonsense; war is human. War is a conflict of wills, not something that can be solved by law or philosophy. . . . In the time between birth and death this conflict of wills will go on until men by their relationship to God receive the disposition of the Son of God, which is holiness.

Shade of His Hand, 1203 L

Our Lord insists on the inevitableness of peril. He says "You must lay your account with war, with hatred, and with death." Men may have lived undisturbed over a volcano for a long while, when suddenly an eruption occurs. Jesus Christ did not say—"You will understand why war has come," but—"Don't be scared when it does come; do not be in a panic."

The Shadow of an Agony, 1171 L

WARNING

"Enter ye in at the strait gate: for wide is the gate, and broad is the way, that leadeth to destruction, and many there be which go in thereat: Because strait is the gate, and narrow is the way, which leadeth unto life, and few there be that find it" (Matthew 7:13–14).

Our Lord continually used proverbs and sayings that were familiar to His hearers, but He put an altogether new meaning to them. Here He uses an allegory that was familiar in His day, and He lifted it by His inspiration to embody His patient warnings. Always distinguish between warning and threatening. God never threatens; the devil never warns.

Studies in the Sermon on the Mount, 1466 L

A warning is a great arresting statement of God's, inspired by His love and patience. This throws a flood of light on the vivid statements of Jesus Christ, such as those in Matthew 23. Jesus is stating the inexorable consequence, "How can ye escape the damnation of hell?" (Matthew 23:33). There is no element of personal vindictiveness. Be careful how you picture our Lord when you read His terrible utterances. Read His denunciations with Calvary in your mind.

Studies in the Sermon on the Mount, 1466 L

You can never warn a pleased person. Satisfaction in any shape or form is impregnable to warning; personal uprightness is always alert to the voice of warning.

Notes on Jeremiah, 1400 R

WILL

We talk about people having a weak will or a strong will; it is a misleading idea. When we speak of a man having a weak will, we mean he is without any impelling passion; he is the creature of every dominating influence; with good people he is good, with bad people he is bad, not because he is a hypocrite, but because he has no ruling passion, and any strong personality knits him into shape. Will is the essential element in God's creation of a man. I cannot *give up* my will: I must exercise it.

The Moral Foundations of Life, 693 L

Always remember that Jesus Christ's statements force an issue of will and conscience first, and only as we obey is there the understanding with the mind (see John 7:17).

Biblical Ethics, 101 L

"And He went down with them, and came to Nazareth" (Luke 2:51).

This is an illustration of the way Jesus used His will all through His life (see John 6:38). He "advanced in wisdom" by applying His will to the will of His Father. "For Christ also pleased not Himself." To do what we like always ends in immorality; to do what God would have us do always ends in growth in grace.

Bringing Sons Unto Glory, 221 R

The Gospel of Jesus always forces an issue of will.

The Place of Help, 1035 R

A preacher has no business to stir up emotions without giving his hearers some issue of will on which to transact.

The Place of Help, 1049 L

If you have been born from above and the Spirit of God is discerning in you the "old man," the disposition of sin, then make it an issue of will with Him, tell Him that you want to be identified with the death of Christ until you know that your "old man" is crucified with Christ. If you have gone through that issue of will, then stand clear for Christ and Christ only, until "I have been crucified with Christ" is not a sentiment, but a sensible fact in daily living, walk, and conversation, stamped with the otherworldliness of the life hid with Christ in God.

Facing Reality, 33 R

The paralysis of refusing to act leaves a man exactly where he was before; when once he acts, he is never the same.

My Utmost for His Highest, November 4, 841 L

The battle is lost or won in the secret places of the will before God, never first in the external world. . . . The battle may take one minute or a year, that will depend on me, not on God; but it must be wrestled out alone before God, and I must resolutely go through the hell of a renunciation before Him. Nothing has any power over the man who has fought out the battle before God and won there.

My Utmost for His Highest, December 27, 859 R

WILL: FREE WILL

God has so constituted us that there must be a free willingness on our part. This power is at once the most fearful and the most glorious power. A human soul can withstand the devil successfully, and it can also withstand God successfully.

Biblical Psychology, 154 R

The subject of human free will is apt to be either understated or overstated. No man has the power to act an act of pure, unadulterated, free will. God is the only Being Who can act with absolute free will. The Bible reveals that man is free to choose, but it nowhere teaches that man is fundamentally free. The freedom man has is not that of power but of choice; consequently he is accountable for choosing the course he takes. For instance, we can choose whether or not we will accept the proposition of salvation which God puts before us; whether or not we will let God rule our lives; but we have not the power to do exactly what we like. This is easily demonstrated when we think of the number of vows that are made every New Year and so quickly broken.

The Moral Foundations of Life, 699 L

Jeremiah states that God's omnipotence will not enforce moral truth upon an unwilling mind; there must be an open mind and heart before the truth of God can be received.

Notes on Jeremiah, 1398 L

Our destiny is not determined for us, but it is determined by us. Man's free will is part of God's sovereign will. We have freedom to take which course we choose, but not freedom to determine the end of that choice. God makes clear what He desires: we must choose, and the result of the choice is not the inevitableness of law, but the inevitableness of God.

Conformed to His Image, 362 L

Within the limits of birth and death I can do as I like; but I cannot make myself unborn, neither can I escape death; those two limits are there. I have nothing to do with placing the limits, but within them I can produce what my disposition chooses.

Shade of His Hand, 1201 R

WILL: PERMISSIVE WILL OF GOD

God cannot do certain things without the co-operation of man. We continually ask, "Why doesn't God do the thing instead of waiting for me?" He cannot. It is the same problem as the difference between God's order and His permissive will. His permissive will allows the devil to do his worst and allows me to sin as I choose, until I choose to resist the devil, quit sinning, and come to God in the right relationship of a covenant with Him through Jesus Christ.

Our Portrait in Genesis, 966 L

We say there ought not to be war, there ought to be no devil, no suffering, and we fuss and fume; but these things *are!* If we lived in the clouds, it would be different; but we are here. "If only I was not where I am!" It is in the present dilemma that practical wisdom is required.

Shade of His Hand, 1196 R

There is a difference between God's order and God's permissive will. We say that God will see us through if we trust Him—"I prayed for my boy, and he was spared in answer to my prayer." Does that mean that the man who was killed was not prayed for, or that prayers for him were not answered? It is wrong to say that in the one case the man was delivered by prayer but not in the other. It is a misunderstanding of what Jesus Christ reveals. Prayer alters a man on the inside, alters his mind and his attitude to things. The point of praying is not that we get things from God, but that we learn by prayer to detect the difference between God's order and God's permissive will.

Shade of His Hand, 1200 R

God's order is—no pain, no sickness, no devil, no war, no sin: His permissive will is all these things, the "soup" we are in just now. What a man needs to do is to get hold of God's order in the kingdom on the inside, and then he will begin to see how to handle the riddle of the universe on the outside.

Shade of His Hand, 1200 R

God's order is—no sin, no sickness, no devil, no war: His Permissive will is things as they are.

Shade of His Hand, 1196 L

The fact that God makes good come out of my wrong does not make my wrong any better; I have simply utilised God's permissive will to go in a circle when I should have gone straight.

Not Knowing Whither, 892 L

WILL: WILL OF GOD

The joy of Jesus lay in knowing that every power of His nature was in such harmony with His Father that He did His Father's will with delight. Some of us are slow to do God's will; we do it as if our shoes were iron and lead; we do it with a great sigh and with the corners of our mouths down, as if His will were the most arduous thing on earth. But when our wills are rectified and brought into harmony with God, it is a delight, a superabounding joy, to do God's will.

The Moral Foundations of Life, 732 L

There is a distinct period in our experience when we cease to say—"Lord, show me Thy will," and the realisation begins to dawn that we *are* God's will, and He can do with us what He likes. We wake up to the knowledge that we have the privilege of giving ourselves over to God's will. It is a question of being yielded to God.

Facing Reality, 35 L

Supernatural voices, dreams, ecstasies, visions, and manifestations may or may not be an indication of the will of God. The words of Scripture, the advice of the saints, strong impressions during prayer may or may not be an indication of the will of God. The one test given in the Bible is discernment of a personal God and a personal relationship to Him, witnessed to ever after in walk and conversation.

Christian Disciplines, Volume 1,
The Discipline of Divine Guidance, 269 R

The striking thing in Our Lord's life was that He was not more eager to do the will of His Father than His Father was for Him to do it. He was the Saviour of the world, everything depended upon Him, and yet for thirty years He did nothing wonderful. "His doing nothing wonderful was in itself a kind of wonder" (Bonaventura). Our Lord's life is the exhibition of *the will of* God, not of *doing* the will of God.

Not Knowing Whither, 869 R

The will of God is the gladdest, brightest, most bountiful thing possible to conceive, and yet some of us talk of the will of God with a terrific sigh—"Oh well, I suppose it is the will of God," as if His will were the most calamitous thing that could befall us.

If Thou Wilt Be Perfect, 573 R

(Continued)

WILL: WILL OF GOD
(Continued)

In testing circumstances saints decide differently—may all the different decisions be correct? Unquestionably they may, for the decisions are made on the basis of personal character in its responsibility to God. The blunder of the saint lies in saying, "Because I decide thus in this crisis, therefore that is the rule for all." Nonsense! God is Sovereign, and His ways are discernible according to the attainment of the particular character. One of the most fallacious lines of reasoning is on the line of an hypothesis in the matter of God's will. No saint knows what he will do in circumstances he has never been in. "I would have you without carefulness," says the apostle Paul. A saint is a creature of vast possibilities, knit into shape by the ruling personality of God.

> *Christian Disciplines, Volume 1,*
> *The Discipline of Divine Guidance, 269 R*

Beware of thinking (no matter what you say) that God guided you in your decisions; the thought leads to spiritual hypocrisy. God holds His children responsible for the way in which they interpret His will. We only discern God's will by being renewed in the spirit of our minds in every circumstance we are in.

> *Not Knowing Whither, 869 L*

There is a great snare especially in evangelical circles of knowing the will of God as expressed in the Bible without the slightest practical working of it out in the life.

> *Conformed to His Image, 360 R*

We have to be continually renewed in the spirit of our minds, refusing to be conformed to the spirit of the age in which we live; then we shall "prove"—literally, make out in obedience—"what is that good, and acceptable, and perfect will of God."

> *Not Knowing Whither, 866 L*

"Because I have had more experience of life than you have, therefore I can discern God's will better than you can." Not at all. Whenever I put my experience of life, or my intelligence, or anything other than dependence on God, as the ground of understanding the will of God I rob Him of glory.

> *Disciples Indeed, 390 L*

How am I going to find out what the will of God is? In one way only: by not trying to find out. If you are born again of the Spirit of God, you *are* the will of God, and your ordinary common-sense decisions are God's will for you unless He gives an inner check. When He does, call a halt immediately and wait on Him. Be renewed in the spirit of your mind that you may make out His will, not in your mind, but in practical living.

> *Not Knowing Whither, 898 L*

We become spiritual whiners and talk pathetically about "suffering the will of the Lord." Where is the majestic vitality and might of the Son of God about that!

> *Our Brilliant Heritage, 946 R*

Doing God's will is never hard. The only thing that is hard is *not* doing His will. All the forces of nature and of grace are at the back of the man who does God's will because in obedience we let God have His amazing way with us.

> *Our Brilliant Heritage, 955 R*

"If you want to be perfect, perfect as I am, perfect as your Father in Heaven is"—then come the conditions. Do we really want to be perfect? Beware of mental quibbling over the word "perfect." Perfection does not mean the full maturity and consummation of a man's powers, but perfect fitness for doing the will of God (cf. Philippians 3:12–15).

> *If Thou Wilt Be Perfect, 602 L*

WISDOM

Plans made apart from trusting God's wisdom are rotten.

Our Portrait in Genesis, 969 L

Always beware when you can reasonably account to yourself for the action you are about to take, because the source of such clear reasoning is the enthroning of human understanding.

Our Portrait in Genesis, 969 L

The reason we know so little about God's wisdom is that we will only trust him as far as we can work things out according to our own reasonable commonsense.

Our Portrait in Genesis, 969 R

It is important to notice the difference between the Wisdom of the Hebrews and the Wisdom of the Greeks. The Wisdom of the Hebrews is based on an accepted belief in God; that is, it does not try to find out whether or not God exists; all its beliefs are based on God, and in the actual whirl of things as they are, all its mental energy is bent on practical living. The Wisdom of the Greeks, which is the wisdom of our day, is speculative; that is, it is concerned with the origin of things, with the riddle of the universe, etc.; consequently the best of our wits is not given to practical living.

Shade of His Hand, 1194 L

The record of the whirl of things as they are is marvellously stated in these Books of Wisdom: Job—how to suffer; Psalms—how to pray; Proverbs—how to act; Ecclesiastes—how to enjoy; Song of Solomon—how to love.

Shade of His Hand, 1194 R

In the Book of Psalms, Wisdom is applied to things as they are and to prayer. The Book of Proverbs applies Wisdom to the practical relationships of life, and Ecclesiastes applies Wisdom to the enjoyment of things as they actually are; there is no phase of life missed out, and it is shown that enjoyment is only possible by being related to God.

Shade of His Hand, 1194 R

At the basis of Hebrew wisdom, first of all is confidence in God; and second, a terrific sigh and sob over the human race as a magnificent ruin of what God designed it to be.

Shade of His Hand, 1219 R

We have to live depending on Jesus Christ's wisdom, not on our own. He is the Master, and the problem is His, not ours. We have to use the key He gives us, the key of prayer. Our Lord puts the key into our hands, and we have to learn to pray under His direction. That is the simplicity which He says His Father will bless.

So Send I You, 1325 R

WITNESS

The regenerating and sanctifying work of the Holy Spirit is to incorporate us into Christ until we are living witnesses to Him. S. D. Gordon* put it well when he said, "We have the Bible bound in morocco, bound in all kinds of beautiful leather; what we need is the Bible bound in shoe leather." That is exactly the teaching of our Lord. After the disciples had received the Holy Spirit they became witnesses to Jesus; their lives spoke more eloquently than their lips—"and they took knowledge of them, that they had been with Jesus."

Biblical Ethics, 132 L
*Samuel Dickey Gordon (1859–1936),
American writer and lecturer, known for his
Quiet Talks book series.

(Continued)

WITNESS (Continued)

God will never answer our prayer to be baptised by the Holy Ghost for any other reason than to be a witness for Jesus. "Ye shall receive power, after that the Holy Ghost is come upon you: and ye shall be witnesses unto Me." Not witnesses of what Jesus can do, that is an elementary witness; but "witnesses unto Me; you will be instead of Me, you will take everything that happens, praise or blame, persecution or commendation, as happening to Me." No one can stand that unless he is constrained by the majesty of the personal power of Jesus. Paul says, "I am constrained by the love of Christ, held as in a fever, gripped as by a disease; that is why I act as I do; you may call me mad or sober, I do not care; I am after only one thing—to persuade men of the judgment seat of Christ and of the love of God."

Approved Unto God, 10 R

If God has done something for you, you will know it unmistakably; but if He has not, never say He has for the sake of other people.

Baffled to Fight Better, 59 R

Jesus preached His first sermon in Nazareth, "where He had been brought up," and He told His disciples they were to begin "in Jerusalem." Did Jesus Christ have such great success in Nazareth where He was known? No, He had exactly the opposite. When they heard Him speak they were so filled with wrath that they broke up the service and tried to kill Him. Our Lord insists that we begin at Jerusalem for the sake of our own character, and our "Jerusalem" is unquestionably among the bounties of our own particular flesh and blood relations. It is infinitely easier to offer the "sacrifice of praise" before strangers than amongst our own flesh and blood.

Biblical Psychology, 187 R

When we talk to a soul, we talk like a tract! When Jesus talked to the woman of Samaria He did not use a prescribed form of address; He told her Divine truth and made her aware of her sin. When He talked to the disciples on the road to Emmaus, their hearts burned within them. The characteristic of the man of God's method is that he can speak to a sinner and win him before the sinner knows where he is; he can speak to saints and make their hearts burn.

God's Workmanship, 430 R

"If thou knewest the gift of God, and who it is that saith to thee, Give me to drink; thou wouldest have asked of Him, and He would have given thee living water" (John 4:10).

Jesus surprised the woman of Samaria by His extraordinary generosity of mind—"How is it that Thou, being a Jew, askest drink of me, which am a woman of Samaria? for the Jews have no dealings with the Samaritans." Our Lord knew who the woman was, but He did not talk with the smile of a superior person, "My poor ignorant woman, when will you understand what I say?" He let her talk about what she knew, and she talked with a growing wonder behind it. The first thing Jesus did was to awaken in her a sense of need of more than she had, and until she got the length of asking—"Sir, give me this water," He did not say a word about her sin.

He Shall Glorify Me, 480 R

We don't take Jesus Christ's way; our first aim is to convict people of sin; Jesus Christ's aim was to get at them where they lived. No man can stand the revelation of what he really is in God's sight unless he is handled by Jesus Christ first.

He Shall Glorify Me, 480 R

Christianity is a personal history with Jesus. "And ye shall be My witnesses." The baptism of the Holy Ghost does not mean that we are put into some great and successful venture for God, but that we are a satisfaction to Jesus wherever we are placed. It is not a question of service done, but that our living relationship to Him is a witness that satisfies Him.

He Shall Glorify Me, 482 R

Our Lord was never impatient. He simply planted seed thoughts in their minds and surrounded them with the atmosphere of His own life. He did not attempt to convince them, but left mistakes to correct themselves, because He knew that eventually the truth would bear fruit in their lives. How differently we would have acted! We get impatient and take men by the scruff of the neck and say: "You must believe this and that." You cannot make a man see moral truth by persuading his intellect. "When He, the Spirit of truth, is come, He shall guide you into all the truth."

The Love of God—The Making of a Christian, 676 L

Our Lord uses in illustration the most conspicuous things known to men, viz., salt, light, and a city set on a hill, and He says—"Be like that in your home, in your business, in your church; be conspicuously a Christian for ridicule or respect according to the mood of the people you are with." Again, in Matthew 10:26–28, our Lord taught the need to be conspicuous proclaimers of the truth and not to cover it up for fear of wolfish men.

Studies in the Sermon on the Mount, 1442 L

Just as Our Lord was a witness Who satisfied His Father; so a Christian witness is one who satisfies his Master. "Ye shall be My witnesses;" "not witnesses to what I can do, but witnesses who satisfy Me in any circumstances I put you in." "I reckon on you for extreme service, with no complaining on your part and no explanation on Mine."

So Send I You, 1314 R

We have been taken up with creeds and doctrines, and when a man is hit we do not know what to give him; we have no Jesus Christ, we have only theology. For one man who can introduce another to Jesus Christ by the way he lives and by the atmosphere of his life, there are a thousand who can only talk jargon about Him. Whenever you come across a man or woman who in your time of distress introduces you to Jesus Christ, you know you have struck the best friend you ever had, one who has opened up the way of life to you.

The Shadow of an Agony, 1167 R

The word has to be sown in living touch with the Lord of the harvest, sown in touch with Him in solitude and prayer, and He will bring the folks round—black and white, educated and uneducated, rich and poor. They are all there, "white already to harvest," but most of us are so keen on our own notions that we do not recognise that they are ripe for reaping. If we are in touch with Jesus Christ, He says all the time—This is the moment; this one here, that one there, is ready to be reaped. We say—"Oh, but I want to go and get scores of heathen saved; I do not want to be the means of reaping my brother"; but your brother happens to be the one who is white to harvest.

So Send I You, 1328 L

"Give Me to drink." How many of us are set upon Jesus Christ slaking our thirst when we ought to be satisfying Him? We should be pouring out now, spending to the last limit, not drawing on Him to satisfy us. "Ye shall be witnesses unto Me"—that means a life of unsullied, uncompromising, and unbribed devotion to the Lord Jesus, a satisfaction to Him wherever He places us.

My Utmost for His Highest, January 18, 740 R

WONDER, SENSE OF

Emotion is not simply an overplus of feeling; it is life lived at white-heat, a state of wonder. To lose wonder is to lose the true element of religion. Has the sense of wonder been dying down in your religious life? If so, you need to get back to the Source. If you have lost the fervour of delight in God, tell Him so.

The Highest Good—The Pilgrim's Song Book,
535 L

The old Divines used to ask God for the grace of trembling, i.e., the sense of wonder. When wonder goes out of natural love, something or someone is to be severely blamed; wonder ought never to go. With a child the element of wonder is always there, a freshness and spontaneity, and the same is true of those who follow Jesus Christ's teaching and become as little children.

The Highest Good—The Pilgrim's Song Book,
535 L

We are too free from wonder nowadays, too easy with the Word of God; we do not use it with the breathless amazement Paul does. Think what sanctification means—*Christ in me; made like Christ;* as He is, so are we.

Our Brilliant Heritage, 922 R

WORK

The more we talk about work, the less we work, and the same with prayer.

Disciples Indeed, 405 R

True enjoyment is not in what we do but in our relationships. If a man is true to God, everything between birth and death will work out on the line of joy. If we bank on what we do, whether it is good or bad, we are off the track; the one thing that matters is personal relationship.

Shade of His Hand, 1207 L

Solomon's counsel is—"Whatsoever thy hand attaineth to do by thy strength that do." He is not recommending work for work's sake, but because through the drudgery of work the man himself is developed. When you deify work, you apostatise from Jesus Christ. In the private spiritual life of many a Christian it is work that has hindered concentration on God. When work is out of its real relation it becomes a means of evading concentration on God.

Shade of His Hand, 1237 L

We lose by the way we do our work the very thing it is intended to bring us. At the back of all is the one thing God is after, what a man is, not what he does, and Solomon keeps that in view all the time. It is what we are in our relation to things that counts, not what we attain to in them. If you put attainment as the end you may reap a broken heart and find that all your outlay ends in disaster; death cuts it short, or disease, or ruin.

Shade of His Hand, 1237 L

WORK, ROUTINE (*See* DRUDGERY)

WORKING FOR GOD

The one mastering obligation of our life as a worker is to persuade men for Jesus Christ, and to do that we have to learn to live amongst facts: the fact of human stuff as it is, not as it ought to be; and the fact of Bible revelation, whether it agrees with our doctrines or not.

Approved Unto God, 10 L

We are not here to work for God because we have chosen to do so, but because God has apprehended us. Natural ability has nothing to do with service; consequently there is never any thought of, "Oh, well, I am not fitted for this."

Approved Unto God, 10 R

How many people have you made homesick for God?

Disciples Indeed, 410 L

The value of our work depends on whether we can direct men to Jesus Christ.

Disciples Indeed, 410 L

The curse of much modern Christian work is its determination to preserve itself.

Disciples Indeed, 410 L

As workers for God, feed your heart and mind on this truth: that as individuals we are mere iotas in the great purpose of God. Every evangelical "craze" is an attempt to confine God to our notions, whereas the Holy Spirit constrains us to be what God wants us to be.

Disciples Indeed, 410 R

Where would you be if God took away all your Christian work? Too often it is our Christian work that is worshipped and not God.

Disciples Indeed, 410 R

We take on a tremendous amount of stuff which we call work for God, and God puts the sentence of death on it for we are exhausted by it without being recuperated, because our strength is drawn from some-where other than the Highest. The sign that what we are doing is God's work is that we know the supernatural recuperation.

God's Workmanship, 453 L

We rush through life and call ourselves practical; we mistake activity for real life; consequently when the activity stops we go out like a vapour; it has not been based on the great fundamental energy of God.

Disciples Indeed, 410 R

Beware of Christian *activities* instead of Christian *being*. The reason workers come to stupendous collapses is that their work is the evidence of a heart that evades facing the truth of God for itself—"I have no time for prayer, for Bible study; I must be always at it."

Disciples Indeed, 411 L

Have we ever got into the way of letting God work, or are we so amazingly important that we really wonder in our nerves and ways what the Almighty does before we are up in the morning! We are so certain we know what is right, and if we don't always keep at it God cannot get on. Compare that view with the grand, marvellous working of God in the life of the Lord Jesus. Our Lord did not work for God; He said, "The Father that dwelleth in Me, He doeth the works." Have we any faith in God at all? Do we really expect God to work in us the good pleasure of His will, or do we expect He will only do it as we pray and plead and sacrifice? All these things shut the door to God working.

If Thou Wilt Be Perfect, 587 L

The whole basis of modern Christian work is the great impulsive desire to evade concentration on God. We will work for Him any day rather than let Him work in us.

If Thou Wilt Be Perfect, 587 L

(Continued)

WORKING FOR GOD
(Continued)

To-day in Christian work we are suffering from a phase of spiritual dyspepsia that emphasises *doing*. The great thing *to do* is *to be* a believer in Jesus. With Jesus it is never "*Do, do*," but "*Be, be* and I will do through you*."

Our Brilliant Heritage, 930 R

Many of us are imitators of other people; we do Christian work because someone has asked us to do it. We must receive our ministry, which is to testify the gospel of the grace of God, from Jesus Christ Himself, not from other Christians.

The Psychology of Redemption, 1077 L

In our Lord's presentation, prayer is the point where the Reality of God merges with human life. Until we are born from above, prayer with us is honestly nothing more than a mere exercise; but in all our Lord's teaching and in His own personal life, as well as in the emphasis laid on prayer by the Holy Ghost after He had gone, prayer is regarded as *the* work (see John 14:11–13).

The Psychology of Redemption, 1082 R

In work for God it is not sufficient to be awake to the need, to be in earnest, to want to do something; it is necessary to prove from every standpoint, moral, intellectual, and spiritual, that the only way to live is in personal relationship to God. It is the individual men and women living a life rooted and grounded in God who are fulfilling God's purpose in the world.

So Send I You, 1321 L

Beware of any work for God which enables you to evade concentration on Him. A great many Christian workers worship their work. The one concern of a worker should be concentration on God, and this will mean that all the other margins of life, mental, moral and spiritual, are free with the freedom of a child—a worshipping child, not a wayward child. A worker without this solemn, dominant note of concentration on God is apt to get his work on his neck; there is no margin of body, mind, or spirit free, consequently he becomes spent out and crushed. There is no freedom, no delight in life; nerves, mind, and heart are so crushingly burdened that God's blessing cannot rest. But the other side is just as true—when once the concentration is on God, all the margins of life are free and under the dominance of God alone. There is no responsibility on you for the work; the only responsibility you have is to keep in living, constant touch with God, and to see that you allow nothing to hinder your co-operation with Him.

My Utmost for His Highest, April 23, 773 L

Occasionally it may happen in your life as a worker that all you have been trying honestly and eagerly to do for God falls about your ears in ruins, and in your utterly crushed and discouraged condition God brings slowly to your mind this truth—"I have been using your work as scaffolding to perfect you to be a worker for Myself; now arise, shake off the dust, and it shall be told you what you must do."

Approved Unto God, 8 R

WORLD / WORLDLY

". . . *by whom the world is crucified unto me, and I unto the world*" (Galatians 6:14).

What is the world? The set of people with the ambitions, religious or otherwise, that are not identified with the Lord Jesus Christ. Paul says, "I am crucified to that world, and that world is crucified to me." When the world comes before us with its fascination and its power, it finds us dead to it, if we have agreed with God on His judgement about sin and the world. These are not only statements made in God's Book, they are meant to be real, definite experiences in our lives.

Facing Reality, 33 R

To love the world as it is is the wrong kind of love; it is that sentiment which is "the enemy of God," because it means I am the friend of the system of things which does not take God into account. We are to love the world in the way God loves it, and be ready to spend and be spent until the wrong and evil are removed from it.

Biblical Ethics, 99 L

Lot was the only one who stood as a representative of God in Sodom, and while he was free from the abominations of Sodom, he was not far from its worldly mind. His was the doubting heart which soon turns to double ways. Lot's position arises from having borrowed most of his piety (Genesis 12:4). Weak faith chooses the visible things instead of enduring as seeing Him Who is invisible, and slowly and surely such faith settles down between mammon and righteousness. In the supreme test Lot trusted his wits; Abraham worshipped and waited.

Not Knowing Whither, 889 L

To be "of" the world means to belong to the set that organises its religion, its business, its social life and pleasures without any concern as to how it affects Jesus Christ; as to whether He lived or died matters nothing at all.

Biblical Ethics, 99 L

It is easy to denounce wrong in the world outside me—anyone without a spark of the grace of God can do that; easy to denounce the sins of others while all the time I may be allowing all sorts of worldly things in my own religious life. We must be continually renewed in the spirit of our mind so that the slightest beginning of compromise with the spirit of the world is instantly detected.

Biblical Ethics, 99 R

"Well, what's the harm; there's nothing wrong in it"—when you hear that you know you have the spirit of the world, because the spirit that comes from Jesus says, "Does this glorify God?"

Biblical Ethics, 99 R

"Otherworldly" is simply a coined word to express what Our Lord prayed for in John 17—"I pray not that Thou shouldest take them out of the world, but that Thou shouldest keep them from the evil"—"I don't ask You to take them out of the world, away from the society of men, but to keep them out of compromise with the evil one who works in the world."

Biblical Ethics, 99 R

To be "a friend of the world" means that we take the world as it is and are perfectly delighted with it—the world is all right and we are very happy in it. Never have the idea that the worldling is unhappy; he is perfectly happy, as thoroughly happy as a Christian. The people who are unhappy are the worldlings or the Christians if they are not at one with the principle which unites them. If a worldling is not a worldling at heart, he is miserable; and if a Christian is not a Christian at heart, he carries his Christianity like a headache instead of something worth having, and not being able to get rid of his head, he cannot get rid of his headache.

Biblical Ethics, 98 R

"*Be careful for nothing*" (*Philippians 4:6*). The enemy of saintliness is carefulness over the wrong thing. The culture of the Christian life is to learn to be carefully careless over everything saving our relationship to God. It is not sin that keeps us from going on spiritually, but "the cares of the world . . . the lusts of other things" that crowd out any consideration of God.

Conformed to His Image, 376 L

(Continued)

WORLD / WORLDLY
(Continued)

You often find people in the world are more desirable, easier to get on with, than people in the Kingdom. There is frequently a stubbornness, a self-opinionativeness, in Christians not exhibited by people in the world.

Disciples Indeed, 393 L

The popular evangelical idea that we are to be against the world, in the sense of a pitched battle with it, is simply an expression of the spirit of the world dressed up in a religious guise. Our Lord was not against the world in that sense; He submitted to its providential order of tyranny, but there was no compromise in His spirit, and the model of the Christian's spirit is Christ Himself.

God's Workmanship, 433 R

It is easy to say we believe in God as long as we remain in the little world we choose to live in; but get out into the great world of facts, the noisy world where people are absolutely indifferent to you, where your message is nothing more than a crazy tale belonging to a bygone age, can you believe God there?

God's Workmanship, 447 R

Jesus Christ's outward life was densely immersed in the things of the world, yet He was inwardly disconnected; the one irresistible purpose of His life was to do the will of His Father.

The Moral Foundations of Life, 700 L

If we can stand before God apart from Jesus Christ, we have proved that Calvary is not needed. Immediately Jesus Christ comes in, He produces havoc, because the whole world system is arrayed against His Redemption. It was the world system of His day, and particularly the religious system, that killed the Son of God.

The Psychology of Redemption, 1090 L

Most of us are surrounded with Christian fellowship and live such sheltered lives that we forget there are those who have to live a life of unspotted holiness in the midst of moral abominations, and God does not take them out of it.

The Place of Help, 1007 R

With regard to all the pleasures and sciences and interests of this life, push this simple consideration, "Is this the kind of thing the Son of God is doing in the world, or is it what the prince of this world is doing?" Not, "Is it right?" but "Is it the kind of thing the Son of God would be doing in the world?" If it is not, then don't touch it.

The Psychology of Redemption, 1089 L

If we give the best we have got to worldliness, we shall one day wake up to the revelation of what we have done and shall experience the wrath of God, mingled with ungovernable despair—"I gave the best I had got, not to God, but to the world, and I can't alter now." This is not only true with individuals, but with the whole of civilised life. Take the good, thoroughgoing, prosperous, worldly business men of any country who have worshipped at the shrine of a pagan worldliness, you will find exactly what Jesus says: their hearts fail them— "men fainting for fear, and for expectation of the things which are coming on the world" (Luke 21:26 RV).

The Servant as His Lord, 1274 R

A false religion grew up in the Middle Ages which taught, "You must get out of the world, deny sex, and cut yourself off from everything around." The stamp of false religion is that it denies that these sensibilities have any nobility in them. It is spiritual cowardice to deny these things because they have been made sordid and bestial; if they cannot be controlled for the glory of God, Jesus Christ has misled us. Remember that we have to live a Christian life in these bodies, to get the right alloy which will produce the thing Jesus Christ stood for. The Incarnation reveals the amalgam of the Divine and the human, the right alloy, i.e., that which makes the Divine serviceable for current use.

The Shadow of an Agony, 1176 R

When you are right with God, you become contemptible in the eyes of the world. Put into practice any of the teaching of the Sermon on the Mount and you will be treated with amusement at first; then if you persist, the world will get annoyed and will detest you.

Studies in the Sermon on the Mount, 1457 L

"Ye cannot serve God and mammon" (Matthew 6:24). What is mammon? The system of civilised life which organises itself without considering God. We have to stand absolutely true to God's line of things.

Studies in the Sermon on the Mount, 1457 R

WORRY

The only rest there is is in abandon to the love of God. There is security from yesterday—"Thou hast beset me behind"; security for to-morrow—"and before"; and security for to-day—"and laid Thine hand upon me." It was this knowledge that gave our Lord the imperturbable peace He always had. We must be like a plague of mosquitoes to the Almighty, with our fussy little worries and anxieties, and the perplexities we imagine, all because we won't get into the elemental life with God which Jesus came to give.

Biblical Ethics, 119 L

Think what simple things Jesus Christ says will choke His word—"the cares of this world . . . the lusts of other things." Once become worried and the choking of the grace of God begins. If we have really had wrought into our hearts and heads the

amazing revelation which Jesus Christ gives that God is love and that we can never remember anything He will forget, then worry is impossible. Notice how frequently Jesus Christ warns against worry. The "cares of this world" will produce worry, and the "lusts of other things" entering in will choke the word God has put in.

Biblical Psychology, 180 L

My soul's horizon reports, like Elijah's servant, "There is nothing." Every door of opportunity seems closed. Keep me unhurried.

Knocking at God's Door, September 12, 647 R

"All power is given unto Me in heaven and in earth" (Matthew 28:18). All power is given—unto whom? To the Being who lived a humble, obscure life in Nazareth; the One who says "Come unto Me, all ye that labour and are heavy laden, and I will give you rest." If all power is given to Jesus Christ, what right have I to insult Him by worrying? If we will let these words of Jesus come into our heart, we shall soon see how contemptible our unbelief is.

Bringing Sons Unto Glory, 237 L

Fretting is sinful if you are a child of God. Get back to God and tell Him with shame that you have been bolstering up that stupid soul of yours with the idea that your circumstances are too much for Him. Ask Him to forgive you and say, "Lord, I take Thee into my calculation as the biggest factor NOW!"

God's Workmanship, 443 R

(Continued)

WORRY (Continued)

*"Commit thy way unto the Lord; trust
also in Him; and He shall bring it to pass"
(Psalm 37:5).*

Don't calculate without God. God seems
to have a delightful way of upsetting the
things we have calculated on without taking
Him into account. . . . The one thing that
keeps us from the possibility of worrying is
bringing God in as the greatest factor in all
our calculations.

My Utmost for His Highest, July 5, 798 L

Jesus Christ will do anything for us in
keeping with His own character; the power
that comes from Him is stamped with His
nature. Will I say sceptically, "What does
Jesus Christ know about my circumstances?
Is His power and understanding sufficient
to manage things for me?" To talk like that
is the way to realise the size of our unbelief,
and to see why Jesus Christ was so stern in
condemning it.

Bringing Sons Unto Glory, 237 L

All our fret and worry is caused by calculating without God.

My Utmost for His Highest, July 4, 798 L

*"Behold the fowls of the air: for they sow not,
neither do they reap, nor gather into barns; yet
your heavenly Father feedeth them. Are ye not
much better than they? . . . Consider the lilies
of the field, how they grow; they toil not, neither do they spin: and yet I say unto you, That
even Solomon in all his glory was not arrayed
like one of these" (Matthew 6:26–29).*

Jesus does not use the illustration of
the birds and the flowers by accident; He
uses it purposely in order to show the utter
unreasonableness from His standpoint of
being so anxious about the means of living.
Imagine the sparrows and blackbirds and
thrushes worrying about their feathers! Jesus
says they do not trouble about themselves
at all; the thing that makes them what they
are is not their thought for themselves, but
the thought of the Father in heaven. A bird
is a hard-working little creature, but it does
not work for its feathers; it obeys the law of
its life and becomes what it is. Jesus Christ's
argument is that if we concentrate on the
life He gives us, we will be perfectly free
for all other things because our Father is
watching the inner life. We have to maintain obedience to the Holy Spirit, Who is
the real principle of our life, and God will
supply the "feathers," for are we not "much
better than they"?

Studies in the Sermon on the Mount, 1458 L

Worry means there is something over which
we cannot have our own way, and is in reality personal irritation with God. Jesus Christ
says, "Don't worry about your life; don't fear
them which kill the body; be afraid only of
not doing what the Spirit of God indicates
to you."

If Ye Shall Ask, 609 L

As we go on we learn to see God's rule in all
the ordinary haphazard circumstances of a
common-sense life, and to say, "I shall never
think of anything my Heavenly Father will
forget, then why should I worry?"

The Psychology of Redemption, 1069 R

*"Fret not thyself, it tendeth only to evil-doing"
(Psalm 37:8 RV).*

It is so easy, we think, to "rest in the
Lord," and to "wait patiently for Him,"
until the nest is upset; until we live, as
many are living to-day, in tumult and
anguish—is it possible then? If this "Don't"
does not work then, it will not work at any
time. Resting in the Lord does not depend
upon external circumstances, but on the
relationship of the life of God in me to God

Himself. Fussing generally ends in sin. We imagine that a little anxiety and worry is an indication of how wise we really are; it may be an indication of how wicked we really are.

God's Workmanship, 443 L

It is not only wrong to worry, it is real infidelity because it means we do not believe God can look after the little practical details of our lives; it is never anything else that worries us.

Studies in the Sermon on the Mount, 1459 R

Every time we have gone back in spiritual communion it has been because we have impertinently known better than Jesus Christ. We have allowed the cares of the world to come in, and have forgotten the "much more" of our Heavenly Father. . . .

"Consider the lilies of the field"—they grow where they are put. Many of us refuse to grow where we are put; consequently we take root nowhere. Jesus says that if we obey the life God has given us, He will look after all the other things.

My Utmost for His Highest, January 26, 743 L

A warning which needs to be reiterated is that the cares of this world, the deceitfulness of riches, and the lust of other things entering in, will choke all that God puts in. We are never free from the recurring tides of this encroachment. If it does not come on the line of clothes and food, it will come on the line of money or lack of money; of friends or lack of friends; or on the line of difficult circumstances. It is one steady encroachment all the time, and unless we allow the Spirit of God to raise up the standard against it, these things will come in like a flood.

My Utmost for His Highest, January 27, 743 R

Are the terrors that are abroad producing panic—panic born of cowardice and selfishness? You never saw anybody in a panic who did not grab for themselves, whether it was sugar or butter or nations. Jesus would never allow His disciples to be in a panic. The one great crime on the part of a disciple, according to Jesus Christ, is worry. Whenever we begin to calculate without God we commit sin.

"Fret not thyself, it tendeth only to evildoing" (Psalm 37:8 RV). Face facts. Very few of us will face facts; we prefer our fictions.

Christian Disciplines, Volume 1,
The Discipline of Peril, 292 R

Notion your mind with the idea that God is there. If once the mind is notioned along that line, then when you are in difficulties it is as easy as breathing to remember—Why, my Father knows all about it!

My Utmost for His Highest, July 16, 801 R

WORSHIP

Worship is giving to God the best He has given us, and He makes it His and ours for ever. What is the best God has given you? Your right to yourself. "Now," He says, "sacrifice that to Me." If you do, He will make it yours and His for ever. If you do not, it will spell death to you.

Facing Reality, 28 R

Isaac was the gift of God to Abraham, but God said, "Offer him . . . for a burnt offering." Abraham obeyed, and in the end received the illumination of true sacrifice and true worship of God. The best I have is my claim to my right to myself, my body. If I am born again of the Spirit of God, I will give up that body to Jesus Christ. "I beseech you therefore, brethren, by the mercies of God, that ye present your bodies a living sacrifice, holy, acceptable unto God, which is your reasonable service" (Romans 12:1).

Facing Reality, 28 R

(Continued)

WORSHIP (Continued)

Whenever you get a blessing from God, give it back to Him as a love gift. Take time to meditate before God and offer the blessing back to Him in a deliberate act of worship. If you hoard a thing for yourself, it will turn into spiritual dry rot, as the manna did when it was hoarded. God will never let you hold a spiritual thing for yourself; it has to be given back to Him that He may make it a blessing to others.

My Utmost for His Highest, January 6, 736 R

Beware of outstripping God by your very longing to do His will. We run ahead of Him in a thousand and one activities; consequently we get so burdened with persons and with difficulties that we do not worship God, we do not intercede. If once the burden and the pressure come upon us and we are not in the worshipping attitude, it will produce not only hardness toward God but despair in our own souls.

My Utmost for His Highest, April 1, 765 R

WRATH OF GOD

The love of God and the wrath of God are obverse sides of the same thing, like two sides of a coin. The wrath of God is as positive as His love. God cannot be in agreement with sin. When a man is severed from God, the basis of his moral life is chaos and wrath, not because God is angry like a Moloch*—it is His constitution of things. The wrath of God abides all the time a man persists in the way that leads away from God; the second he turns, he is faced with His love. Wrath is the dark line in God's face, and is expressive of His hatred of sin.

Conformed to His Image, 345 L

*A tyrannical power requiring sacrifice to be appeased.

When we speak of the wrath of God we must not picture Him as an angry sultan on the throne of heaven, bringing a lash about people when they do what He does not want. There is no element of personal vindictiveness in God. It is rather that God's constitution of things is such that when a man becomes severed from God his life tumbles into turmoil and confusion, into agony and distress; it is hell at once, and he will never get out of it unless he turns to God; immediately he turns, chaos is turned into cosmos, wrath into love, distress into peace. "Knowing therefore the terror of the Lord" we persuade men to keep in touch with Him.

Conformed to His Image, 363 L

YOUTH

Another thing to bear in mind is the difference between a young life and a mature life. A boy or girl just emerging from the "teens" is always chaotic; if a young life is normal it is a chunk of chaos; if it is not, there is something wrong; there ought to be the chaotic element.

Biblical Ethics, 94 L

One of the greatest benefits when a young life is trying to express itself is to have something to work at with the hands, to model in wax, to paint, or write, or dig, anything that will give an opportunity of expression.

Biblical Psychology, 210 R

The defects of a growing life are one thing; the vices of a mature life are another. Be as merciless as God can make you towards the vices of a mature life, but be very gentle and patient with the defects of a growing life.

Biblical Ethics, 94 R

God holds us responsible for the way we judge a young life; if we judge it by the standards by which we would judge a mature life, we will be grossly unjust.

Biblical Ethics, 94 L

The body has an enormous influence on the soul, and the soul on the body. When the body is developing into manhood or womanhood there is a sudden awakening of the soul to religious influences, and it is always a dangerous time. What is looked upon as evidence of the grace of God at work is merely the opening up of the soul in the process of development. God never places any importance on that phase. Over and over again people have built up hope on the religious promise of boys and girls in their teens and after a while it fades away and the unwise say, he, or she, has backslidden. . . . We are apt to place our faith on the years when we are in the making, whereas lives ought to be allowed to develop along a right line to the point of reliability.

Bringing Sons Unto Glory, 222 L

When a young life is trying to express itself, it experiences exquisite suffering; music is run to, theatres are run to, literature is run to—anything to try and get the power to express what is there in longing.

Biblical Psychology, 210 R

The boy who gives the grandest promise does not always become what you expect, while the lad who is stodgy to begin with may come out top. One of the finest commentators on the Bible was an ignorant dunce as a lad, with no promise at all to begin with. There is always an incalculable element in everyone.

Shade of His Hand, 1237 R

It is an appalling thing to see a young man with an old head on his shoulders; a young man ought not to be careful but to be full of cheer. "Rejoice, O young man, in thy youth." Solomon is not advocating the sowing of wild oats, but that a man should enter into his life fully and remember that he must pay the price in the right way, not the wrong.

Shade of His Hand, 1243 L

Solomon's counsel is robust and strong— "Let thy heart cheer thee in the days of thy youth, and walk in the ways of thine heart." The young man who cannot enjoy himself is no good; he has a sinister attitude to life. The man who can enjoy himself is not pretending to be what he is not.

Shade of His Hand, 1243 R

~ ANNOTATED BIBLIOGRAPHY ~

Oswald Chambers' Spoken Messages

God's Bible School, Cincinnati, Ohio, and
summer Camp Meetings in the U.S.
(1906–1910)
League of Prayer, Britain (1907–1915)
The Bible Training College, London
(1911–1915)
YMCA work with British Commonwealth
soldiers, Egypt (1915–1917)

The Complete Works of Oswald Chambers

*Each entry below gives the title, publication date,
theme, and spoken source for each of Oswald
Chambers' books.*

Approved Unto God, combined volume
(1946)
Includes:
* **Approved Unto God** (1936)
  Theme: Christian service; being a
  worker for God
  Lectures at the Bible Training College
  in London
* **Facing Reality** (1939)
  Theme: Belief
  Messages given at League of Prayer
  meetings in Britain and at the Bible
  Training College; talks to British
  Commonwealth troops in Egypt

As He Walked
See **Our Brilliant Heritage**

Baffled to Fight Better (1917) – Now
published as **Our Ultimate Refuge**
Theme: Job and the problem of suffering
Talks to soldiers in Egypt

Biblical Ethics (1947)
Theme: Christian ethics, morality,
philosophy
Lectures at the Bible Training College and
at League of Prayer meetings; talks to
soldiers in Egypt

Biblical Psychology (1912, 1936)
Theme: Soul, spirit, personality; the origins
of man
Lectures at the Bible Training College

Bringing Sons Unto Glory (1944)
Theme: Studies in the life of Christ, the
meaning of His life for us
Lectures at the Bible Training College and
evening classes in London

Called of God (1936)
Theme: The missionary call
Selections from **My Utmost for His Highest**

Christian Disciplines (Published in various
forms 1907–1968)
Themes: Divine guidance, suffering, peril,
prayer, loneliness, and patience
Talks given in Britain and the U.S.

Conformed to His Image (1950)
Theme: Christian thinking, faith
Classes taught at the Bible Training College;
sermons and talks in Britain, the U.S.,
and Egypt

Disciples Indeed (1955)
Themes: Belief, the Bible, the call of God,
the character of God, experience, the
Holy Spirit, the moral law, personality,
personal relationship, prayer, preaching,
preparation, redemption, sin, study, the
teaching of Jesus, temptation, testimony,
thinking, and workers for God
Talks in the Sermon Class at the Bible
Training College

Facing Reality
See **Approved Unto God**

The Fighting Chance
See **The Servant as His Lord**

Gems from Genesis (1989)
See **Not Knowing Whither** (1934) and **Our
Portrait in Genesis** (1957)

God's Workmanship (1953)
    Theme: Practical Christian living
    Lectures and sermons given in England and
        Egypt, 1910–1917

The Graciousness of Uncertainty
    See **The Love of God**

Grow Up Into Him
    See **Our Brilliant Heritage**

He Shall Glorify Me (1946)
    Theme: Three chapters on the Holy Spirit,
        then miscellaneous sermons
    Lectures at the Bible Training College; talks
        to soldiers in Egypt

The Highest Good
    Includes:
    • **The Highest Good** (1938)
        Theme: Righteousness, morality, and
          ethics
        Lectures from Christian Ethics class at
          the Bible Training College
    • **The Pilgrim's Song Book** (1940)
        Theme: Psalms 120–128; the Pilgrim
          Psalms; the Psalms of Ascent
        Talks in Wensleydale District, summer
          1915, before leaving for Egypt
    • **Thy Great Redemption** (1937)
        Theme: Redemption
        Lectures given at the Bible Training
          College

If Thou Wilt Be Perfect (1939)
    Theme: Spiritual philosophy, mystic writers
    Lectures on Biblical Philosophy given at
        the Bible Training College

If Ye Shall Ask (1937) – Now published as
    If You Will Ask
    Theme: Prayer
    Lectures given at the Bible Training College
        and at League of Prayer meetings; talks to
        soldiers in Egypt

Knocking at God's Door (1957) – first
    published as **A Little Book of Prayers**
    (1938)
    Theme: A prayer for each day of the year
    Oswald Chambers' personal prayers gleaned
        from his journals

A Little Book of Prayers
    See **Knocking at God's Door**

The Love of God (1938)
    Theme: Three chapters on the love of God
    Two talks on the love of God from Dunoon
        years; one talk from Egypt
    Includes:
    • **The Ministry of the Unnoticed** (1936)
        Theme: Service in ordinary
          circumstances
        Three devotional talks to students at
          the Bible Training College
    • **The Message of Invincible Consolation**
        (1931)
        Theme: Difficulties, suffering
        Two talks on 2 Corinthians 4:16–18,
          given at annual meeting of the
          League of Prayer
    • **The Making of a Christian** (1918,
        1935)
        Theme: New birth, right thinking and
          living
        Talks at the Bible Training College and
          in Egypt
    • **Now Is It Possible** (1923, 1934)
        Theme: Holy living, faith, discipleship
        Three talks given at the Bible Training
          College
    • **The Graciousness of Uncertainty**
        (1938)
        Theme: Faith, facing the unknown
        Talk to soldiers in Egypt

The Making of a Christian
    See **The Love of God**

The Message of Invincible Consolation
    See **The Love of God**

The Ministry of the Unnoticed
See *The Love of God*

The Moral Foundations of Life (1936)
Theme: Ethical principles of Christian life
Lectures at the Bible Training College

My Utmost for His Highest (U.K. 1927;
U.S. 1935)
Theme: Practical Christian living; a reading
for each day of the year
Compiled by Mrs. Chambers from all her
notes of Oswald's talks

Notes on Ezekiel (1949)
Theme: Abbreviated exposition of Ezekiel
1–34
Lectures at the Bible Training College

Notes on Isaiah (1941)
Theme: The character of God from Isaiah
1–53
Lectures at the Bible Training College

Notes on Jeremiah (1936)
Theme: Lessons about God and man from
Jeremiah 1–29
Lectures at the Bible Training College

Not Knowing Whither (1934)
Theme: Faith; facing the unknown; lessons
from the life of Abraham, Genesis 12–25
Lectures on Genesis at the Bible Training
College

Now Is It Possible
See *The Love of God*

The Pilgrim's Song Book
See *The Highest Good*

Our Portrait in Genesis (1957)
Theme: Exposition of Genesis 1–6; 26–37
Lectures on Genesis at the Bible Training
College

Our Brilliant Heritage, combined volume
(1965)
Includes:
 • **Our Brilliant Heritage** (1929)
  Theme: The gospel mystery of
   sanctification
  Talks to League of Prayer meetings
 • **Grow Up Into Him** (1931)
  Theme: Christian habits
  Lectures at the Bible Training College
 • **As He Walked** (1930)
  Theme: Christian experience
  Lectures at the Bible Training College

The Philosophy of Sin (1937)
Theme: Studies in the problems of man's
moral life
Lectures at the Bible Training College

The Place of Help (1935)
Theme: Practical Christian living
Miscellaneous talks, many in Egypt
identified by date and place

The Psychology of Redemption, subtitled
Making All Things New (1922; 2nd
edition, 1930; 3rd edition, 1935)
Theme: Parallels between the life of Christ
and the Christian's life of faith
Lectures at the Bible Training College, at
the League of Prayer convention, and in
classes in Egypt

Run Today's Race (1968)
Theme: "Seed Thoughts," a sentence for
each day
Drawn from previously published articles
and books

The Sacrament of Saints
See *The Servant as His Lord*

The Saints in the Disaster of Worldliness
See *The Servant as His Lord*

The Servant as His Lord, combined volume (1959) of four previously published booklets
Includes:
- **The Fighting Chance** (1935)
  Theme: Exposition of Romans 8:35–39
  Talks given at a League of Prayer meeting
- **The Soul of a Christian** (1936)
  Theme: Personal relationship with God
  Lectures at the Bible Training College
- **The Saints in the Disaster of Worldliness** (1939)
  Theme: Perseverance, patience
  Lectures to soldiers in Egypt
- **The Sacrament of Saints** (1934)
  Theme: Being made "broken bread" in the hands of God
  Lectures in the Sermon Class at the Bible Training College

Shade of His Hand (1924)
  Theme: "Is Life Worth Living?" – themes from Ecclesiastes
  Talks to soldiers in Egypt

The Shadow of an Agony (1918)
  Theme: War, upheaval, facing the tragedies of life
  Talks to soldiers in Egypt

So Send I You (1930), subtitled **The Secret of the Burning Heart**
  Theme: The call, preparation, service of a missionary
  Lectures at the Bible Training College

The Soul of a Christian
  See **The Servant as His Lord**

Studies in the Sermon on the Mount (1915, 1929)
  Theme: Study of Matthew 5–7
  Talks at League of Prayer convention and the Bible Training College

Thy Great Redemption
  See **The Highest Good**

Workmen of God (1937), subtitled **The Cure of Souls**
  Theme: Dealing with the spiritual conditions of others
  Talks at a League of Prayer meeting

Currently Available

The following Oswald Chambers books are currently in print and available from Discovery House Publishers:

Biblical Ethics
Biblical Psychology
Christian Disciplines
Complete Works of Oswald Chambers
Conformed to His Image / The Servant as His Lord
If You Will Ask
The Love of God
My Utmost for His Highest
Our Brilliant Heritage / If You Will Be Perfect / Disciples Indeed
Our Ultimate Refuge (original title: **Baffled to Fight Better**)
So Send I You / Workmen of God
Studies in the Sermon on the Mount

Also available, the biography of Oswald Chambers:

Oswald Chambers: Abandoned to God
by David McCasland

SCRIPTURE INDEX

~ SUBJECT INDEX ~

NOTE TO THE READER

The publisher invites you to share your response to the

message of this book by writing Discovery House Publishers,

P.O. Box 3566, Grand Rapids, MI 49501, U.S.A.

For information about other Discovery House books,

music, videos, or DVDs, contact us at the same address or

call 1-800-653-8333. Find us on the Internet at

http://www.dhp.org/ or send e-mail to books@dhp.org.